STERLING
Test Prep

MCAT©

Organic Chemistry
& Biochemistry

Practice Questions

with detailed explanations

5th edition

www.Sterling-Prep.com

5   4   3   2   1

ISBN-13: 978-1-9475562-3-2

Sterling Test Prep products are available at special quantity discounts for sales, promotions, premed counseling offices, and other educational purposes.

For more information, contact our Sales Department at:

Sterling Test Prep
6 Liberty Square #11
Boston, MA 02109

info@sterling-prep.com

© 2020 Sterling Test Prep

Published by Sterling Test Prep

MCAT® is a registered trademark of the American Association of Medical Colleges (AAMC). AAMC neither endorses nor sponsors this product and is not associated with Sterling Test Prep.

Dear Future Physician!

Congratulations on choosing this book as part of your MCAT® preparation!

Organic chemistry and biochemistry are challenging disciplines that are heavily tested on the MCAT as part of "Chemical and Physical Foundations of Biological Systems" section and, to a much smaller extent, "Biological and Biochemical Foundations of Living Systems" section of the MCAT. This book provides 720 high-yield practice questions that test your knowledge of all organic chemistry and biochemistry topics on the MCAT.

The explanations to these questions provide detailed solutions and cover a broad spectrum of concepts that you must be well-versed in to be able to answer related questions on the test and get a high score. By reading these explanations carefully and understanding how they apply to solve the question, you will learn important concepts and the relationships between them. This will prepare you for the test, and you will significantly increase your score.

Scoring well on the MCAT is extremely important for admission to medical school. To achieve a high score, you need to develop skills to properly apply the knowledge you have and quickly choose the correct answer. Understanding key concepts, having the ability to extract information from the passages and distinguishing between similar answer choices is more valuable than simply memorizing terms. That is why you must solve numerous practice questions.

All the content of our publications is prepared by our writers and editors to ensure strict adherence to the topics and skills outlined by the AAMC for the redesigned MCAT. Our editors possess extensive credentials, were educated at top colleges and universities and have been admitted to medical school with stellar MCAT scores. They are experts on teaching, preparing students for the MCAT and have coached thousands of premeds on admission strategies.

We wish you great success in your future medical profession and look forward to being an important part of your successful preparation for the MCAT!

Sterling Test Prep Team

191101gdx

Our Commitment to the Environment

Sterling Test Prep is committed to protecting our planet's resources by supporting environmental organizations with proven track records of conservation, ecological research and education and preservation of vital natural resources. A portion of our profits is donated to help these organizations so they can continue their critical missions. These organizations include:

 Ocean Conservancy For over 40 years, Ocean Conservancy has been advocating for a healthy ocean by supporting sustainable solutions based on science and cleanup efforts. Among many environmental achievements, Ocean Conservancy laid the groundwork for an international moratorium on commercial whaling, played an instrumental role in protecting fur seals from overhunting and banning the international trade of sea turtles. The organization created national marine sanctuaries and served as the lead non-governmental organization in the designation of 10 of the 13 marine sanctuaries.

 For 25 years, Rainforest Trust has been saving critical lands for conservation through land purchases and protected area designations. Rainforest Trust has played a central role in the creation of 73 new protected areas in 17 countries, including the Falkland Islands, Costa Rica and Peru. Nearly 8 million acres have been saved thanks to Rainforest Trust's support of in-country partners across Latin America, with over 500,000 acres of critical lands purchased outright for reserves.

 Since 1980, Pacific Whale Foundation has been saving whales from extinction and protecting our oceans through science and advocacy. As an international organization, with ongoing research projects in Hawaii, Australia, and Ecuador, PWF is an active participant in global efforts to address threats to whales and other marine life. A pioneer in non-invasive whale research, PWF was an early leader in educating the public, from a scientific perspective, about whales and the need for ocean conservation.

With your purchase, you support environmental causes around the world.

Table of Contents

Visit www.MasterMCAT.com for online MCAT simulated practice tests

Our advanced testing platform allows you to take the tests in the same CBT (computer-based test) format as the AAMC's official MCAT.

- Assess your knowledge of different subjects and topics
- Receive a Scaled Score and Diagnostics Reports with your performance analysis
- Learn important scientific topics and concepts
- Improve your test-taking skills by simulating testing under time constraints
- Comprehensive and cost-effective complete MCAT® science preparation
- Prepare and learn anywhere on your schedule

To access these and other MCAT questions online
at a special pricing for book owners, see page 451

We want to hear from you

Your feedback is important to us because we strive to provide the highest quality prep materials. Email us if you have any questions, comments or suggestions, so we can incorporate your feedback into future editions.

Customer Satisfaction Guarantee

If you have any concerns about this book, including printing issues, contact us and we will resolve any issues to your satisfaction.

info@onlinemcatprep.com

We reply to all emails – please check your spam folder

Thank you for choosing our products to achieve your educational goals!

Please, leave your Customer Review on Amazon

MCAT: Chemical and Physical Foundations of Biological Systems

General Information

The Medical College Admission Test (MCAT) is a standardized, multiple-choice, computer-based exam offered by The Association of American Medical Colleges (AAMC) that does not include a writing section. The MCAT is multi-disciplinary in nature and is composed of four different sections, one of which is the Chemical and Physical Foundations of Biological Systems.

This section is organized around two foundational concepts. Sufficient discipline knowledge and appropriate demonstrations of scientific inquiry and reasoning skills, research methods, and statistics skills are required to score well. Assessment is made based on the professional recommendations from both medical educators and physicians who indicate the prerequisite skills and medical knowledge needed for students to be successful in medical school and the practice of medicine. The tested concepts reflect those typically encountered in introductory college-level biology, biochemistry, general chemistry, organic chemistry, inorganic chemistry, and physics courses.

Information about this content will be covered in more detail later in this guide. The general format of the entire MCAT and the breakdown of the questions for the Chemical and Physical Foundations of Biological Systems section are detailed in the charts below.

MCAT Format		
Section	**Number of Questions**	**Time Limit**
Examinee Agreement	-	8 minutes
Tutorial (optional)	-	10 minutes
Chemical and Physical Foundations of Biological Systems	59	95 minutes
Break (optional)	-	10 minutes
Critical Analysis and Reasoning Skills	53	90 minutes
Mid-Exam Break (optional)	-	30 minutes
Biological and Biochemical Foundations of Living Systems	59	95 minutes
Break (optional)	-	10 minutes
Psychological, Social and Biological Foundations of Behavior	59	95 minutes

Void Question	-	5 minutes
Satisfaction Survey (optional)	-	5 minutes
Total Exam Questions	230	
Total Content Time	-	6 hours 15 minutes
Total Exam Time*	-	~7 hours 33 minutes
*Does not include the time required to check in at the testing center		

Chemical and Physical Foundations of Biological Systems Section Discipline Composition	
Discipline	*Approximate Percentage of Test**
Biochemistry (first semester)	25%
Biology (introductory)	5%
General Chemistry	30%
Organic Chemistry	15%
Physics (introductory)	25%
*Percentages are approximated to the nearest 5% with variance existing between test versions	

Chemical and Physical Foundations of Biological Systems Section Question Format Overview	
Question Type	*Number of Questions*
Passage-Based	4-6 questions per set (10 sets)
Discrete (Independent)	15

Passage-based questions can be readily identified by the presence of at least one paragraph of content preceding associated with a group of multiple-choice questions. Discrete questions are much shorter and do not require much reading comprehension to recognize what is being asked. They may prompt you to correctly complete the sentence or ask a direct question in 1-2 sentences.

Given the 59 questions that must be answered within 95 minutes, it is recommended that you allot not more than approximately 1 minute 36 seconds to answer each question.

Some of the questions included will not be scored as they are experimental questions being field-tested for future versions of the MCAT. There will be no indication given as to which questions count towards your score and which will not.

Tested Skills

The Chemical and Physical Foundations of Biological Systems MCAT section requires enough demonstration of four skills. These skills, their approximate percentage weighing on the section and explanations on how to successfully demonstrate them are detailed in the charts below. Sample questions are also provided.

Assessed Skills	
Skill 1: Knowledge of Scientific Concepts and Principles (35%)	demonstrate an understanding of scientific concepts and principles
	identify the relationships between closely related concepts
Skill 2: Scientific Reasoning and Problem Solving (45%)	demonstrate reasoning about scientific principles, theories, and models
	analyze and evaluate scientific explanations and predictions
Skill 3: Reasoning about the Design and Execution of Research (10%)	demonstrate an understanding of important components of scientific research
	demonstrate reasoning about ethical issues in research
Skill 4: Data-Based and Statistical Reasoning (10%)	interpret patterns in data presented in tables, figures, and graphs
	reasoning about data and concluding them

Skill 1 Competencies: Knowledge of Scientific Concepts and Principles

- Recognize correct scientific principles

- Identify the relationships among closely related concepts

- Identify the relationships between different representations of concepts

- Identify examples of observations that illustrate scientific principles

- Use mathematical equations to solve problems

Skill 2 Competencies: Scientific Reasoning and Problem Solving

- Demonstrate reasoning about scientific principles, theories, and models

- Analyze and evaluate scientific explanations and predictions

- Evaluate arguments about causes and consequences

- Utilize theory, observations, and evidence to draw conclusions

- Identify scientific findings that challenge or invalidate a scientific theory or model

- Determine and use scientific formulas to solve problems

Skill 3 Competencies: Reasoning about the Design and Execution of Research

- Recognize the role of theory, past findings, and observations in scientific questioning

- Identify testable research questions and hypotheses

- Differentiate between samples and populations and between results that do and do not support generalizations about populations

- Ascertain the relationships among variables in a study

- Demonstrate reasoning about the appropriateness, precision, and accuracy of tools used to conduct research in the natural sciences

- Demonstrate reasoning about the appropriateness, reliability, and validity of tools used to conduct research in the behavioral and social sciences

- Demonstrate reasoning about the features of research studies that imply associations between variables or causal relationships between them

- Demonstrate reasoning about ethical issues in scientific research

Skill 4 Competencies: Data-Based and Statistical Reasoning

- Utilize, analyze and interpret data in figures, graphs, and tables

- Evaluate if representations make sense for scientific observations and data

- Use measures of central tendency (mean, median and mode) and measures of dispersion (range, interquartile range, and standard deviation) to describe data

- Demonstrate reasoning about the random and systemic error

- Demonstrate reasoning about statistical significance and uncertainty

- Utilize data to explain relationships between variables or make predictions

- Utilize data to answer research questions and draw conclusions

- Recognize conclusions that are supported by research results

- Ascertain the implications of results for hypothetical situations

Tested Content

Below are the complete organic chemistry and select biochemistry content outline based on the information released by the AAMC to test-takers and higher education institutions. Some of the tested biochemistry concepts are more closely related to biology, rather than organic chemistry discipline, and therefore, those topics are not listed in this table and are not included in this book.

The content is organized into four Foundational Concepts. Each Foundational Concept has several content areas with associated topics and subtopics.

Note that the Foundational Concepts are numbered 1, 3, 4 and 5. This is because other numbers are tested on other sections of the MCAT and pertain to other sciences.

Foundational Concept 1: Biomolecules have unique properties that determine how they contribute to the structure and function of cells, and how they participate in the processes necessary to maintain life.	
Amino Acids	**Description** Absolute configuration at the α position Amino acids as dipolar ions Classifications • Acidic or basic • Hydrophobic or hydrophilic **Reactions** Sulfur linkage for cysteine and cystine Peptide linkage: polypeptides and proteins Hydrolysis
Protein Structure	**Structure** 1° structure of proteins 2° structure of proteins 3° structure of proteins; role of proline, cystine, hydrophobic bonding 4° structure of proteins **Conformational stability** Denaturing and folding Hydrophobic interactions Solvation layer (entropy) **Separation techniques** Isoelectric point Electrophoresis

Carbohydrates	**Description**
	Nomenclature and classification, common names
	Absolute configuration
	Cyclic structure and conformations of hexoses
	Epimers and anomers
	Hydrolysis of the glycoside linkage
	Monosaccharides
	Disaccharides
	Polysaccharides

Foundational Concept 3: Complex systems of tissues and organs sense the internal and external environments of multicellular organisms, and through integrated functioning, maintain a stable internal environment within an ever-changing external environment.

Lipids	**Description; structure**
	Steroids
	Terpenes and terpenoids
	Lipid components of plasma membrane
	• Phospholipids (and phosphatides)
	• Steroids
	• Waxes

Foundational Concept 4: Complex living organisms transport materials, sense their environment, process signals, and respond to changes using processes that can be understood in terms of physical principles.

Molecular Structure and Absorption Spectra	**Infrared region**
	Intramolecular vibrations and rotations
	Recognizing common characteristic group absorptions, fingerprint region
	Visible region
	Absorption in visible region gives complementary color (e.g., carotene)
	Effect of structural changes on absorption (e.g., indicators)
	Ultraviolet region
	π-Electron and non-bonding electron transitions
	Conjugated systems
	NMR spectroscopy
	Protons in a magnetic field; equivalent protons
	Spin-spin splitting

Foundational Concept 5: The principles that govern chemical interactions and reactions form the basis for a broader understanding of the molecular dynamics of living systems.	
Covalent Bond	**Stereochemistry of covalently bonded molecules** Isomers • Structural isomers • Stereoisomers (e.g., diastereomers, enantiomers, cis/trans isomers) • Conformational isomers The polarization of light, specific rotation The absolute and relative configuration • Conventions for writing *R* and *S* forms • Conventions for writing *E* and *Z* forms
Separations and Purifications	**Extraction: distribution of a solute between two immiscible solvents** **Distillation** **Chromatography: basic principles involved in the separation process** Column chromatography • Gas-liquid chromatography • High-pressure liquid chromatography Paper chromatography Thin-layer chromatography **Separation and purification of peptides and proteins** Electrophoresis Quantitative analysis Chromatography • Size-exclusion • Ion-exchange • Affinity **Racemic mixtures, separation of enantiomers**
Amino Acids, Peptides, Proteins	**Amino acids: description** Absolute configuration at the α position Dipolar ions Classification • Acidic or basic • Hydrophilic or hydrophobic Synthesis of α-amino acids • Strecker Synthesis • Gabriel Synthesis **Peptides and proteins: reactions** Sulfur linkage for cysteine and cystine Peptide linkage: polypeptides and proteins Hydrolysis

	General Principles The primary structure of proteins The secondary structure of proteins The tertiary structure of proteins Isoelectric point
Lipids	**Description, Types** Storage 　• Triacylglycerols 　• Free fatty acids: saponification Structural 　• Phospholipids and phosphatides 　• Sphingolipids 　• Waxes Signals/cofactors 　• Fat-soluble vitamins 　• Steroids 　• Prostaglandins
Carbohydrates	**Description** Nomenclature and classification, common names Absolute configuration Cyclic structure and conformations of hexoses Epimers and anomers **Hydrolysis of the glycoside linkage** **Keto-enol tautomerism of monosaccharides** **Disaccharides** **Polysaccharides**
Aldehydes and Ketones	**Description** Nomenclature Physical properties **Important reactions** Nucleophilic addition reactions at C=O bond 　• Acetal, hemiacetal 　• Imine, enamine 　• Hydride reagents 　• Cyanohydrin Oxidation of aldehydes Reactions at adjacent positions: enolate chemistry 　• Keto-enol tautomerism (α-racemization) 　• Aldol condensation, retro-aldol 　• Kinetic versus thermodynamic enolate

	General principles
	Effect of substituents on the reactivity of C=O; steric hindrance
	The acidity of α-H; carbanions
Alcohols	**Description**
	Nomenclature
	Physical properties (acidity, hydrogen bonding)
	Important reactions
	Oxidation
	Substitution reactions: S_N1 or S_N2
	Protection of alcohols
	Preparation of mesylates and tosylates
Carboxylic Acids	**Description**
	Nomenclature
	Physical properties
	Important reactions
	Carboxyl group reactions
	• Amides (and lactam), esters (and lactone), anhydride formation
	• Reduction
	Decarboxylation
	Reactions at 2-position, substitution
Acid Derivatives (Anhydrides, Amides, Esters)	**Description**
	Nomenclature
	Physical properties
	Important reactions
	Nucleophilic substitution
	Transesterification
	Hydrolysis of amides
	General principles
	Relative reactivity of acid derivatives
	Steric effects
	Electronic effects
	Strain (e.g., β-lactams)
Phenols	**Oxidation and reduction (e.g., hydroquinone, ubiquinone):**
	biological 2 e⁻ redox centers
Polycyclic and Heterocyclic Aromatic Compounds	**Biological aromatic heterocycles**

MCAT Scores

MCAT Raw Scoring

Test takers receive a total of five MCAT scores – one score for each of the four sections and a combined total score.

For each of the four sections, scores range from a low of 118 to a high of 132 (125 midpoint).

The combined score ranges from a low of 472 to a high of 528 (500 midpoint).

Scoring Methodology and Converted Scores

Raw scores are determined based only on the number of correct answers provided. Wrong answers do not subtract from the figure. Thus, wrong answers and unanswered questions are weighed equally. Raw scores are then converted to scaled scores (which compensate for small difficulty variations between sets of questions).

Since different exam versions contain different sets of questions, the exact conversion is not constant. Additionally, the MCAT is not graded on a curve. The Association of American Medical Colleges (AAMC) accounts for any difficulty differences among test versions in the score converting process.

Score Release Dates

MCAT scores are made available 30 to 35 days after the date on which the test was administered. These dates vary slightly year-to-year, so refer to the AAMC MCAT website for further information. They are released by 5 pm Eastern Time (ET) on the indicated day.

Percentile Rank

The percentile rank you will receive represents the percentage of test takers who scored the same or lower than you. Yearly, on May 1, data from one or more testing years are used to update the percentile ranks. This ensures a current and accurate indication of percentile ranks.

MCAT Strategies

Preparation Strategies

- Plan to devote between 3 and 6 months to study for the MCAT before your examination date. The MCAT can be challenging even when the appropriate study has been dedicated, so it will be guaranteed to be difficult if preparation has been inadequate.

  If circumstances require that you hold down a part-time or full-time job, err on the side of giving yourself more versus less time to study. If you can go without employment, 3 months' preparation should be enough if you commit to studying as though it were roughly a typical 9-to-5 shift (advice ranges from devoting 6-8 hours a day, 5-6 days a week). Advice concerning the total number of hours needed to prepare ranges from a low of 405 to a high of 1,300; it depends on how strong your prior knowledge background is.

- Do not study too far in advance. This can inadvertently result in poor knowledge retention. Studying more than 6 months ahead of time is usually not advised, provided this is your first time taking the MCAT, and you completed all required coursework successfully.

- During this preparation period, it is wise to temporarily remove or postpone as many distractions as you can from your life. With that in mind, it is also crucial to not completely neglect physical activity or your social life. The goal should be to prepare robustly, but not to jeopardize your health and emotional well-being – balance is key.

- Develop a realistic study and practice schedule. Cramming 12 hours a day is not only unfeasible; it will likely burn you out which is detrimental to your intended efforts. Once a realistic study and practice schedule is determined, commit to it.

- When studying, focus on developing an understanding over memorization. The redesigned MCAT is intended to measure your understanding of concepts.

- When studying, devote blocks of time to each of the four MCAT sections. At the end of each study block, write a one-page outline of the topics you covered. The act of writing increases knowledge retention.

- Alternate the days you commit to studying, and the days you commit to practicing. This will result in a steady increase in knowledge retention, aid in identifying problem areas that require further study, and accustom you to the challenging nature of the test.

- Consider using homemade flash cards to develop knowledge retention and to quiz what you know. Do not opt for flash cards sold on the MCAT books market because the act of making them is very beneficial for retaining knowledge.

- Consider occasionally studying with a friend who is also preparing for the MCAT. This can not only be a source of encouragement but also bolster your competence.

  Explaining concepts to help your study partner comprehend them can improve and fine-tune your degree of understanding.

- Take practice tests. You shouldn't take them too early in your preparation before you develop a broad and deep understanding of concepts, but you should not postpone them to the last couple of weeks before your test.

  If you find you are not scoring well on practice tests, you want to have enough time left to fill in your gaps without much stress.

- During practice tests, it is a good idea to replicate the test center conditions you might encounter. This includes sitting at a desk and working at a plug-in keyboard computer, wearing earplugs (which are provided at testing centers), eating the sorts of snacks or light meals you will likely bring on your test day, endeavoring to limit your breaks to those allowed by testing centers, not using your cell phone, studying under both hotter and colder temperatures than you prefer (since you cannot control the test center thermostat), etc.

  It may also be wise to situate yourself in a study environment where background noise is present. During the exam, you will likely hear sniffles, coughs, shifting in seats and pencil or finger tapping, among other noises.

  Even with available earplugs being provided at the test center, you will want to be adept at tuning these noises out as much as possible.

- During practice tests, develop a consistent pace at which you answer questions. Getting your response time reliably down to not more than 1 minute 36 seconds per question will ensure that you complete the MCAT sections on time when you take the official test.

- Develop a healthy sleep, exercise and dietary regimen to optimize your physical and mental condition. Some people require more sleep, others less. The same applies to physical activity and dietary needs. Commit to getting the amount of sleep, exercise, and nutrition appropriate for your personal needs.

Test Day Strategies

- Ensure a restful mental and physical state by getting a full night's sleep before the test.

- Avoid foods and drinks that lead to drowsiness (foods heavy in carbohydrates and protein) and sweets or drinks loaded with sugar.

- Arrive at the testing center early. This will give you ample time to both check-in and arrive at a place of mental calm before the test begins. Starting off the right way is an advantage you should give yourself.

- Uphold a positive attitude and avoid falling to mental spirals of negative emotions. Too much concern can lead to underperformance.

- Do not concern yourself with what other test takers are doing. If some appear to be proceeding rapidly through the test, that should not matter to you. For all you know, they may be guessing on every other question. Focus only on your progress.

- Do not skip the available breaks. Even if you perceive your stamina to be Herculean, giving yourself these moments of rest will help you finish strong. The test is long and demanding; your mind and body will appreciate the breaks in the second half.

- Eat a light meal or snack during the allowed breaks to replenish your energy.

- Close your eyes and consider taking a waking-nap or moment of meditation during the allowed breaks to give your eyes and mind a brief respite. Just be sure to rouse yourself when the time approaches to go back in.

Test-taking Strategies

There are strategies, approaches, and perspectives that you should learn to apply on the MCAT®. On the test, you need to think and analyze information quickly. This skill cannot be gained from a college course, a review prep course, or a textbook. However, you can develop it through repetitive practice and focus.

Intimidation by information. Test developers usually select material for the test that will be completely unknown to most test takers. Don't be overwhelmed, intimidated, or discouraged by unfamiliar concepts.

While going through a question, try to understand all the relevant material available, while disregarding the distracter information. Being exposed to topics and terms that you are not familiar with is normal for this test.

Do not feel stressed out if you're not very familiar with the topic. If you have done your preparation, then most other test takers are not familiar with it either. So, stay calm and work through the questions. Don't turn this into a learning exercise either by trying to memorize the information (in a passage or question) that was not known to you before because your objective on the test is to answer questions by selecting the correct answers.

Find your pace. Everybody reads and processes information at a different rate. You should practice finding your optimal rate, so you can read fast and still comprehend the information. If you have a good pace and don't invest too much time in any one question, you should have enough time to complete each section at a comfortable rate. Avoid two extremes where you either work too slowly, reading every word carefully, or act panicky and rush through the material without understanding.

When you find your own pace that allows you to stay focused and calm, you will have enough time for all the questions. It is important to remember that you are trying to achieve optimal, not maximum, comprehension. If you spend the time necessary to achieve a maximum comprehension of a passage or question, you will most likely not have enough time for the whole section.

Don't overinvest in one question. The test is timed, and you cannot spend too much time on any one question. Get away from thinking that if you spent just one more minute on the question, you'd get it right. You can get sucked into a question so that you lose track of time and end up rushing through the rest of the test (which may cause you to miss even more questions). If you spend your allocated per-question time and are still not sure of the answer, select the best option, note the question number and move on. The test allows you to return to any question and change your answer choice. If you have extra time left after you answered all other questions on that section, return to that question and take a fresh look. Unless you have a sound reason to change your original answer, don't change your answer choice.

You shouldn't go into the MCAT thinking that you must get every question right. Accept the fact that you will have to guess on some questions (and maybe get them wrong) and still have time for every question. Your goal should be to answer as many questions correctly as you possibly can.

Factually correct, but actually wrong. Often MCAT questions are written in a way that the incorrect answer choice may be factually correct on its own but doesn't answer the question. When you are reading the answer choices, and one choice jumps out at you because it is factually correct, be careful. Make sure to go back to the question and verify that the answer choice actually answers the question being asked. Some incorrect answer choices will seem to answer the question asked and are even factually correct but are based on extraneous information within the question stem.

Narrow down your choices. Use the process of elimination to narrow the possible answer choices if you cannot identify the one correct answer with certainty. For example, if answer choices "A" and "C" can be quickly identified as incorrect for a question, you will have increased your chances of guessing the correct answer from 25% to 50%. Using this method as a last possible recourse will increase your likelihood of receiving a higher score.

When you find two answer choices that are direct opposites, it is very likely that the correct answer choice is one of the two. You can typically rule out the other two answer choices (unless they are also direct opposites of each other) and narrow down your search for the correct choice that answers the question.

Experiments. If you encounter a passage that describes an experiment, ask some basic questions including: "What is the experiment designed to find out?", "What is the experimental method?", "What are the variables?", "What are the controls?" Understanding this information will help you use the presented information to answer the question associated with the passage.

Multiple experiments. The best way to remember three variations of the same experiment is to focus on the differences between the experiments. What changed between the first and second experiment? What was done differently between the second and the third experiment? This will help you organize the information in your mind.

Look for units. When solving a problem that you don't know the formula for, try to solve for the units in the answer choices. The units in the answer choices are your clues for understanding the relationship between the question and the correct answer. Review what value is being sought in the question. Sometimes you can eliminate some wrong answers because they contain improper units.

Don't fall for the familiar. When in doubt, it is easy to choose what you are familiar with. If you recognize a term in one of the four answer choices, you may be tempted to pick that choice. But don't go with familiar answers just because they are familiar. Think through the other answer choices and how they relate to the question before making your selection.

Roman numerals. Some questions will present three or four statements and ask which of them are correct. For example:

> A. I only
> B. III only
> C. I and II only
> D. I and III only

Notice that statement II doesn't have an answer choice dedicated to it. It is likely that statement II is wrong, and you can eliminate answer choice C. This narrows your search to three choices. However, if you are confident that statement II is part of the answer, you can disregard this strategy.

Passage-Based Questions

- Pay attention to the notes after a passage. The information provided in those notes is usually necessary to answer some questions associated with that passage. Notes are there for a reason and often contain information necessary to answer at least one of the questions.

- Read through the passage once briefly to understand what items it deals with and take mental notes of some key points. Then look at the questions. You might find that you can answer some questions without using the information in the passage.

  With other questions, once you know what exactly is being asked, you can read through the passage more effectively looking for an answer. This technique will help you save some time that you otherwise would have overinvested in processing the information that had no benefit to you.

- Assuming you possess an adequate understanding of the basic framework of the science, assess what information is realistic about the scientific method and experimental design.

- Read the passage in its entirety and quickly make a 4-6-word summary of each paragraph (you can do this on scratch paper if you prefer). This forces you to cut to the heart of the content, eliminate distracting details, and in doing so, it makes you evaluate the main ideas of each paragraph.

- Be cautious of questions that contain the words *all*, *none* or *except*. Questions with these words require you to answer them in particular ways that may not be immediately apparent.

- Use reasoning skills when answering questions. If an answer choice does not reasonably make sense, trust your gut and consider that it is likely not correct.

- If after reading a passage-based question twice you still are uncertain to its meaning or stumped on how to answer it, mark this question as one to revisit later and proceed to the next question.

Extra Tips

- With fact questions that require selecting among numbers, don't go with the smallest or largest number unless you have a reason to believe it is the answer.

- Do not rely on gut feelings alone to quickly answer questions. Understand and recognize the difference between *knowing* an answer and having a *gut feeling* about the answer.

  Gut feelings should only be utilized after conducting a process of elimination.

- Use estimation rather than exact computation when possible. In most instances, estimating will enable the correct answer to be identified much more quickly than if exact computations are made.

- Don't fall for answers that sound "clever" and don't go with "bizarre" choices. Only choose them if you are confident that the choice is correct.

- None of these strategies will replace the importance of preparation. However, knowing and using them will help you utilize your test time more productively and increase your probability for successful guessing when you don't know the answer.

Other MCAT products by Sterling Test Prep

MCAT Practice Tests

- **MCAT Physical & Chemical Foundations of Biological Systems + Biological & Biochemical Foundations of Living Systems (8 practice tests)**
- **MCAT Physical & Chemical Foundations of Biological Systems (4 practice tests)**
- **MCAT Biological & Biochemical Foundations of Living Systems (4 practice tests)**

MCAT Practice Questions

- **MCAT Physics Practice Questions**
- **MCAT General Chemistry Practice Questions**
- **MCAT Biology & Biochemistry Practice Questions**

MCAT Content Review

- **Physics Review**
- **General Chemistry Review**
- **Biology and Biochemistry Review**
- **Organic Chemistry and Biochemistry Review**
- **Psychology and Sociology Review**

Diagnostic Tests

Diagnostic Test #1

This Diagnostic Test is designed for you to assess your proficiency on each topic and not to mimic the actual test. Use your test results and identify areas of your strength and weakness to adjust your study plan and enhance your fundamental knowledge.

The length of the Diagnostic Tests is proven to be optimal for a single study session.

#	Answer:				Review	#	Answer:				Review
1:	A	B	C	D	___	31:	A	B	C	D	___
2:	A	B	C	D	___	32:	A	B	C	D	___
3:	A	B	C	D	___	33:	A	B	C	D	___
4:	A	B	C	D	___	34:	A	B	C	D	___
5:	A	B	C	D	___	35:	A	B	C	D	___
6:	A	B	C	D	___	36:	A	B	C	D	___
7:	A	B	C	D	___	37:	A	B	C	D	___
8:	A	B	C	D	___	38:	A	B	C	D	___
9:	A	B	C	D	___	39:	A	B	C	D	___
10:	A	B	C	D	___	40:	A	B	C	D	___
11:	A	B	C	D	___	41:	A	B	C	D	___
12:	A	B	C	D	___	42:	A	B	C	D	___
13:	A	B	C	D	___	43:	A	B	C	D	___
14:	A	B	C	D	___	44:	A	B	C	D	___
15:	A	B	C	D	___	45:	A	B	C	D	___
16:	A	B	C	D	___	46:	A	B	C	D	___
17:	A	B	C	D	___	47:	A	B	C	D	___
18:	A	B	C	D	___	48:	A	B	C	D	___
19:	A	B	C	D	___	49:	A	B	C	D	___
20:	A	B	C	D	___	50:	A	B	C	D	___
21:	A	B	C	D	___	51:	A	B	C	D	___
22:	A	B	C	D	___	52:	A	B	C	D	___
23:	A	B	C	D	___	53:	A	B	C	D	___
24:	A	B	C	D	___	54:	A	B	C	D	___
25:	A	B	C	D	___	55:	A	B	C	D	___
26:	A	B	C	D	___	56:	A	B	C	D	___
27:	A	B	C	D	___	57:	A	B	C	D	___
28:	A	B	C	D	___	58:	A	B	C	D	___
29:	A	B	C	D	___	59:	A	B	C	D	___
30:	A	B	C	D	___	60:	A	B	C	D	___

Notes

1. Which of the following is the IUPAC name for this compound?

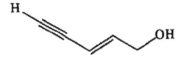

    A. (*Z*)-pent-3-en-1-yn-5-ol   **C.** (*Z*)-pent-2-en-4-yn-1-ol
    B. (*E*)-pent-3-en-1-yn-5-ol   **D.** (*E*)-pent-2-en-4-yn-1-ol

2. Identify the number of carbon atoms for each hybridization in the molecule.

    $O=CH–CH_2–CH=C=C=CH_2$

	sp	sp^2	sp^3
A.	1	4	1
B.	2	3	1
C.	0	3	3
D.	1	3	2

3. What is the relationship between the following molecules?

$$
\begin{array}{c}
CH_2CH_3 \quad\quad\quad CH_3 \\
| \quad\quad\quad\quad\quad | \\
CH_2 \quad\quad\quad\quad CHCH_3 \\
| \quad\quad\quad\quad\quad\quad | \\
CH_3CH_2-CH-CH-CH_2-CH-CH-CH_3 \\
| \quad\quad\quad\quad\quad\quad | \\
CH_3 \quad\quad\quad\quad CH_2CH_3
\end{array}
$$

$$
\begin{array}{c}
CH_3 \\
| \\
CHCH_3 \quad\quad\quad CH_2CH_3 \\
| \quad\quad\quad\quad\quad\quad | \\
CH_3CH_2-CH-CH-CH_2-CH-CH-CH_2CH_2CH_3 \\
| \quad\quad\quad\quad\quad\quad | \\
CH_3 \quad\quad\quad\quad CH_3
\end{array}
$$

    A. Diastereomers   **C.** Identical
    B. Structural isomers   **D.** Enantiomers

4. Which of the following is NOT true?

    A. NMR spectroscopy utilizes magnetic fields
    B. IR spectroscopy utilizes light of wavelength 200-400 nm
    C. UV spectroscopy utilizes molecular vibrations within molecules
    D. Mass spectrometry utilizes fragmentation of the sample

5. In thin-layer chromatography (TLC), which of the following best describes the behavior of a polar component within a sample in an ether solvent?

    A. The polar component moves downward compared to the solvent

    B. The polar component moves a similar distance compared to the solvent

    C. The polar component moves less distance compared to the solvent

    D. Neither the solvent nor the polar component moves because of the differences in polarity

6. Which of the following undergoes bimolecular nucleophilic substitution at the fastest rate?

    A. 1-chloro-2,2-diethylcyclopentane

    B. 1-chlorocyclopentane

    C. 1-chlorocyclopentene

    D. 1-chloro-1-ethylcyclopentane

7. What is the major product formed from the reaction of 2-bromo-2-methylpentane with sodium ethoxide?

    A. 2-methylpent-2-ene

    B. 2-methylpent-3-ene

    C. 2-methyl-2-methoxypentane

    D. 2-methylpentene

8. Which of the following is the major product of this reaction?

$+$ 1) BH$_3$, THF $+$ 2) $^-$OH, H$_2$O$_2$, H$_2$O $\rightarrow$

9. Which of the following statements is supported by the table below?

	Solubility (g/L H_2O)	Melting point (°C)
para-nitrophenol	10	112
meta-nitrophenol	2.7	98
ortho-nitrophenol	0.8	47

A. *Meta*- and *para*-nitrophenol form intramolecular hydrogen bonds

B. *Ortho*-nitrophenol does not form intermolecular hydrogen bonds

C. *Ortho*-nitrophenol has the greatest intramolecular hydrogen bonding

D. *Para*-nitrophenol has the weakest intermolecular hydrogen bonding

10. When (*R*)-2-hexanol is subjected to PBr_3, the compound it produces is:

A. (*R*)-2-bromohexane   C. (*R/S*)-2-bromohexane

B. (*S*)-2-bromohexane   D. (*S*)-2-bromopentane

11. Which of the following are enol forms of 2-butanone ($CH_3COCH_2CH_3$)?

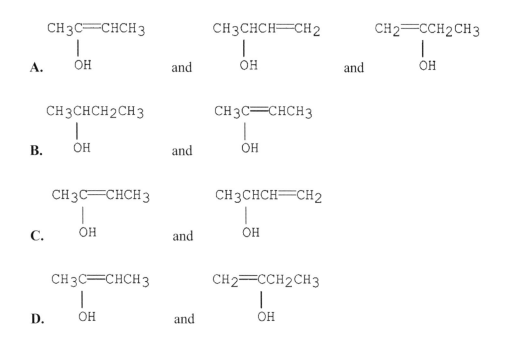

12. Which of the following acids is likely to have the weakest conjugate base?

A. $CH_3Cl_2CCO_2H$

B. $CH_3CH_2CH_2CO_2H$

C. $(CH_3CH_2)_3CCO_2H$

D. $CH_3HNCH_2CH_2CH_2CO_2H$

13. Which of the following products may be formed in the reaction below?

$+ H_2O / H_3O^+ \rightarrow$?

A. $HOCH_2CH(CH_3)_2$
B. $CH_3CH(CH_3)_2$

C. $HOOCCH_2CH(CH_3)_2$
D. $CH_3CH=CHCHO$

14. Dodecylamine, $CH_3(CH_2)_{10}CH_2NH_2$, is insoluble in water, but it can be converted to water-soluble form. Which of the species below represents a water-soluble form of this compound?

A. $CH_3(CH_2)_{10}CH_2NHCH_3$
B. $CH_3(CH_2)_{10}CH_2NH_3^+Cl^-$

C. $CH_3(CH_2)_{10}CH_2NH_2–OH$
D. $CH_3(CH_2)_{10}CH_2NH_2–Cl$

15. What is the name of the following compound?

$$H_3CCH_2CH_2CH_2CH_2CONH_2$$

A. 1-hexanamide   **B.** hexanamide   **C.** hexanamine   **D.** hexamine

16. Identify the correctly drawn arrows:

A.

B.

C.

D.

17. Which of the following best describes the geometry about the carbon-carbon double bond in the alkene below?

A. *E*   **B.** *Z*   **C.** *cis*   **D.** *S*

18. The IR absorption at 1710 cm^{-1} most likely indicates the presence of which of the following functional groups?

A. carbon-carbon double bond
B. ketone

C. alcohol
D. ether

19. Which of the following laboratory techniques is most convenient for the separation of acetone from octane?

    A. column chromatography   **C.** distillation

    B. thin layer chromatography   **D.** crystallization

20. Which of the following is the best leaving group?

    A. Cl^- **B.** NH_2^- **C.** ^-OH **D.** Br^-

21. What reagents can best be used to accomplish the following transformation?

    A. 1) $Hg(OAc)_2$, H_2O/THF; 2) $NaBH_4$
    B. 1) $Hg(O_2CCF_3)_2$, CH_3OH; 2) $NaBH_4$
    C. 1) BH_3·THF; 2) HO^-, H_2O_2
    D. H^+, H_2O

22. Which of the following statements correctly describes the general reactivity of alkynes?

    A. Unlike alkenes, alkynes fail to undergo electrophilic addition reactions
    B. Alkynes are generally more reactive than alkenes
    C. An alkyne is an electron-rich molecule and therefore reacts as a nucleophile
    D. The σ bonds of alkynes are higher in energy than the π bonds, and thus are more reactive

23. Which of the molecules shown below is NOT an *aromatic* compound?

    A.   Benzimidazole

    B.   Thiophene

    C.   Quinoline

    D.   Thiazole

24. Which of the following reactions yields an ester?

A. $C_6H_5OH + CH_3CH_2Br$

B. $CH_3COOH + C_2H_5OH + H_2SO_4$

C. $CH_3COOH + SOCl_2$

D. $2\ CH_3OH + H_2SO_4$

25. Which statement is true regarding the major differences between aldehydes and ketones as compared to other carbonyl compounds?

A. The carbonyl group carbon atom in aldehydes and ketones is bonded to atoms that do not attract electrons strongly

B. The polar carbon-oxygen bond in aldehydes and ketones is less reactive than the hydrocarbon portion of the molecule

C. The carbonyl carbon in aldehydes and ketones has bond angles of 120°, unlike the comparable bond angles in other carbonyl compounds

D. The molar masses in aldehydes and ketones are much less than in the other types of compounds

26. The boiling point of acetic acid is 119 °C and that of methyl acetate is 57 °C. What is the reason that acetic acid boils at a much higher temperature than methyl acetate?

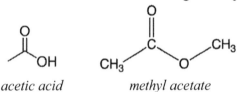

acetic acid   *methyl acetate*

A. molecular mass

B. presence of an ester linkage

C. hydrophobic interactions

D. hydrogen bonding

27. Which is the most reactive of the four derivatives of a carboxylic acid?

A. anhydride   **B.** acid bromide   **C.** amide   **D.** ester

28. Which of the following molecules represents a tertiary amine?

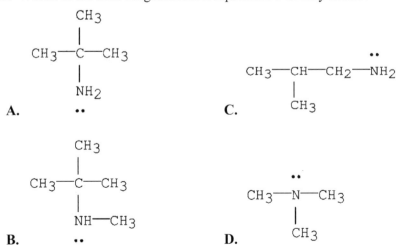

29. Which of the following is NOT a proper condensed structural formula for an alkane?

A. $CH_3CHCH_3CH_2CH_3$

C. $CH_3CH_3CH_3$

B. $CH_3CH_2CH_2CH_2CH_3$

D. $CH_3CH_2CH_2CH_3$

30. Triethylamine, $(CH_3CH_2)_3N$, is a molecule in which the nitrogen atom is [ ] hybridized, and the molecular shape is [ ].

A. sp^3 ... trigonal pyramidal

C. sp^2 ... tetrahedral

B. sp^3 ... tetrahedral

D. sp^2 ... trigonal planar

31. Which of the following is a structural isomer of 2-methylbutane?

A. *n*-propane   **B.** 2-methylpropane   **C.** *n*-butane   **D.** *n*-pentane

32. A compound with a broad, deep IR absorption at 3300 cm^{-1} indicates the presence of:

A. acyl halide   **B.** alcohol   **C.** alkene   **D.** ketone

33. Which of the following is an example of the termination step for a free-radical chain reaction?

A. Cl–Cl + hv → 2 Cl·

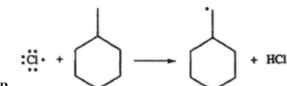

B.

C. Cl· + Cl· → Cl$_2$

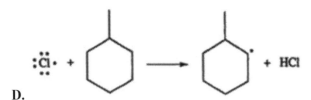

D.

34. Heating a(n) [ ] results in a Cope elimination.

A. amine oxide   **B.** imine   **C.** enamine   **D.** oxime

35. What is the major product when C_2H_4 undergoes an addition reaction with 1 mole equivalent of Br$_2$ in CCl$_4$?

A. $C_2H_2 + H_2$ **B.** $C_2H_4Br_2$ **C.** $C_2HBr + HBr$ **D.** C_2H_3Br

36. What is the degree of unsaturation for benzene?

A. 1   **B.** 2   **C.** 3   **D.** 4

37. What is the major product of the reaction of 2,2-dimethylcyclohexanol with HBr?

A.   **B.**   **C.**   **D.**

38. Which series of reactions best facilitates the following conversion?

A. 1) KMnO$_4$ (*aq*); 2) Hg(OAc)$_2$ (*aq*); 3) NaBH$_4$ / ⁻OH

B. 1) NaBH$_4$; 2) H$_3$PO$_4$ / Δ

C. 1) H$_3$C-MgBr; 2) H$_2$O / H$_3$O$^+$

D. 1) NaBH$_4$; 2) HBr (*g*); 3) Mg / ether; 4) H$_2$O / H$_3$O$^+$

39. The pK_a of acetic acid (CH$_3$COOH) is 4.8. If the pH of an aqueous solution of CH$_3$COOH and CH$_3$COO⁻ is 4.8, then:

A. [CH$_3$COOH] = [CH$_3$COO⁻]   **C.** CH$_3$COOH is completely ionized

B. [CH$_3$COOH] < [CH$_3$COO⁻]   **D.** [CH$_3$COOH] > [CH$_3$COO⁻]

40. What are the products of a hydrolysis reaction of an ester?

A. Alcohol and alkane   **C.** Ether and alkene

B. Carboxylic acid and alcohol   **D.** Ketone and aldehyde

41. Which of the following sequences ranks the following isomers in order of increasing boiling points?

    1   2   3

A. 1 < 3 < 2   **B.** 3 < 2 < 1   **C.** 2 < 1 < 3   **D.** 2 < 3 < 1

42. The name of the following alkyl group is ~$CH_2CH_2CH_3$:

A. ethyl   **B.** propyl   **C.** isopropyl   **D.** *sec*-butyl

43. Which of the following is the most stable cation?

A.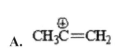

C.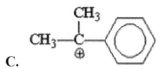

B. $CH_3CH=\overset{\oplus}{C}-$⬡

D. $H_3C-\overset{\oplus}{C}$(with CH_3, CH_3 groups)

44. Which of the following statements about *cis-* / *trans-*isomers is NOT correct?

A. Conversion between *cis–* and *trans–* isomers occurs by rotation around the double bond
B. In the *trans–* isomer, the groups of interest are on opposite sides across the double bond
C. In the *cis–* isomer, the reference groups are on the same side of the double bond
D. There are no *cis–* / *trans–* isomers in alkynes

45. What is the name given to the localized bending and folding of a polypeptide backbone of a protein molecule?

A. primary structure   **C.** tertiary structure
B. secondary structure   **D.** quaternary structure

46. Which molecule is NOT a fatty acid?

A. $CH_3(CH_2)_{14}COOH$
B. $CH_3CH_2(CH=CHCH_2)_3(CH_2)_6COOH$
C. $(CH_3)_2CH(CH_2)_3COOH$
D. $CH_3(CH_2)_7CH=CH(CH_2)_7COOH$

47. Disaccharides are best characterized as:

A. two monosaccharides linked by a nitrogen bond
B. two peptides linked by a hydrogen bond
C. two monosaccharides linked by an oxygen bond
D. two amino acids linked by a peptide bond

48. DNA is a(n):

A. peptide   **B.** protein   **C.** nucleic acid   **D.** enzyme

49. Which of the following macromolecules are composed of polypeptides?

    A. amino acids   **B.** proteins   **C.** carbohydrates   **D.** fats

50. The chemical composition of lipids are esters of glycerol with three:

    A. long chain alcohols and fatty acids
    B. identical saturated fatty acids
    C. identical unsaturated fatty acids
    D. predominantly saturated fatty acids

51. If Benedict's reagent is used to test for reducing sugars, tartaric acid yields:

    A. positive result only in the open-chain configuration
    B. ambiguous result
    C. negative result
    D. positive result

52. Which of the following amine bases is NOT present in DNA?

    A. adenine   **B.** cytosine   **C.** guanine   **D.** uracil

53. Which amino acid can form covalent sulfur-sulfur bonds?

    A. proline   **B.** methionine   **C.** cysteine   **D.** glycine

54. Which of the following is NOT a function of lipids within the body?

    A. cushioning to prevent injury   **C.** energy reserve
    B. insulation   **D.** precursor for glucose catabolism

55. Maltose is a:

    A. trisaccharide   **B.** polysaccharide   **C.** monosaccharide   **D.** disaccharide

56. In transcription:

    A. the mRNA contains the genetic information from DNA
    B. uracil pairs with thymine
    C. a double helix containing one parent strand and one daughter strand is produced
    D. the mRNA produced is identical to the parent DNA

57. Which amino acid is a secondary amine with its nitrogen and alpha carbon joined as part of a ring structure?

    A. lysine   **B.** proline   **C.** alanine   **D.** aspartic acid

58. Which of the following lipids is an example of a simple lipid?

    A. oil   **B.** wax   **C.** fat   **D.** terpene

59. Which molecule shown is a D-isomer?

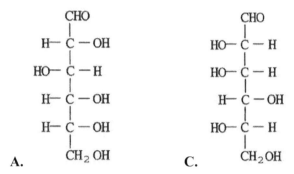

    A.   **C.**

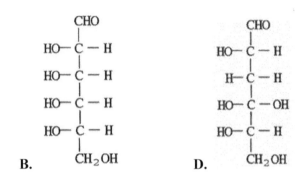

    B.   **D.**

60. The two strands of the double helix of DNA are held together by:

    A. disulfide bridges   **C.** hydrogen bonds
    B. ionic bonds   **D.** covalent bonds

Check your answers using the answer key. Then, go to the explanations section and review the explanations in detail, paying attention to questions you didn't answer correctly or marked for review. Note the topic that those questions belong to.

We recommend that you do this BEFORE taking the next Diagnostic Test.

Diagnostic Test #1 – Answer Key

1	D	Nomenclature	31	D	Stereochemistry
2	B	Covalent bond	32	B	Molecular structure & spectra
3	C	Stereochemistry	33	C	Alkanes & alkyl halides
4	B	Molecular structure & spectra	34	A	Alkenes
5	C	Separations & purifications	35	B	Alkynes
6	B	Alkanes & alkyl halides	36	D	Aromatic compounds
7	A	Alkenes	37	B	Alcohols
8	C	Alkynes	38	B	Aldehydes & ketones
9	C	Aromatic compounds	39	A	Carboxylic acids
10	B	Alcohols	40	B	COOH derivatives
11	D	Aldehydes & ketones	41	A	Amines
12	A	Carboxylic acids	42	B	Nomenclature
13	A	COOH derivatives	43	C	Covalent bond
14	B	Amines	44	A	Stereochemistry
15	B	Nomenclature	45	B	Amino acids, peptides, proteins
16	B	Covalent bond	46	C	Lipids
17	B	Stereochemistry	47	C	Carbohydrates
18	B	Molecular structure & spectra	48	C	Nucleic acids
19	C	Separations & purifications	49	B	Amino acids, peptides, proteins
20	D	Alkanes & alkyl halides	50	D	Lipids
21	C	Alkenes	51	C	Carbohydrates
22	C	Alkynes	52	D	Nucleic acids
23	A	Aromatic compounds	53	C	Amino acids, peptides, proteins
24	B	Alcohols	54	D	Lipids
25	A	Aldehydes & ketones	55	D	Carbohydrates
26	D	Carboxylic acids	56	A	Nucleic acids
27	B	COOH derivatives	57	B	Amino acids, peptides, proteins
28	D	Amines	58	D	Lipids
29	C	Nomenclature	59	A	Carbohydrates
30	A	Covalent bond	60	C	Nucleic acids

Diagnostic Test #2

This Diagnostic Test is designed for you to assess your proficiency on each topic and not to mimic the actual test. Use your test results and identify areas of your strength and weakness to adjust your study plan and enhance your fundamental knowledge.

The length of the Diagnostic Tests is proven to be optimal for a single study session.

#	Answer:				Review	#	Answer:				Review
1:	A	B	C	D	___	31:	A	B	C	D	___
2:	A	B	C	D	___	32:	A	B	C	D	___
3:	A	B	C	D	___	33:	A	B	C	D	___
4:	A	B	C	D	___	34:	A	B	C	D	___
5:	A	B	C	D	___	35:	A	B	C	D	___
6:	A	B	C	D	___	36:	A	B	C	D	___
7:	A	B	C	D	___	37:	A	B	C	D	___
8:	A	B	C	D	___	38:	A	B	C	D	___
9:	A	B	C	D	___	39:	A	B	C	D	___
10:	A	B	C	D	___	40:	A	B	C	D	___
11:	A	B	C	D	___	41:	A	B	C	D	___
12:	A	B	C	D	___	42:	A	B	C	D	___
13:	A	B	C	D	___	43:	A	B	C	D	___
14:	A	B	C	D	___	44:	A	B	C	D	___
15:	A	B	C	D	___	45:	A	B	C	D	___
16:	A	B	C	D	___	46:	A	B	C	D	___
17:	A	B	C	D	___	47:	A	B	C	D	___
18:	A	B	C	D	___	48:	A	B	C	D	___
19:	A	B	C	D	___	49:	A	B	C	D	___
20:	A	B	C	D	___	50:	A	B	C	D	___
21:	A	B	C	D	___	51:	A	B	C	D	___
22:	A	B	C	D	___	52:	A	B	C	D	___
23:	A	B	C	D	___	53:	A	B	C	D	___
24:	A	B	C	D	___	54:	A	B	C	D	___
25:	A	B	C	D	___	55:	A	B	C	D	___
26:	A	B	C	D	___	56:	A	B	C	D	___
27:	A	B	C	D	___	57:	A	B	C	D	___
28:	A	B	C	D	___	58:	A	B	C	D	___
29:	A	B	C	D	___	59:	A	B	C	D	___
30:	A	B	C	D	___	60:	A	B	C	D	___

Notes

1. Ethyl propanoate is a(n):

    A. ester   **B.** alcohol   **C.** aldehyde   **D.** carboxyl alcohol

2. Acetone is a common solvent used in organic chemistry laboratories. Which of the following statements is/are correct regarding acetone?

Acetone

    I. One atom is sp^3 hybridized and tetrahedral
    II. One atom is sp^2 hybridized and trigonal planar
    III. The carbonyl carbon contains an unshared pair of electrons

    A. I only   **B.** II only   **C.** I and II only   **D.** II and III only

3. Which of the following statement(s) for the compound *meso*-tartaric acid is/are true?

    I. achiral
    II. the polarimeter reads a zero deflection
    III. racemic mixture

    A. I only   **B.** II only   **C.** III only   **D.** I and II only

4. Which of the following compounds generates only one signal on its ^{1}H NMR spectrum?

    A. *tert*-butyl alcohol   **C.** toluene
    B. 1,2-dibromoethane   **D.** methanol

5. When placed in an electric field for separation by gel electrophoresis, which of the following molecules migrates toward the cathode at physiological pH 7.35?

    A. $HOOCCHNH_2CH_2–S–S–CH_2CHNH_2COOH$ **C.** $H_2NCH_2CHNH_2COOH$
    B. $HOCCH_2CH_2CHNH_2COOH$ **D.** $HN(CH_3)COOH$

6. Halogenation of alkanes proceeds by the mechanism shown below:

    I. $Br_2 + h\nu \rightarrow 2\ Br\cdot$
    II. $Br\cdot + RH \rightarrow HBr + R\cdot$
    III. $R\cdot + Br_2 \rightarrow RBr + Br\cdot$

Which of these steps involve chain propagation?

    A. I only   **B.** III only   **C.** I and II only   **D.** II and III only

7. When $CH_3–CH=CH_2$ is reacted with water in the presence of a catalytic amount of acid, a new compound is formed. What might be the product of this reaction?

A. $CH_3-\overset{\overset{\text{O}}{\|}}{C}-CH_3$ **B.** $H_3C\overset{\overset{\text{OH}}{|}}{}CH_3$ **C.** HO OH   **D.** $CH_3–CH–CH_2$

8. Which of the alkyne addition reactions below involve(s) an enol intermediate?

     I. hydroboration/oxidation
     II. treatment with $HgSO_4$ in dilute H_2SO_4
     III. hydrogenation

A. I only   **B.** II only   **C.** III only   **D.** I and II only

9. If bromobenzene is treated with sulfur trioxide (SO_3) and concentrated H_2SO_4, what is/are the major product(s)?

  A. *ortho-* and *para*-bromobenzenesulfonic acid
  B. benzene
  C. benzenesulfonic acid
  D. *meta*-bromobenzenesulfonic acid

10. When (*R*)-2-heptanol is subjected to a two-step mechanism of tosyl chloride followed by Cl^-, the product is:

  A. (*R*)-2-chloroheptane   **C.** (*R/S*)-2-chloroheptane
  B. heptene   **D.** (*S*)-2-chloroheptane

11. Of the following, which is the best solvent for an aldol addition?

  A. acetone   **C.** propanol
  B. methyl acetate   **D.** dimethyl ether

12. Which of the following are the preferred reagents used in the following synthesis?

  A. 1) $NaBH_4$ / THF; 2) H_3O^+
  B. 1) Mg / ether; 2) dry CO_2; 3) H_3O^+
  C. 1) $LiAlH_4$ / THF; 2) H_3O^+
  D. 1) Hot $KMnO_4$; 2) H_3O^+

13. What is the major ring-containing product of this reaction?

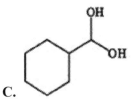 + KOH, $H_2O/\Delta \rightarrow H^+$ workup $\rightarrow$?

A.

C.
OH
OH

B.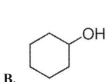
OH

D.

14. Which of the following amines is the most basic in the gas phase?

  A. NH_3 **C.** $(CH_3)_3N$

  B. $(CF_3)_3N$ **D.** H_2NCH_3

15. Provide the common name of the compound:

CH₃
H₃C
Cl

  A. isoheptyl chloride
  B. *tert*-heptyl chloride
  C. neoheptyl chloride
  D. *sec*-heptyl chloride

16. Which of the following molecules represents the most stable carbocation?

A. $H_2C=C(H)-CH_2^{\oplus}$ **C.** $CH_3CH=C(H)-CH_2^{\oplus}$

B. $H_2C=C(CH_3)-CH_2^{\oplus}$ **D.** $CH_3C(CH_3)=C(H)-CH_2^{\oplus}$

17. Which of the following molecules are identical?

I. CH₂OH / =O / HO—H / H—OH / H—OH / CH₂OH   II. (structure)   III. (structure)

A. I and II   **C.** II and III
B. I and III   **D.** I, II and III

18. Both methyl salicylate and aspirin exhibit a strong absorption for IR at 1735 cm⁻¹. This absorption indicates the presence of:

A. ester   **C.** alcohol
B. aromatic ring   **D.** phenol

19. Which of the following molecules are probably isolated closest to the top of a fractionating tower during distillation?

A. $C_{10}H_{22}$ **C.** C_4H_{10}
B. $C_{20}H_{42}$ **D.** C_8H_{18}

20. What statement(s) is/are true about an S_N2 reaction?

    I. A carbocation intermediate is formed
    II. The rate-determining step is bimolecular
    III. The mechanism has two steps

A. I only   **C.** I and III only
B. II only   **D.** II and III only

21. What is the product of the following reaction?

$+ H_2SO_4 / \Delta \rightarrow$?

A. (structure)   **B.** (structure)   **C.** (structure)   **D.** (structure)

22. Which of the following is the final and major product of this reaction?

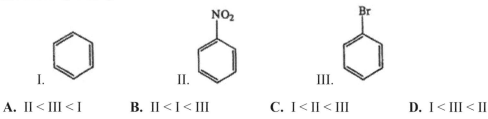

$+ H_2O, H_2SO_4 / HgSO_4 \rightarrow ?$

A.

C.

B.

D.

23. Rank the following three molecules in increasing order according to the rate at which they react with $Br_2 / FeBr_3$.

I.

II.

III.

A. II < III < I   **B.** II < I < III   **C.** I < II < III   **D.** I < III < II

24. Phenol exists predominantly:

A. in the keto form because its keto tautomer is antiaromatic
B. in the keto form because its keto tautomer is nonaromatic
C. in the enol form because its keto tautomer is antiaromatic
D. in the enol form because its keto tautomer is nonaromatic

25. All of the following statements about oxidation of carbonyls are true, EXCEPT:

A. Benedict's test involves the reduction of Cu^{2+}
B. Tollens' test involves the reduction of Ag^+
C. oxidation of primary alcohols produces secondary alcohols
D. oxidation of secondary alcohols produces ketones

26. Which of the following molecules is the strongest acid?

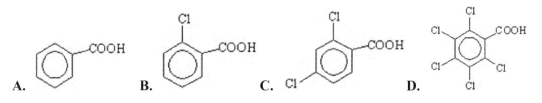

A.   B.   C.   D.

---

27. What is the name of the product formed by the reaction of butanoic acid with methylamine?

    A. *N*-methylbutamide   **C.** pentanone

    B. *N*-methylbutanamide   **D.** pentylamine

28. All of the following are properties of amines, EXCEPT:

    A. amines react with acids to form amides at low temperatures

    B. amines with low molecular weights are soluble in water

    C. amines that form hydrogen bonds have higher boiling points relative to their molecular mass

    D. amines frequently have offensive odors

29. What is the IUPAC name of the molecule shown?

    A. 2-ethyl-5-hexene   **C.** 5-methyl-1-heptene

    B. 5-ethyl-1-hexene   **D.** 3-methyl-6-heptene

$CH_2{=}CH{-}CH_2{-}CH_2{-}CH{-}CH_3$

                                     CH_2

                                     CH_3

30. Which of the following pairs are resonance structures?

    A. and

    B. and

    C. and

    D. and

31. Which of the following molecules contains a chiral carbon?

    A. $CH_3{-}CH{-}CH_2CH_3$ with CH_3 **C.** $CH_3{-}C{-}CH_2CH_3$ with O

    B. $CH_3{-}CH{-}CH_2CH_3$ with OH **D.** $CH_3{-}CH{-}CH_3$ with OH

32. Absorption of what type of electromagnetic radiation results in electronic transitions?

    A. X-rays   **B.** radio waves   **C.** microwaves   **D.** ultraviolet light

33. Which of the following compounds undergo(es) a substitution reaction?

    I. C_2H_6 II. C_2H_2 III. C_2H_4

    A. I only   **B.** II only   **C.** I and II only   **D.** II and III only

34. Alkenes are more acidic than alkanes. What is the best explanation of this property?

　A. The sp^2 hybridized orbitals in alkenes stabilize the negative charge generated when a proton is abstracted

　B. The sp^2 hybridized orbitals in alkenes destabilize the negative charge generated when a proton is abstracted

　C. The sp^3 hybridized orbitals in alkenes stabilize the negative charge generated when a proton is abstracted

　D. The sp^3 hybridized orbitals in alkenes destabilize the negative charge generated when a proton is abstracted

35. If the compound C_5H_7NO contains 1 ring, how many *pi* bonds are there in this compound?

　A. 0　　　　　**B.** 1　　　　　**C.** 2　　　　　**D.** 3

36. Which of the following is true about the benzene molecule?

　A. It is a saturated hydrocarbon
　B. The *pi* electrons of the ring move around the ring and have resonance
　C. It is a hydrocarbon with the molecular formula of C_nH_{2n+2}
　D. It contains heterocyclic oxygen

37. Treatment of salicylic acid with methanol and nonaqueous acid yields an:

Salicylic acid　　+ CH_3OH + H_2SO_4 → ?

　A. acetal　　　　**B.** ether　　　　**C.** ester　　　　**D.** hemiacetal

38. The reaction of ethylmagnesium bromide with which of the following compounds yields a tertiary alcohol after quenching with aqueous acid?

　A. ethylene oxide　　**B.** $(CH_3)_2CO$　　　**C.** CH_3CHO　　　**D.** H_2CO

39. The water solubility of compounds containing the carboxylic acid group can be increased by reaction with:

　A. water　　　　**B.** sodium hydroxide　**C.** nitric acid　　　**D.** sulfuric acid

40. Amides are less basic than amines because the:

　A. carbonyl group donates electrons by resonance
　B. carbonyl group withdraws electrons by resonance
　C. nitrogen does not have a lone pair of electrons
　D. nitrogen has a full positive charge

41. Which of the compounds shown form hydrogen bonds between a mixture of the molecules?

    A. $(CH_3)_3N$ **B.** $CH_3CH_2OCH_3$ **C.** $CH_3CH_2CH_2F$ **D.** $CH_3NHCH_2CH_3$

42. Which name is NOT correct?

    A. 2,2-dimethylbutane   **C.** 2,3,3-trimethylbutane
    B. 2,3-dimethylpentane   **D.** 2,3,3-trimethylpentane

43. Which of the following is closest to the C–O–C bond angle in CH_3–O–CH_3?

    A. 109.5°   **B.** 90°   **C.** 180°   **D.** 120°

44. What is the relationship between the following compounds?

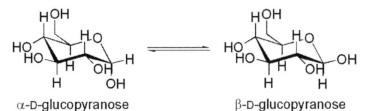

    A. conformational isomers   **C.** diastereomers
    B. constitutional isomers   **D.** enantiomers

45. Collagen is an example of a (an):

    A. storage protein   **C.** enzyme
    B. transport protein   **D.** structural protein

46. When dietary triglycerides are hydrolyzed, the products are:

    A. glycerol and lipids   **C.** amino acids
    B. carbohydrates   **D.** glycerol and fatty acids

47. The diagram below shows a step in which of the following processes?

α-D-glucopyranose   β-D-glucopyranose

    A. anomerization   **C.** hemiacetal formation
    B. mutarotation   **D.** aldehyde formation

48. The one cyclic amine base that occurs in DNA but not in RNA is:

    A. cystine   **B.** guanine   **C.** thymine   **D.** uracil

49. The coiling of a chain of amino acids describes a protein's:

    A. primary structure   **C.** tertiary structure
    B. secondary structure   **D.** quaternary structure

50. Unsaturated fatty acids have lower melting points than saturated fatty acids, because:

    A. their molecules fit closely together
    B. *cis*-double bonds give them an irregular shape
    C. they have fewer hydrogen atoms
    D. they have more hydrogen atoms

51. The compound shown is best described as:

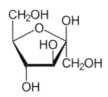

    A. furanose form of an aldopentose   **C.** pyranose form of a ketopentose
    B. pyranose form of an aldopentose   **D.** furanose form of a ketopentose

52. In the synthesis of mRNA, an adenine in the DNA pairs with:

    A. guanine   **B.** thymine   **C.** uracil   **D.** adenine

53. The laboratory conditions typically used to hydrolyze a protein are:

    A. dilute acid and room temperature   **C.** concentrated acid and heat
    B. dilute base and room temperature   **D.** concentrated base and heat

54. Which of the following is commonly known as glycerol?

    A. $CH_2-CH-CH-CH_2$ with OH, OH, OH, OH

    C. $CH_2-CH-CH_2$ with OH, OH, OH

    B. $CH_2-CH_2-CH_2$ with OH, OH

    D. $CH_2-CH_2-CH_3$ with OH

55. To what class of compounds does glucose belong?

A. cyclic acetal

B. cyclic hemiacetal

C. cyclic ketone

D. cyclic aldehyde

56. Nucleic acids determine the:

A. quantity and type of prions

B. number of mitochondria in a cell

C. sequence of amino acids

D. pH of the cell nucleus

57. Which of the following is an essential amino acid?

A. aniline   **B.** arginine   **C.** glycine   **D.** serine

58. How many fatty acids are in a phospholipid molecule?

A. 0   **B.** 1   **C.** 2   **D.** 3

59. Glucose undergoes an isomerization to yield fructose 1,6-bisphosphate. Which of the following is an isomerization reaction?

A. $CH_3CH_2COCl + H_2O \rightarrow CH_3CH_2COOH + HCl$

B. $CH_2CH_2OHCOOCH_2 + CH_3OH \rightarrow CHCH_2OHCOOCH_3 + CH_3CH_2OH$

C. $CH_2OHCOCH_2CH_2CH_3 \rightarrow CHOCHOHCH_2CH_2CH_3$

D. $CH_3CH_2CH_2CHOHCH_3 \rightarrow CH_3CH_2CHCHCH_3$

60. What type of biological compound is characterized by alcohol and amine functional groups?

A. nucleic acid   **B.** lipid   **C.** carbohydrate   **D.** protein

Check your answers using the answer key. Then, go to the explanations section and review the explanations in detail, paying attention to questions you didn't answer correctly or marked for review. Note the topic that those questions belong to.

We recommend that you do this BEFORE taking the next Diagnostic Test.

Please, leave your Customer Review on Amazon

Diagnostic Test #2 – Answer Key

1	A	Nomenclature	31	B	Stereochemistry
2	B	Covalent bond	32	D	Molecular structure & spectra
3	D	Stereochemistry	33	A	Alkanes & alkyl halides
4	B	Molecular structure & spectra	34	A	Alkenes
5	C	Separations & purifications	35	C	Alkynes
6	D	Alkanes & alkyl halides	36	B	Aromatic compounds
7	B	Alkenes	37	C	Alcohols
8	D	Alkynes	38	B	Aldehydes & ketones
9	A	Aromatic compounds	39	B	Carboxylic acids
10	D	Alcohols	40	B	COOH derivatives
11	D	Aldehydes & ketones	41	D	Amines
12	C	Carboxylic acids	42	C	Nomenclature
13	B	COOH derivatives	43	A	Covalent bond
14	C	Amines	44	B	Stereochemistry
15	A	Nomenclature	45	D	Amino acids, peptides, proteins
16	D	Covalent bond	46	D	Lipids
17	A	Stereochemistry	47	B	Carbohydrates
18	A	Molecular structure & spectra	48	C	Nucleic acids
19	C	Separations & purifications	49	B	Amino acids, peptides, proteins
20	B	Alkanes & alkyl halides	50	B	Lipids
21	A	Alkenes	51	D	Carbohydrates
22	A	Alkynes	52	C	Nucleic acids
23	A	Aromatic compounds	53	C	Amino acids, peptides, proteins
24	D	Alcohols	54	C	Lipids
25	C	Aldehydes & ketones	55	B	Carbohydrates
26	D	Carboxylic acids	56	C	Nucleic acids
27	B	COOH derivatives	57	B	Amino acids, peptides, proteins
28	A	Amines	58	C	Lipids
29	C	Nomenclature	59	C	Carbohydrates
30	C	Covalent bond	60	A	Nucleic acids

Notes

Diagnostic Test #3

This Diagnostic Test is designed for you to assess your proficiency on each topic and not to mimic the actual test. Use your test results and identify areas of your strength and weakness to adjust your study plan and enhance your fundamental knowledge.

The length of the Diagnostic Tests is proven to be optimal for a single study session.

#	Answer:				Review	#	Answer:				Review
1:	A	B	C	D	___	31:	A	B	C	D	___
2:	A	B	C	D	___	32:	A	B	C	D	___
3:	A	B	C	D	___	33:	A	B	C	D	___
4:	A	B	C	D	___	34:	A	B	C	D	___
5:	A	B	C	D	___	35:	A	B	C	D	___
6:	A	B	C	D	___	36:	A	B	C	D	___
7:	A	B	C	D	___	37:	A	B	C	D	___
8:	A	B	C	D	___	38:	A	B	C	D	___
9:	A	B	C	D	___	39:	A	B	C	D	___
10:	A	B	C	D	___	40:	A	B	C	D	___
11:	A	B	C	D	___	41:	A	B	C	D	___
12:	A	B	C	D	___	42:	A	B	C	D	___
13:	A	B	C	D	___	43:	A	B	C	D	___
14:	A	B	C	D	___	44:	A	B	C	D	___
15:	A	B	C	D	___	45:	A	B	C	D	___
16:	A	B	C	D	___	46:	A	B	C	D	___
17:	A	B	C	D	___	47:	A	B	C	D	___
18:	A	B	C	D	___	48:	A	B	C	D	___
19:	A	B	C	D	___	49:	A	B	C	D	___
20:	A	B	C	D	___	50:	A	B	C	D	___
21:	A	B	C	D	___	51:	A	B	C	D	___
22:	A	B	C	D	___	52:	A	B	C	D	___
23:	A	B	C	D	___	53:	A	B	C	D	___
24:	A	B	C	D	___	54:	A	B	C	D	___
25:	A	B	C	D	___	55:	A	B	C	D	___
26:	A	B	C	D	___	56:	A	B	C	D	___
27:	A	B	C	D	___	57:	A	B	C	D	___
28:	A	B	C	D	___	58:	A	B	C	D	___
29:	A	B	C	D	___	59:	A	B	C	D	___
30:	A	B	C	D	___	60:	A	B	C	D	___

Notes

1. Which of the following is *cis*-2,3-dichloro-2-butene?

A.

B.

C.

D.

2. Which of the following compounds exhibits the greatest dipole moment?

    A. (1*S*,2*S*)-1,2-dichloro-1,2-diphenylethane

    B. 1,2-dichlorobutane

    C. (1*R*,2*S*)-1,2-dichloro-1,2-diphenylethane

    D. (*E*)-1,2-dichlorobutene

3. Which of the following is a result of the reaction below?

    (*S*)-3-bromo-3-methylhexane + HCN

    A. loss of optical activity   **C.** retention of optical activity

    B. mutarotation   **D.** inversion of absolute configuration

4. What type of spectroscopy would be the LEAST useful in distinguishing dimethyl ether from bromoethane?

    A. UV spectroscopy   **C.** IR spectroscopy

    B. mass spectrometry   **D.** ^{1}H NMR spectroscopy

5. At atmospheric pressure, a certain organic liquid has a boiling point of 180 °C and decomposes at 170 °C, while its isomer, also a liquid, boils at 220 °C and decomposes at 195 °C. These isomers can be separated by:

    A. sublimation   **C.** vacuum distillation

    B. fractional distillation   **D.** simple distillation

6. Which of the following is the most stable conformer of *trans*-1-isopropyl-3-methylcyclohexane?

    A. methyl and isopropyl are axial

    B. methyl and isopropyl are equatorial

    C. methyl is axial and isopropyl is equatorial

    D. methyl is equatorial and isopropyl is axial

7. The reaction below can be classified as a(n):

cis-pent-2-ene → pentane

A. tautomerization   **B.** elimination   **C.** oxidation   **D.** reduction

8. What is the major product of this reaction?

$+ CH_3CH_2MgBr →$

A.

C.

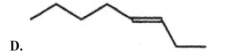

B.

D.

9. The reason why complete hydrogenation of benzene to cyclohexane requires H_2, a rhodium (Rh) catalyst and 1,000 psi pressure at 100 °C is because:

A. the double bonds in benzene have the same reactivity as *pi* bonds of non-aromatic alkenes
B. hydrogenation produces an aromatic compound
C. the double bonds in benzene are more reactive than a typical alkene
D. the double bonds in benzene are less reactive than a typical alkene

10. Which of the following molecules has the most acidic proton?

A. 2-pentanol   **B.** 3-pentyne   **C.** 2-pentene   **D.** pentane

11. Oxidation of an aldehyde produces a:

A. tertiary alcohol   **C.** primary alcohol
B. secondary alcohol   **D.** carboxylic acid

12. Which of the following reactions will NOT result in the formation of a carboxylic acid?

A. Oxidation of a secondary alcohol
B. Oxidation of a primary alcohol
C. Hydrolysis of nitriles
D. Grignard reagents reacting with CO_2

13. Which of the following compounds is the most susceptible to nucleophilic attack by ⁻OH?

    A. propionyl bromide   **C.** propanal
    B. benzyl bromide   **D.** butanoic acid

14. What is the conjugate acid of CH_3NH_2?

    A. NH_4^+ **B.** NH_2^- **C.** $CH_3NH_3^+$ **D.** CH_3NH^-

15. Which of the following is the IUPAC name for this compound?

    A. 3-ethylhexan-2-one   **C.** 3-propylpentan-2-one
    B. 4-ethylhexan-5-one   **D.** 3-propylpentan-4-one

16. Draw a structural formula for benzene. How many σ bonds are in the molecule?

    A. 14   **B.** 18   **C.** 6   **D.** 12

17. If two chlorine atoms replace two of the hydrogen atoms in butane, how many different dichlorobutane constitutional isomers can there be?

    A. 4   **B.** 6   **C.** 2   **D.** 1

18. What 1H NMR spectral data is expected for the compound shown?

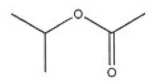

    A. 4.9 (1H, sextet), 4.3 (3H, singlet), 3.0 (6H, doublet)
    B. 3.6 (3H, singlet), 2.8 (3H, septet), 1.2 (6H, doublet)
    C. 4.3 (1H, septet), 3.3 (3H, singlet), 1.2 (6H, doublet)
    D. 3.8 (1H, septet), 2.2 (3H, singlet), 1.0 (6H, doublet)

19. A compound which dissolves in hydrochloric acid, and not in neutral water, is:

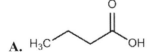

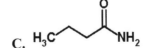

    B. $H_3C–CH_2–CH_2–NH_2$ **D.** $H_3C–CH_2–O–H$

20. Which of the following compounds readily undergoes E_1, S_N1 and E_2 reactions, but not S_N2 reactions?

A. $(CH_3CH_2CH_2)_3CBr$ **C.** $(CH_3CH_2)_3COH$

B. $CH_3CH_2CH_2CH_3$ **D.** $CH_3CH_2CH_2CH_2Br$

21. The major product of the following reaction will likely be the result of a(n) [   ] mechanism?

2-bromobutane + *tert*-butyl alkoxide

A. E_2 **B.** E_1 **C.** S_N2 **D.** S_N1

22. Which of the following is the product for the reaction?

$+ H_2O + HgSO_4 / H_2SO_4 \rightarrow$

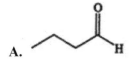

A.

C.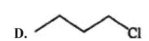

B. $CH_3CH_2CH_2CH{=}CHOH$

D. $CH_3CH_2CH_2CH_2CHO$

23. Which of the following reactions is NOT an electrophilic aromatic substitution reaction?

A. $CH_3C_6H_5 + C_6H_5CH_2CH_2Cl / AlCl_3$

B. $CH_3C_6H_5 + Br_2 / FeBr_3$

C. $CH_3C_6H_5 + CH_3CH_2CH_2COCl / AlCl_3$

D. $CH_3C_6H_5 + H_2, Rh / C$

24. What is the major product of this reaction?

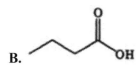

A.

C.

B.

D.

25. Which of the following will alkylate a lithium enolate most rapidly?

    A. methyl bromide   **C.** neopentyl bromide

    B. isopropyl bromide   **D.** bromobenzene

26. Which acid would be expected to have the lowest boiling point?

    A. oxalic   **B.** formic   **C.** benzoic   **D.** acetic

27. What is the major organic product of this reaction?

    A.   **C.**

    B.   **D.**

28. Which amine has the lowest boiling point?

    A.   **C.**

    B.   **D.**

29. Name the structure shown below:

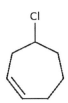

    A. 1-chloro-3-cycloheptene   **C.** 4-chlorocyclohexene

    B. 4-chlorocycloheptene   **D.** 1-chloro-3-cyclohexene

30. Which is the formal charge of nitrogen in NH_4?

    A. −2   **B.** −1   **C.** 0   **D.** +1

31. How many asymmetric centers are present in the compound shown below?

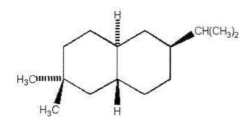

A. 1   **B.** 2   **C.** 3   **D.** 4

32. Which of the following compounds absorbs the longest wavelength of UV-visible light?

A. (Z)-1,3-hexadiene   **C.** (Z)-but-2-ene
B. (E)-1,3,5-hexatriene   **D.** (E)-but-2-ene

33. The complete combustion of one mole of nonane in oxygen would produce [ ] moles of CO_2 and [ ] moles of H_2O?

A. 9 … 10   **B.** 9 … 9   **C.** 9 … 4.5   **D.** 4.5 … 4.5

34. What is the major product from the following reaction?

+ HBr → ?

A. ⌀—CH₂Br   **C.** HO—CH(CH₃)—CH₂—Br

B. Me—CHBr—CH₂—OH   **D.** H_3C—C(=O)—CH_3

35. What is the product from the reaction of one mole of acetylene and two moles of bromine vapor?

A. 1,1,2,2-tetrabromoethene   **C.** 1,2-dibromoethene
B. 1,1,2,2-tetrabromoethane   **D.** 1,2-dibromoethane

36. Which two steps may be used to synthesize 1-chloro-4-nitrobenzene, starting from benzene?

A. 1) Na / NH_3; 2) Cl_2 / $FeCl_3$ **C.** 1) HCl / H_2O; 2) HNO_3 / H_2SO_4
B. 1) HNO_3 / H_2SO_4; 2) Cl_2 / $FeCl_3$ **D.** 1) Cl_2 / $FeCl_3$; 2) HNO_3 / H_2SO_4

37. Which of the following alcohols dehydrates with the fastest rate?

A.

C.

B.

D.

38. In Benedict's test:

    I. an aldehyde is oxidized

    II. a red/brown precipitate is formed

    III. copper (II) ion is reduced

  A. I only   **B.** II only   **C.** III only   **D.** I, II and III

39. The reaction of butanoic acid with ethanol produces:

  A. butyl ethanamide   **B.** ethyl butanamide   **C.** butyl ethanoate   **D.** ethyl butanoate

40. What reagent(s) are needed to complete the following reaction?

  A. H_2, Pd   **C.** 1) $LiAlH_4$; 2) H_3O^+

  B. 1) DIBAL–H; 2) H_3O^+ **D.** 1) $NaBH_4$; 2) H_3O^+

41. In water, does the molecule lysergic acid diethylamide act as:

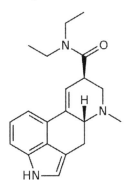

    I. acid   II. base   III. neither acid nor base

  A. I only   **B.** II only   **C.** III only   **D.** I and II only

42. Provide the IUPAC name of the compound:

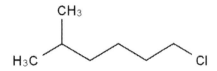

A. 1,1-dimethyl-5-chloropentane
B. 6-chloro-2-methylhexane

C. 1-chloro-5-methylhexane
D. 2-methyl-chloro-heptane

43. The nitrogen's lone pair in pyrrolidine is occupying which type of orbital?

A. *s*
B. *sp³*
C. *sp²*
D. *sp*

44. What is the relationship between the structures shown below?

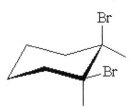

A. identical compounds
B. configurational isomers

C. diastereomers
D. enantiomers

45. Considering the acid/base character of many amino acid side chains, why do changes in pH interfere with the function of proteins?

    I. at high pH, the acidic side chains of amino acids such as glutamic acid and tyrosine become negatively charged as they lose a hydrogen ion
    II. a change in pH can result in a change in the type of molecular attractions that occur among amino acids within a polypeptide
    III. at low pH, the alkaline side chains of amino acids such as lysine and histidine become positively charged as they gain a hydrogen ion

A. I only
B. II only

C. III only
D. I, II and III

46. A molecule that has both polar and nonpolar parts is:

A. an isomer
B. amphipathic

C. an enantiomer
D. hydrophobic

47. How many degrees of unsaturation are present in acarbose?

A. 1   **B.** 3   **C.** 4   **D.** 5

48. Which of the following is NOT part of a nucleotide?

A. cyclic nitrogenous base   **C.** phosphate group
B. fatty acid   **D.** cyclic sugar

49. A particular polypeptide can be represented as Gly-Ala-Phe-Cys-Gly-Ala-Phe-Cys. How many sites with positive or negative charges are in this polypeptide?

A. 8   **B.** 7   **C.** 4   **D.** 2

50. Saturated fats are [ ] at room temperature and are obtained from [ ]?

A. liquids; plants   **C.** solids; plants
B. liquids; animals   **D.** solids; animals

51. Which group of carbohydrates CANNOT be hydrolyzed to give smaller molecules?

A. oligosaccharide   **C.** disaccharide
B. trisaccharide   **D.** monosaccharide

52. Which of the following types of linkage is found in a nucleic acid?

A. phosphate linkage   **C.** glycoside linkage
B. ester linkage   **D.** peptide linkage

53. Which one of the following amino acids do(es) NOT contain a basic side chain?

     I. arginine   II. lysine   III. threonine

A. I only   **B.** II only   **C.** III only   **D.** I and III only

54. Which of the following is NOT found in a lipid wax?

A. saturated fatty acid   **C.** glycerol

B. long-chain alcohol   **D.** ester linkage

55. D-ribulose has the following structural formula. To what carbohydrate class does ribulose belong?

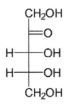

A. ketotetrose   **B.** ketopentose   **C.** aldotetrose   **D.** aldopentose

56. Which of the following codes for an amino acid during protein synthesis?

A. RNA nucleotide   **C.** DNA nucleotide

B. RNA trinucleotide   **D.** DNA trinucleotide

57. The isoelectric point of an amino acid is the:

A. pH at which it exists in the zwitterion form   **C.** pH at which it exists in the basic form

B. pH equal to its pK_a **D.** pH at which it exists in the acid form

58. How many molecules of fatty acid are needed to produce one molecule of a fat or oil?

A. 1   **B.** 1.5   **C.** 2   **D.** 3

59. Carbohydrate can be defined as a molecule:

A. composed of carbon atoms bonded to water molecules

B. composed of amine groups and carboxylic acid groups bonded to a carbon skeleton

C. composed mostly of hydrocarbons and soluble in non-polar solvents

D. that is an aldehyde or ketone and has more than one hydroxyl group

60. How does RNA differ from DNA?

A. RNA is double-stranded, while DNA is single-stranded

B. RNA is a polymer of amino acids, while DNA is a polymer of nucleotides

C. RNA contains uracil, while DNA contains thymine

D. In RNA G pairs with T, while in DNA G pairs with C

Check your answers using the answer key. Then, go to the explanations section and review the explanations in detail, focusing attention to questions you didn't answer correctly or marked for review. Note the topic that those questions belong to.

We recommend that you do this BEFORE taking the next Diagnostic Test.

Diagnostic Test #3 – Answer Key

1	D	Nomenclature	31	C	Stereochemistry
2	C	Covalent bond	32	B	Molecular structure & spectra
3	A	Stereochemistry	33	A	Alkanes & alkyl halides
4	A	Molecular structure & spectra	34	B	Alkenes
5	C	Separations & purifications	35	B	Alkynes
6	C	Alkanes & alkyl halides	36	D	Aromatic compounds
7	D	Alkenes	37	C	Alcohols
8	A	Alkynes	38	D	Aldehydes & ketones
9	D	Aromatic compounds	39	D	Carboxylic acids
10	A	Alcohols	40	C	COOH derivatives
11	D	Aldehydes & ketones	41	B	Amines
12	A	Carboxylic acids	42	C	Nomenclature
13	A	COOH derivatives	43	B	Covalent bond
14	C	Amines	44	C	Stereochemistry
15	A	Nomenclature	45	D	Amino acids, peptides, proteins
16	D	Covalent bond	46	B	Lipids
17	B	Stereochemistry	47	D	Carbohydrates
18	D	Molecular structure & spectra	48	B	Nucleic acids
19	B	Separations & purifications	49	D	Amino acids, peptides, proteins
20	A	Alkanes & alkyl halides	50	D	Lipids
21	A	Alkenes	51	D	Carbohydrates
22	C	Alkynes	52	A	Nucleic acids
23	D	Aromatic compounds	53	C	Amino acids, peptides, proteins
24	A	Alcohols	54	C	Lipids
25	A	Aldehydes & ketones	55	B	Carbohydrates
26	B	Carboxylic acids	56	B	Nucleic acids
27	C	COOH derivatives	57	A	Amino acids, peptides, proteins
28	A	Amines	58	D	Lipids
29	B	Nomenclature	59	D	Carbohydrates
30	D	Covalent bond	60	C	Nucleic acids

Notes

Diagnostic Test #4

This Diagnostic Test is designed for you to assess your proficiency on each topic and not to mimic the actual test. Use your test results and identify areas of your strength and weakness to adjust your study plan and enhance your fundamental knowledge.

The length of the Diagnostic Tests is proven to be optimal for a single study session.

#	Answer:				Review	#	Answer:				Review
1:	A	B	C	D	___	31:	A	B	C	D	___
2:	A	B	C	D	___	32:	A	B	C	D	___
3:	A	B	C	D	___	33:	A	B	C	D	___
4:	A	B	C	D	___	34:	A	B	C	D	___
5:	A	B	C	D	___	35:	A	B	C	D	___
6:	A	B	C	D	___	36:	A	B	C	D	___
7:	A	B	C	D	___	37:	A	B	C	D	___
8:	A	B	C	D	___	38:	A	B	C	D	___
9:	A	B	C	D	___	39:	A	B	C	D	___
10:	A	B	C	D	___	40:	A	B	C	D	___
11:	A	B	C	D	___	41:	A	B	C	D	___
12:	A	B	C	D	___	42:	A	B	C	D	___
13:	A	B	C	D	___	43:	A	B	C	D	___
14:	A	B	C	D	___	44:	A	B	C	D	___
15:	A	B	C	D	___	45:	A	B	C	D	___
16:	A	B	C	D	___	46:	A	B	C	D	___
17:	A	B	C	D	___	47:	A	B	C	D	___
18:	A	B	C	D	___	48:	A	B	C	D	___
19:	A	B	C	D	___	49:	A	B	C	D	___
20:	A	B	C	D	___	50:	A	B	C	D	___
21:	A	B	C	D	___	51:	A	B	C	D	___
22:	A	B	C	D	___	52:	A	B	C	D	___
23:	A	B	C	D	___	53:	A	B	C	D	___
24:	A	B	C	D	___	54:	A	B	C	D	___
25:	A	B	C	D	___	55:	A	B	C	D	___
26:	A	B	C	D	___	56:	A	B	C	D	___
27:	A	B	C	D	___	57:	A	B	C	D	___
28:	A	B	C	D	___	58:	A	B	C	D	___
29:	A	B	C	D	___	59:	A	B	C	D	___
30:	A	B	C	D	___	60:	A	B	C	D	___

Notes

1. What is the IUPAC name for the following structure?

    A. 5,6-dimethyl cyclohexane   **C.** *trans*-1,2-dimethyl cyclohexane

    B. *cis*-1,2-dimethyl cyclohexane   **D.** 1,2-dimethyl cyclohexane

2. C=C, C=O, C=N and N=N bonds are observed in many organic compounds. However, C=S, C=P, C=Si and other similar bonds are not often found. What is the most probable explanation for this observation?

    A. the comparative sizes of $3p$ atomic orbitals make effective overlap between them less likely than between two $2p$ orbitals

    B. S, P and Si do not undergo hybridization of orbitals

    C. S, P and Si do not form π bonds due to the lack of occupied p orbitals in their ground state electron configurations

    D. carbon does not combine with elements found below the second row of the periodic table

3. Which of the following compounds share the same absolute configuration?

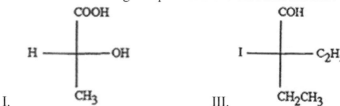

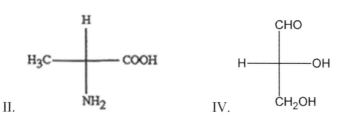

    A. I and III only   **B.** I and II only   **C.** I and IV only   **D.** II, III and IV only

4. Which of the following compounds is NOT IR active?

    A. Cl_2 **B.** CO   **C.** $CH_3CH_2CH_2OH$ **D.** CH_3Br

5. Which of the following techniques would be most suitable in the separation and analysis of two miscible liquids with boiling points of 60 °C and 140 °C?

    A. Simple distillation and gas chromatography

    B. Vacuum distillation and electrophoresis

    C. Recrystallization and electrophoresis

    D. Recrystallization and gas chromatography

6. Ethers can be formed from ethyl bromide in a reaction whereby the incoming ⁻OR group represents a(n):

A. substrate **B.** electrophile **C.** nucleophile **D.** leaving group

7. Products A, B, and C of the following reaction are, respectively:

2-methyl-2-butene + HBr $\rightarrow$ product A

2-methyl-2-butene + HBr / H_2O_2 $\rightarrow$ product B

2-methyl-2-butene + H_2O / H^+ / heat $\rightarrow$ product C

Product A	Product B	Product C
A. 2-bromo-2-methylbutane	2-bromo-3-methylbutane	2-methyl-2-butanol
B. 3-methyl-2-bromobutene	3-methyl-2-bromobutane	2-methyl-2-butanol
C. 2-bromo-2-methylbutane	2-bromo-2-methylbutane	3-methyl-2-butanol
D. 1-bromo-2-methyl-2-butene	2-bromo-2-methylbutane	2-methyl-2-butane

8. Which is the most stable product for the reaction below:

+ 1) BH_3 / THF 2) ⁻OH, H_2O_2, H_2O

A.

B. $CH_3CH_2CH_2CH=CHOH$

C.

D.

9. Which of the following compounds is least susceptible to electrophilic aromatic substitution?

A. *p*-H_3CCH_2O–C_6H_4–O–CH_2CH_3

B. *p*-O_2N–C_6H_4–NH–CH_3

C. *p*-Cl–C_6H_4–NH_3^+

D. *p*-CH_3CH_2–C_6H_4–CH_2CH_3

10. Which of the following would have the highest boiling point?

A. 1-hexyne **B.** 1-hexene **C.** hexane **D.** 1-hexanol

11. All of the statements concerning the carbonyl group in aldehydes and ketones are true, EXCEPT:

A. in condensed form, the aldehyde group can be written as –CHO

B. since the bond is polar, carbonyl groups readily form hydrogen bonds with each other

C. the bond angles about the central carbon atom are 120°

D. the bond is polar with a slight negative charge on the oxygen atom

12. Which of the following molecules would be expected to be the most soluble in water?

A. $CH_3(CH_2)_6CO_2H$

C. CH_3CO_2H

B. $CH_3(CH_2)_{12}CO_2H$

D. $CH_3CH_2CH_2CO_2H$

13. Which of the following type of a bond is depicted below?

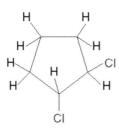

A. amide bond

B. glycosidic bond

C. ester bond

D. ether bond

14. What is the conjugate base of CH_3NH_2?

A. NH_2^-

B. NH_4^+

C. CH_3NH^-

D. $CH_3NH_3^+$

15. Give the IUPAC name for the following structure:

A. 4-isopropyloctane

B. 5-isopropyloctane

C. 3-ethyl-2-methylheptane

D. 2-methyl-3-ethylheptane

16. How many σ bonds are in cyclohexane (C_6H_{12}), a saturated cyclic hydrocarbon?

A. 12

B. 14

C. 16

D. 18

17. What is the correct IUPAC name for the following structure?

A. *trans*-1,2-dichlorocyclopentane

B. 1,2-dichlorocyclopentane

C. *cis*-1,2-dichlorocyclopentane

D. *trans*-dichlorocyclopentane

18. Which sequence correctly ranks the regions of the electromagnetic spectrum in order of increasing energy?

      1) infrared   2) ultraviolet   3) radio wave

  A. $3 < 1 < 2$ **B.** $3 < 2 < 1$ **C.** $2 < 1 < 3$ **D.** $1 < 3 < 2$

19. The solvent diethyl ether can be mixed with water but only by shaking the two liquids together. After the shaking is stopped, the liquids separate into two layers. The protonated form of the alkaloid caffeine is readily soluble in water but not in diethyl ether. Suggest what may happen to the caffeine of a caffeinated beverage if the beverage is first made alkaline with sodium hydroxide and then shaken with diethyl ether.

  A. The diethyl ether and water would mix into one layer
  B. The caffeine would transform into the free acid and transfer into the diethyl ether
  C. The caffeine would transform into the free base and become more soluble in the diethyl ether
  D. The water layer would turn a pink color, indicating an alkaline pH

20. Which of the following compounds can most easily undergo both E_1 and S_N2 reactions?

  A. $(CH_3CH_2CH_2)_2CHBr$ **C.** $(CH_3CH_2CH_2)_3CCH_2Cl$
  B. $(CH_3CH_2CH_2)_3CBr$ **D.** $(CH_3CH_2CH_2)_2CHCN$

21. Which of the following is vinyl chloride?

  A. $CH_2{=}CHCl$ **B.** $CH_2{=}CHCH_2Cl$ **C.**   **D.**

22. The compound 1-butyne contains:

  A. a ring structure   **B.** a triple bond   **C.** a double bond   **D.** all single bonds

23. Which of the following statements is NOT correct about benzene?

  A. The carbon-carbon bond lengths are the same
  B. The carbon-hydrogen bond lengths are the same
  C. All of the carbon atoms are *sp* hybridized
  D. It has delocalized electrons

24. The functional group C=O is found in all the species below, EXCEPT:

  A. amides   **B.** ethers   **C.** aldehydes   **D.** ketones

25. Which of the following compound is most soluble in water?

  A. acetone   **B.** cyclohexanone   **C.** 2-butanone   **D.** 3-butanone

26. Which of the following molecule is the most polar?

    A. butane   **B.** butanoic acid   **C.** cyclohexane   **D.** ethanol

27. The compound below has which functional groups?

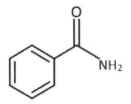

    A. aromatic and alcohol   **C.** aromatic and amide
    B. aromatic and amine   **D.** aromatic and carboxylic acid

28. A functional group containing nitrogen is found in:

    A. carboxylic acids   **C.** alcohols
    B. amines   **D.** alkenes

29. Which name is NOT correct for IUPAC nomenclature?

    A. 2,2-dimethylbutane   **C.** 2,3,3-trimethylbutane
    B. 2,3-dimethylpentane   **D.** 2,3,4-trimethylpentane

30. Triethylamine [$(CH_3CH_2)_3N$] is a molecule in which the nitrogen atom is [   ] hybridized, and the C–N–C bond angle is approximately [   ].

    A. sp^3, > 109.5°   **C.** sp^2, > 109.5°
    B. sp^3, 109.5°   **D.** sp^2, < 109.5°

31. Which of the following compounds is NOT chiral?

    A. 1,2-dichlorobutane   **C.** 2,3-dibromobutane
    B. 1,4-dibromobutane   **D.** 1,3-dibromobutane

32. In the UV-visible spectrum of (*E*)-1,3,5-hexatriene, the lowest energy absorption corresponds to a:

    A. π to σ^* transition   **C.** σ to π transition
    B. σ to σ^* transition   **D.** π to π^* transition

33. Which of the following molecules has the lowest boiling point?

    A. *cis*-2-pentene   **C.** pentane
    B. 2-pentyne   **D.** neopentane

34. What reagent(s) is/are needed to accomplish the following transformation?

A. BH_3 / THF

B. 1) BH_3 / THF 2) ^-OH, H_2O_2, H_2O

C. H_2O / H_2O_2

D. H_2O / H^+

35. The *pi* bond of an alkyne is [ ] and [ ] than the *pi* bond of an alkene.

A. longer; stronger

B. longer; weaker

C. shorter; stronger

D. shorter; weaker

36. Which reaction is NOT characteristic of aromatic compounds?

A. addition   **B.** halogenation   **C.** nitration   **D.** sulfonation

37. Which of the following is an allylic alcohol?

A. $CH_3CH=CHCH_2OH$

B. $HOCH=CHCH_2CH_3$

C. $CH_2=CHCH_2CH_3$

D. $CH_2=CHCH_2OCH_3$

38. Treatment of a nitrile with a Grignard reagent, followed by hydrolysis, results in:

A. ester   **B.** ketone   **C.** aldehyde   **D.** ether

39. The most common reactions of carboxylic acid or its derivative involve:

A. replacement of the group bonded to the carbonyl atom

B. oxidation of the R group

C. addition across the double bond between carbon and oxygen

D. replacement of the oxygen atom in the carbonyl group

40. What are the products of an acid-catalyzed hydrolysis reaction of amides and water?

A. an alcohol and an alkane

B. an amine and a ketone

C. a carboxylic acid and an amine salt

D. an ester and an ether

41. Which of the following is NOT correct about amines?

A. Amines are bases (proton acceptors)

B. Amines are converted to ammonium salts by reaction with HCl

C. Amines are organic derivatives of ammonia

D. Amines are very water soluble

42. Which compound has the common name s*ec*-butylamine?

    A. 1-butanamine   **C.** *N*-methyl-1-propanamine
    B. 2-butanamine   **D.** *N*-methyl-2-propanamine

43. How many distinct and degenerate *p* orbitals exist in the second electron shell, where n = 2?

    A. 3   **B.** 2   **C.** 1   **D.** 0

44. The specific rotation of a pure enantiomeric substance is –6.30°. What is the percentage of this enantiomer in a mixture with an observed specific rotation of –3.15°?

    A. 75%   **B.** 80%   **C.** 25%   **D.** 50%

45. What is the best description of the linkage shown in the following polypeptide?

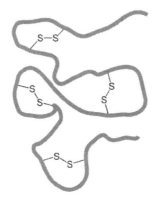

    A. disulfide linkage   **C.** hemiacetal
    B. glucosidic linkage   **D.** acetal

46. The chemical bond that links glycerol to fatty acid is an example of what type of linkage?

    A. ester   **B.** ionic   **C.** ether   **D.** peptide

47. In the sucrose molecule shown below, which bond joins the disaccharide?

    A. α-glucosidic linkage   **C.** acetal
    B. β-glucosidic linkage   **D.** hemiacetal

48. The attractive force between the cyclic amine bases in DNA is/are:

A. disulfide bridges
B. hydrogen bonding
C. hydrophobic stacking
D. ionic interactions of salt bridges

49. A particular polypeptide can be represented as Gly-Ala-Ala-Phe-Cys-Gly-Ala-Cys-Phe-Cys. How many peptide bonds are there in this polypeptide?

A. 9   **B.** 10   **C.** 8   **D.** 6

50. A molecule that has both hydrophobic and hydrophilic portions is:

A. amphoteric   **B.** enantiomeric   **C.** amphiprotic   **D.** amphipathic

51. What is the major biological function of the glycogen biomolecule?

A. It is used to synthesize disaccharides
B. It is the building block of proteins
C. It stores glucose in animal cells
D. It is a storage form of sucrose

52. The three-base sequence in mRNA specifying the amino acid is called:

A. rRNA   **B.** an anticodon   **C.** a codon   **D.** tRNA

53. Hydrophobic interactions help to stabilize the [ ] structure(s) of a protein.

A. primary
B. secondary
C. secondary and tertiary
D. tertiary and quaternary

54. The products of the base-catalyzed breakdown of fat are:

A. salts of fatty acids
B. salts of fatty acids and glycerol
C. esters of fatty acids
D. terpenes

55. What is the minimal number of chiral centers necessary for a *meso* carbohydrate?

A. 0   **B.** 1   **C.** 2   **D.** 3

56. Which of the following is an RNA codon for protein synthesis?

     I. GUA   II. CGU   III. ACG

A. I only   **B.** II only   **C.** III only   **D.** I, II and III

57. The side chains, or *R* groups, of amino acids can be classified into each of the following categories EXCEPT:

    A. acidic   **B.** isoelectric   **C.** non-polar   **D.** polar

58. The potassium or sodium salt of a long chain carboxylic acid is called a(n):

    A. emollient   **B.** ether   **C.** triglyceride   **D.** soap

59. A carbohydrate that gives two molecules when it is completely hydrolyzed is known as a:

    A. polysaccharide   **C.** monosaccharide
    B. starch   **D.** disaccharide

60. During DNA replication, an adenine base on the template strand codes for which base on the complementary strand?

    A. thymine   **C.** cytosine
    B. guanine   **D.** adenine

Check your answers using the answer key. Then, go to the explanations section and review the explanations in detail, paying attention to questions you didn't answer correctly or marked for review. Note the topic that those questions belong to.

We recommend that you do this BEFORE taking the next Diagnostic Test.

Diagnostic Test #4 – Answer Key

1	B	Nomenclature	31	B	Stereochemistry
2	A	Covalent bond	32	D	Molecular structure & spectra
3	C	Stereochemistry	33	D	Alkanes & alkyl halides
4	A	Molecular structure & spectra	34	B	Alkenes
5	A	Separations & purifications	35	D	Alkynes
6	C	Alkanes & alkyl halides	36	A	Aromatic compounds
7	A	Alkenes	37	A	Alcohols
8	D	Alkynes	38	B	Aldehydes & ketones
9	C	Aromatic compounds	39	A	Carboxylic acids
10	D	Alcohols	40	C	COOH derivatives
11	B	Aldehydes & ketones	41	D	Amines
12	C	Carboxylic acids	42	B	Nomenclature
13	A	COOH derivatives	43	A	Covalent bond
14	C	Amines	44	A	Stereochemistry
15	A	Nomenclature	45	A	Amino acids, peptides, proteins
16	D	Covalent bond	46	A	Lipids
17	A	Stereochemistry	47	A	Carbohydrates
18	A	Molecular structure & spectra	48	B	Nucleic acids
19	C	Separations & purifications	49	A	Amino acids, peptides, proteins
20	A	Alkanes & alkyl halides	50	D	Lipids
21	A	Alkenes	51	C	Carbohydrates
22	B	Alkynes	52	C	Nucleic acids
23	C	Aromatic compounds	53	D	Amino acids, peptides, proteins
24	B	Alcohols	54	B	Lipids
25	A	Aldehydes & ketones	55	C	Carbohydrates
26	B	Carboxylic acids	56	D	Nucleic acids
27	C	COOH derivatives	57	B	Amino acids, peptides, proteins
28	B	Amines	58	D	Lipids
29	C	Nomenclature	59	D	Carbohydrates
30	B	Covalent bond	60	A	Nucleic acids

Diagnostic Test #5

This Diagnostic Test is designed for you to assess your proficiency on each topic and not to mimic the actual test. Use your test results and identify areas of your strength and weakness to adjust your study plan and enhance your fundamental knowledge.

The length of the Diagnostic Tests is proven to be optimal for a single study session.

#	Answer:				Review	#	Answer:				Review
1:	A	B	C	D	___	31:	A	B	C	D	___
2:	A	B	C	D	___	32:	A	B	C	D	___
3:	A	B	C	D	___	33:	A	B	C	D	___
4:	A	B	C	D	___	34:	A	B	C	D	___
5:	A	B	C	D	___	35:	A	B	C	D	___
6:	A	B	C	D	___	36:	A	B	C	D	___
7:	A	B	C	D	___	37:	A	B	C	D	___
8:	A	B	C	D	___	38:	A	B	C	D	___
9:	A	B	C	D	___	39:	A	B	C	D	___
10:	A	B	C	D	___	40:	A	B	C	D	___
11:	A	B	C	D	___	41:	A	B	C	D	___
12:	A	B	C	D	___	42:	A	B	C	D	___
13:	A	B	C	D	___	43:	A	B	C	D	___
14:	A	B	C	D	___	44:	A	B	C	D	___
15:	A	B	C	D	___	45:	A	B	C	D	___
16:	A	B	C	D	___	46:	A	B	C	D	___
17:	A	B	C	D	___	47:	A	B	C	D	___
18:	A	B	C	D	___	48:	A	B	C	D	___
19:	A	B	C	D	___	49:	A	B	C	D	___
20:	A	B	C	D	___	50:	A	B	C	D	___
21:	A	B	C	D	___	51:	A	B	C	D	___
22:	A	B	C	D	___	52:	A	B	C	D	___
23:	A	B	C	D	___	53:	A	B	C	D	___
24:	A	B	C	D	___	54:	A	B	C	D	___
25:	A	B	C	D	___	55:	A	B	C	D	___
26:	A	B	C	D	___	56:	A	B	C	D	___
27:	A	B	C	D	___	57:	A	B	C	D	___
28:	A	B	C	D	___	58:	A	B	C	D	___
29:	A	B	C	D	___	59:	A	B	C	D	___
30:	A	B	C	D	___	60:	A	B	C	D	___

Notes

1. The compound below is named:

    A. pentanone
    B. pentanal

    C. butanaldehyde
    D. pentaketone

2. Which of the compounds listed below is linear?

    A. 1,3,5-heptatriene
    B. acetylene

    C. 2-butyne
    D. dichloromethane

3. How many structural isomers of $C_4H_8Cl_2$ exhibit optical activity?

    A. 0   **B.** 1   **C.** 2   **D.** 3

4. Infrared spectroscopy provides a scientist with information about:

    A. molecular weight
    B. distribution of protons

    C. functional group
    D. conjugation

5. Which of the following factors usually increase(s) the solubility of a molecule in a given solvent?

    I. higher temperature
    II. similar polarities
    III. greater molecular weight of the molecule

    A. I only   **B.** II only   **C.** III only   **D.** I and II only

6. What is the most likely mechanism for the reaction between 1-bromobutane and sodium cyanide?

    A. E_1 **B.** E_2 **C.** S_N1 **D.** S_N2

7. Which of the following reactions will NOT occur?

Reaction 1: butene + NBS → 2-bromobutane
Reaction 2: 2-methylbutane + 8 O_2 + heat → 5 CO_2 + 6 H_2O
Reaction 3: 2-methylbutane + Br_2 + *hv* → 2-bromo-2-methylbutane
Reaction 4: 2-methyl-2-butene + Br_2 + CCl_4 → (*S*)-1,2-dibromo-2-methylbutane (+ enantiomer)

    A. Reaction 1   **B.** Reaction 2   **C.** Reaction 3   **D.** Reaction 4

8. For isomers with the formula $C_{10}H_{16}$, which of the following structural features are NOT possible within this set of molecules?

A. 2 rings and 1 double bond

B. 2 double bonds and 1 ring

C. 2 triple bonds

D. 1 ring and 1 triple bond

9. Which of the following molecules reacts the slowest in electrophilic nitration?

A. Toluene

B. Aniline

C. Anisole (methoxybenzene)

D. Bromobenzene

10. Which is a product of the oxidation of CH_3–CH_2–CH_2–O–H?

A. CH_3–CH_2–CH_3

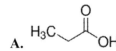

B.

C.

D.

11. Which of the following functional groups represents a ketone?

A.

B.

C.

D.

12. When a small amount of hexanoic acid [$CH_3(CH_2)_4CO_2H$, $pK_a \approx 4.8$] is added to a separatory funnel which contains the organic solvent diethyl ether and water with a pH of 11.0, it is found mainly in the [ ] phase as [ ]:

A. water; $CH_3(CH_2)_4CO_2H$

B. ether; $CH_3(CH_2)_4CO_2H$

C. water; $CH_3(CH_2)_4CO_2^-$

D. ether; $CH_3(CH_2)_4CO_2^-$

13. The reaction of benzoic acid with thionyl chloride followed, by treatment with ammonia, yields which of the following compounds?

A. *p*-chlorobenzamide

B. *m*-chlorobenzamide

C. benzamide

D. *p*-aminobenzaldehyde

14. The compound, trimethylamine is a(n) [   ] and has the formula [   ]:

A. base, $(CH_3)_3N$ B. acid, $(CH_3)_2NH$ C. base, $(CH_3)_2NH$ D. acid, $(CH_3)_3N$

15. Provide the common name of the compound:

$$CH_3 \quad CH_3$$
$$H_3C \longrightarrow N$$
$$CH_3 \quad CH_3$$

A. neobutyldimethylamine

B. *sec*-butyldimethylamine

C. *tert*-butyldimethylamine

D. isobutyldimethylamine

16. How many single and double bonds are in the benzene molecule (not including the C–H bonds)?

A. 6 single, 3 double

B. 5 single, 2 double

C. 6 single, 0 double

D. 5 single, 0 double

17. How many chiral carbon atoms are in this structure?

$$CH_2-CH-CH-CHCH_3$$
$$\;\;\; OH \;\; OH \;\; Br \;\;\; Cl$$

A. 6 B. 5 C. 3 D. 4

18. In the mass spectrum of 3,3-dimethyl-2-butanone, the base peak occurs at *m/z*:

A. 43 B. 58 C. 84 D. 85

19. Which of the three compounds is soluble in aqueous sodium bicarbonate?

salicylic acid

methyl salicylate

acetylsalicylic acid

I. salicylic acid II. methyl salicylate III. acetylsalicylic acid

A. I only B. II only C. I and II only D. I and III only

20. Which of the following alkyl halogens reacts the fastest with NaOH?

A. *t*-butyl bromide   **C.** *t*-butyl fluoride
B. *t*-butyl iodide   **D.** *t*-butyl chloride

21. Give the possibilities in the structure for a compound with a formula of C_6H_{10}:

A. no rings; no double bonds; no triple bonds
B. one double bond; or one ring
C. two rings; two double bonds; one double bond and one ring; or one triple bond
D. three rings; three double bonds; two double bonds and one ring; one ring and two double bonds; one triple bond and one ring; or one double bond and one ring

22. What is the product from the reaction of one mole of acetylene and one mole of hydrogen gas using platinum catalyst?

A. propane   **B.** propene   **C.** ethane   **D.** ethene

23. In electrophilic aromatic substitution, the aromatic ring acts as a(n):

A. leaving group   **B.** dienophile   **C.** nucleophile   **D.** electrophile

24. Which of the following has the highest boiling point?

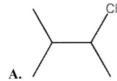

25. All of the following statements about oxidation of carbonyls are true, EXCEPT:

A. oxidation of aldehydes produces carboxylic acids
B. ketones do not react with mild oxidizing agents
C. Tollens' test involves the oxidation of Ag^+
D. Benedict's test involves the reduction of Cu^{2+}

26. Which of the following compounds acts as an acid?

A. CH_3COCH_3 **C.** C_2H_5OH
B. $(CH_3)_2NH$ **D.** C_2H_5COOH

27. The compound capsaicin below has which functional groups?

A. aldehyde and amine
B. carboxylic acid and amine

C. nitro and amine
D. amide and ether

28. Which compound is an example of an amine salt?

A. sulfanilamide
B. thioacetamide

C. dimethylammonium bromide
D. histamine

29. What is the correct IUPAC name for the following compound?

A. 2-oxocyclohex-3-ene-1-carboxylic acid
B. 5-formylcyclohex-2-enone-oic acid
C. 2-formylcyclohex-5-enone
D. 3-oxocyclohex-4-enoic acid

30. Determine the number of *pi* bonds in CH_3CN:

A. 0   B. 1   C. 2   D. 3

31. Which of the following is a true statement?

A. A mixture of achiral compounds is optically inactive
B. All molecules that possess a single chirality center of the *S* configuration are levorotatory
C. All achiral molecules are *meso*
D. All chiral molecules possess a plane of symmetry

32. The protons marked H_a and H_b in the molecule below are:

A. diastereotopic
B. heterotopic

C. homotopic
D. enantiotopic

33. Acetate can react with a tertiary alkyl chloride to form an ester. The reaction occurs more rapidly in water than in dimethylsulfoxide (DMSO) because water stabilizes the:

A. intermediate racemates   **C.** carbocation intermediate

B. configuration inversion   **D.** acetate

34. Which of the following is/are the most stable diene?

 A.   **C.**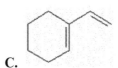

 B.   **D.**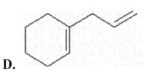

35. Which of the species below is less basic than an acetylide?

     I. CH_3Li II. CH_3MgBr III. CH_3ONa

A. I only   **B.** II only   **C.** III only   **D.** I and II only

36. What is the effect of –F substituents on electrophilic aromatic substitution?

A. *meta*-directing with activation

B. *meta*-directing with deactivation

C. *ortho-* / *para*-directing with activation

D. *ortho-* / *para*-directing with deactivation

37. What compound is formed by the oxidation of 2-hexanol?

A. hexanal   **C.** 2-hexanone

B. hexanoic acid   **D.** 2-hexene

38. Which of the following classes of compounds has a carbonyl group?

A. phenol   **C.** amine

B. ether   **D.** none of the above

39. All of the statements concerning citric acid are true, EXCEPT it:

A. is produced only by plants

B. is used in many consumer products

C. is extremely soluble in water

D. contains three carboxylic acid groups because its carbon skeleton is branched

40. What is the name of the product formed by the reaction of propanoic acid with ethanol?

A. ethyl propanoate
B. pentanal

C. pentyl ester
D. ethyl propyl ketone

41. Which statement about the differences between an amine and an amide is NOT correct?

A. Amides act as proton acceptors, while amines do not
B. Amines are basic and amides are neutral
C. Amines form ammonium salts when treated with acid; amides do not
D. The lone pair of electrons on amides is held more tightly than the lone pair on amines

42. What is the IUPAC name of the compound shown?

$$CH_3-CH-CH-CH_2-CH-CH_3$$

A. 3,4,6-trimethylheptane
B. 2,4,5-trimethylheptane

C. 3,5-dimethyl-2-ethylhexane
D. 2-ethyl-3,5-dimethylhexane

43. Give the hybridization, shape, and bond angle for carbon in ethene:

A. sp^3, tetrahedral, 120°
B. sp^3, tetrahedral, 109.5°

C. sp^2, trigonal planar, 120°
D. sp^2, trigonal planar, 109.5°

44. Which of the following best describes the geometry about the carbon-carbon double bond in the alkene below?

A. *E*   B. *Z*   C. *cis*   D. *R*

45. Which of the following compounds is an amino acid?

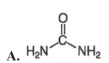

46. Lipids are naturally occurring compounds which all:

A. contain fatty acids as structural units
B. are water-insoluble, but soluble in nonpolar solvents

C. contain ester groups
D. contain cholesterol

47. Which functional group is not usually found in carbohydrates?

A. hydroxyl   **B.** ether   **C.** amide   **D.** aldehyde

48. What is the sugar component in RNA called?

A. fructose   **B.** galactose   **C.** glucose   **D.** ribose

49. The most basic functional group of aspartame is the:

Aspartame (Asp-Phe)

A. amide nitrogen
B. amino group

C. ester carbonyl oxygen
D. aromatic ring

50. Hydrogenation of vegetable oils converts them into what type of molecule?

A. esters   **B.** ethers   **C.** hemiacetals   **D.** saturated fats

51. The linkage between Subunits 2 and 3 in acarbose is best described as which of the following?

A. β-(1→4)   **B.** β-(1→2)   **C.** α-(1→6)   **D.** α-(1→4)

52. What is the process in which the DNA double helix unfolds, and each strand serves as a template for the synthesis of a new strand?

    A. translation   **C.** transcription

    B. replication   **D.** complementation

53. What is the major product of the following reaction series?

COOH + $PBr_3 \rightarrow$? + excess $NH_3 \rightarrow$?

    A. Ala   **B.** Gly   **C.** Val   **D.** Ile

54. A polyunsaturated fatty acid contains more than one:

    A. double bond   **C.** hydroxyl group

    B. carbonyl group   **D.** carboxyl group

55. A monosaccharide consisting of 5 carbon atoms, one of which is a ketone, is classified as a(n):

    A. aldohexose   **C.** aldotetrose

    B. ketopentose   **D.** aldopentose

56. If NADH is the reduced form of the high energy intermediate dinucleotide, which of the following is the oxidized form of this important biomolecule?

    A. NAD^{+2} **C.** NAD^+

    B. NAD   **D.** $NADH_2$

57. The protein conformation determined mostly from interactions between R groups is:

    A. tertiary structure   **C.** primary structure

    B. quaternary structure   **D.** secondary structure

58. The molecule shown can be classified as a(an):

    A. steroid   **C.** wax

    B. eicosanoid   **D.** glycerophospholipid

59. The monosaccharide shown below is a(n)

    A. aldohexose   **C.** ketohexose

    B. aldopentose   **D.** ketopentose

60. Which of the following illustrates the direction of flow for protein synthesis?

    A. RNA → protein → DNA   **C.** RNA → DNA → protein

    B. DNA → protein → RNA   **D.** DNA → RNA → protein

Check your answers using the answer key. Then, go to the explanations section and review the explanations in detail, paying attention to questions you didn't answer correctly or marked for review. Note the topic that those questions belong to.

We recommend that you do this BEFORE taking the next Diagnostic Test.

Diagnostic Test #5 – Answer Key

1	B	Nomenclature	31	A	Stereochemistry
2	B	Covalent bond	32	C	Molecular structure & spectra
3	D	Stereochemistry	33	C	Alkanes & alkyl halides
4	C	Molecular structure & spectra	34	C	Alkenes
5	D	Separations & purifications	35	C	Alkynes
6	D	Alkanes & alkyl halides	36	D	Aromatic compounds
7	A	Alkenes	37	C	Alcohols
8	C	Alkynes	38	D	Aldehydes & ketones
9	D	Aromatic compounds	39	A	Carboxylic acids
10	D	Alcohols	40	A	COOH derivatives
11	D	Aldehydes & ketones	41	A	Amines
12	C	Carboxylic acids	42	B	Nomenclature
13	C	COOH derivatives	43	C	Covalent bond
14	A	Amines	44	A	Stereochemistry
15	C	Nomenclature	45	B	Amino acids, peptides, proteins
16	A	Covalent bond	46	B	Lipids
17	C	Stereochemistry	47	C	Carbohydrates
18	A	Molecular structure & spectra	48	D	Nucleic acids
19	D	Separations & purifications	49	B	Amino acids, peptides, proteins
20	B	Alkanes & alkyl halides	50	D	Lipids
21	C	Alkenes	51	D	Carbohydrates
22	D	Alkynes	52	B	Nucleic acids
23	C	Aromatic compounds	53	C	Amino acids, peptides, proteins
24	D	Alcohols	54	A	Lipids
25	C	Aldehydes & ketones	55	B	Carbohydrates
26	D	Carboxylic acids	56	C	Nucleic acids
27	D	COOH derivatives	57	A	Amino acids, peptides, proteins
28	C	Amines	58	C	Lipids
29	A	Nomenclature	59	A	Carbohydrates
30	C	Covalent bond	60	D	Nucleic acids

Notes

Diagnostic Test #6

This Diagnostic Test is designed for you to assess your proficiency on each topic and not to mimic the actual test. Use your test results and identify areas of your strength and weakness to adjust your study plan and enhance your fundamental knowledge.

The length of the Diagnostic Tests is proven to be optimal for a single study session.

#	Answer:				Review	#	Answer:				Review
1:	A	B	C	D	___	31:	A	B	C	D	___
2:	A	B	C	D	___	32:	A	B	C	D	___
3:	A	B	C	D	___	33:	A	B	C	D	___
4:	A	B	C	D	___	34:	A	B	C	D	___
5:	A	B	C	D	___	35:	A	B	C	D	___
6:	A	B	C	D	___	36:	A	B	C	D	___
7:	A	B	C	D	___	37:	A	B	C	D	___
8:	A	B	C	D	___	38:	A	B	C	D	___
9:	A	B	C	D	___	39:	A	B	C	D	___
10:	A	B	C	D	___	40:	A	B	C	D	___
11:	A	B	C	D	___	41:	A	B	C	D	___
12:	A	B	C	D	___	42:	A	B	C	D	___
13:	A	B	C	D	___	43:	A	B	C	D	___
14:	A	B	C	D	___	44:	A	B	C	D	___
15:	A	B	C	D	___	45:	A	B	C	D	___
16:	A	B	C	D	___	46:	A	B	C	D	___
17:	A	B	C	D	___	47:	A	B	C	D	___
18:	A	B	C	D	___	48:	A	B	C	D	___
19:	A	B	C	D	___	49:	A	B	C	D	___
20:	A	B	C	D	___	50:	A	B	C	D	___
21:	A	B	C	D	___	51:	A	B	C	D	___
22:	A	B	C	D	___	52:	A	B	C	D	___
23:	A	B	C	D	___	53:	A	B	C	D	___
24:	A	B	C	D	___	54:	A	B	C	D	___
25:	A	B	C	D	___	55:	A	B	C	D	___
26:	A	B	C	D	___	56:	A	B	C	D	___
27:	A	B	C	D	___	57:	A	B	C	D	___
28:	A	B	C	D	___	58:	A	B	C	D	___
29:	A	B	C	D	___	59:	A	B	C	D	___
30:	A	B	C	D	___	60:	A	B	C	D	___

Notes

1. A compound with the molecular formula C_3H_6 is:

   A. butane   **B.** butyne   **C.** 2-methylpropane   **D.** cyclopropane

2. Which of the following is the least stable carbocation? (Use Ph = phenyl group)

   A. PhH_2C^+ **B.** $CH_3CH_2CH_2{}^+$ **C.** Ph_3C^+ **D.** Ph_2HC^+

3. If two of the hydrogen atoms in ethylene, $H_2C=CH_2$, are replaced by two chlorine atoms to form dichloroethylene, how many different dichloroethylene isomers are there?

   A. 3   **B.** 4   **C.** 1   **D.** 2

4. A compound with nine carbon atoms produces a single NMR signal. What is a possible structural formula for the compound?

   A. $(CH_3)_3CCCl_2C(CH_3)_3$
   B. $(CH_3)_2CHCH_2CH_2CH(CH_3)CH_2CH_3$
   C. $(CH_3)_2CHCH_2(CH_2)_4CH_3$
   D. $CH_3(CH_2)_7CH_3$

5. In a fractionating column, the crude oil vapors pass from a pipe into the column. Tar and lubricating stock are the first components to be pulled off at the bottom. From the remaining hydrocarbons, the natural gas is the first fraction collected, followed by gasoline and then kerosene. From this information, which has a higher boiling point, gasoline or kerosene?

   A. Fractional distillation components are pulled off based on molecular weight, so it is not possible to determine which has the higher boiling point from the information given
   B. their boiling points are the same, but kerosene has the greatest density
   C. Kerosene has a higher boiling point
   D. Gasoline has a higher boiling point

6. If propane was reacted with Cl_2 in the presence of UV light, what products form and what are their approximate percentages?

   A. Propyl chloride yields 100%
   B. Propyl chloride yields 42%, and isopropyl chloride yields 58%
   C. Propyl chloride yields 75%, and isopropyl chloride yields 25%
   D. Propyl chloride yields 90%, and isopropyl chloride yields 10%

7. Which of the following reactions does NOT proceed through a bromonium ion intermediate?

   A. $CH_3CH=CH_2 + Br_2 + H_2O \rightarrow CH_3CH_2OHCH_2Br + HBr$
   B. $CH_2=CHCH_2CH_2CH=CH_2 + Br_2 \rightarrow CH_2BrCHBrCH_2CH_2CHBrCH_2Br$
   C. $CH_3CH_2CH=CH_2 + Br_2 \rightarrow CH_3CH_2CHBrCH_2Br$
   D. $CH_3CH_2CH=CH_2 + HBr \rightarrow CH_3CH_2CHBrCH_3$

8. What is the general molecular formula for the alkyne class of compounds?

   I. C_nH_{2n+2} II. C_nH_{2n} III. C_nH_{2n-2}

A. I only   **B.** II only   **C.** III only   **D.** II and III only

9. What is the effect of each of –Cl substituents on electrophilic aromatic substitution?

A. *meta*-directing with deactivation   **C.** *ortho-/para*-directing with deactivation
B. *meta*-directing with activation   **D.** *ortho*-directing with activation

10. Which of the following alcohols has the lowest boiling point?

A. hexanol   **C.** propanol
B. 2-methyl-1-propanol   **D.** ethanol

11. Which of the following pairs have the most similar chemical properties?

A. alkanes and carboxylic acids   **C.** amines and esters
B. alkenes and aromatics   **D.** ketones and aldehydes

12. Which of the following compounds is the strongest acid?

A. $HOOCCH_2F$ **C.** $HOOCCH_2Br$
B. $HOOCCH_3$ **D.** $HOOCCH_2OCH_3$

13. Which of the following products might be formed if benzoyl chloride was treated with excess CH_3CH_2MgBr?

A. $C_6H_5CH_2CHO$ **C.** C_6H_5COOH
B. $C_6H_5C(CH_2CH_3)OHCH_2CH_3$ **D.** $C_6H_5COOCH_2CH_3$

14. Why is an amine salt more soluble in water than the corresponding free amine?

A. The negative charge on the nitrogen atom increases water solubility
B. It has a higher molecular weight than the corresponding amine
C. It is ionic and therefore more soluble than covalent compounds with the same structure
D. All amines are insoluble in water

15. What is the correct IUPAC name for the following compound?

A. 2-ethyl-4-methylhexane   **C.** 4-ethyl-2-methylhexane
B. 2,4-dimethylhexane   **D.** 3,5-dimethylheptane

16. The energy of a sp^3 hybridized orbital for a carbon atom is:

    A. lower in energy than both the $2s$ and the $2p$ atomic orbitals
    B. higher in energy than both the $2s$ and the $2p$ atomic orbitals
    C. higher in energy than the $2p$ atomic orbital, but lower in energy than the $2s$ atomic orbital
    D. higher in energy than the $2s$ atomic orbital, but lower in energy than the $2p$ atomic orbital

17. The enantiomer of the compound below is:

```
        CHO
         |
    H —— C —— OH
         |
    H —— C —— OH
         |
        CH2OH
```

```
        CHO                    CHO                     CHO                    CHO
         |                      |                       |                      |
    H —— C —— OH          HO —— C —— H            HO —— C —— H           H —— C —— OH
         |                      |                       |                      |
   HO —— C —— H           HO —— C —— H             H —— C —— OH           H —— C —— OH
         |                      |                       |                      |
        CH2OH                  CH2OH                   CH2OH                  CH2OH
A.                     B.                       C.                     D.
```

18. In mass spectrometry plots, the relative abundance is the unit along the y-axis in a mass spectrum. What are the units on the x-axis?

    A. mass / charge (m/z)   **C.** molecular weight (amu)
    B. mass (m)   **D.** frequency (ν)

19. How does fractional distillation function to separate molecules?

    A. It utilizes differences in melting points
    B. It utilizes the fraction of carbon in the isomers
    C. It utilizes the different weight of molecules
    D. It utilizes the different boiling points of molecules

20. What is true about an S_N1 reaction?

        I. A carbocation intermediate is formed
        II. The rate determining step is bimolecular
        III. The mechanism has two steps

    A. I only   **C.** I and II only
    B. II only   **D.** I and III only

21. When reacted with HBr, *cis*-3-methyl-2-hexene most likely undergoes:

    A. *anti*-Markovnikov *syn*- and *anti*-addition
    B. *anti*-Markovnikov *syn*-addition
    C. Markovnikov *syn*- and *anti*-addition
    D. Markovnikov *syn*-addition

22. Among the following compounds, which acids are stronger than ammonia?

    I. water   II. ethane   III. butyne   IV. but-2-yne

    A. I and II only   **C.** I and III only
    B. II only   **D.** II and III only

23. 1,3-cyclopentadiene reacts with sodium metal at low temperatures according to:

What is the best explanation for this observation?

    A. Aromaticity stabilizes the anion
    B. Sodium metal is highly selective for cycloalkenes
    C. Aromaticity stabilizes the carbocation
    D. The reactant is more unstable at reduced temperatures

24. The reaction of $(CH_3)_2CHCH_2OH$ with concentrated HBr using controlled heating yields:

    A. $(CH_3)_2CHCH_2OBr$ **C.** $CH_3CH_2CH_2Br$
    B. $(CH_3)_2CHCH_4^+Br^-$ **D.** $(CH_3)_2CHCH_2Br$

25. Which compound gives a positive Tollens' test?

    A. pentane   **B.** pentanal   **C.** 3-pentanone   **D.** 2-pentanone

26. Explain why caprylic acid $CH_3(CH_2)_6COOH$ dissolves in a 5% aqueous solution of sodium hydroxide, but caprylaldehyde, $CH_3(CH_2)_6CHO$, does not.

    A. Caprylic acid reacts to form the water-soluble salt
    B. Caprylaldehyde behaves as a reducing agent, which neutralizes the sodium hydroxide
    C. Caprylaldehyde can form more hydrogen bonds to water than caprylic acid
    D. With two oxygens, caprylic acid is about twice as polar as caprylaldehyde

27. The compound below has which functional groups?

CH₂OH

A. lactone and alcohol
B. ether and alcohol

C. ester and hemiacetal
D. ester and acetal

28. Based on the properties of the attached functional group, which compound below interacts most strongly with water, thus making it the most soluble compound?

A. $CH_3–CH_2–I$ B. $CH_3–O–CH_3$ C. $CH_3–CH_2–NH_2$ D. $CH_3–CH_2–H$

29. Name the following structure according to IUPAC nomenclature:

A. 3-ethyl-3-hexene
B. 4-methylenehexane

C. 2-propyl-1-butene
D. 2-ethyl-1-pentene

30. Which of the following pairs are resonance structures?

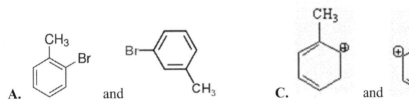

31. Which of the statements correctly describes an achiral molecule?

A. The molecule has an enantiomer
B. The molecule may be a *meso* form
C. The molecule has a non-superimposable mirror image
D. The molecule exhibits optical activity when it interacts with plane-polarized light

32. How many nuclear spin states are allowed for the ^1H nucleus?

    A. 1   **B.** 2   **C.** 3   **D.** 4

33. The most stable conformational isomer of 1,2-dibromoethane is:

    A. eclipsed, *anti*   **C.** staggered, *anti*
    B. staggered, *gauche*   **D.** eclipsed, *gauche*

34. All of the following are examples of addition reactions of alkenes, EXCEPT:

    A. ozonolysis   **C.** oxidation
    B. hydration   **D.** bromination

35. In the reduction of alkynes using sodium in liquid ammonia, which of the species below is NOT an intermediate in the commonly accepted mechanism?

    A. vinyl anion   **C.** anion
    B. vinyl cation   **D.** vinyl radical

36. What is the major product of this electrophile aromatic substitution (EAS) reaction?

$+ \text{HNO}_3 / \text{H}_2\text{SO}_4 \rightarrow$?

37. When propanol is subjected to PBr_3, the compounds undergo:

    A. an S_N1 elimination reaction to form propene
    B. oxidation to form an aldehyde
    C. an S_N1 reaction to produce an alkyl halide
    D. addition, elimination and then substitution to form bromopropane

38. Consider the equilibrium of each of the carbonyl compounds with HCN to produce cyanohydrins. Which is the correct ranking of compounds in order of increasing K_{eq} for this equilibrium?

A. 2-methylcyclohexanone < cyclohexanone < CH_3CHO < H_2CO
B. CH_3CHO < 2-methylcyclohexanone < cyclohexanone < H_2CO
C. cyclohexanone < 2-methylcyclohexanone < H_2CO < CH_3CHO
D. cyclohexanone < 2-methylcyclohexanone < CH_3CHO < H_2CO

39. All of the statements about carboxylic acids are true, EXCEPT:

A. they react with bases to form salts which are often more soluble than the original acid
B. they form hydrogen bonds, causing their boiling points to be higher than expected on the basis of molecular weight
C. when they behave as acids, the ^-OH group is lost, leaving the CO^- ion
D. they undergo substitution reactions involving the ^-OH group

40. Benzoyl chloride, $PhC(O)Cl$, reacts with water to form benzoic acid, $PhCO_2H$. In this addition–elimination reaction:

A. water acts as a nucleophile, benzoyl chloride acts as an electrophile, and chloride acts as a leaving group
B. water acts as an electrophile, benzoyl chloride acts as a nucleophile, and chloride acts as a leaving group
C. both water and benzoyl chloride act as electrophiles
D. there are no nucleophiles or electrophiles

41. Assuming roughly equivalent molecular weights, which of the following has the highest boiling point?

A. alcohol
B. ether

C. tertiary amine
D. quaternary ammonium salt

42. What is the IUPAC name for the following structure?

A. *cis*-methylcyclohexane
B. *cis*-1-chloro-2-methylcyclopentane
C. *Z*-chloro-methylcyclohexane
D. *cis*-2-chloro-2-methylcyclohexane

43. Due to electron delocalization, the carbon-oxygen bond in acetamide, CH_3CONH_2:

    A. is longer than the carbon-oxygen bond of dimethyl ether, $(CH_3)_2O$

    B. is longer than the carbon-oxygen bond of acetone, $(CH_3)_2CO$

    C. is nonpolar

    D. has more double bond character than the carbon-oxygen bond of acetone, $(CH_3)_2CO$

44. Which of the following statements does NOT correctly describe *cis*-1,2-dimethylcyclopentane?

    A. Its diastereomer is *trans*-1,2-dimethylcyclopentane   **C.** It is achiral

    B. It contains two asymmetric carbons   **D.** It has an enantiomer

45. All of the bonds below are apparent in the secondary and tertiary structure of a protein, EXCEPT:

    A. electrostatic interactions   **C.** hydrogen bonding

    B. peptide bonds   **D.** hydrophobic interactions

46. Triacylglycerols are compounds which contain combined:

    A. cholesterol and other steroids   **C.** fatty acids and glycerol

    B. fatty acids and phospholipids   **D.** fatty acids and choline

47. Each of the following yields a positive Benedict's test for reducing sugars, EXCEPT:

    A. α-1,1-glucose-glucose   **C.** glucose

    B. β-1,4-glucose-glucose   **D.** fructose

48. What is the main function of the structural difference of the sugar that makes up RNA, compared to the sugar of DNA?

    A. It stabilizes the RNA outside the nucleus

    B. It acts as an energy source to produce proteins

    C. It allows the RNA to be easily digested by enzymes

    D. It keeps the RNA from binding tightly to DNA

49. Proteins are polymers. They consist of monomer units which are:

    A. keto acids   **B.** amide   **C.** amino acids   **D.** ketones

50. The name of the reaction that occurs when a fat reacts with sodium hydroxide and water is:

    A. oxidation   **C.** reduction

    B. hydration   **D.** saponification

51. How many stereoisomers do carbohydrates have?

    A. 2^n, where n is the number of chiral centers
    B. $2^n - 1$, where n is the number of chiral centers
    C. $2n$, where n is the number of chiral centers
    D. $2n - 1$, where n is the number of chiral centers

52. The double helix of DNA is stabilized mainly by:

    A. ionic bonds   **C.** ion–dipole bonds
    B. hydrogen bonds   **D.** ester bonds

53. Proteins migrate the smallest distance during gel electrophoresis when the protein is at:

    A. high pH   **C.** low pH
    B. neutral pH   **D.** their isoelectric point

54. Which of the following molecules produce fat from an esterification reaction?

    I. $CH_3(CH_2)_{14}COOH$
    II. $CH_3(CH_2)_7CH=CH(CH_2)_7COCH_2CH_3$
    III. $HOCH_2CHO$
    IV. $HOCH_2CH(OH)CH_2OH$

    A. I and IV only   **C.** II and IV only
    B. II and III only   **D.** I and III only

55. Which of the following molecules is a disaccharide?

    A. fructose   **B.** cellulose   **C.** lactose   **D.** glucose

56. Which of the following is the correct listing of DNA's constituents in the order of increasing size?

    A. Nucleotide, codon, gene, nucleic acid
    B. Nucleic acid, nucleotide, codon, gene
    C. Nucleotide, codon, nucleic acid, gene
    D. Gene, nucleic acid, nucleotide, codon

57. Why might a change in pH cause a protein to denature?

    A. The hydrogen bonds between the hydrophobic portions of the protein collapse due to extra protons
    B. The disulfide bridges open
    C. The functional groups that give the protein its shape become protonated or deprotonated
    D. The water hardens and causes the protein's shape to change

58. Oils are generally [   ] at room temperature and are obtained from [   ]:

    A. liquids … plants   **C.** solids … plants

    B. liquids … animals   **D.** solids … animals

59. Ribose can be classified as a(n):

    A. aldoketose   **C.** aldohexose

    B. aldopentose   **D.** ketopentose

60. The number of adenines in a DNA molecule is equal to the number of thymines because:

    A. adenines are paired opposite of guanine in a DNA molecule

    B. of the strong attraction between the nucleotides of adenine and thymine

    C. the structure of adenine is similar to uracil

    D. adenine is paired to cytosine in a DNA molecule

Check your answers using the answer key. Then, go to the explanations section and review the explanations in detail, paying attention to questions you didn't answer correctly or marked for review. Note the topic that those questions belong to.

We recommend that you do this BEFORE taking the next Diagnostic Test.

Please, leave your Customer Review on Amazon

Diagnostic Test #6 – Answer Key

1	D	Nomenclature	31	B	Stereochemistry
2	B	Covalent bond	32	B	Molecular structure & spectra
3	A	Stereochemistry	33	C	Alkanes & alkyl halides
4	A	Molecular structure & spectra	34	A	Alkenes
5	C	Separations & purifications	35	B	Alkynes
6	B	Alkanes & alkyl halides	36	B	Aromatic compounds
7	D	Alkenes	37	D	Alcohols
8	C	Alkynes	38	A	Aldehydes & ketones
9	C	Aromatic compounds	39	C	Carboxylic acids
10	D	Alcohols	40	A	COOH derivatives
11	D	Aldehydes & ketones	41	D	Amines
12	A	Carboxylic acids	42	B	Nomenclature
13	B	COOH derivatives	43	B	Covalent bond
14	C	Amines	44	D	Stereochemistry
15	B	Nomenclature	45	B	Amino acids, peptides, proteins
16	D	Covalent bond	46	C	Lipids
17	B	Stereochemistry	47	A	Carbohydrates
18	A	Molecular structure & spectra	48	C	Nucleic acids
19	D	Separations & purifications	49	C	Amino acids, peptides, proteins
20	D	Alkanes & alkyl halides	50	D	Lipids
21	C	Alkenes	51	A	Carbohydrates
22	C	Alkynes	52	B	Nucleic acids
23	A	Aromatic compounds	53	D	Amino acids, peptides, proteins
24	D	Alcohols	54	A	Lipids
25	B	Aldehydes & ketones	55	C	Carbohydrates
26	A	Carboxylic acids	56	A	Nucleic acids
27	A	COOH derivatives	57	C	Amino acids, peptides, proteins
28	C	Amines	58	A	Lipids
29	D	Nomenclature	59	B	Carbohydrates
30	C	Covalent bond	60	B	Nucleic acids

Notes

Diagnostic Test #7

This Diagnostic Test is designed for you to assess your proficiency on each topic and not to mimic the actual test. Use your test results and identify areas of your strength and weakness to adjust your study plan and enhance your fundamental knowledge.

The length of the Diagnostic Tests is proven to be optimal for a single study session.

#	Answer:				Review	#	Answer:				Review
1:	A	B	C	D	___	31:	A	B	C	D	___
2:	A	B	C	D	___	32:	A	B	C	D	___
3:	A	B	C	D	___	33:	A	B	C	D	___
4:	A	B	C	D	___	34:	A	B	C	D	___
5:	A	B	C	D	___	35:	A	B	C	D	___
6:	A	B	C	D	___	36:	A	B	C	D	___
7:	A	B	C	D	___	37:	A	B	C	D	___
8:	A	B	C	D	___	38:	A	B	C	D	___
9:	A	B	C	D	___	39:	A	B	C	D	___
10:	A	B	C	D	___	40:	A	B	C	D	___
11:	A	B	C	D	___	41:	A	B	C	D	___
12:	A	B	C	D	___	42:	A	B	C	D	___
13:	A	B	C	D	___	43:	A	B	C	D	___
14:	A	B	C	D	___	44:	A	B	C	D	___
15:	A	B	C	D	___	45:	A	B	C	D	___
16:	A	B	C	D	___	46:	A	B	C	D	___
17:	A	B	C	D	___	47:	A	B	C	D	___
18:	A	B	C	D	___	48:	A	B	C	D	___
19:	A	B	C	D	___	49:	A	B	C	D	___
20:	A	B	C	D	___	50:	A	B	C	D	___
21:	A	B	C	D	___	51:	A	B	C	D	___
22:	A	B	C	D	___	52:	A	B	C	D	___
23:	A	B	C	D	___	53:	A	B	C	D	___
24:	A	B	C	D	___	54:	A	B	C	D	___
25:	A	B	C	D	___	55:	A	B	C	D	___
26:	A	B	C	D	___	56:	A	B	C	D	___
27:	A	B	C	D	___	57:	A	B	C	D	___
28:	A	B	C	D	___	58:	A	B	C	D	___
29:	A	B	C	D	___	59:	A	B	C	D	___
30:	A	B	C	D	___	60:	A	B	C	D	___

Notes

1. The IUPAC name for the compound $H_2C=CH–CH=CH_2$ is:

A. 1,3-butadiene

B. butane-1,3

C. butene-2

D. 1,3-dibutene

2. Draw a structural formula for cyclohexane, a cyclic saturated hydrocarbon (C_6H_{12}). How many π bonds are in a cyclohexane molecule?

A. 3   **B.** 4   **C.** 0   **D.** 2

3. Which of the following compounds is an isomer of $CH_3CH_2CH_2CH_2OH$?

A. $CH_3CH_2CH_2OH$

B. $CH_3(OH)CHCH_3$

C. $CH_3CH_2CH_2CHO$

D. $CH_3CH_2(OH)CHCH_3$

4. A clear liquid is subjected to infrared spectroscopy and produces a spectrum with a prominent, broad peak at approximately 3000 cm^{-1} and a sharp peak at 1710 cm^{-1}, as well as several smaller peaks between 1420 cm^{-1} and 940 cm^{-1}. This substance is most likely:

A. ketone

B. carboxylic acid

C. alcohol

D. aldehyde

5. Which of the following factors usually increase(s) the solubility of a molecule in a given solvent?

    I. higher temperature

    II. similar polarities

    III. lower density of the solvent

A. I only

B. II only

C. III only

D. I and II only

6. Which of the compounds listed below has the lowest boiling point?

A. 3-methylheptane

B. 2,4-dimethylhexane

C. octane

D. 2,2,4-trimethylpentane

7. Which of the following compounds is/are geometric isomers?

    I. Isobutene

    II. (*E*)-2-butene

    III. *cis*-2-butene

    IV. *trans*-2-butene

A. I and II only

B. II and III only

C. III and IV only

D. II, III and IV only

8. When 2,2-dibromobutane is heated to 200 °C in the presence of molten KOH, what is the major organic product?

A. but-1-yne

B. but-2-yne

C. 1-bromobut-1-yne

D. 1-bromobut-2-yne

9. Derivatives of the compound shown below are currently being examined for their effectiveness in treating drug addiction and metabolic syndrome. Which sequence ranks the aromatic rings of this compound in order of increasing reactivity (slowest to fastest reacting) in an electrophilic aromatic substitution reaction?

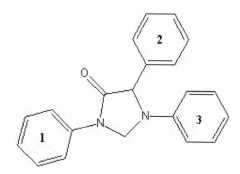

A. 2 < 1 < 3

B. 2 < 3 < 1

C. 3 < 2 < 1

D. 3 < 1 < 2

10. Which of the following has the highest boiling point?

A. ethyl methyl ether

B. dihexyl ether

C. dimethyl ether

D. diethyl ether

11. Which compound gives a positive indicator with the Tollens' reagent?

A. $H-\overset{\overset{O}{\|}}{C}-O-CH_2-CH_3$

C. $CH_3-\overset{\overset{O}{\|}}{C}-CH_2-CH_3$

B. $H-\overset{\overset{OH}{|}}{C}-CH_2-CH_3$

D. $CH_3-\overset{\overset{O}{\|}}{C}-H$

12. Which of the functional groups below contain(s) a hydroxyl group as a part of its/their structure?

I. anhydride   II. carboxylic acid   III. ester

A. I only

B. II only

C. III only

D. I and II only

13. Which functional group(s) below indicate(s) the presence of two atoms connected by a triple bond?

I. ester   II. nitrile   III. alkyne

A. I only   **C.** III only
B. II only   **D.** II and III only

14. The functional group C=O is found in all the species below, EXCEPT:

A. amines   **C.** carboxylic acids
B. amides   **D.** aldehydes

15. What is the IUPAC name for salicylic acid shown below:

A. 2-hydroxybenzoic acid   **C.** 1-hydroxybenzoic acid
B. α-hydroxybenzoic acid   **D.** *meta*-hydroxybenzoic acid

16. The N–H bond in the ammonium ion, NH_4^+, is formed by the overlap of which two orbitals?

A. sp^2–s **B.** sp^2–sp^2 **C.** sp^3–s **D.** sp^3–sp^3

17. If two of the hydrogen atoms in ethylene, $H_2C=CH_2$, are replaced by one chlorine atom and one fluorine atom to form chlorofluoroethene, C_2H_2ClF, how many different chlorofluoroethene isomers are there?

A. 4   **B.** 3   **C.** 2   **D.** 1

18. Which of the following laboratory techniques is used primarily as a compound identification procedure?

A. extraction   **C.** crystallization
B. NMR spectroscopy   **D.** distillation

19. The best method to separate each volatile isomer product from the reaction mixture is:

A. extraction   **C.** fractional distillation
B. crystallization   **D.** thin-layer chromatography

20. Which of the following is NOT a feature of S$_N$2 reactions?

A. single-step mechanism   **C.** bimolecular kinetics

B. pentacoordinate transition state   **D.** carbocation intermediate

21. Consider the following alcohol A.

The major product resulting from the dehydration of A is:

A.

C.

B.

D.

22. What class of organic product results when 1-heptyne is treated with a mixture of mercuric acetate [Hg(OAc)$_2$] in aqueous sulfuric acid (H$_2$SO$_4$), followed by sodium borohydride (NaBH$_4$)?

A. diol   **C.** aldehyde

B. ether   **D.** ketone

23. The major aromatic product of the following reaction is:

A. methyl ketone substitutes in the *ortho / para* position
B. methyl ketone substitutes in the *meta* position
C. methyl ketone replacing the bromine
D. formation of phenol

24. Based on the properties of the attached functional group, which compound interacts most strongly with water, thus making it the most soluble compound?

A. CH₃–CH₂–S–H

B. CH₃–CH₂–I

C. CH₃–CH₂–O–H

D. CH₃–CH₂–Cl

25. Reduction of aldehydes and ketones is a [ ] reaction involving the [ ] ion(s).

A. two-step; H⁻ and H⁺

B. two-step; OH⁻ and H⁺

C. one-step; H⁻

D. one-step; H⁺

26. Which acid is expected to have the lowest boiling point?

A. formic, HCO₂H

B. oxalic, (CO₂H)₂

C. acetic, CH₃CO₂H

D. benzoic, C₆H₅CO₂H

27. Which of these molecules is an ester?

A.

C.

B.

D.

28. A quaternary ammonium salt does NOT carry out substitution reactions with alkyl halides, because the nitrogen atom is not:

A. an electrophile

B. a nucleophile

C. negatively charged

D. saturated

29. What is the common name for the simplest ketone, propanone?

A. acetal

B. acetone

C. carbanone

D. formalin

30. Among the hydrogen halides, the strongest bond is in [ ], and the longest bond is in [ ]?

A. HI ... HI

B. HI ... HF

C. HF ... HI

D. HF ... HF

31. In the Fischer projection below, what are the configurations of the two asymmetric centers?

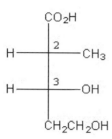

A. 2*S*, 3*S*   B. 2*S*, 3*R*   C. 2*R*, 3*S*   D. 2*R*, 3*R*

32. While the carbonyl stretching frequency for simple aldehydes, ketones, and carboxylic acids is about 1710 cm^{-1}, the carbonyl stretching frequency for esters is about:

A. 1660 cm^{-1} B. 1700 cm^{-1} C. 1735 cm^{-1} D. 1800 cm^{-1}

33. Which conformer is at a local energy minimum on the potential energy diagram in the chair-chair interconversion of cyclohexane?

A. boat   B. twist-boat   C. half-chair   D. planar

34. What is the major product of the following reaction?

+ Br$_2$ / H$_2$O → ?

A.   C.

B.   D.

35. Which of the following describes the reaction below?

H$_3$C≡CH$_3$ + H$_2$, Pd, CaCo$_3$, quinolone, hexane →

A. oxidation   C. substitution
B. reduction   D. catalytic hydration

36. In electrophilic aromatic substitution reactions, an extremely reactive electrophile is typically used because the aromatic ring is:

A. a poor electrophile   **C.** reactive

B. nonpolar   **D.** a poor nucleophile

37. What is the product of the following reaction?

A.

B.

C.

D.

38. Which of the following is the best Michael acceptor?

A.

B.

C.

D.

39. Which of the following molecules is acidic?

I.   II.   III.

A. I only   **C.** I and II only

B. II only   **D.** I and III only

40. The products of basic hydrolysis of an ester are:

A. acid + water

B. alcohol + water

C. carboxylate salt + alcohol

D. another ester + water

41. Amines are most similar in chemical structure and behavior to:

A. sodium hydroxide

B. a primary alcohol

C. the hydronium ion

D. ammonia

42. The name of the compound shown below is:

A. 3-ethyltoluene

B. 2-ethyltoluene

C. 1-ethyl-4-methylbenzene

D. 1-ethyl-2-methylbenzene

43. Which of the following is the most stable carbocation?

A.

C.

B.

D.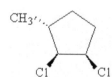

44. Which of the following terms best describes the pair of compounds shown?

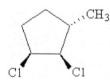

A. same molecule

B. conformational isomers

C. enantiomers

D. diastereomers

45. Proteins are characterized by the fact that they:

    A. always have quaternary structures
    B. retain their conformation above 35-40 °C
    C. have a primary structure formed by covalent linkages
    D. are composed of a single peptide chain

46. Lipids are compounds that are soluble in:

    A. glucose solution   **C.** distilled water
    B. organic solvents   **D.** normal saline solution

47. If one of the carboxylic acids of tartaric acid is reduced to an aldehyde and the other is replaced with a CH_2OH group, which of the following results?

    A. aldotetrose   **C.** ketotriose
    B. aldotriose   **D.** aldopentose

48. What type of biological compound is a polymer composed of a sugar, a base, and phosphoric acid?

    A. nucleic acid   **C.** carbohydrate
    B. lipid   **D.** protein

49. The reaction mechanism by which 2,4-dinitrofluorobenzene reacts with a protein is:

    A. addition   **C.** nucleophilic aromatic substitution
    B. S_N2 **D.** electrophilic aromatic substitution

50. Which statement regarding fatty acids is NOT correct? Fatty acids:

    A. are always liquids
    B. are long-chain carboxylic acids
    C. are usually unbranched chains
    D. usually have an even number of carbon atoms

51. The cyclic structure shown below is classified as a(n):

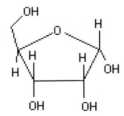

    A. ketose   **C.** pentose
    B. aldehyde   **D.** hexose

52. What is the term for the process by which a DNA molecule synthesizes an identical molecule of DNA?

A. transcription

C. duplication

B. translation

D. replication

53. Members of which class of biomolecules is the building blocks of proteins?

A. fatty acids

C. glycerols

B. amino acids

D. monosaccharides

54. Unsaturated triacylglycerols are usually [ ] because [ ]?

A. liquids … they have relatively short fatty acid chains

B. liquids … the kinks in their fatty acid chains prevent their fitting together closely

C. liquids … they contain impurities from their natural sources

D. solids … they have relatively long fatty acid chains

55. An acyclic sugar shown by a Fischer projection is classified as a D-isomer if the hydroxyl group on the chiral carbon:

A. nearest to the carbonyl group points to the left

B. nearest to the carbonyl group points to the right

C. farthest from the carbonyl group points to the left

D. farthest from the carbonyl group points to the right

56. The bonds that link the base pairs in the DNA double helix are [ ] bonds?

A. hydrophobic

C. peptide

B. hydrogen

D. ionic

57. If a hair stylist is about to apply a reducing agent to a client with fine hair who wants to have his hair curly, should the reducing agent be regular strength, concentrated, or diluted?

A. diluted, so as not to cause the hair to fall apart completely

B. concentrated, in order to add more disulfide cross-linking

C. concentrated, in order to add more hydrogen bonding

D. concentrated because in thin hair each strand is made of fewer cysteine amino acids

58. Two families of fatty acids that are significant in nutrition are Ω-6 and Ω-3 fatty acids. Which of the following structures would be classified as a Ω-3 fatty acid?

A.

B.

C.

D.

59. What is the structural difference between deoxyribose and ribose?

A. methyl group   **C.** carboxyl group

B. hydroxyl group   **D.** carbonyl group

60. Translation is the process whereby:

A. protein is synthesized from DNA   **C.** DNA is synthesized from DNA

B. protein is synthesized from mRNA   **D.** DNA is synthesized from mRNA

Check your answers using the answer key. Then, go to the explanations section and review the explanations in detail, paying attention to questions you didn't answer correctly or marked for review. Note the topic that those questions belong to.

We recommend that you do this BEFORE taking the next Diagnostic Test.

Diagnostic Test #7 – Answer Key

1	A	Nomenclature	31	D	Stereochemistry
2	C	Covalent bond	32	C	Molecular structure & spectra
3	D	Stereochemistry	33	B	Alkanes & alkyl halides
4	B	Molecular structure & spectra	34	B	Alkenes
5	D	Separations & purifications	35	B	Alkynes
6	D	Alkanes & alkyl halides	36	D	Aromatic compounds
7	D	Alkenes	37	B	Alcohols
8	B	Alkynes	38	D	Aldehydes & ketones
9	A	Aromatic compounds	39	D	Carboxylic acids
10	B	Alcohols	40	C	COOH derivatives
11	D	Aldehydes & ketones	41	D	Amines
12	B	Carboxylic acids	42	A	Nomenclature
13	D	COOH derivatives	43	D	Covalent bond
14	A	Amines	44	C	Stereochemistry
15	A	Nomenclature	45	C	Amino acids, peptides, proteins
16	C	Covalent bond	46	B	Lipids
17	B	Stereochemistry	47	A	Carbohydrates
18	B	Molecular structure & spectra	48	A	Nucleic acids
19	C	Separations & purifications	49	C	Amino acids, peptides, proteins
20	D	Alkanes & alkyl halides	50	A	Lipids
21	A	Alkenes	51	C	Carbohydrates
22	D	Alkynes	52	D	Nucleic acids
23	A	Aromatic compounds	53	B	Amino acids, peptides, proteins
24	C	Alcohols	54	B	Lipids
25	A	Aldehydes & ketones	55	D	Carbohydrates
26	A	Carboxylic acids	56	B	Nucleic acids
27	A	COOH derivatives	57	A	Amino acids, peptides, proteins
28	B	Amines	58	D	Lipids
29	B	Nomenclature	59	B	Carbohydrates
30	C	Covalent bond	60	B	Nucleic acids

Diagnostic Test #8

This Diagnostic Test is designed for you to assess your proficiency on each topic and not to mimic the actual test. Use your test results and identify areas of your strength and weakness to adjust your study plan and enhance your fundamental knowledge.

The length of the Diagnostic Tests is proven to be optimal for a single study session.

#	Answer:				Review	#	Answer:				Review
1:	A	B	C	D	___	31:	A	B	C	D	___
2:	A	B	C	D	___	32:	A	B	C	D	___
3:	A	B	C	D	___	33:	A	B	C	D	___
4:	A	B	C	D	___	34:	A	B	C	D	___
5:	A	B	C	D	___	35:	A	B	C	D	___
6:	A	B	C	D	___	36:	A	B	C	D	___
7:	A	B	C	D	___	37:	A	B	C	D	___
8:	A	B	C	D	___	38:	A	B	C	D	___
9:	A	B	C	D	___	39:	A	B	C	D	___
10:	A	B	C	D	___	40:	A	B	C	D	___
11:	A	B	C	D	___	41:	A	B	C	D	___
12:	A	B	C	D	___	42:	A	B	C	D	___
13:	A	B	C	D	___	43:	A	B	C	D	___
14:	A	B	C	D	___	44:	A	B	C	D	___
15:	A	B	C	D	___	45:	A	B	C	D	___
16:	A	B	C	D	___	46:	A	B	C	D	___
17:	A	B	C	D	___	47:	A	B	C	D	___
18:	A	B	C	D	___	48:	A	B	C	D	___
19:	A	B	C	D	___	49:	A	B	C	D	___
20:	A	B	C	D	___	50:	A	B	C	D	___
21:	A	B	C	D	___	51:	A	B	C	D	___
22:	A	B	C	D	___	52:	A	B	C	D	___
23:	A	B	C	D	___	53:	A	B	C	D	___
24:	A	B	C	D	___	54:	A	B	C	D	___
25:	A	B	C	D	___	55:	A	B	C	D	___
26:	A	B	C	D	___	56:	A	B	C	D	___
27:	A	B	C	D	___	57:	A	B	C	D	___
28:	A	B	C	D	___	58:	A	B	C	D	___
29:	A	B	C	D	___	59:	A	B	C	D	___
30:	A	B	C	D	___	60:	A	B	C	D	___

Notes

1. The compound $CH_3(CH_2)_5CH_3$ is known as:

    A. heptane   **B.** hexene   **C.** hexane   **D.** pentane

2. Which of the following is NOT a resonance structure of the species shown?

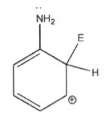

  A.   **C.**

  B.   **D.**

3. How many isomers are there of butane, C_4H_{10}?

    A. 3   **B.** 4   **C.** 1 (no isomers)   **D.** 2

4. Which of the following compounds gives the greatest number of proton NMR peaks?

    A. 3,3-dichloropentane   **C.** 1-chlorobutane
    B. 4,4-dichloroheptane   **D.** 1,4-dichlorobutane

5. After completing the synthesis of 3-methylpentanoic acid, which of the following treatments neutralizes the mineral acids and facilitates the distribution of the organic acid from the organic layer to the aqueous extraction layer?

    A. Extraction with aqueous NaCl   **C.** Extraction with aqueous $NaHCO_3$
    B. Extraction with ether   **D.** Extraction with water

6. Which of the following statements best describes the mechanism of the unimolecular elimination of *tert*-butyl chloride with ethanol?

    A. The reaction is a concerted single-step process

    B. The reaction involves homolytic cleavage of the C–Cl bond

    C. The rate-determining step is the formation of $(CH_3)_3C\cdot$

    D. The rate-determining step is the formation of $(CH_3)_3C^+$

7. Which of the following is NOT an example of a conjugated system?

    A. 1,2-butadiene   **C.** benzene

    B. cyclobutadiene   **D.** 2,4-cyclohexadiene

8. What reagents are used to convert 1-hexyne into 2-hexanone?

    A. 1) Si_2BH; 2) H_2O_2, NaOH   **C.** 1) O_3; 2) $(CH_3)_2S$

    B. Hg^{2+}, H_2SO_4, H_2O **D.** 1) CH_3MgBr; 2) CO_2

9. What is the most likely regiochemistry of this electrophilic aromatic substitution reaction?

$+ Br_2 / FeBr_3 \rightarrow$?

10. Compounds with the –OH group attached to a saturated alkane-like carbon are known as:

    A. ethers   **C.** alcohols

    B. hydroxyls   **D.** alkyl halides

11. Which of the following reactions does NOT yield a ketone product?

A. [structure: cyclohexyl–C≡CH] + 1) Sia_2BH/THF; 2) $H_2O_2/\,^-OH \rightarrow$

B. [structure: isobutyl–C≡N] + 1) CH_3CH_2MgBr; 2) $H_3O^+ \rightarrow$

C. [structure: carboxylic acid with OH] + 1) 2 CH_3CH_2Li; 2) $H_3O^+ \rightarrow$

D. [benzene ring] + [H_3C–C(=O)–Cl] + $AlCl3 \rightarrow$

12. Identify the carboxylic acid and alcohol from which the following ester was made.

[structure: H_3C–C(=O)–O–CH_3 (ethyl acetate drawn as H3C-CO-O-CH2CH3)]

A. $CH_3CH_2CO_2H$ and CH_3CH_2OH
B. CH_3CO_2H and CH_3CO_2H
C. CH_3CO_2H and CH_3CH_2OH
D. $CH_3CH_2CO_2H$ and $CH_3CH_2CH_2OH$

13. Identify the functional group:

[structure: –C–C(=O)–N–]

A. anhydride
B. amine
C. amide
D. ester

14. Which of the following compounds has the lowest boiling point?

A. dimethylamine
B. *sec*-butylamine
C. diethylamine
D. *n*-butylamine

15. Name the following structure:

A. 2-methylene-4-pentene

B. 2-methyl-1,4-pentadiene

C. 2-methyl-2,4-pentadiene

D. 4-methyl-1,4-pentadiene

16. In an aqueous environment, which bond requires the most energy to break?

A. hydrogen

B. dipole-dipole

C. *sigma*

D. ionic

17. What is the relationship between the following compounds?

A. constitutional isomers

B. structural isomers

C. geometric isomers

D. conformational isomers

18. Where would one expect to find the ^{1}H NMR signal for the carboxyl group's hydrogen in propanoic acid?

A. δ 4.1-5.6 ppm

B. δ 10-13 ppm

C. δ 8-9 ppm

D. δ 6.1-7.8 ppm

19. Where in a petroleum fractionating tower would a chemist locate the molecules with the strongest intermolecular forces?

A. near the top

B. near the middle

C. near the bottom

D. no specific location because fractional distillation does not utilize molecular weight

20. Which of the following best describes the process of an S_N1 reaction in which the leaving group is on a chiral carbon atom?

A. inversion of stereochemistry

B. double inversion of stereochemistry

C. racemic mixture

D. retention of stereochemistry

21. Which of the following would show the LEAST regioselectivity for HBr addition?

A. $(CH_3)_2C=C(CH_3)CH_2CH_3$

B. $H_2C=C(CH_3)CH_2CH_3$

C. $CH_2HC=C(CH_3)CH_2CH_3$

D. $(CH_3)_2C=CHCH_2CH_3$

22. What is the major product of this reaction?

$$H_3C-C\equiv C-CH_3 + Na\ (s),\ NH_3\ (l) \rightarrow\ ?$$

A.

C.

B.

D.

23. A compound is a six-carbon cyclic hydrocarbon. It is inert to bromine in water and bromine in dichloromethane, yet it decolorizes bromine in carbon tetrachloride when a small quantity of $FeBr_3$ is added. Which of the following is the identity of the compound?

A. 1,4-cyclohexadiene

B. 1,3-cyclohexadiene

C. benzene

D. cyclohexane

24. When (*S*)-2-heptanol is subjected to $SOCl_2$ / pyridine, the compound is transformed into:

A. (*R/S*)-2-chloroheptane

B. (*R*)-2-chloroheptane

C. (*S*)-2-chloroheptane

D. 2-heptone

25. What reagents are needed to complete the following synthesis?

A. 1) NaOH / heat; 2) HCl (*aq*)

B. 1) NaOH / Br₂

C. 1) warm conc. KMnO₄ / NaOH; 2) HCl (*aq*)

D. 1) Ag(NH₃)₂OH; 2) HCl (*aq*)

26. Which of the following has the highest boiling point?

A. ethyl alcohol, CH_3CH_2OH

B. acetic acid, CH_3COOH

C. ethane, CH_3CH_3

D. dimethyl ketone, CH_3COCH_3

27. Which of the following is a product of this reaction?

$$CH_3-C-OCH_2CH_2CH_3 + NaOH \rightarrow\ ?$$

A. CH_3COOH

B. $CH_3CH_2COO^-\ Na^+$

C. CH_3CH_2-OH

D. $CH_3COO^-\ Na^+$

28. Which of these molecules is a tertiary amine?

A. RNH_2 　　　　**B.** R_2NH 　　　　**C.** R_3N 　　　　**D.** R_3NH^+

29. Name the structure:

A. (Z)-3-ethyl-5-hydroxymethyl-3-penten-1-ynal
B. (E)-3-ethyl-5-hydroxymethyl-3-penten-1-ynal
C. (Z)-3-ethyl-2-hydroxymethyl-2-penten-4-ynal
D. (E)-3-ethyl-2-hydroxymethyl-2-penten-4-ynal

30. The nitrogen atom of trimethylamine is [ ] hybridized which is reflected in the C–N–C bond angle of [ ]:

A. sp, 180° 　　**B.** sp^2, 120° 　　**C.** sp^2, 108° 　　　**D.** sp^3, 108°

31. Which of the following compounds are isomers?

I. $CH_3CH_2OCH_3$ 　　　　III. $CH_2COHCH_2CH_3$
II. $CH_3CH_2CH_2OH$ 　　　IV. $CH_3CH_2OCH_2CH_3$

A. I and II only 　　　　**C.** III and IV only
B. II and III only 　　　**D.** I, II and III only

32. While the carbonyl stretching frequency for simple aldehydes, ketones, and carboxylic acids is about 1710 cm^{-1}, the carbonyl stretching frequency for acid chlorides is about:

A. 1700 cm^{-1} 　　　　**C.** 1800 cm^{-1}
B. 1735 cm^{-1} 　　　　**D.** 1660 cm^{-1}

33. Which of the following is true regarding S_N1 and S_N2 reactions?

A. The rates of S_N1 reactions depend mostly on steric factors, while the rates of S_N2 reactions depend mostly on electronic factors
B. S_N1 reactions proceed more readily with a tertiary alkyl halide substrate, while S_N2 reactions proceed more readily with a primary alkyl halide substrate
C. Both S_N1 and S_N2 reactions produce rearrangement products
D. S_N1 reactions proceed via a carbocation intermediate, while S_N2 reactions proceed via a carbocation intermediate under certain conditions

34. Which statement is true in the oxymercuration-reduction of an alkene?

    A. *Anti*-Markovnikov orientation and *anti*-addition occur

    B. *Anti*-Markovnikov orientation and *syn*-addition occur

    C. Markovnikov orientation and *anti*-addition occur

    D. Markovnikov orientation and *syn*-addition occur

35. What is the major product of the following acid/catalyzed hydration reaction?

$+ H_2O / H_2SO_4, HgSO_4 \rightarrow ?$

    A.

    B.

    C.

    D.

36. While electron-withdrawing groups (such as $-NO_2$ and $-CO_2R$) are *meta*-directing with regard to electrophilic aromatic substitution reactions, they are *ortho-* / *para*-directing in nucleophilic aromatic substitution reactions. This observation would best be explained by using which concept?

    A. tautomerism   **C.** hydrogen bonding

    B. aromaticity   **D.** resonance

37. The ester prepared by heating 1-pentanol with acetic acid in the presence of an acidic catalyst is named:

    A. 1-pentyl acetate   **C.** acetic pentanoate

    B. acetyl 1-pentanoate   **D.** pentanoic acetate

38. A compound with an –OH group and an ether-like –OR group bonded to the same carbon atom is:

    A. hemiacetal   **C.** aldol

    B. diol   **D.** acetal

39. The ion formed from a carboxylic acid is called the:

    A. ester cation   **C.** carboxylate cation

    B. ester anion   **D.** carboxylate anion

40. Which sequence correctly ranks each carbonyl group in order of increasing reactivity toward nucleophilic addition?

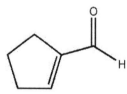

    A. 1 < 2 < 3   **C.** 3 < 1 < 2

    B. 2 < 3 < 1   **D.** 1 < 3 < 2

41. Which formula best represents the form an amine takes in acidic solution?

    A. RNH_2^- **B.** RNH_2^+ **C.** RNH_2 **D.** RNH_3^+

42. What is the complete systematic IUPAC name for the following compound?

    A. isopropyl-(4-isopropyl-4-methylbut-2-enyl) ether

    B. (*E*)-4-isopropoxy-4,5-dimethylhex-2-ene

    C. 4-(1-methylethoxy)-4-isopropyl-4-methylpent-2-ene

    D. 4-isopropyl-2,4-dimethylhept-5-en-3-ol

43. Which of the following statements concerning the cyclic molecule shown is NOT true?

    A. It contains a σ molecular orbital formed by the overlap of a carbon *p* atomic orbital with an oxygen sp^3 atomic orbital

    B. It contains a σ molecular orbital formed by the overlap of carbon sp^3 hybrid atomic orbitals

    C. It contains a σ molecular orbital formed by the overlap of carbon sp^2 hybrid atomic orbitals

    D. It contains a π molecular orbital formed by the overlap of a carbon *p* atomic orbital with an oxygen *p* atomic orbital

44. The cause of *cis-trans* isomerism is:

    A. short length of the double bond
    B. strength of the double bond

    C. lack of rotation of the double bond
    D. stability of the double bond

45. At pH 8, which of the following is true for aspartame shown below?

    A. Both the acid and amino group are protonated
    B. Both the acid and ester group are deprotonated
    C. The acid group is deprotonated, and the amino group is protonated
    D. The amino group is deprotonated, and the acid group is protonated

46. Which of the following molecules is an omega-3 fatty acid?

    A. oleic acid
    B. linolenic acid

    C. linoleic acid
    D. palmitic acid

47. Fructose does not break apart into smaller units because it is a(n):

    A. monosaccharide
    B. polysaccharide

    C. hexose
    D. aldose

48. During DNA transcription, a guanine base on the template strand codes for which base on the growing RNA strand?

    A. guanine
    B. thymine

    C. adenine
    D. cytosine

49. Non-polar *R* groups on amino acids are said to be [ ] because they are not attracted to water molecules.

    A. ionized
    B. unreactive

    C. hydrophilic
    D. hydrophobic

50. Which of the following is a lipid?

    A. lactose
    B. aniline

    C. nicotine
    D. estradiol

51. Two cyclic isomeric sugars that only differ in the position of the –OH group attached to the hemiacetal carbon are called:

A. enantiomers   **C.** anomers

B. mutarotation   **D.** epimers

52. Cellular respiration produces the same products as:

A. do nucleic acids   **C.** does catabolism

B. does campfire   **D.** does anabolism

53. Which of the following amino acids has its isoelectric point at the lowest pH?

A. arginine   **B.** aspartic acid   **C.** valine   **D.** glycine

54. Which of the following terms best describes the interior of a soap micelle in water?

A. hard   **B.** saponified   **C.** hydrophobic   **D.** hydrophilic

55. Which molecule is a reducing sugar?

A. sucrose   **B.** maltose   **C.** starch   **D.** glycogen

56. What intermolecular force connects strands of DNA in the double helix?

A. hydrogen bonds   **C.** amide bonds

B. ionic bonds   **D.** ester bonds

57. In biosynthesis, which amino acid serves as the source of the amino group for other amino acids?

A. D-phenylalanine   **C.** racemic phenylalanine

B. L-phenylalanine   **D.** L-glutamic acid

58. Which best describes the lipid shown below?

R = $(CH_2)_{10}CH_3$

A. saturated fatty acid   C. wax

B. unsaturated fatty acid   D. triglyceride

59. The glycosidic bond that connects the two monosaccharides in lactose is:

A. $\alpha(1\rightarrow6)$ C. $\alpha(1\rightarrow4)$

B. $\alpha,\beta(1\rightarrow2)$ D. $\beta(1\rightarrow4)$

60. How are codons and anticodons related?

A. Codons are the base pairs on a tRNA that bind to complementary strands of DNA and produce proteins

B. Anticodons are the codons on the mRNA used to bind to DNA

C. Codons start the process of transcription; anticodons end the process

D. Codons and anticodons are complementary base pairs that encode for an amino acid

---

Check your answers using the answer key. Then, go to the explanations section and review the explanations in detail, paying attention to questions you didn't answer correctly or marked for review. Note the topic that those questions belong to.

We recommend that you do this BEFORE taking the next Diagnostic Test.

Diagnostic Test #8 – Answer Key

1	A	Nomenclature	31	A	Stereochemistry
2	D	Covalent bond	32	C	Molecular structure & spectra
3	D	Stereochemistry	33	B	Alkanes & alkyl halides
4	C	Molecular structure & spectra	34	C	Alkenes
5	C	Separations & purifications	35	C	Alkynes
6	D	Alkanes & alkyl halides	36	D	Aromatic compounds
7	A	Alkenes	37	A	Alcohols
8	B	Alkynes	38	A	Aldehydes & ketones
9	D	Aromatic compounds	39	D	Carboxylic acids
10	C	Alcohols	40	B	COOH derivatives
11	A	Aldehydes & ketones	41	D	Amines
12	C	Carboxylic acids	42	B	Nomenclature
13	C	COOH derivatives	43	A	Covalent bond
14	A	Amines	44	C	Stereochemistry
15	B	Nomenclature	45	C	Amino acids, peptides, proteins
16	C	Covalent bond	46	B	Lipids
17	C	Stereochemistry	47	A	Carbohydrates
18	B	Molecular structure & spectra	48	D	Nucleic acids
19	C	Separations & purifications	49	D	Amino acids, peptides, proteins
20	C	Alkanes & alkyl halides	50	D	Lipids
21	A	Alkenes	51	C	Carbohydrates
22	A	Alkynes	52	B	Nucleic acids
23	C	Aromatic compounds	53	B	Amino acids, peptides, proteins
24	B	Alcohols	54	C	Lipids
25	B	Aldehydes & ketones	55	B	Carbohydrates
26	B	Carboxylic acids	56	A	Nucleic acids
27	D	COOH derivatives	57	D	Amino acids, peptides, proteins
28	C	Amines	58	D	Lipids
29	C	Nomenclature	59	D	Carbohydrates
30	D	Covalent bond	60	D	Nucleic acids

Diagnostic Test #9

This Diagnostic Test is designed for you to assess your proficiency on each topic and not to mimic the actual test. Use your test results and identify areas of your strength and weakness to adjust your study plan and enhance your fundamental knowledge.

The length of the Diagnostic Tests is proven to be optimal for a single study session.

#	Answer:				Review	#	Answer:				Review
1:	A	B	C	D	___	31:	A	B	C	D	___
2:	A	B	C	D	___	32:	A	B	C	D	___
3:	A	B	C	D	___	33:	A	B	C	D	___
4:	A	B	C	D	___	34:	A	B	C	D	___
5:	A	B	C	D	___	35:	A	B	C	D	___
6:	A	B	C	D	___	36:	A	B	C	D	___
7:	A	B	C	D	___	37:	A	B	C	D	___
8:	A	B	C	D	___	38:	A	B	C	D	___
9:	A	B	C	D	___	39:	A	B	C	D	___
10:	A	B	C	D	___	40:	A	B	C	D	___
11:	A	B	C	D	___	41:	A	B	C	D	___
12:	A	B	C	D	___	42:	A	B	C	D	___
13:	A	B	C	D	___	43:	A	B	C	D	___
14:	A	B	C	D	___	44:	A	B	C	D	___
15:	A	B	C	D	___	45:	A	B	C	D	___
16:	A	B	C	D	___	46:	A	B	C	D	___
17:	A	B	C	D	___	47:	A	B	C	D	___
18:	A	B	C	D	___	48:	A	B	C	D	___
19:	A	B	C	D	___	49:	A	B	C	D	___
20:	A	B	C	D	___	50:	A	B	C	D	___
21:	A	B	C	D	___	51:	A	B	C	D	___
22:	A	B	C	D	___	52:	A	B	C	D	___
23:	A	B	C	D	___	53:	A	B	C	D	___
24:	A	B	C	D	___	54:	A	B	C	D	___
25:	A	B	C	D	___	55:	A	B	C	D	___
26:	A	B	C	D	___	56:	A	B	C	D	___
27:	A	B	C	D	___	57:	A	B	C	D	___
28:	A	B	C	D	___	58:	A	B	C	D	___
29:	A	B	C	D	___	59:	A	B	C	D	___
30:	A	B	C	D	___	60:	A	B	C	D	___

Notes

1. Which of the following compounds is named correctly?

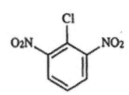

A. *meta*-fluorobenzoic acid

C. 2-iodo-1-bromobenzene

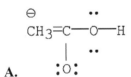

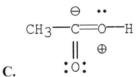

B. 2,5-dinitro-1-chlorobenzene

D. 1,3,dichloro-2-nitrobenzene

2. Which of the following is the most stable resonance contributor to acetic acid?

$$CH_3 \!-\! C \!-\! O \!-\! H$$

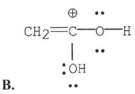

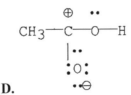

A.

C.

B.

D.

3. $CH_3\!-\!CH_2\!-\!O\!-\!H$ and $CH_3\!-\!O\!-\!CH_3$ are a pair of compounds that are:

A. isomers   **C.** anomers

B. epimers   **D.** allotropes

4. A researcher recorded the NMR spectra of each of the following compounds. Disregarding chemical shifts, which possesses a spectrum significantly different from the others?

A. 1,1,2-tribromobutane   **C.** 3,3-dibromoheptane

B. bromobutane   **D.** dibutyl ether

5. Various hydrocarbons can be separated from a crude oil mixture by:

A. precipitation

B. fractional distillation

C. filtration

D. chromatography

6. The rate of an S_N2 reaction depends on:

A. neither the concentration of the nucleophile nor the substrate

B. the concentration of both the nucleophile and the substrate

C. the concentration of the substrate only

D. the concentration of the nucleophile only

7. Which of the following has the lowest heat of hydrogenation per mole of H_2 absorbed?

A. 1,2-hexadiene

B. 1,3,5-heptatriene

C. 1,3-hexadiene

D. 1,5-hexadiene

8. Given that 1-butyne has a boiling point of 8.1 °C, what is the phase of propyne at room temperature and 1 atm pressure?

A. solid   **B.** supercritical fluid   **C.** gas   **D.** liquid

9. In the electrophilic aromatic substitution of phenol, substituents add predominantly in which position(s)?

    I. *ortho* to the hydroxyl group

    II. *meta* to the hydroxyl group

    III. *para* to the hydroxyl group

A. I only   **B.** II only   **C.** III only   **D.** I and III only

10. The compound below has which functional groups?

A. ether, alkene and alcohol

B. ester, alkene and alcohol

C. aromatic, alcohol and ether

D. aromatic, alcohol and ester

11. Which observation denotes a positive Benedict's test?

A. A mirror-like deposit forms from a colorless solution

B. A purple solution yields a brown precipitate

C. A red precipitate forms from a blue solution

D. A red-brown solution becomes clear and colorless

12. Which fatty acid is expected to have the highest boiling point?

    A. oxalic, $(CO_2H)_2$ **C.** benzoic, $C_6H_5CO_2H$

    B. stearic, $CH_3(CH_2)_{16}CO_2H$ **D.** acetic, CH_3CO_2H

13. Esters and amides are most easily made by nucleophilic acyl substitution reactions on:

    A. acid chlorides   **C.** carboxylates

    B. acid anhydrides   **D.** carboxylic acids

14. Which of the compounds listed is the strongest organic base that functions as a proton acceptor?

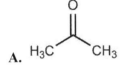

    A.   **C.** CH_3–CH_2–NH_2

    B.   **D.**

15. Name the compound shown below.

    A. *cis*-1,3-dichlorocyclohexane   **C.** *cis*-1,2-dichlorocyclohexane

    B. *trans*-1,3-dichlorocyclohexane   **D.** *trans*-1,2-dichlorocyclohexane

16. The compound methylamine, CH_3NH_2, contains a C–N bond. In this bond, which of the following best describes the charge on the nitrogen atom?

    A. uncharged   **C.** +1

    B. slightly negative   **D.** slightly positive

17. What is the relationship between the two structures shown below?

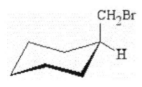 and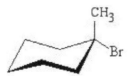

    A. conformational isomers   **C.** enantiomers

    B. configurational isomers   **D.** constitutional isomers

18. Which compound(s) show(s) intense IR absorption at 1680 cm^{-1}?

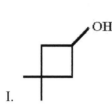

I.

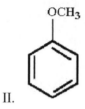

II.

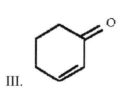

III.

A. I only
B. II only

C. III only
D. II and III only

19. Which one of the species below is soluble in dilute HCl (*aq*)?

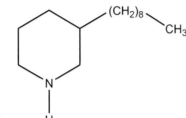

A.

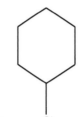

C.

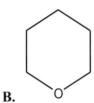

B.

D.

20. The heat of combustion of propane is –530 kcal/mol. A reasonable approximation for the heat of combustion for heptane is:

A. –432 kcal/mol
B. –682 kcal/mol

C. –865 kcal/mol
D. –1158 kcal/mol

21. Which of the following is the best solvent for the addition of HCl to 3-hexene?

A. 3-hexene
B. CH₃COOH

C. CH₃OH
D. H₂O

22. How many moles of hydrogen are required to convert a mole of pentyne to pentane?

A. 0
B. 1
C. 2
D. 3

23. Which of the following is NOT aromatic?

A.

C.

B.

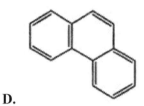

D.

24. Which compound is NOT an unsaturated compound?

A. $H_2C=CH-Cl$
B. CH_3-CH_2-O-H

C. $H_2C=CH_2$
D. $CH_3-CH=CH_2$

25. A ylide is a molecule that can be described as a:

A. carbanion bound to a positively charged heteroatom
B. carbocation bound to a positively charged heteroatom
C. carbocation bound to a carbon radical
D. carbocation bound to a diazonium ion

26. Which formula correctly illustrates the form taken by the acetic acid in a basic solution?

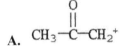

27. The reaction of an amine and a carboxylic acid produces what kind of compound?

A. amine
B. amide

C. anhydride
D. ketone

28. Which of the following behaves like a base?

I. $CH_3CONHCH_3$ II. $(CH_3)_2NH$ III. $C_2H_5CONHCH_3$

A. I only   **B.** II only   **C.** III only   **D.** I and II only

143

29. What is the IUPAC name of the compound shown?

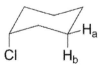

    A. 2,2-dimethyl-4-butanol   **C.** 2-methyl-4-pentanol

    B. 4,4-dimethyl-2-butanol   **D.** 4-methyl-2-pentanol

30. Which of the following molecules is the most polar?

    A. acetaldehyde   **C.** ethane

    B. acetic acid   **D.** ethylene

31. Among the butane conformers, which occur at energy minima on a graph of potential energy versus dihedral angle?

    A. *anti*   **C.** *gauche*

    B. eclipsed   **D.** eclipsed and *gauche*

32. What is the relationship between H$_a$ and H$_b$ in the following structure?

    A. diastereotopic   **C.** homotopic

    B. enantiotopic   **D.** isotopic

33. Which compound is least soluble in water?

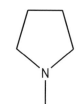

    A.   **C.**

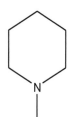

    B.   **D.**

34. What is the major product of the following reaction?

$+ \ H^+ / \ H_2O \rightarrow \ ?$

A.

C.

B.

D.

35. What is the product of the reaction of one mole of acetylene and one mole of bromine vapor?

A. 1,1,2,2-tetrabromoethane
B. 1,1,2,2-tetrabromoethene

C. 1,2-dibromoethane
D. 1,2-dibromoethene

36. Which of these molecules is aromatic?

A.

C.

B.

D.

37. Compounds of the type R₃C–OH are referred to as [ ] alcohols.

A. primary
B. secondary

C. tertiary
D. quaternary

38. Which of the following represents the correct ranking in terms of increasing the boiling point?

    A. *n*-butane < 1-butanol < diethyl ether < 2-butanone
    B. *n*-butane < 2-butanone < diethyl ether < 1-butanol
    C. 2-butanone < *n*-butane < diethyl ether < 1-butanol
    D. *n*-butane < diethyl ether < 2-butanone < 1-butanol

39. When an alcohol reacts with a carboxylic acid, the major product is a(n):

    A. salt   **B.** ester   **C.** amine   **D.** amide

40. Penicillin can be taken orally if the compound can survive degradation by the low pH of the stomach. The amide bond between the *R* group and 6-APA of dicloxacillin is stable at low pH, because:

    A. high hydroxide concentration promotes amide stability
    B. amide bonds do not easily undergo hydrolysis
    C. hydrogen bonding has stabilization effects
    D. aromatic compounds are unaffected by changes in pH

41. The reaction of an amine with water is best represented by:

    A. $R\text{–}NH_2 + H_2O \leftrightarrow R\text{–}NH_3^+ + OH^-$
    B. $R\text{–}NH_2 + 2\ H_2O \leftrightarrow R\text{–}NH_4^{2+} + 2\ OH^-$
    C. $R\text{–}NH_2 + 2\ H_2O \leftrightarrow R\text{–}N^{2-} + 2\ H_3O^+$
    D. $R\text{–}NH_2 + H_2O \leftrightarrow R\text{–}NH^- + H_3O^+$

42. What is the IUPAC name of the compound shown below?

    A. (1*R*,4*S*)-1,4-dichloro-1-ethyl-4-methylcyclopentane
    B. (1*R*,3*S*)-1,3-dichloro-1-ethyl-3-methylcyclopentane
    C. (1*S*,3*S*)-1,3-dichloro-1-ethyl-3-methylcyclopentane
    D. (1*R*,3*S*)-1,3-dichloro-1-methyl-3-ethylcyclopentane

43. A molecule of acetylene (C_2H_2) has a [   ] geometry and a molecular dipole moment that is [   ].

    A. bent, zero   **C.** linear, zero
    B. linear, nonzero   **D.** bent, nonzero

44. How many different isomers are there for dibromobenzene, $C_6H_4Br_2$?

A. 0   **B.** 1   **C.** 2   **D.** 3

45. The proton on the nitrogen of saccharin is much more acidic than the proton on the amide nitrogen of aspartame. This is best explained by the fact that:

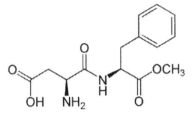

        Aspartame (Asp-Phe)   *Saccharin*

     A. extra resonance stabilization of the resulting anion is provided by the sulfone group
     B. the saccharin nitrogen is *sp* hybridized
     C. the adjacent sulfone group stabilizes the anion because it is an electron-donating group
     D. cyclic amides are more acidic than acyclic amides

46. Which fatty acid is a saturated fatty acid?

     A. oleic acid   **C.** arachidonic acid
     B. linoleic acid   **D.** myristic acid

47. Which of the following is correct regarding the classification of carbohydrate isomers?

     A. Each D-aldohexose has exactly two anomers
     B. There are 16 D-aldohexose stereoisomers
     C. There are 8 aldohexose stereoisomers
     D. Glucose has the same number of stereoisomers as fructose

48. Which of these nitrogenous base pairs is found in DNA?

     A. adenine-guanine   **C.** adenine-cytosine
     B. adenine-uracil   **D.** guanine-cytosine

49. 2,4-dinitrofluorobenzene is used in protein analysis to determine the:

     A. most reactive amino acid in the protein
     B. amino acid at the *C*-terminus
     C. amino acid at the *N*-terminus
     D. most frequent amino acid found in the protein

50. Commercially, liquid vegetable oils are converted to solid fats such as margarine by:

A. oxidation   **C.** hydrolysis

B. hydration   **D.** hydrogenation

51. Which of the following contains α(1→6) branches?

A. cellulose   **C.** amylose

B. sucrose   **D.** glycogen

52. If one strand of a DNA double helix has the sequence AGTACTG, what is the sequence of the other strand?

A. GACGTCA   **C.** GTCATGA

B. AGTACTG   **D.** TCATGAC

53. Insulin is an example of a(n):

A. hormone   **C.** structural protein

B. storage protein   **D.** enzyme

54. The biochemical roles of lipids are:

A. short-term energy storage, transport of molecules and structural support

B. storage of excess energy, component of cell membranes and chemical messengers

C. catalysis, protection against outside invaders, motion

D. component of cell membranes, catalysis, and structural support

55. Humans cannot digest cellulose because they:

A. have intestinal flora which use up β(1→4) glycosidic bonds

B. are poisoned by β(1→4) glycosidic bonds

C. are allergic to β(1→4) glycosidic bonds

D. lack the necessary enzymes to break β(1→4) glycosidic bonds

56. The main role of DNA is to provide instructions on how to build:

      I. lipids   II. carbohydrates   III. proteins

A. I only   **B.** II only   **C.** III only   **D.** I and II only

57. What type of protein structure corresponds to a spiral alpha helix of amino acids?

A. primary   **C.** tertiary

B. secondary   **D.** quaternary

58. Which fatty acid composition yields a triglyceride that is most likely an oil?

A. 3 palmitic acid units

B. 2 palmitic and 1 oleic acid units

C. 2 linoleic and 1 stearic acid units

D. 3 stearic acid units

59. Mutarotation is a process where:

A. glucose undergoes reaction to form an equilibrium mixture of anomers

B. glucose reacts with alcohol forming a cyclic acetal

C. the aldehyde group present in sugar is converted to a hemiacetal

D. two glucose molecules react to form a disaccharide

60. Nucleic acids are polymers of [   ] monomers.

A. monosaccharide

B. fatty acid

C. DNA

D. nucleotide

Check your answers using the answer key. Then, go to the explanations section and review the explanations in detail, paying attention to questions you didn't answer correctly or marked for review. Note the topic that those questions belong to.

We recommend that you do this BEFORE taking the next Diagnostic Test.

Please, leave your Customer Review on Amazon

Diagnostic Test #9 – Answer Key

1	D	Nomenclature	31	A	Stereochemistry
2	D	Covalent bond	32	A	Molecular structure & spectra
3	A	Stereochemistry	33	D	Alkanes & alkyl halides
4	C	Molecular structure & spectra	34	C	Alkenes
5	B	Separations & purifications	35	D	Alkynes
6	B	Alkanes & alkyl halides	36	A	Aromatic compounds
7	C	Alkenes	37	C	Alcohols
8	C	Alkynes	38	D	Aldehydes & ketones
9	D	Aromatic compounds	39	B	Carboxylic acids
10	A	Alcohols	40	B	COOH derivatives
11	C	Aldehydes & ketones	41	A	Amines
12	B	Carboxylic acids	42	B	Nomenclature
13	A	COOH derivatives	43	C	Covalent bond
14	C	Amines	44	D	Stereochemistry
15	A	Nomenclature	45	A	Amino acids, peptides, proteins
16	B	Covalent bond	46	D	Lipids
17	D	Stereochemistry	47	A	Carbohydrates
18	C	Molecular structure & spectra	48	D	Nucleic acids
19	A	Separations & purifications	49	C	Amino acids, peptides, proteins
20	D	Alkanes & alkyl halides	50	D	Lipids
21	A	Alkenes	51	D	Carbohydrates
22	C	Alkynes	52	D	Nucleic acids
23	C	Aromatic compounds	53	A	Amino acids, peptides, proteins
24	B	Alcohols	54	B	Lipids
25	A	Aldehydes & ketones	55	D	Carbohydrates
26	B	Carboxylic acids	56	C	Nucleic acids
27	B	COOH derivatives	57	B	Amino acids, peptides, proteins
28	B	Amines	58	C	Lipids
29	D	Nomenclature	59	A	Carbohydrates
30	B	Covalent bond	60	D	Nucleic acids

Diagnostic Test #10

This Diagnostic Test is designed for you to assess your proficiency on each topic and not to mimic the actual test. Use your test results and identify areas of your strength and weakness to adjust your study plan and enhance your fundamental knowledge.

The length of the Diagnostic Tests is proven to be optimal for a single study session.

#	Answer:				Review	#	Answer:				Review
1:	A	B	C	D	___	31:	A	B	C	D	___
2:	A	B	C	D	___	32:	A	B	C	D	___
3:	A	B	C	D	___	33:	A	B	C	D	___
4:	A	B	C	D	___	34:	A	B	C	D	___
5:	A	B	C	D	___	35:	A	B	C	D	___
6:	A	B	C	D	___	36:	A	B	C	D	___
7:	A	B	C	D	___	37:	A	B	C	D	___
8:	A	B	C	D	___	38:	A	B	C	D	___
9:	A	B	C	D	___	39:	A	B	C	D	___
10:	A	B	C	D	___	40:	A	B	C	D	___
11:	A	B	C	D	___	41:	A	B	C	D	___
12:	A	B	C	D	___	42:	A	B	C	D	___
13:	A	B	C	D	___	43:	A	B	C	D	___
14:	A	B	C	D	___	44:	A	B	C	D	___
15:	A	B	C	D	___	45:	A	B	C	D	___
16:	A	B	C	D	___	46:	A	B	C	D	___
17:	A	B	C	D	___	47:	A	B	C	D	___
18:	A	B	C	D	___	48:	A	B	C	D	___
19:	A	B	C	D	___	49:	A	B	C	D	___
20:	A	B	C	D	___	50:	A	B	C	D	___
21:	A	B	C	D	___	51:	A	B	C	D	___
22:	A	B	C	D	___	52:	A	B	C	D	___
23:	A	B	C	D	___	53:	A	B	C	D	___
24:	A	B	C	D	___	54:	A	B	C	D	___
25:	A	B	C	D	___	55:	A	B	C	D	___
26:	A	B	C	D	___	56:	A	B	C	D	___
27:	A	B	C	D	___	57:	A	B	C	D	___
28:	A	B	C	D	___	58:	A	B	C	D	___
29:	A	B	C	D	___	59:	A	B	C	D	___
30:	A	B	C	D	___	60:	A	B	C	D	___

Notes

1. Provide the IUPAC name of the following compound:

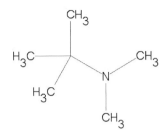

    A. *N,N,*2-trimethyl-2-propanamine   **C.** *N,N,*1,1-tetramethylethanamine
    B. *N,N,*2-trimethylpropanamine   **D.** *N,N*-dimethyl-2-butanamine

2. Identify the most stable carbocation:

    A. $H_2C{=}CH \oplus$ **C.**

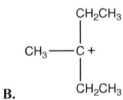

    B.   **D.**

3. When two compounds are made up of the same number and kind of atom but differ in their molecular structure, they are known as:

    A. hydrocarbons   **C.** homologs
    B. isomers   **D.** isotopes

4. Which NMR signal represents the most deshielded proton?

    A. δ 2.0   **B.** δ 3.8   **C.** δ 6.5   **D.** δ 7.3

5. The temperatures in a fractionating tower at an oil refinery are important, but so are the pressures. Where might the pressure in a fractional distillation tower be greatest, at the bottom or the top, and why?

    A. At the bottom, because the lower temperature means a greater number of vaporized molecules
    B. At the top, because the lower temperature means a greater number of vaporized molecules
    C. At the bottom, because the higher temperature means a greater number of vaporized molecules
    D. At the top, because the higher temperature means a greater number of vaporized molecules

6. An alkyl halide forms a carbocation that is more stable than the carbocation formed from isopropyl bromide. Which of the following alkyl halides forms the most stable carbocation?

A. *n*-propyl chloride
B. *tert*-butyl chloride

C. methyl chloride
D. ethyl chloride

7. The rate law for the addition of HBr to many simple alkenes may be approximated as rate = k [alkene]·[HBr]. This rate law indicates all of the following EXCEPT that the reaction:

A. occurs in a single step involving one HBr molecule and one alkene molecule
B. involves one HBr molecule and one alkene molecule in the rate-determining step, and may involve many steps
C. is first order in HBr
D. is second order overall

8. Which of the following does NOT properly describe the physical properties of an alkyne?

A. Less dense than water
B. Insoluble in most organic solvents
C. Relatively nonpolar
D. Nearly insoluble in water

9. Of the following, which reacts most readily with Br_2 / $FeBr_3$ in an electrophilic aromatic substitution?

A.

C.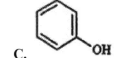
OH

B.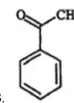

D.
OH

10. The functional group, –OH, is found in which one of these types of organic compounds?

A. amines   B. alcohols   C. alkanes   D. alkenes

11. Which of the following organic compounds is most likely NOT a ketone?

A. estradiol (female hormone)
B. progesterone (female hormone)

C. androsterone (male hormone)
D. cortisone (adrenal hormone)

12. Which acid is expected to have the highest boiling point?

   A. formic   **B.** oxalic   **C.** acetic   **D.** stearic

13. What are the major organic products of the reaction shown?

$+ H_2O / H_2SO_4 \rightarrow$?

   A. $CH_3COOH + HOCH_2CH_2CH_3$
   B. $CH_3CH_2CH_2OH + CH_3CH_2OH$
   C. $CH_3CH_2COOH + HOCH_2CH_3$
   D. $CH_3CH_2CH_2COO^- + {}^+H_2OCH_2CH_3$

14. *p*-toluidine is somewhat soluble in water due to the polarity of:

   A. its aromatic ring structure   **C.** *p*-toludinoic acid
   B. its amine group   **D.** benzene

15. Name the following structure:

   A. *cis*-3,4-dimethyl-3-hepten-7-ol   **C.** *cis*-4,5-dimethyl-4-hepten-1-ol
   B. *trans*-4,5-dimethyl-4-hepten-1-ol   **D.** *trans*-3,4-dimethyl-3-hepten-7-ol

16. Consider the interaction of two hydrogen $1s$ atomic orbitals of the same phase. Which of the statements below is NOT a correct description of this interaction?

   A. The molecular orbital formed is cylindrically symmetric
   B. The molecular orbital formed has a node between the atoms
   C. The molecular orbital formed is lower in energy than a hydrogen $1s$ atomic orbital
   D. A *sigma* bonding molecular orbital is formed

17. Identify the relationship between the compounds:

   A. constitutional isomers   **C.** identical
   B. configurational isomers   **D.** conformational isomers

18. The mass spectrum of alcohols often fails to exhibit detectable M peaks, instead showing relatively large [ ] peaks.

  A. M–18   **B.** M+2   **C.** M–16   **D.** M–17

19. Which of the following pairs of alkenes has the same physical properties?

  A. 2-butene and isobutene   **C.** 1-butene and 2-butene
  B. 1-butene and isobutene   **D.** None of the above

20. Which of the following reactions is most likely to proceed by an S_N2 mechanism?

  A. *t*-butyl iodide with ethanol   **C.** 2-bromo-2-methyl pentane with HCl
  B. 2-bromo-3-methyl pentane with methanol   **D.** 1-bromopropane with NaOH

21. Which reactant is used to convert propene to 1,2-dichloropropane?

  A. HCl   **B.** NaCl   **C.** H_2 **D.** Cl_2

22. What are the two products from the complete combustion of an alkyne?

  A. CO_2 and H_2O **C.** CO and H_2O
  B. CO_2 and H_2 **D.** CO and H_2

23. In the molecular orbital representation of benzene, how many π molecular orbitals are present?

  A. 1   **B.** 2   **C.** 4   **D.** 6

24. What is the major product of this reaction?

PhOH + $Na_2Cr_2O_7 / H_2SO_4 \rightarrow$?

  A. 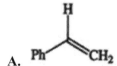   **C.**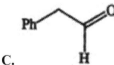

  B. 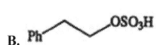   **D.**

25. The reagent(s) that convert(s) a carbonyl group of a ketone into a methylene group is:

  A. Na, NH_3, CH_3CH_2OH **C.** $NaBH_4$, CH_3CH_2OH
  B. $LiAlH_4$ **D.** Zn(Hg), conc. HCl

26. The reaction of a carboxylic acid with a base such as sodium hydroxide, NaOH, gives:

  A. alcohol   **C.** alkoxide salt
  B. ester   **D.** carboxylate salt

27. What are the products of this reaction?

$$CH_3CH_2CONHCH_2CH_3 + NaOH \rightarrow ?$$

  A. $CH_3CH_2COO^- Na^+ + CH_3CH_2NH_2$
  B. $CH_3CH_2CH_2OH + CH_3CH_2NH_3^- Na^+$
  C. $CH_3CH_2COO^- Na^+ + CH_3CH_2NH_3^+ Cl^-$
  D. $CH_3CH_2COOH + CH_3CH_2NH_2$

28. Which of the following does NOT contain a polar carbonyl group?

  A. an amine   **C.** an ester
  B. a carboxylic acid   **D.** a ketone

29. What is the systematic name for the following compound?

  A. 3-methyl-2-pentanol   **C.** 2-methyl-3-pentenol
  B. 4-methyl-3-pentanol   **D.** 2-methyl-3-pentanol

30. In *trans*-hept-4-en-2-yne the shortest carbon-carbon bond is between carbons:

  A. 1 and 2   **C.** 3 and 4
  B. 2 and 3   **D.** 4 and 5

31. Which of the following carbons in the molecule below are chiral carbons?

  A. carbons 1 and 5   **C.** carbons 2, 3 and 4
  B. carbons 3 and 4   **D.** all carbons are chiral

32. In ^1H NMR, protons on the α-carbon of amines typically resonate between:

  A. 0.5 and 1.0 ppm   **C.** 3.0 and 4.0 ppm
  B. 2.0 and 3.0 ppm   **D.** 6.0 and 7.0 ppm

33. Which of the following molecules can rotate freely around its carbon-carbon bond?

A. acetylene

B. cyclopropane

C. ethane

D. ethylene

34. Using Zaitsev's rule, choose the most stable alkene among the following:

A. 1-methylcyclohexene

B. 3-methylcyclohexene

C. 4-methylcyclohexene

D. 3,4-dimethylcyclohexene

35. The compound propyne consists of how many carbon atoms and how many hydrogen atoms?

A. 3C, 2H

B. 3C, 6H

C. 3C, 4H

D. 2C, 2H

36. Which of the following structures is aromatic?

A.

B.

C.

D.

37. Which of the following reagents is best to convert methyl alcohol to methyl chloride?

A. Cl^-

B. $SOCl_2$

C. Cl_2/CCl_4

D. $Cl_2/h\nu$

38. The reaction of ethylmagnesium bromide with which of the following compounds yields a secondary alcohol after quenching with aqueous acid?

A. $(CH_3)_2CO$

B. ethylene oxide

C. H_2CO

D. CH_3CHO

39. What are the products from the reaction of ethanoic acid and methanol with sulfuric acid catalyst?

$$CH_3COOH + CH_3OH + H_2SO_4 \rightarrow ?$$

A. $CH_3CH_2COOH + H_2O$

B. $CH_3COOCH_3 + H_2O$

C. $CH_3COCH_3 + H_2O$

D. $CH_3CH_2CHO + H_2O$

40. Which product is formed during a reaction of acetic acid (CH₃COOH) with ammonia (NH₃)?

    A. ethylammonium hydroxide   **C.** acetamide

    B. amino acetate   **D.** ammonium acetate

41. When comparing amine compounds of different classes but similar molar masses, which type most likely has the highest boiling point?

    A. primary amines   **C.** tertiary amines

    B. secondary amines   **D.** quaternary ammonium salts

42. Which condensed structural formula is known as the isopropyl group?

A.   **C.**

B.   **D.**

43. What two atomic orbitals (or hybrid atomic orbitals) overlap to form the C=C π bond in ethylene?

    A. C sp^2 + C p **B.** C p + C p **C.** C sp^3 + C sp^2 **D.** C sp^3 + C sp^3

44. How many different stereoisomers can the following compound have?

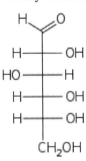

D-glucose

    A. 2   **B.** 4   **C.** 8   **D.** 16

45. Amino acids are linked to one another in a protein by which of the following bonds?

    A. amide bonds   **C.** ester bonds

    B. carboxylate bonds   **D.** amine bonds

46. Cholesterol belongs to the [   ] group of lipids.

A. prostaglandin

B. triacylglycerol

C. saccharides

D. steroid

47. Galactose has the structure shown below. It can be classified as a(n):

A. monosaccharide

B. disaccharide

C. ketose

D. ribose

48. The nucleotide sequence, T-A-G, stands for

A. threonine-alanine-glutamine

B. thymine-adenine-guanine

C. tyrosine-asparagine-glutamic acid

D. thymine-adenine-glutamine

49. Which of the following amino acids is most likely present in the hydrophobic binding region of a protein?

A. tyrosine   **B.** glutamine   **C.** valine   **D.** serine

50. In chemical terms, soaps are best described as:

A. simple esters of fatty acids

B. mixed esters of fatty acids

C. salts of carboxylic acids

D. long chain acids

51. The three elements found in all carbohydrates are [   ], [   ] and [   ]:

A. nitrogen, oxygen, hydrogen

B. carbon, hydrogen, oxygen

C. carbon, hydrogen, water

D. nitrogen, oxygen, carbon

52. The two new DNA molecules formed in replication:

A. contain one parent and one daughter strand

B. both contain only the parent DNA strands

C. both contain only two new daughter DNA strands

D. are complementary to the original DNA

53. Identify the functional groups in the following compound.

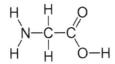

A. alcohol and ketone

B. alcohol, amine and ketone

C. amine and carboxylic acid

D. amine, hydroxide and ketone

54. The function of cholesterol in a cell membrane is to:

A. act as a precursor to steroid hormones

B. take part in the reactions that produce bile acids

C. maintain structure due to its flat rigid characteristics

D. attract hydrophobic molecules to form solid deposits

55. When a monosaccharide forms a cyclic hemiacetal, the carbon atom that contained the carbonyl group is identified as the [ ] carbon atom because [ ]:

A. D ... the carbonyl group is drawn to the right

B. L ... the carbonyl group is drawn to the left

C. anomeric ... its substituents can assume an α or β position

D. acetal ... it forms bonds to an –OR and an –OR'

56. Which of the following is found in an RNA nucleotide?

    I. phosphoric acid

    II. nitrogenous base

    III. ribose sugar

A. I only   **B.** II only   **C.** III only   **D.** I, II and III

57. The pH at which the positive and negative charges of an amino acid balance is:

A. isotonic point

B. isobestic point

C. isobaric point

D. isoelectric point

58. Which of the following terms best describes the compound below?

$$
\begin{array}{l}
CH_2 - O - \overset{\overset{\displaystyle O}{\|}}{C} - (CH_2)_{18}CH_3 \\[2ex]
CH - O - \overset{\overset{\displaystyle O}{\|}}{C} - (CH_2)_{16}CH_3 \\[2ex]
CH_2 - O - \overset{\overset{\displaystyle O}{\|}}{C} - (CH_2)_{18}CH_3
\end{array}
$$

A. unsaturated triglyceride

B. saturated triglyceride

C. terpene

D. prostaglandin

59. Which of the following is a non-reducing sugar?

A. mannose   **B.** sucrose   **C.** lactose   **D.** glucose

60. Which of the following descriptions of the nucleoside uridine does NOT apply to the structure of the molecule?

A. The uracil base is directly bonded to the 1' position of ribofuranose in the α position

B. The ribofuranose moiety is only found in the D configuration

C. Nitrogen, at position 1 in the uracil base, is directly bonded to the ribofuranose moiety

D. The 5'–OH group is replaced with phosphate(s) in the nucleotide structure

Check your answers using the answer key. Then, go to the explanations section and review the explanations in detail, paying attention to questions you didn't answer correctly or marked for review. Note the topic that those questions belong to.

We recommend that you do this BEFORE taking the next Diagnostic Test.

Diagnostic Test #10 – Answer Key

1	A	Nomenclature	31	B	Stereochemistry
2	B	Covalent bond	32	B	Molecular structure & spectra
3	B	Stereochemistry	33	C	Alkanes & alkyl halides
4	D	Molecular structure & spectra	34	A	Alkenes
5	C	Separations & purifications	35	C	Alkynes
6	B	Alkanes & alkyl halides	36	A	Aromatic compounds
7	A	Alkenes	37	B	Alcohols
8	B	Alkynes	38	D	Aldehydes & ketones
9	C	Aromatic compounds	39	B	Carboxylic acids
10	B	Alcohols	40	C	COOH derivatives
11	A	Aldehydes & ketones	41	A	Amines
12	D	Carboxylic acids	42	A	Nomenclature
13	C	COOH derivatives	43	B	Covalent bond
14	B	Amines	44	D	Stereochemistry
15	B	Nomenclature	45	A	Amino acids, peptides, proteins
16	B	Covalent bond	46	D	Lipids
17	B	Stereochemistry	47	A	Carbohydrates
18	A	Molecular structure & spectra	48	B	Nucleic acids
19	D	Separations & purifications	49	C	Amino acids, peptides, proteins
20	D	Alkanes & alkyl halides	50	C	Lipids
21	D	Alkenes	51	B	Carbohydrates
22	A	Alkynes	52	A	Nucleic acids
23	D	Aromatic compounds	53	C	Amino acids, peptides, proteins
24	D	Alcohols	54	C	Lipids
25	D	Aldehydes & ketones	55	C	Carbohydrates
26	D	Carboxylic acids	56	D	Nucleic acids
27	A	COOH derivatives	57	D	Amino acids, peptides, proteins
28	A	Amines	58	B	Lipids
29	D	Nomenclature	59	B	Carbohydrates
30	B	Covalent bond	60	A	Nucleic acids

Notes

Diagnostic Test #11

This Diagnostic Test is designed for you to assess your proficiency on each topic and not to mimic the actual test. Use your test results and identify areas of your strength and weakness to adjust your study plan and enhance your fundamental knowledge.

The length of the Diagnostic Tests is proven to be optimal for a single study session.

#	Answer:				Review	#	Answer:				Review
1:	A	B	C	D	___	31:	A	B	C	D	___
2:	A	B	C	D	___	32:	A	B	C	D	___
3:	A	B	C	D	___	33:	A	B	C	D	___
4:	A	B	C	D	___	34:	A	B	C	D	___
5:	A	B	C	D	___	35:	A	B	C	D	___
6:	A	B	C	D	___	36:	A	B	C	D	___
7:	A	B	C	D	___	37:	A	B	C	D	___
8:	A	B	C	D	___	38:	A	B	C	D	___
9:	A	B	C	D	___	39:	A	B	C	D	___
10:	A	B	C	D	___	40:	A	B	C	D	___
11:	A	B	C	D	___	41:	A	B	C	D	___
12:	A	B	C	D	___	42:	A	B	C	D	___
13:	A	B	C	D	___	43:	A	B	C	D	___
14:	A	B	C	D	___	44:	A	B	C	D	___
15:	A	B	C	D	___	45:	A	B	C	D	___
16:	A	B	C	D	___	46:	A	B	C	D	___
17:	A	B	C	D	___	47:	A	B	C	D	___
18:	A	B	C	D	___	48:	A	B	C	D	___
19:	A	B	C	D	___	49:	A	B	C	D	___
20:	A	B	C	D	___	50:	A	B	C	D	___
21:	A	B	C	D	___	51:	A	B	C	D	___
22:	A	B	C	D	___	52:	A	B	C	D	___
23:	A	B	C	D	___	53:	A	B	C	D	___
24:	A	B	C	D	___	54:	A	B	C	D	___
25:	A	B	C	D	___	55:	A	B	C	D	___
26:	A	B	C	D	___	56:	A	B	C	D	___
27:	A	B	C	D	___	57:	A	B	C	D	___
28:	A	B	C	D	___	58:	A	B	C	D	___
29:	A	B	C	D	___	59:	A	B	C	D	___
30:	A	B	C	D	___	60:	A	B	C	D	___

Notes

1. Ignoring geometric isomers, what is the IUPAC name for the following compound:

$CH_3–CH=CH–CH_3$, is:

A. but-2-yne

B. but-2-ene

C. butene-3

D. butene-2

2. Which of the following is an allylic cation?

A.

B.

C.

D.

3. What is the relationship between the following molecules?

A. different molecules

B. enantiomers

C. identical

D. isomers

4. Free-radical chlorination of propane gives two isomeric monochlorides: 1-chloropropane and 2-chloropropane. How many NMR signals does each of these compounds display, respectively?

A. 3, 2   **B.** 3, 3   **C.** 2, 2   **D.** 2, 3

5. Which of the choices below lists a possible sequence through which the three molecules shown (initially in a chloroform $CHCl_3$ solution) may be separated?

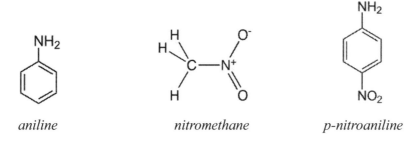

aniline   *nitromethane*   *p-nitroaniline*

    A. Extraction with a strongly acidic aqueous solution → extraction with an even stronger acidic aqueous solution → distillation

    B. Extraction with a strongly basic solution of NaOH → extraction with a weakly acidic aqueous solution of benzoic acid → distillation

    C. Extraction with a weakly acidic aqueous solution of benzoic acid → extraction with a strongly acidic HCl aqueous solution → distillation

    D. Extraction with a strongly acidic HCl aqueous solution → extraction with a weakly acidic aqueous solution → distillation

6. The rate of an S_N1 reaction depends on:

    A. the concentration of both the nucleophile and the electrophile

    B. neither the concentration of the nucleophile nor of the electrophile

    C. the concentration of the nucleophile only

    D. the concentration of the electrophile only

7. Which of the following correctly ranks the halides in order of increasing rate of addition to 3-hexene in a nonpolar aprotic solvent?

    A. HI < HBr < HCl   **C.** HCl < HI < HBr

    B. HBr < HCl < HI   **D.** HCl < HBr < HI

8. What is the term for a family of unsaturated hydrocarbon compounds with a triple bond?

    A. alkynes   **C.** alkanes

    B. arenes   **D.** alkenes

9. What is the effect of an ammonium substituent on electrophilic aromatic substitution?

    A. *ortho/para*-directing with activation   **C.** *meta*-directing with activation

    B. *ortho/para*-directing with deactivation   **D.** *meta*-directing with deactivation

10. Which formula is an alcohol?

A. R—O—H

B.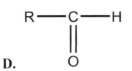

C.

D.

11. Which of the following reagents quantitatively converts an enolizable ketone to its enolate salt?

A. lithium hydroxide

B. lithium diisopropylamide

C. methyllithium

D. diethylamine

12. Which type of compound is shown below?

A. ester   **B.** carboxylic acid   **C.** ketone   **D.** aldehyde

13. Hydrolysis of the ester ethyl acetate produces:

A. butanal and ethanol

B. ethanal and acetic acid

C. ethanol and acetic acid

D. butanoic acid

14. Which of the following can be synthesized from an arenediazonium salt?

I. C_6H_5Br II. C_6H_5CN III. C_6H_5OH

A. I only   **B.** I and II only   **C.** I and III only   **D.** I, II and III

15. What is the IUPAC name for the following structure:

A. (*Z*)-3-ethyl-5-hydroxymethyl-3-penten-1-ynal

B. (*E*)-3-ethyl-5-hydroxymethyl-3-penten-1-ynal

C. (*Z*)-3-ethyl-2-hydroxymethyl-2-penten-4-ynal

D. (*E*)-3-ethyl-2-hydroxymethyl-2-penten-4-ynal

16. Which of the following best approximates the C–C–C bond angle of propene?

A. 90° **B.** 109° **C.** 120° **D.** 150°

17. What is the relationship between the structures shown below?

A. geometric isomers
B. conformational isomers
C. constitutional isomers
D. diastereomers

18. Which of the following transitions is usually observed in the UV spectra of ketones?

A. n to π^* **B.** n to π **C.** σ to n **D.** σ to σ^*

19. Which of these statements correctly describes the separation of caffeine from heptanoic acid by extraction into dichloromethane (CH_2Cl_2) and water?

Caffeine   Heptanoic acid

A. In a basic solution, heptanoic acid is more soluble in CH_2Cl_2 than in H_2O
B. In an acidic solution, heptanoic acid is more soluble in H_2O than in CH_2Cl_2
C. In an acidic solution, caffeine is more soluble in CH_2Cl_2 than in H_2O
D. In a basic solution, caffeine is more soluble in CH_2Cl_2 than in H_2O

20. Which of the following properties is NOT characteristic of alkanes?

A. They are tasteless and colorless
B. They have strong hydrogen bonds
C. Their melting points increase with molecular weight
D. They are generally less dense than water

21. The carbon–carbon single bond in 1,3-butadiene has a bond length that is shorter than a carbon–carbon single bond in an alkane. This is a result of the:

A. overlap of two sp^3 orbitals
B. overlap of one sp^2 and one sp^3 orbital
C. partial double-bond character due to the σ electrons
D. overlap of two sp^2 orbitals

22. Which of the following molecular formulas correspond(s) to an alkyne?

I. $C_{10}H_{18}$ II. $C_{10}H_{20}$ III. $C_{10}H_{22}$

A. I only   **B.** II only   **C.** III only   **D.** I and II only

23. Which of the following compounds undergoes Friedel-Crafts alkylation with $(CH_3)_3CCl$, $AlCl_3$ most rapidly?

A. toluene   **C.** acetophenone

B. iodobenzene   **D.** benzenesulfonic acid

24. The alcohol and carboxylic acid required to form propyl ethanoate are [ ] and [ ]:

A. 1-propanol ... ethanoic acid   **C.** ethanol ... propionic acid

B. propanol ... propanoic acid   **D.** methanol ... propionic acid

25. Which type of compound is shown below?

A. ester   **C.** ketone

B. carboxylic acid   **D.** aldehyde

26. Which carboxylic acid is used to prepare the ester shown?

A. $(CH_3)_2CHCH_2COOH$ **C.** CH_3COOH

B. $(CH_3)_2CHCOOH$ **D.** CH_3CH_2COOH

27. What class of compound has the following general structure?

A. ester   **C.** aldehyde

B. ketone   **D.** anhydride

28. Methyl bromide can generate the corresponding methylamine through alkyl halide ammonolysis. The nitrile reduction pathway generates the corresponding:

A. ethylmethylamide   **C.** reduced methylene group

B. ethylamine   **D.** dehalogenated methyl group

29. Give the IUPAC name for the following structure:

A. 1-chloro-4-methylcyclohexanol

B. 5-chloro-2-methylcyclohexanol

C. 3-chloro-2-methylcyclohexanol

D. 2-methyl-5-chlorocyclohexanol

30. What determines the polarity of a covalent bond?

A. The difference in the total number of protons

B. The difference in the total number of valence electrons

C. The difference in atomic size

D. The difference in electronegativity

31. What is the relationship between the following compounds?

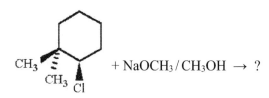

A. conformational isomers

C. enantiomers

B. diastereomers

D. constitutional isomers

32. What is the relative area of each peak in a quartet spin-spin splitting pattern?

A. 1:1:1:1   B. 1:3:3:1   C. 1:2:1   D. 1:2:2:1

33. Predict the most likely mechanism for the reaction shown below:

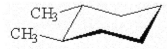

A. E_2 B. E_1 C. S_N2 D. S_N1

34. What is the name of the major organic product of the following reaction?

$(CH_3)_2C=C(CH_3)_2 + H^+/H_2O \rightarrow$?

A. 2,3-dimethyl-2-butanol

C. 3,3-dimethyl-1-butanol

B. 2,3-dimethyl-1-butanol

D. 3,3-dimethyl-2-butanol

35. What is the product from the reaction of one mole of acetylene and two moles of hydrogen gas using platinum catalyst?

    A. propene   **C.** ethene

    B. propane   **D.** ethane

36. Which sequence correctly ranks the following aromatic rings in order of increasing rate of reactivity in an electrophilic aromatic substitution reaction?

I.   II.   III.

    A. I < II < III   **B.** II < III < I   **C.** III < I < II   **D.** II < I < III

37. Which compound has the highest boiling point?

    A. $CH_3CH_2CH_2CH_2OH$ **C.** $CH_3CH_2CH_2CH_2CH_2OH$

    B. $CH_3CH_2CH_2CH_3$ **D.** $CH_3CH_2CH_2CH_2CH_3$

38. Which of the following carbonyl compounds may be synthesized from 1,3-dithiane?

    I. methyl vinyl ketone   III. 3,3-dimethyl-2-butanone

    II. 2-pentanone   IV. 2-phenylethanal

    A. I and IV only   **C.** II and III only

    B. II only   **D.** II and IV only

39. When an amine reacts with a carboxylic acid at high temperature, the major product is a(n):

    A. ether   **B.** thiol   **C.** amide   **D.** ester

40. What functional group is NOT present in the following structure for thyroxine (i.e., thyroid hormone)?

    A. organic halide   **C.** carboxylic acid

    B. ether   **D.** anhydride

41. Amines are classified by the:

    A. number of carbons present in the molecule
    B. number of carbons attached to the carbon bonded to the nitrogen
    C. number of hydrogens attached to the nitrogen
    D. number of alkyl groups attached to the nitrogen

42. What is the name of the following compound?

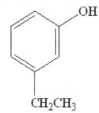

    A. *p*-ethylphenol   **B.** *m*-ethylbenzene   **C.** *o*-ethylphenol   **D.** *m*-ethylphenol

43. What is the molecular geometry of an open-chain noncyclical hydrocarbon with the generic molecular formula C_nH_{2n-2}?

    A. trigonal pyramidal   **B.** trigonal planar   **C.** tetrahedral   **D.** linear

44. Which of the following is NOT true of enantiomers?

    A. Enantiomers have the same chemical reactivity with non-chiral reagents
    B. Enantiomers have the same direction of specific rotation
    C. Enantiomers have the same melting point
    D. Enantiomers have the same boiling point

45. The linear sequence of amino acids along a peptide chain determines its:

    A. primary structure   **C.** tertiary structure
    B. secondary structure   **D.** quaternary structure

46. All of the fatty acids below contain between sixteen and eighteen carbons and range from saturated to three double bonds. Which has the lowest melting point?

    A. palmitic acid (saturated)   **C.** linoleic acid (two double bonds)
    B. oleic acid (one double bond)   **D.** linolenic acid (three double bonds)

47. Amylose is a form of starch which has:

    A. both α(1→4) and β(1→4) glycosidic linkages between glucose units
    B. glycosidic linkages joining glucose units
    C. only β(1→4) glycosidic linkages between glucose units
    D. only α(1→4) glycosidic linkages between glucose units

48. What is the complementary DNA sequence to ATATGGTC?

    A. CGCGTTGA   **B.** GCGCAACT   **C.** TATACCAG   **D.** TUTUCCAG

49. Polar *R* groups, along with acidic and basic *R* groups, are said to be [ ] because they are attracted to water molecules.

    A. unreactive   **B.** ionized   **C.** hydrophobic   **D.** hydrophilic

50. Which of the following statements correctly describe(s) the relationship between the structure of a fatty acid and its melting point?

    I. Saturated fatty acids melting points increase gradually with the molecular weights
    II. As the number of double bonds in a fatty acid increases, its melting point decreases
    III. The presence of a *trans* double bond in the fatty acid has a greater effect on its melting point than does the presence of a *cis* double bond

    A. I only   **B.** II only   **C.** III only   **D.** I and II only

51. Fructose can be classified as a(n):

    A. ketohexose   **B.** aldopentose   **C.** aldohexose   **D.** ketopentose

52. What happens to DNA when it is placed into an aqueous solution at physiological pH?

    A. Individual DNA molecules repel each other due to the presence of positive charges
    B. DNA molecules bind to negatively charged proteins
    C. Individual DNA molecules attract each other due to the presence of positive and negative charges
    D. Individual DNA molecules repel each other due to the presence of negative charges

53. An amino acid whose *R* group is predominantly hydrocarbon is classified as:

    A. acidic   **B.** basic   **C.** nonpolar   **D.** polar

54. The hydrocarbon end of a soap molecule is:

    A. hydrophilic and attracted to grease   **C.** hydrophilic and attracted to water
    B. hydrophobic and attracted to grease   **D.** hydrophobic and attracted to water

55. All of the statements concerning monosaccharides are correct, EXCEPT:

    A. the number of stereoisomers possible is 2^n, where n is the number of chiral carbon atoms in the molecule
    B. monosaccharides with 5 or 6 carbon atoms exist in solution in the cyclic form
    C. the two different cyclic forms of a monosaccharide are called tautomers
    D. a molecule is classified as a D or L isomer by the position of the hydroxyl group on the chiral center farthest from the carbonyl group

56. What is the term for the process by which a DNA molecule synthesizes a complementary single strand of RNA?

A. translation

B. transcription

C. replication

D. duplication

57. There are [   ] different types of major biomolecules used by humans.

A. a few dozen

B. four

C. several thousand

D. several million

58. It is important to have cholesterol in one's body because:

A. it breaks down extra fat lipids

B. it serves as the starting material for the biosynthesis of most other steroids

C. it is the starting material for the building of glycogen

D. the brain is made almost entirely of cholesterol

59. Which of the following statements describes most monosaccharides?

A. They are unsaturated compounds

B. They are rarely found as monomers in nature

C. They are composed of carbon, hydrogen, and oxygen with each carbon bound to at least one oxygen

D. They are insoluble

60. Consider the following types of compounds:

I. amino acid

II. nitrogen-containing base

III. phosphate group

IV. five-carbon sugar

From which of the above compounds are the monomers (i.e., nucleotides) of nucleic acids formed?

A. I only

B. I and II only

C. II and IV only

D. II, III and IV only

Check your answers using the answer key. Then, go to the explanations section and review the explanations in detail, paying attention to questions you didn't answer correctly or marked for review. Note the topic that those questions belong to.

We recommend that you do this BEFORE taking the next Diagnostic Test.

Diagnostic Test #11 – Answer Key

1	B	Nomenclature	31	C	Stereochemistry
2	B	Covalent bond	32	B	Molecular structure & spectra
3	C	Stereochemistry	33	A	Alkanes & alkyl halides
4	A	Molecular structure & spectra	34	A	Alkenes
5	C	Separations & purifications	35	D	Alkynes
6	D	Alkanes & alkyl halides	36	D	Aromatic compounds
7	D	Alkenes	37	C	Alcohols
8	A	Alkynes	38	D	Aldehydes & ketones
9	D	Aromatic compounds	39	C	Carboxylic acids
10	A	Alcohols	40	D	COOH derivatives
11	B	Aldehydes & ketones	41	D	Amines
12	B	Carboxylic acids	42	D	Nomenclature
13	C	COOH derivatives	43	D	Covalent bond
14	D	Amines	44	B	Stereochemistry
15	C	Nomenclature	45	A	Amino acids, peptides, proteins
16	C	Covalent bond	46	D	Lipids
17	C	Stereochemistry	47	D	Carbohydrates
18	A	Molecular structure & spectra	48	C	Nucleic acids
19	D	Separations & purifications	49	D	Amino acids, peptides, proteins
20	B	Alkanes & alkyl halides	50	D	Lipids
21	D	Alkenes	51	A	Carbohydrates
22	A	Alkynes	52	D	Nucleic acids
23	A	Aromatic compounds	53	C	Amino acids, peptides, proteins
24	A	Alcohols	54	B	Lipids
25	C	Aldehydes & ketones	55	C	Carbohydrates
26	A	Carboxylic acids	56	B	Nucleic acids
27	A	COOH derivatives	57	B	Amino acids, peptides, proteins
28	B	Amines	58	B	Lipids
29	B	Nomenclature	59	C	Carbohydrates
30	D	Covalent bond	60	D	Nucleic acids

Notes

Diagnostic Test #12

This Diagnostic Test is designed for you to assess your proficiency on each topic and not to mimic the actual test. Use your test results and identify areas of your strength and weakness to adjust your study plan and enhance your fundamental knowledge.

The length of the Diagnostic Tests is proven to be optimal for a single study session.

#	Answer:				Review	#	Answer:				Review
1:	A	B	C	D	___	31:	A	B	C	D	___
2:	A	B	C	D	___	32:	A	B	C	D	___
3:	A	B	C	D	___	33:	A	B	C	D	___
4:	A	B	C	D	___	34:	A	B	C	D	___
5:	A	B	C	D	___	35:	A	B	C	D	___
6:	A	B	C	D	___	36:	A	B	C	D	___
7:	A	B	C	D	___	37:	A	B	C	D	___
8:	A	B	C	D	___	38:	A	B	C	D	___
9:	A	B	C	D	___	39:	A	B	C	D	___
10:	A	B	C	D	___	40:	A	B	C	D	___
11:	A	B	C	D	___	41:	A	B	C	D	___
12:	A	B	C	D	___	42:	A	B	C	D	___
13:	A	B	C	D	___	43:	A	B	C	D	___
14:	A	B	C	D	___	44:	A	B	C	D	___
15:	A	B	C	D	___	45:	A	B	C	D	___
16:	A	B	C	D	___	46:	A	B	C	D	___
17:	A	B	C	D	___	47:	A	B	C	D	___
18:	A	B	C	D	___	48:	A	B	C	D	___
19:	A	B	C	D	___	49:	A	B	C	D	___
20:	A	B	C	D	___	50:	A	B	C	D	___
21:	A	B	C	D	___	51:	A	B	C	D	___
22:	A	B	C	D	___	52:	A	B	C	D	___
23:	A	B	C	D	___	53:	A	B	C	D	___
24:	A	B	C	D	___	54:	A	B	C	D	___
25:	A	B	C	D	___	55:	A	B	C	D	___
26:	A	B	C	D	___	56:	A	B	C	D	___
27:	A	B	C	D	___	57:	A	B	C	D	___
28:	A	B	C	D	___	58:	A	B	C	D	___
29:	A	B	C	D	___	59:	A	B	C	D	___
30:	A	B	C	D	___	60:	A	B	C	D	___

Notes

1. Name the structure:

CH₃CH₂   CH₂CH₂CH₂Cl

C=C

CH₃CH₂   CH₃

A. *cis*-7-chloro-3-ethyl-4-methyl-3-heptene   **C.** 1-chloro-5-ethyl-4-methyl-3-heptene

B. 1-chloro-3-pentenyl-2-pentene   **D.** 7-chloro-3-ethyl-4-methyl-3-heptene

2. Which of the following is a benzylic cation?

A.

C.

B.   ⊕CH₂

D.

3. Butene, C_4H_8, is a hydrocarbon with one double bond. How many isomers are there of butene?

A. two   **B.** three   **C.** four   **D.** five

4. In the proton NMR, in what region of the spectrum does one typically observe hydrogens bound to the aromatic ring?

A. 1.0-1.5 ppm   **B.** 2.0-3.0 ppm   **C.** 4.5-5.5 ppm   **D.** 6.0-8.0 ppm

5. Which of the following factors usually increase(s) the solubility of a compound in a given solvent?

    I. higher temperature   III. higher molecular weight of the compound
    II. similar polarities   IV. lower density of the solvent

A. I only   **B.** I and II only   **C.** I, II and III only   **D.** I, II and IV only

6. A nucleophile is:

A. an oxidizing agent   **C.** a Lewis base
B. electron deficient   **D.** a Lewis acid

7. Both (*E*)- and (*Z*)-hex-3-ene can be subjected to a hydroboration-oxidation sequence. How are the products from these two reactions related?

   A. The products of the two isomers are diastereomers

   B. The products of the two isomers are constitutional isomers

   C. The (*E*)- and (*Z*)-isomers generate the same products in the same amounts

   D. The (*E*)- and (*Z*)-isomers generate the same products but in differing amounts

8. What is the major organic product that results when 3-heptyne is subjected to excess hydrogen and a platinum catalyst?

   A. heptane   **C.** (*Z*)-2-heptene

   B. (*Z*)-3-heptene   **D.** 2-heptyne

9. What is the major product of this reaction?

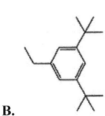

$+ C(CH_3)_3Br + FeBr \rightarrow$?

   A.

   B.

   C.

   D.

10. Which of the following alcohols has the highest boiling point?

   A. 2-methyl-1-propanol   **C.** ethanol

   B. hexanol   **D.** propanol

11. Oxidation of a ketone produces:

   A. a secondary alcohol   **C.** a carboxylic acid

   B. an aldehyde   **D.** no reaction

12. Which of the following functional groups does this organic compound contain?

A. amide   B. amine   C. carboxylic acid   D. ester

13. The compound below is which type of compound?

A. amide   B. amino acid   C. amine   D. aldehyde

14. Which compound is a primary amine?

A. *N*, *N*-dimethylethylamine   C. diethylamine
B. isopropylamine   D. trimethylamine

15. What is the IUPAC name for the following compound?

A. 1-methyl-4-cyclohexene   C. 4-methylcyclohexene
B. 1-methyl-3-cyclohexene   D. 5-methylcyclohexene

16. Which orbitals overlap to create the H–C bond in CH_3^+?

A. $s–p$ B. $s–sp^2$ C. $sp^3–sp^3$ D. $sp^2–sp^3$

17. Which of the following compounds has an asymmetric center?

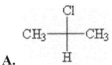

A.

C.

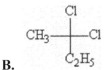

B.   D.

18. ^{1}H nuclei located near electronegative atoms are [ ] relative to ^{1}H nuclei which are not near them.

    A. coupled   **B.** split   **C.** shielded   **D.** deshielded

19. Separation by thin-layer chromatography is based primarily on:

    A. relative specific rotations (+/−) of the sample
    B. comparative refractive indices (R_f) of the sample and the solvent
    C. relative attraction of the sample towards the stationary and mobile phases
    D. the molecular weight of the sample

20. Identify the number of tertiary carbons in the following structure:

    A. 4   **B.** 5   **C.** 2   **D.** 3

21. What is the major product of this reaction?

$+ D_2 / Pt \rightarrow ?$

A.

C.

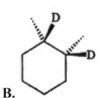
B.

D.

22. In the addition of hydrogen bromide to alkynes in the absence of peroxides, which of the following species is thought to be an intermediate?

    A. carbene   **C.** vinyl cation
    B. vinyl radical   **D.** vinyl anion

23. All of the following are common reactions of benzene, EXCEPT:

    A. nitration   **C.** chlorination

    B. hydrogenation   **D.** bromination

24. When phenol acts as an acid, a [ ] ion is produced.

    A. phenoxide   **C.** phenyl

    B. benzol   **D.** benzyl

25. (*S*)-2-methylbutanal [ ] upon sitting in an acidic or basic aqueous solution.

    A. racemizes   **C.** inverts completely to the *R* configuration

    B. esterifies   **D.** hydrolyzes

26. What is the major organic product of the reaction shown?

$$CH_3(CH_2)_3COOH + CH_3C(OH)HCH_3 \rightarrow ?$$

    A. $CH_3CH_2CH_2COOCH(CH_3)_2$ **C.** $CH_3CH_2CH_2CH_2COOCHCH_2CH_3$

    B. $CH_3CH_2CH_2CH_2C(OH)OCH(CH_3)_2$ **D.** $CH_3CH_2CH_2CH_2COOCH(CH_3)_2$

27. The products of acid hydrolysis of an ester are:

    A. alcohol + water   **C.** another ester + water

    B. acid + water   **D.** alcohol + acid

28. Which organic functional group is important for its basic properties?

    A. carbonyl   **B.** hydroxyl   **C.** amine   **D.** aromatic

29. Give the formula of the structure below:

    A. C_8H_{14} **B.** C_8H_{12} **C.** C_8H_{10} **D.** C_8H_8

30. Which of the following structures, including formal charges, is correct for diazomethane, CH_2N_2?

    A. $H_2C=N^+=N^-$ **C.** $H_2C=N^-=N^+$

    B. $H_2C=N^+\equiv N^-$ **D.** $^-CH_2-N\equiv N:$

31. How many stereoisomers are possible for the structure below?

A. 2 **B.** 4 **C.** 8 **D.** 16

32. Which compound is expected to show intense IR absorption at 1715 cm^{-1}?

A. $(CH_3)_2CHNH_2$ **C.** 2-methylhexane
B. hex-1-yne **D.** $(CH_3)_2CHCO_2H$

33. If the concentration of ^-OH doubles in a reaction with bromopropane, then the reaction rate:

A. quadruples **C.** remains the same
B. doubles **D.** is halved

34. Give the best product for the following reaction:

35. Which of the following molecular formulas correspond(s) to an acyclic alkyne?

I. C_9H_{20} II. C_9H_{18} III. C_9H_{16}

A. I only **B.** II only **C.** III only **D.** I and II only

36. How many pairs of degenerate π molecular orbitals are found in benzene?

A. 6 **B.** 2 **C.** 4 **D.** 3

37. When an alcohol reacts with phosphoric acid, the product is referred to as a:

A. pyrophosphate   **C.** phosphate ester
B. phosphate anion   **D.** phosphate salt

38. What is an ester reduced to with diisobutylaluminum hydride (DIBAL)?

A. 1° alcohol   **C.** ketone
B. alkane   **D.** aldehyde

39. What products are formed upon the reaction of benzoic acid with sodium hydroxide, NaOH?

A. Sodium bicarbonate and sodium benzoate
B. Sodium bicarbonate and benzaldehyde
C. Sodium benzoate and water
D. Benzaldehyde and water

40. Which of the following reactions is favorable, in the direction indicated, under common laboratory conditions?

41. The following is an example of a:

A. quaternary ammonium salt
B. tertiary ammonium

C. quaternary amide salt
D. tertiary amine

42. Which structure is *para*-dibromobenzene?

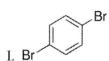

A. I only   B. II only   C. III only   D. I and II only

43. What chemical reaction was used by German chemist Friedrich Wohler to synthesize urea for the first time?

A. Heating ammonium cyanide
B. Combining the elements carbon, hydrogen, oxygen and nitrogen
C. Evaporating urine
D. Heating ammonium cyanate

44. *Cis-trans* isomerism occurs when:

A. each carbon in an alkene double bond has two different substituent groups
B. the carbons in the *para* position of an aromatic ring have the same substituent groups
C. a branched alkane has a halogen added to two adjacent carbon atoms
D. an alkene is hydrated according to Markovnikov's Rule

45. Name the amino acid produced when propanoic acid is subjected to the following sequence of reagents:

1) PBr$_3$, Br$_2$
2) H$_2$O
3) NH$_3$, Δ

A. alanine
B. aspartic acid

C. glutamic acid
D. valine

46. The molecule shown can be classified as a(n):

$$H_2C-O-\overset{\overset{O}{\|}}{C}-(CH_2)_6-CH_3$$
$$HC-O-\overset{\overset{O}{\|}}{C}-(CH_2)_7-CH=CH-(CH_2)_7-CH_3$$
$$H_2C-O-\overset{\overset{O}{\|}}{C}-O-P-O_3^{2-}$$

A. sphingolipid   C. wax

B. eicosanoid   D. glycerophospholipid

47. The conversion of cyclic glucose between the alpha and beta form is called:

A. dimerization   C. mutarotation

B. cyclization   D. polymerization

48. Which of the following statements describes cellular activity that happens during both transcription and translation?

A. Protein is formed   C. The DNA helix uncoils

B. Transfer RNA is used to link peptides   D. Nucleotides bind to complementary bases

49. What type of molecular attraction is expected to dominate between two threonine amino acids within a folding polypeptide chain?

$$H_3C-\overset{\overset{OH}{|}}{C}H-\overset{\overset{O}{\|}}{C}-OH$$
$$\underset{NH_2}{|}$$

A. dipole–induced dipole   C. ion–dipole

B. induced dipole–induced dipole   D. dipole–dipole

50. Which molecule is a fatty acid?

A. CH_3COOH C. $(CH_3)_2CH(CH_2)_3COOH$

B. $CH_2=CHCOOH$ D. $CH_3(CH_2)_7CH=CH(CH_2)_7COOH$

51. Common reducing reactions of monosaccharides are due to:

A. their cyclic structures

B. the presence of at least one hydroxyl group

C. the presence of more than one hydroxyl group

D. the presence of a carbonyl group, usually on carbon #1

52. The two strands of DNA in the double helix are held together by:

A. dipole–dipole attractions

B. metallic bonds

C. ionic bonds

D. covalent bonds

53. Which of the standard amino acids is achiral?

A. lysine

B. glycine

C. valine

D. alanine

54. What is the purpose of the plasma membrane?

A. Storing of the genetic material of the cell

B. Retaining water in the cell to prevent it from dehydrating

C. Acting as a cell wall to give the cell structure and support

D. Acting as a boundary, but also letting molecules in and out

55. What type of biological compound is characterized by an aldehyde or ketone and alcohol functional groups?

A. nucleic acid

B. fatty acid

C. sugar

D. amino acid

56. What is the major difference between nucleotides of deoxyribonucleic acid and ribonucleic acid?

A. The ribose nucleic acid is missing a hydroxyl group on the sugar

B. The ribose nucleic acid is missing a hydroxyl group on the nitrogenous base

C. The deoxyribose nucleic acid is missing a hydroxyl group on the sugar

D. The deoxyribose nucleic acid is missing a hydroxyl group on the nitrogenous base

57. Which of the following amino acids does NOT contain an aromatic *R*-group?

A. tyrosine

B. phenylalanine

C. tryptophan

D. none of the above

58. Given a single triglyceride containing three identical and fully saturated fatty acid residues, which of the following terms accurately describes it?

A. optically inactive

B. *meso*

C. optically active

D. chiral

59. Identify the C_3 epimer of the sugar below drawn in its open-chain (acyclic) Fischer projection.

A.

```
        CHO
    H ——— OH
    H ——— OH
   HO ——— H
    H ——— OH
       CH₂OH
```

C.

```
        CHO
    H ——— OH
   HO ——— H
   HO ——— H
    H ——— OH
       CH₂OH
```

B.

```
        CHO
   HO ——— H
    H ——— OH
   HO ——— H
    H ——— OH
       CH₂OH
```

D.

```
        CHO
   HO ——— H
   HO ——— H
    H ——— OH
   HO ——— H
       CH₂OH
```

60. In biochemical reactions, the reduction of carbonyl groups is carried out by:

A. pyruvic acid

B. NADH

C. LiAlH₄

D. NaBH₄

Diagnostic Test #12 – Answer Key

1	D	Nomenclature	31	D	Stereochemistry
2	D	Covalent bond	32	D	Molecular structure & spectra
3	C	Stereochemistry	33	B	Alkanes & alkyl halides
4	D	Molecular structure & spectra	34	D	Alkenes
5	B	Separations & purifications	35	C	Alkynes
6	C	Alkanes & alkyl halides	36	B	Aromatic compounds
7	C	Alkenes	37	C	Alcohols
8	A	Alkynes	38	D	Aldehydes & ketones
9	C	Aromatic compounds	39	C	Carboxylic acids
10	B	Alcohols	40	A	COOH derivatives
11	D	Aldehydes & ketones	41	A	Amines
12	C	Carboxylic acids	42	A	Nomenclature
13	A	COOH derivatives	43	D	Covalent bond
14	B	Amines	44	A	Stereochemistry
15	C	Nomenclature	45	A	Amino acids, peptides, proteins
16	B	Covalent bond	46	D	Lipids
17	D	Stereochemistry	47	C	Carbohydrates
18	D	Molecular structure & spectra	48	D	Nucleic acids
19	C	Separations & purifications	49	D	Amino acids, peptides, proteins
20	D	Alkanes & alkyl halides	50	D	Lipids
21	B	Alkenes	51	D	Carbohydrates
22	C	Alkynes	52	A	Nucleic acids
23	B	Aromatic compounds	53	B	Amino acids, peptides, proteins
24	A	Alcohols	54	D	Lipids
25	A	Aldehydes & ketones	55	C	Carbohydrates
26	D	Carboxylic acids	56	C	Nucleic acids
27	D	COOH derivatives	57	D	Amino acids, peptides, proteins
28	C	Amines	58	A	Lipids
29	A	Nomenclature	59	C	Carbohydrates
30	A	Covalent bond	60	B	Nucleic acids

Detailed
Explanations

Explanations: Diagnostic Test #1

1. D is correct.

Number this five-carbon chain beginning at the highest-priority functional group – the alcohol (functional groups with higher oxidation states are a higher priority). Thus, the alcohol is attached to carbon 1.

The C=C double bond is between carbons 2 and 3, and the C≡C triple bond is between carbons 4 and 5.

The stereochemistry about the alkene is '*E*' (highest priority groups are on opposite sides of the alkene). The priority groups are ranked according to the Cahn-Ingold-Prelog rules for prioritization based for the atomic number of atoms attached to the alkene.

Cis–trans relationship cannot be used to describe the molecule because the substituents across the double bond are different.

2. B is correct.

There are four bonding patterns of carbon described by the three hybridization bonding models.

When carbon forms four single (σ) bonds, it is sp^3 hybridized.

When carbon forms one double (π) bond and two single (σ) bonds, it is sp^2 hybridized.

Carbon is *sp* hybridized when it forms one triple (2–π) bond and one single (σ) bond or it forms two double (π) bonds.

$$O=CH–CH_2–CH=C=C=CH_2$$
$$sp^2 \quad sp^3 \quad sp^2 \quad sp \quad sp \quad sp^2$$

3. C is correct.

Inspection of each molecule reveals that the longest chain in both molecules is 10 carbon atoms.

These molecules have the same root name and the substituents, and the locations of the substituents are the same. Therefore, the molecules represent the same compound.

4. B is correct.

Infrared radiation (IR) is useful in the region of 1500 to 3500 cm^{-1} (called wavenumbers).

In this range, the molecular vibrations of molecules are active and the functional groups are identified by their characteristic absorbance frequencies.

Below 1500 cm^{-1} is the fingerprint region and is used for more detailed analysis once the target molecule(s) have been identified.

A: Nuclear magnetic resonance (NMR) spectroscopy involves a sample containing the compound being subjected to a high-intensity magnetic field and scanning through the radio-frequency range of the electromagnetic spectrum for particular absorptions.

NMR relies on the magnetic properties of certain atomic nuclei and determines the physical and chemical properties of atoms within molecules. NMR can be used to deduce the structure (connectivity) of the atoms within the molecule.

C: The UV range (not the IR range) of wavelengths is between 200–400 nm and corresponds to the energy required for electronic transitions between the bonding or nonbonding molecular orbitals and antibonding molecular orbitals.

UV spectroscopy is useful for studying compounds that contain double bonds, especially in conjugated (i.e., alternating double and single bond) molecules.

When molecules containing π-electrons (or non-bonding electrons) absorb UV energy, these electrons are promoted (i.e., excited) to higher *anti*-bonding molecular orbitals.

The more easily excited the electrons (i.e., lower energy gap between the *HOMO* and the *LUMO*), the longer the wavelength of UV light it absorbs.

D: MS (mass spectrometry) studies compounds through the fragmentation of molecules, although the unfragmented parent peak also provides useful information.

Note: mass spectrometry destroys (fragments) the sample and is not the preferred method of choice for rare/limited samples.

5. C is correct.

For thin-layer chromatography (TLC), a mixture is spotted onto the thin layer of absorbent, which is affixed to plastic or glass (polar) plates.

The spotted TLC plate is placed upright in a developing chamber that contains a solvent.

The solvent is typically a nonpolar liquid, such as ether.

Capillary action draws the solvent up the TLC plate, as well as portions of the mixture (sample spotted onto the plate) that are miscible (dissolved) by the solvent.

Solubility (i.e., migrations along with the solvent) of the sample depends on the affinity of the sample to adhere to the polar plates compared to its solubility in the nonpolar (e.g., ether) solvent.

The R_f value (i.e., retention factor) is a physical reference value for that molecule.

The distance traveled by the sample is divided into the distance traveled by the solvent.

The fraction is then multiplied by 100% and expressed as a percentage between 0% (highly polar molecules that do not migrate) to 100% (highly non-polar molecules that dissolve into and then migrate along with the solvent).

6. B is correct.

Bimolecular nucleophilic substitution (S_N2) occurs at the fastest rate when the substrate is the least hindered.

The relative reactivity of the alkyl halides for S_N2 is methyl > primary > secondary >> tertiary.

S_N2 reactions do not occur on sterically hindered tertiary substrates.

A: 1-chloro-2,2-diethylcyclopentane is a secondary alkyl halide. This substrate does not undergo S_N2 substitution as rapidly as 1-chlorocyclopentane because the presence of branching adjacent to the carbon containing the leaving group reduces the rate of S_N2 reactions since the approach of the nucleophile is impeded, compared to a straight-chain molecule.

C: 1-chlorocyclopentene does not undergo nucleophilic substitution because it has a halogen attached to a vinylic (i.e., on a double bond) carbon.

D: 1-chloro-1-ethylcyclopentane is a tertiary halide and does not undergo S_N2 nucleophilic substitution. The mechanism is S_N1 (with a carbocation intermediate).

7. A is correct.

Tertiary alkyl halides form alkenes with strong bases, via E_2, such as sodium ethoxide ($NaOCH_2CH_3$).

The most substituted alkene is the major (Zaitsev) product that is internal or more substituted.

The least substituted alkene is the minor (Hofmann) product that is terminal or less substituted.

B: 2-methylpent-3-ene is a molecule whereby the alkene does not connect to carbon that had the bromine or with an adjacent carbon. Rearrangement does not occur in E_2 reactions because rearrangement requires a carbocation (S_N1 or E_1) intermediate.

C: 2-methyl-2-methoxypentane is the product of substitution. Tertiary alkyl halides do not undergo substitution with Lewis bases; elimination is the mechanism for product formation.

D: 2-methylpentene is a less substituted alkene and only occurs with a bulky base (e.g., tert-butyl oxide or LDA).

8. C is correct.

Alkynes can be oxidized to aldehydes or ketones as follows:

Disiamylborane (BH₃) is used for the hydroboration of alkynes (and alkenes) and involves peroxides in step 2.

The hydration of the alkyne (or alkene) proceeds through an *anti*-Markovnikov addition; the preference for the *anti*-Markovnikov addition is due to the minimization of steric interactions.

The peroxide (H_2O_2) and ⁻OH converts the RBH_2 bond to an enol (C=C–OH) of the *anti*-Markovnikov product.

The enol (alkene and alcohol attached to the same carbon atom) is less stable and tautomerizes (i.e., migration of a proton) to the aldehyde (aldehyde or ketone are referred to as keto) and is not the final product of the reaction.

The keto and enol form are structural isomers with the keto form more than 99% of the final yield due to stability.

9. C is correct.

Each molecule has nitro (~NO_2) and hydroxyl (~OH) functional groups that can hydrogen-bond.

Proximity is needed for either intramolecular (within the molecule) or intermolecular (between molecules) bonding. Alignment of the functional groups to permit hydrogen bonding depends on the shape of the individual molecule.

The melting points (transition from packed molecules in a solid to liquid phase), boiling points (transition from associated molecules in a liquid to independent molecules in the gas phase) and water solubility of polar molecules are related to the presence and quantity of intermolecular hydrogen bonding.

The *meta*- and *para*-nitrophenol are more water-soluble and have higher melting points than *ortho*-nitrophenol because *ortho*-nitrophenol tends to form intramolecular hydrogen bonds instead of intermolecular hydrogen bonds.

Intramolecular hydrogen bonds for *ortho*-nitrophenol make the molecule independent so that it takes less energy to disrupt the lattice structure of the molecules (melting). Likewise, intramolecular hydrogen bonding reduces the molecule's ability to form hydrogen bonds with water, and therefore the molecule is less water-soluble.

A: *meta*- and *para*-nitrophenol form strong intermolecular hydrogen bonds, which leads to a higher melting point. Additionally, the nitro and hydroxyl groups form hydrogen bonds with water, and the molecules are more water-soluble.

B: *ortho*-nitrophenol forms some intermolecular hydrogen bonds, but less than *meta*- and *para*-nitrophenol. *Meta*-nitrophenol forms weak intramolecular bonds due to the large distance between the functional groups.

D: *para*-nitrophenol has the nitro and hydroxyl substituents at opposite ends of the flat molecule and cannot form intramolecular hydrogen bonds.

10. B is correct.

The reaction between (R)-2-hexanol and PBr$_3$ (phosphorous tribromide) proceeds via an S$_N$2 reaction mechanism.

An addition-elimination sequence occurs in the P–Br bond, then substitution by Br$^-$ of the alcohol gives the inverted (S)-2-hexanol product.

11. D is correct.

The correct tautomer forms of the ketone have the carbon-oxygen bond directly bound to the alkene carbon atom.

12. A is correct.

In Brønsted-Lowry theory, an acid is a proton donor, and a base is a proton acceptor.

In solution, a strong acid dissociates its proton and exists predominantly in the deprotonated form as the acid's conjugate base. A strong acid forms a weak conjugate base because the acid's protons dissociated in solution.

The resulting anions of the deprotonated carboxylic acids are stable due to resonance. Resonance is a major contributor to stabilize the anion by delocalizing the negative charge (using *pi* bonds) over several (in this example, two oxygen) atoms.

Acids that contain an electron-withdrawing substituent on the α-carbon (i.e., carbon adjacent to the carbonyl) tend to be stronger acids (donate proton more readily) because induction (via *sigma* bond) pulls the electron density. Induction has a stabilizing effect on the carboxylate anion (the conjugate base of carboxylic acid). Conversely, acids with electron-donating α substituents (i.e., methyl chains) tend to be weaker (less likely to dissociate the H$^+$).

The acid with two chlorine substituents, which are electron-withdrawing, forms the most stable carboxylate anion (when H$^+$ dissociates), and it is, therefore, the strongest acid, meaning that it has the weakest (most stable) conjugate base.

B: CH$_3$CH$_2$CH$_2$CO$_2$H is a carboxylic acid that has only hydrogens and therefore lacks stability influences from electronegative atoms (F, N, O or Cl).

C: (CH$_3$CH$_2$)$_3$CCO$_2$H is a carboxylic acid that has a tertiary butyl substituent which is electron-donating via hyperconjugation (i.e., alkyl chains donate electrons).

D: CH$_3$HNCH$_2$CH$_2$CH$_2$CO$_2$H is a carboxylic acid that has an amino substituent which is strongly electron-withdrawing via electronegativity of the nitrogen, but the nitrogen is located at a large distance from the COO$^-$ and therefore its influence is minimal.

13. A is correct.

The reaction is the acid hydrolysis of an ester.

When esters are hydrolyzed, they yield carboxylic acids and alcohols.

From the hydrolysis of this ester, 2-butenoic acid and isobutanol are formed.

2-butenoic acid   *isobutanol*

B: $CH_3CH(CH_3)_2$ is an alkane, and neither type of compound can be obtained by hydrolyzing an ester.

C: $HOOCCH_2CH(CH_3)_2$ may look like the carboxylic acid produced from the hydrolysis of the ester, but the carbonyl double bond is absent.

D: $CH_3CH=CHCHO$ is an unsaturated aldehyde.

14. B is correct.

Exposing bulky amines to an acid such as HCl allows it to become more soluble in water.

The charged ammonium cation allows for stronger dipole interactions with water compared to the neutral amine form.

15. B is correct.

The longest carbon chain in the molecule contains six carbon atoms.

The highest (and sole) functional group is the amide.

16. B is correct.

Full arrowheads are used to show the movement of a pair of electrons (compared to single headed – fishhook – arrows for radical reactions).

Only movement of the *pi* (π) electrons is responsible for the stable diene structures to the right.

The *pi* electrons must also be in conjugation.

17. B is correct.

When determining whether an alkene is the *Z* / *E* (or *cis* / *trans*) stereoisomer, it is important to identify the higher priority substituent group at each of the two carbon atoms of the alkene.

The priority groups are ranked according to the Cahn-Ingold-Prelog (CIP) rules for prioritization based for the atomic number of atoms attached to the alkene.

If the higher priority groups are positioned on the same side of the double bond, the molecule is *Z* (*cis* notation can be used if the substituents are the same).

If the higher priority groups are positioned on the opposite sides of the double bond, the molecule is *E* (*trans* notation can be used if the substituents are the same).

The stereochemistry about the alkene is '*Z*.' The highest priority groups – Br and Cl across the double bond – are on the same side of the alkene.

Cis–trans relationship cannot be used to describe the molecule because the substituents across the double bond are different.

18. B is correct.

The IR absorbance at 1710 cm^{-1} indicates the presence of the carbonyl group of either a ketone or an aldehyde. The carbonyl is also present in the derivatives of carboxylic acid: acyl halide, anhydride, carboxylic acid, esters, and amide.

NMR can be used to distinguish between an aldehyde (NMR δ 9–10) and a ketone (no characteristic NMR signals).

Aldehydes have additional peaks at 2700–2800 cm^{-1}, while ketones do not.

19. C is correct.

Because of the large difference in molecular weight between acetone and octane, they have different boiling points.

Acetone is a 3-carbon chain with a BP of 56–57 °C, while octane is an 8-carbon chain with a BP of 125–126 °C. The approximate magnitude of the difference (not the exact values) in BP are necessary to solve this type of problems.

In general, a large increase in molecular weight between two compounds results in a large difference in boiling point, and therefore distillation is used to separate the molecules.

Distillation is effective for separating molecules with differences in BP of at least 25 °C.

20. D is correct.

Stable molecules are the best leaving groups. If all the leaving groups are charged, then the bromide ion is the best leaving group, because the anion is stable (due to atomic size).

The order of the halogens as leaving groups: I$^-$ > Br$^-$ > Cl$^-$ > F$^-$

The order of the halogens as nucleophiles: I$^-$ > Br$^-$ > Cl$^-$ > F$^-$

21. C is correct.

An *anti*-Markovnikov addition of water is needed across the alkene double bond.

The reagents are borane, followed by hydrogen peroxide and sodium hydroxide.

$$H_3C-C(CH_3)=CH_2 \quad \text{(box)}$$

Top path: Hg(OAc)₂, H₂O, THF → AcO–C(CH₃)(CH₃)–CH₂–Hg-OAc (OAc = O-COCH₃) → NaBH₄/NaOH → HO–C(CH₃)(CH₃)–CH₂–H **oxymercuration** (Addition / Substitution)

Bottom path: BH₃, ether → H–C(CH₃)(CH₃)–CH₂–B(R)(R) (R = H or C₄H₉) → H₂O₂, NaOH, H₂O → H–C(CH₃)(CH₃)–CH₂–OH **hydroboration**

Comparison of Markovnikov vs. anti-Markovnikov addition reactions for alkenes

Each reaction above occurs in separate steps as indicated by the vertical separation line.

A: the product of oxymercuration-demercuration: 1) Hg(OAc)₂, H₂O / THF; 2) NaBH₄

(structure: phenyl–CH₂CH₂–CH(OH)–CH₃)

22. C is correct. Like alkenes, alkynes are electron rich functional groups and act as nucleophiles that donate electron density to electron-seeking electrophiles.

The reactivity of alkenes and alkynes is similar, and they interact with electrophiles in analogous ways.

23. A is correct.

Hückel's rule predicts that for a monocyclic compound to be aromatic, there must be a fully conjugated *pi* (sp^2 hybridization at each atom in the ring) containing $(4n + 2)$ *pi* electrons.

Two *pi* electrons are contributed by each of the double bonds. The lone pair of electrons on a double bonded N is perpendicular to the *pi* cloud and does not count as the number of *pi* electrons for Hückel's rule. Note: when N is in a single bond, the unshared electrons are parallel to the *pi* system and count toward aromaticity.

Benzimidazoline is not fully conjugated because there is a CH₂ (sp^3) group in the ring. Cyclic conjugation is necessary for a molecule to be aromatic.

B: thiophene has a sp^2 hybridized sulfur (like oxygen) and has a lone pair of electrons counted as in the ring. The total number of *pi* electrons is 6.

C: quinoline has 10 *pi* electrons and therefore is aromatic. The lone pair of electrons on a double bonded N is perpendicular to the *pi* cloud and does not count as the number of *pi* electrons for Hückel's rule.

D: thiazole has 6 *pi* electrons and therefore is aromatic. The lone pair of electrons on a double bonded N is perpendicular to the *pi* cloud and does not count as *pi* electrons for Hückel's rule. Sulfur (like oxygen) is *sp²* hybridized and has a lone pair of electrons counted as in the ring.

24. B is correct.

Esterification occurs when a carboxylic acid reacts with an alcohol under catalytic acidic conditions to form an ester + water.

A: C_6H_5OH and CH_3CH_2Br form an ether via Williamson (S_N2) ether synthesis when the alcohol reacts with the alkyl halide.

C: CH_3COOH + $SOCl_2$ is the S_N2 reaction of a carboxylic acid with thionyl chloride, and an acyl halide is formed.

D: 2 CH_3OH + H_2SO_4, form dimethyl ether from molecules of methanol and catalytic acid (e.g., sulfuric acid).

25. A is correct.

Carboxylic acid derivatives are similar in structure to ketones and aldehydes. However, one of the H or R groups has been replaced with a heteroatom, such as oxygen or nitrogen.

26. D is correct.

Hydrogen bonding a strong type of dipole-dipole interaction and raises the boiling point of organic compounds.

Dimer formed from hydrogen bonding of two carboxylic acids

The carboxylic acid of acetic acid participates in such hydrogen bonding while the ester of methyl acetate does not form similar intermolecular hydrogen bonds.

27. B is correct.

Acid bromides have the best leaving group (i.e., most stable anion), and therefore are the most reactive. Acyl halides (RCOCl or RCOBr) are so reactive that they are not normally found in nature due to the moisture in the atmosphere, which converts them to carboxylic acids.

The rate of reaction depends on factors such as: the leaving group, the steric environment, and the substituents bonded to the carbonyl carbon.

The more stable the leaving group (as an anion), the faster is the reaction. Also, a more electrophilic carbonyl (i.e., induction from neighboring groups) undergoes nucleophile attack more rapidly.

Additionally, steric hindrance (i.e., bulky groups) at the reaction center leads to slower reaction rates.

28. D is correct.

A tertiary amine (R_3N) has three alkyl groups bonded to the nitrogen atom.

A secondary amine (R_2NH) has two alkyl groups bonded to the nitrogen atom.

A primary amine (RNH_2) has one alkyl group bonded to the nitrogen atom.

A and C: are primary amines.

B: is a secondary amine.

29. C is correct. Neutral carbon atoms maintain bonds to four other atoms; therefore, an acyclic hydrocarbon cannot terminate with a methylene ($\sim CH_2 \sim$) group.

Methyl ($\sim CH_3$) groups are at the ends of alkanes and have a formula of $\sim CH_3$.

Using a subscript of n for the number of carbons, the degrees of unsaturation can be determined from the following formulae:

Alkane: C_nH_{2n+2} = 0 degrees of unsaturation

Alkene: C_nH_{2n} = 1 degree of unsaturation

Alkyne: C_nH_{2n-2} = 2 degrees of unsaturation

$CH_3CH_3CH_3$ has 3 carbons and, according to the formula C_nH_{2n+2}, should have 8 hydrogens. This molecule has 9 hydrogens; it is impossible because it would require a carbon with 5 bonds.

A: $CH_3CHCH_3CH_2CH_3$ has 5 carbons and, according to the formula C_nH_{2n+2}, should have 12 hydrogens.

B: $CH_3CH_2CH_2CH_2CH_3$ has 5 carbons and, according to the formula C_nH_{2n+2}, should have 12 hydrogens.

D: $CH_3CH_2CH_2CH_3$ has 4 carbons and, according to the formula C_nH_{2n+2}, should have 10 hydrogens.

30. A is correct. There are four regions of electron density around the nitrogen atom (including the lone pair). Therefore, the nitrogen atom is sp^3 hybridized.

Electron geometry describes the geometry of the electron pairs, groups and domains on the central atom, whether they are bonding or non-bonding. Molecular geometry is the name of the shape used to describe the molecule. When atoms bond to a central atom, they do it in a way that maximizes the distance between bonding electrons. This gives the molecule its overall shape. If no lone pairs of electrons are present, the electronic geometry is the same as the molecular shape. When there is a lone pair, it occupies more space than bonding electrons, so the net effect is to bend the shape of the molecule (although the electron geometry still conforms to the predicted shape).

The shape of this molecule is trigonal pyramidal with bonds of approximately 109.5 degrees due to the bulky ethyl substituents. The presence of three substituents (i.e., ethyls) and the lone pair on the nitrogen result in the pyramidal shape consistent with VESPER theory.

31. D is correct.

Determine the molecular formula of the given molecule. 2-methylbutane has 5 carbon atoms and 12 hydrogen atoms.

Only *n*-pentane has the same molecular formula.

The notation *n*– represents normal (or straight chain).

32. B is correct.

The broad, deep absorption between 3000 cm^{-1} to 3500 cm^{-1} is characteristic for an alcohol.

33. C is correct.

Radical termination steps involve an overall decrease in the number of radicals when comparing the starting materials to the products.

The correct answer involves a decrease in the number of radicals (from two to zero).

A: the number of radicals increases from zero to two, which is an initiation step.

B: the number of radicals (one) does not change, which are propagation steps.

C: the number of radicals decreases from two to zero, which is a termination step.

D: the number of radicals (one) does not change, which are propagation steps.

34. A is correct.

The *Cope elimination* is an intramolecular elimination reaction that occurs when the oxygen atom of the oxide of a tertiary amine removes a proton from an adjacent position.

This results in the formation of a *syn*-alkene.

The reaction requires heat.

The Cope elimination yields the same products as a Hofmann elimination (i.e., exhaustive methylation).

35. B is correct.

In this reaction, the bromine adds to the alkene group of C_2H_4 and forms 1,2–dibromoethane.

The reaction proceeds via *anti*-addition from the 3-membered bridge structure of the bromonium (i.e., halonium) ion.

A: hydrogen gas cannot be generated as a product from this reaction.

Carbon-carbon multibonds do not form from the given reaction conditions, because the reagents do not include any base to eliminate the bromine(s) to form either an alkene or alkyne.

Sample anti-stereochemical products from the addition of bromine to an alkene

Each product has an enantiomer that is not shown.

Bromonium ion as an intermediate:

bromonium ion

The reaction is also regioselective (i.e., where) for the addition of the second nucleophile (i.e., Br^-) to the halonium (i.e., bromonium) structure.

The incoming nucleophile attacks the more substituted atom.

Mechanism of Br_2 addition to an alkene:

bridged halonium ion

The incoming nucleophile attacks the bromonium bridged-structure ion at the most substituted position.

The bromonium ion (i.e., 3-membered bridged-structure) undergoes S_N2 attack for *anti*-addition product formation.

The stereochemical (i.e., *trans*) notation would include wedges and dashes.

trans-1,2 dibromocyclohexane

36. D is correct.

Degrees of unsaturation:

double bonds = 1 degree of unsaturation

triple bonds = 2 degrees of unsaturation

rings = 1 degree of unsaturation

Using the degree of unsaturation calculation:

benzene (1 ring and 3 double bonds) = 4 degrees of unsaturation

37. B is correct.

The hydrobromic acid protonates the secondary alcohol that dissociates as water.

The secondary carbocation, formed as an intermediate, is repositioned to the tertiary position through an alkyl (i.e., methide) shift.

After the methide shift, this more stable tertiary carbocation is then attacked by the bromide ion.

38. B is correct.

A ketone is being converted to an alkene.

The oxidation state of ketones is larger than the oxidation state of alkenes, and therefore the ketone needs to be reduced.

Reduction of a ketone forms a secondary alcohol.

The carbon skeleton rearranges, and this requires the formation of a carbocation.

Exposure to phosphoric acid produces the secondary carbocation, and this is followed by an alkyl shift and deprotonation to yield the alkene product.

39. A is correct.

The pK_a is the pH where half of the acid has dissociated to its conjugate base form.

The concentration of the acid and conjugate base is equal when the pK_a of the compound and the pH of the solution are the same.

Henderson-Hasselbalch equation:

$$pH = pK_a + \log[\text{conjugate base}] / [\text{acid}]$$

40. B is correct.

The hydrolysis of an ester is the reverse process of condensation because water is introduced to the ester to produce a carboxylic acid and an alcohol.

A chemical equilibrium exists for the acid-catalyzed process, and the reaction is driven forward with the use of a large excess of water.

A chemical equilibrium does not exist for the base-promoted process, because the alcohol product is unable to add into the carboxylate to reform the ester.

41. A is correct.

Structure 1: cyclic secondary enamine

Structure 2: secondary amine

Structure 3: cyclic quaternary amine

The secondary amine (2) contains one N–H bond, and therefore, this amine can form hydrogen bonds.

The cyclic amine (3) and the enamine (1) do not contain N–H bonds, so their boiling points are lower.

Aside from hydrogen bonding considerations, molecules with formal charges (molecule 3) interact via electrostatic forces, which increase their boiling point.

42. B is correct.

Because the group has three carbon atoms, the group is known as a propyl group.

Propyl substituents exist as either the *n*-propyl (i.e., normal or straight chain) or the isopropyl group.

Sample common names for organic substituents used in nomenclature

43. C is correct.

Tertiary carbocations are more stable than secondary or primary carbocation because they experience more hyperconjugation effects from the neighboring C–H bonds.

Resonance stabilization also lowers the energy of the cation.

44. A is correct.

For an alkene to experience *cis-trans* isomerization, the *pi* bond of the double bond is broken.

The *pi* bond of the alkene makes the double bond rigid.

Heating the alkene at high temperatures or exposure to electromagnetic radiation (e.g., UV radiation) may cause the *pi* bond to homolytically cleave to 1,2-diradical and rotate about the *sigma* bond to form the diastereomers.

E / *Z* and *cis* / *trans* isomers are geometric isomers and classified as diastereomers.

45. B is correct.

A polypeptide chain can undergo short range bending and folding to form β sheets or α helices.

These structures arise as the peptide bonds can assume a partial double bond character and so adopt different conformations.

The arrangement of groups around the relatively rigid amide bond can cause *R* groups to alternate from side to side and hence interact with one another.

In addition, the carbonyl oxygen in one region of the polypeptide chain could become hydrogen bonded to the amide hydrogen in another region of the polypeptide chain. This interaction often results in the formation of a beta-pleated sheet or an alpha helix.

Localized bending and folding of a polypeptide do not constitute a protein's primary structure.

A: primary structure of a protein is the amino acid sequence; individual amino acids are linked through peptide (i.e., amide) linkages.

C: tertiary structure of a protein is the 3-D shape that arises by further folding of the polypeptide chain.

Usually, these nonrandom folds give the protein a particular conformation and associated function.

D: quaternary structure is the spatial arrangement between two or more associated polypeptide chains (often linked by disulfide bridges between cysteine residues).

46. C is correct.

Fatty acid molecules are composed of long alkyl chains that do not involve branching. This is because each two-carbon segment of the fatty acid straight chain can be enzymatically converted to an acetyl-CoA derivative.

Branching in the alkyl chain may impede the oxidative degradation of these compounds because a beta-ketone must be accessed before cleavage of the chain.

Secondary alkyl groups can be oxidized to alcohols but cannot be converted to ketones for this step.

47. C is correct.

The "di" prefix in the name suggests that there are two smaller subunits.

Monosaccharides are linked together through glycosidic (i.e., oxygen bonded to two ethers) functional groups.

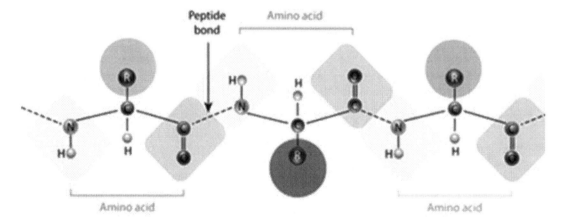

Lactose (above) is a disaccharide formed by a β(1→4) linkage between galactose and glucose.

48. C is correct.

DNA (deoxyribonucleic acid) is a long biological molecule composed of smaller units called nucleotides (i.e., sugar, phosphate, and base).

The sugar is deoxyribose (compared to ribose for RNA), and the bases are either adenine, cytosine, guanine, and thymine (with thymine replaced by uracil in RNA).

The strands that these nucleotides make up are called nucleic acids.

49. B is correct.

Proteins are biological macromolecules composed of amino acids that are bonded to each other with peptide (amide) bonds.

Three amino acids residues of a nascent (i.e., growing) polypeptide chain

50. D is correct.

Lipids (i.e., fats) is a term used to describe long chain ester-linked molecules such as triglycerides. The term "lipid" is sometimes used interchangeably with the word "fat."

However, lipids also include cyclic biomolecules, such as steroids (e.g., cholesterol and its derivatives such as estrogen and testosterone).

Glycerol is a 3-carbon chain with three hydroxyl groups. Each hydroxyl undergoes a condensation reaction with the carboxylic acid end of a fatty acid chain to form a lipid.

Glycerol

Comparison of saturated and unsaturated fatty acids. The unsaturated fatty acid contains one or more double bonds. The unsaturated fatty acid is a *cis* alkene in the above example.

Formation, via dehydration (removal of H₂O), of triglyceride from glycerol and 3 fatty acids

51. C is correct.

Benedict's test (or Tollens' reagent) is used to detect reducing sugars. An oxidized copper reagent is reduced by a sugar's aldehyde, and the aldehyde is oxidized to a carboxylic acid in the process.

Reducing sugars (and alpha hydroxyl ketones) give a positive Benedict's test: a red-brown precipitate forms. Fehling's solution also gives a positive test for reducing sugars by changing from blue to clear and forming a red-brown precipitate.

Tollens' reagent forms silver ions (mirror) as a positive test for reducing sugars.

Tartaric acid has no aldehyde or ketone to react to because its first and last carbons have carboxylic functional groups. Therefore, it cannot reduce the reagent and yields a negative result (Tollens' remains clear while Benedict's and Fehling's remain blue).

52. D is correct.

Ribose is the structural sugar of RNA, while deoxyribose is the sugar for DNA.

Uracil is a nucleotide (i.e., sugar, phosphate, and base) that contains a ribose sugar.

This sugar is similar to deoxyribose; however, one difference is that deoxyribose has one fewer alcohol group (2' position of the sugar) than ribose.

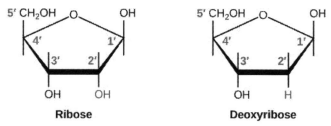

Uracil is a base of RNA and does not appear in DNA strands.

53. C is correct. Sulfur-sulfur bonds are disulfide bonds. The bonds are formed from the dimerization of two cysteine residues.

Cysteine is the only molecule among the common amino acids that possesses a thiol (or SH) group

54. D is correct.

Fat can be produced from glucose, but glucose is not produced from animal fat. The excess of glucose consumption in the body can lead to increased levels of fat in the body.

55. D is correct.

Maltose is a disaccharide composed of two glucose molecules, and the glycosidic linkage is an $\alpha(1\rightarrow4)$ linkage.

56. A is correct.

During transcription, the two nucleic acid strands of DNA dissociate, and mRNA is synthesized (transcription) by using the nitrogen bases of DNA as a template.

Therefore, the mRNA strand is a complementary strand to the DNA strand.

The mRNA then exits the nucleus to be used as a template for the production of proteins (translation).

57. B is correct.

The amino group of all the other common amino acids contains primary amine functional groups.

Proline contains a five-membered ring as part of its structure.

58. D is correct.

There are two overall categories of lipids: long chain lipids (e.g., triglycerides) and smaller, polycyclic lipids, such as steroids (e.g., cholesterol and its derivatives such as estrogen and testosterone).

Terpenes (samples shown below) are small alkene-containing hydrocarbon building blocks that can be combined and cyclized to form steroids. Terpenes are simple lipids.

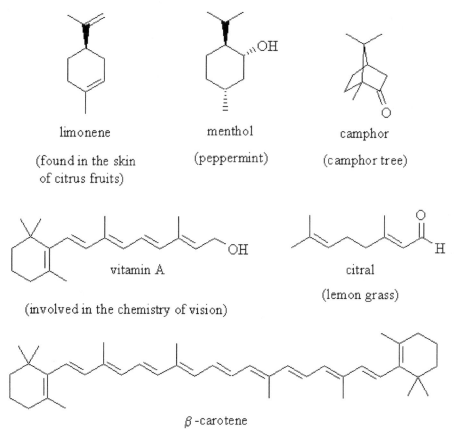

Examples of terpenes

59. A is correct.

For D-sugar monosaccharides, the hydroxyl group of the last asymmetric carbon atom (i.e., furthest from the carbonyl carbon) is oriented to the right.

60. C is correct.

The bonds that make up every single strand of DNA are covalent bonds, and the bonds linking the antiparallel strands of DNA together are hydrogen bonds.

Two hydrogen bonds form between adenine and thymine (A=T).

Three hydrogen bonds form between cytosine and guanine (C≡G).

Explanations: Diagnostic Test #2

1. A is correct.

The suffix ~*oate* signifies an ester functional group as the highest priority group in the molecule.

2. B is correct.

The carbonyl carbon is trigonal planar because the double bonded carbon is sp^2 hybridized.

I: each of the two methyl carbons is sp^3 hybridized and tetrahedral.

III: none of the carbons have an unshared pair of electrons (i.e., carbanions) because carbanions are highly reactive and observed in a limited number of examples (e.g., Grignard reagent, Gillman reagent, acetylide anion) and are not present in stable molecules.

3. D is correct.

A *meso* compound has chiral centers but is not itself chiral because it has an internal plane of symmetry.

A *meso* compound is a single molecule that contains two enantiomers joined together.

Tartaric acid is a four-carbon polyol with two carboxylic acids and two chiral centers. There are three stereoisomers: the (+) form, the (–) form and the *meso* form.

Meso compounds are identical to their mirror images.

Each of the two stereoisomers rotates plane-polarized light as indicated by the notation of (+) or (–), but *meso*-tartaric acid is achiral (i.e., no net rotation of plane-polarized light).

III: racemic mixture refers to a solution that contains enantiomers (i.e., chiral molecules that are mirror images).

4. B is correct.

For NMR, the position that hydrogen absorbs is determined by the chemical environment.

If the chemical environment of two hydrogens is identical, only one signal is produced.

Therefore, equivalent hydrogens could be replaced by another group to yield the same molecule.

The challenge is in determining whether hydrogens are in identical environments (i.e., symmetric molecules).

1,2-dibromoethane

1,2-dibromoethane produces only one absorbance in the NMR spectrum, because a molecule has only one type of hydrogen atom.

A: *tert*-butyl alcohol produces 2 signals.

C: toluene produces 2 signals.

D: methanol produces 2 signals.

5. C is correct.

A molecule must have a net positive charge to migrate to the cathode.

In gel electrophoresis, the cathode is the negatively charged end because it involves an electrolytic rather than a galvanic cell.

Amino acids have amphoteric properties ($+ / -$ regions within the molecule) at physiological pH of 7.35; the carboxylic acid end is negative, while the amino end is positive.

At physiological pH values, the carboxyl terminus of an amino acid with COOH ($pK_a \approx 5$) dissociates to become a negatively charged carboxylate.

At physiological pH, the amino terminus with NH_3 ($pK_a \approx 10$) is protonated and becomes positively charged.

Thus, at physiological pH, an amino acid is a zwitterion (i.e., both positive and negative charges within the same molecule).

Comparison of amino acids: structure 1 is neutral and structure 2 results from protonation/deprotonation to form the zwitterion.

The overall charge of an amino acid depends on the ratio of negatively charged carboxylates to positively charged amino groups.

The molecule that migrates towards the positive cathode is $H_2NCH_2CHNH_2COOH$ which, at physiological pH, exists as $^+H_3NCH_2CH(^+NH_3)COO^-$.

Therefore, the molecule has a net positive charge.

A: the molecule is neutral with two amino groups protonated and two carboxyl groups deprotonated.

B: the molecule is neutral with one amino group protonated and one carboxyl group deprotonated. The alcohol has a pK_a of 17 and is neutral at physiological pH.

D: the molecule is neutral with one amino group protonated and one carboxyl group deprotonated at physiological pH.

6. D is correct.

Free radical halogenation is one of the few reactions (along with combustion) that alkanes undergo and occurs via a highly reactive halogen radical.

A radical is a single, neutrally charged atom which has an unhybridized *p* orbital with a single unpaired electron that causes it to be reactive.

Steps for free radical halogenation:

Step I: initiation is the formation of the free radical from a diatomic molecule (X_2) by homolytic bond cleavage. Initiation is shown in the first reaction equation and is usually catalyzed by ultraviolet light ($h\nu$), heat or by an attack by another free radical.

Step II: propagation involves a radical and a neutral molecule, and the products are a new neutral molecule and new radical. The halogen-free radical attacks the neutral alkane and, via homolytic bond cleavage, produces a new H–X bond and another highly reactive free radical as the alkyl radical.

The alkyl radical reacts with Br_2 to form the alkyl halide and another halogen radical. This new halogen radical then starts the process again, thus causing a chain reaction (propagation).

Step III: termination involves the joining of two radicals. For example, an alkyl radical attacks a halogen radical to produce a new neutral molecule.

I: $Br_2 + h\nu \rightarrow 2\ Br\cdot$ is UV light-induced generation of two free radicals and is the chain initiating step.

II: $Br\cdot + RH \rightarrow HBr + R\cdot$ is a chain propagating step because the reaction advances the chain onward by generating a new neutral product plus a new free radical.

III: $R\cdot + Br_2 \rightarrow RBr + Br\cdot$ is a chain propagating step because the reaction advances the chain onward by generating a new neutral product plus a new free radical.

7. B is correct.

Protonation of the alkene results in the formation of the more stabilized carbocation, and this cation forms at the secondary alkyl position.

The cation is then trapped by water to form the alcohol.

8. D is correct.

Alkynes are oxidized by two common mechanisms to yield either the Markovnikov or *anti*-Markovnikov product.

One of the *pi* bonds of the alkyne undergoes addition to yield an enol intermediate.

The enol tautomerizes to generate the Markovnikov ketone or the *anti*-Markovnikov aldehyde.

9. A is correct.

Benzene is aromatic and undergoes electrophilic aromatic substitution (EAS) with the addition of a Lewis acid (e.g., $AlCl_3$, $FeBr_3$ or H_2SO_4).

The reagents of SO_3 and concentrated H_2SO_4 are used to sulfonate aromatic compounds, whereby an SO_3H group is substituted onto the benzene ring.

Halogens are *ortho* and *para* directing deactivators.

Therefore, the product is a mixture of *ortho-* and *para*-bromobenzenesulfonic acid.

B: the bromine is not displaced from the aromatic benzene ring and replaced with hydrogen to form benzene.

C: the SO_3H group does not substitute for the bromine of bromobenzene.

D: *meta-* is not formed because halogens are *ortho* and *para* directing deactivators.

10. D is correct.

A tosyl group (Tos) is $CH_3C_6H_4SO_2$ (derived from $CH_3C_6H_4SO_2Cl$) and forms esters and amides of tosylic acid.

Tosylates are used to increase the efficiency of the original hydroxyl as a leaving group.

Unlike PBr_3 or $SOCl_2$ (both via S_N2), the reaction mechanism preserves the bond between the carbon and the O of the hydroxyl, and therefore no inversion of stereochemistry occurs (during the first step in this example) with the use of a tosylate.

The first step with the tosylate results in retention of the chiral center and the second step (i.e., Cl^- as a nucleophile) produces an inverted product.

11. D is correct.

Since the aldol reaction involves deprotonation (abstraction of H^+) by a strong base, the preferred solvents are neither acidic nor electrophilic.

Dimethyl ether, unlike the other solvents listed, does not contain an acidic proton.

12. C is correct.

Lithium aluminum hydride (LAH or $LiAlH_4$) is a powerful reducing agent and can reduce carboxylic acids and esters to form primary alcohols and reduces nitro groups to amines.

Sodium borohydride ($NaBH_4$) is a weak reducing agent and is only used for the reduction of aldehydes (to primary alcohols) and ketones (to secondary alcohols).

13. B is correct.

Treatment of the ester with potassium hydroxide and heat results in the nucleophilic attack of hydroxide to the carbonyl in an addition-elimination reaction.

The ring product exists as a negatively charged species (cyclohexanol as the alkoxide) because of the presence of a base (KOH), until the second step of the H^+ workup.

After acidic workup, the alkoxide is protonated to form cyclohexanol.

14. C is correct.

Amines are Brønsted-Lowry and Lewis bases because the lone pair of electrons on nitrogen can bind to a proton.

It is favorable for the amine to abstract a proton from the acid.

Electron-donating groups attached to the nitrogen in the amine make the amine more basic because by donating electron density, they stabilize the positive ion formed.

Therefore, electron-donating groups (alkyl chains via hyperconjugation) destabilize the lone pair of electrons on the amine and make it more reactive.

Conversely, substituents (e.g., electronegative atoms) are electron-withdrawing, and the amine is less basic.

Alkyl groups, compared to hydrogen atoms, are electron-donating, and therefore basicity decreases in the order trimethylamine > methylamine > ammonia in the gas phase.

The gas phase is specified because, in aqueous solutions, hydrogen bonding also plays a role in stabilizing the salt, and thus may result in a different order.

In addition reactions, electronegative atoms, such as the fluorine of $(CF_3)_3N$, strongly reduce the basicity of the amine because of the inductive electron-withdrawing effect of the electronegative atom.

In this example, it is unfavorable for the nitrogen to acquire a positive charge in forming a salt.

15. A is correct.

The longest carbon chain has seven carbon atoms; it has one chlorine and one methyl substituent.

IUPAC recognizes the following 5 common names for the nomenclature of organic molecules:

16. D is correct.

The allylic cation can delocalize the cation at the most substituted position is the most stable molecule.

The other allylic cations are not as stable because the cation is less substituted in the other resonance forms.

17. A is correct.

A racemic mixture contains equal quantities of two enantiomers (i.e., isomers that are non-superimposable mirror images).

Compound I is D-fructose in a Fischer projection.

Compound II is D-fructose in a straight chain.

Compound III is D-glucose in a straight chain.

18. A is correct.

IR absorption between 1630 cm^{-1} and 1740 cm^{-1} is characteristic of carbonyls (e.g., aldehydes, ketones, acid anhydrides, anhydrides, carboxylic acids, esters, and amides).

An IR absorption of 1735 cm^{-1} is characteristic of an ester.

19. C is correct.

For a given class of compounds, the smaller the molecular weight, the lower the boiling point.

For a mixture containing compounds of different boiling points, the smallest and most volatile components have the lowest boiling point.

Molecules with the lowest boiling point vaporize first and travel furthest up the fractionating column.

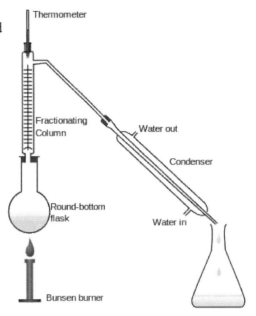

20. B is correct.

As a concerted mechanism, the single step of the S$_N$2 reaction is a simultaneous substitution occurring with the formation of a new bond while the original bond breaks.

S$_N$2 undergoes second-order kinetics.

rate = k [substrate] × [nucleophile]

21. A is correct.

The reaction shown is an acid catalyzed dehydration reaction. An alcohol in the presence of sulfuric acid and heat is characteristic of the E$_1$ mechanism to form an alkene.

The generated cation undergoes a ring expansion to give a more stable tertiary carbocation, which is eliminated to form the tertiary (i.e., trisubstituted) alkene. From the rearranged carbocation, the alpha proton is eliminated by the conjugate base HSO$_4^-$ to regenerate the sulfuric acid.

The ring (i.e., bond angle or Baeyer) strain energy also drives ring expansion.

22. A is correct.

The hydration of the alkyne involves the formation of a carbocation and proceeds through a Markovnikov-type mechanism.

The enol intermediate converts (i.e., tautomerizes) to the keto of the methyl phenyl ketone product.

23. A is correct.

Substituents on an aromatic ring affect the rate at which electrophilic aromatic substitution reactions occur.

Since the ring acts as a nucleophile in these reactions, electron-donating substituents increase the rate of reaction, while electron-withdrawing substituents decrease the rate of reaction.

The bromine substituent (III) is slightly deactivating (due to its electronegativity), making it less reactive than benzene (I).

The nitro group is extremely deactivating (due to resonance), making nitrobenzene (II) less reactive than bromobenzene (III).

24. D is correct.

Aldehydes and ketones tautomerize to exist in equilibrium between the keto and enol forms.

Keto   *Enol*

Most molecules (99%) exist predominantly in the keto form because the carbon oxygen (carbonyl) double bond is more stable than the hydroxyl on the double bond of the enol.

Phenols are one of few aldehydes/ketones that exist predominantly in the enol form in the keto-enol tautomer equilibrium. The conjugated benzene ring system of phenol provides stability for the enol form.

The keto form of phenol lacks conjugation because a carbon in the ring is sp^3 hybridized.

When the phenol molecule assumes the keto form, aromaticity is lost and the molecule becomes less stable.

Enol   Keto

Therefore, the keto form is non-aromatic and thus less stable.

Aromatic molecules are cyclic, planar, have conjugated double bonds (i.e., sp^2 at each atom) and satisfy Hückel's number of *pi* electrons ($4n + 2$, where n is an integer).

Anti-aromatic compounds are also cyclic, planar, have conjugated double bonds, but have 4n (e.g., 4, 8, 12 and so on) *pi* electrons and therefore are unstable.

Nonaromatic compounds do not meet the four criteria needed for aromatic compounds: cyclic, planar, conjugated double bonds and Hückel's number of *pi* electrons.

25. C is correct.

Oxidation of primary alcohols produces aldehydes (by PCC or oxidation in dry conditions).

Oxidation of secondary alcohols commonly produces ketones (e.g., by PCC) or carboxylic acids (e.g., Jones oxidation by CrO_3 in H_2SO_4).

A: Benedict's test (or Tollens' reagent) is used to detect reducing sugars. An oxidized copper reagent is reduced by a sugar's aldehyde, and the aldehyde is oxidized to a carboxylic acid in the process.

Reducing sugars (and alpha hydroxyl ketones) gives a positive Benedict's test: a red-brown precipitate forms.

Fehling's solution also gives a positive test for reducing sugars by changing from blue to clear and forming a red-brown precipitate.

B: Tollens' reagent forms silver ions (i.e., shiny mirror surface) as a positive test for reducing sugars.

26. D is correct.

The chlorine substitution stabilizes the negative charge of the carboxylate through inductive withdrawal of electron density through the *sigma* bonds.

The *ortho* substitution also lowers the pK_a of the acid because of its conjugation with the aryl ring decreases (*ortho* effect).

27. B is correct.

The longest continuing chain in the product is four carbon atoms long.

Therefore, the root name is *butan* and the suffix is *~amide* because it is an amide (i.e., R–$CONR_2$) functional group.

For this example, the nitrogen contains a methyl group.

N-methylbutanamide

28. A is correct.

Amines can be protonated with Brønsted acids to produce ammonium salts.

Amides can be formed from primary and secondary amines by acylation of the nitrogen of primary and secondary amines.

29. C is correct.

The longest carbon chain in the molecule is composed of seven carbon atoms.

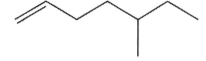

The methyl substituent is at the fifth carbon of the chain.

The alkene *pi* bond is between carbon one and carbon two.

30. C is correct.

Resonance structures are derived from the movement of lone pairs and *pi* electrons.

Generated negative charges are placed on the more electronegative atoms and the positive charges on the less electronegative atoms.

31. B is correct.

The molecule that contains the chiral carbon is the one that has a central carbon with four different groups as substituents.

These carbons are also described as asymmetric (i.e., stereogenic center or chiral carbons).

32. D is correct.

UV light has enough energy to excite electrons to higher energy vacant orbitals to produce photoactivated atoms.

However, this form of radiation generally is not strong enough to eject electrons from atoms of most elements to form ions.

33. A is correct.

Alkanes undergo free radical halogenation to substitute one of the C–H bonds with a C–X bond, where X is a halogen.

Alkenes and alkynes generally undergo addition reactions instead, where an electrophile may add across a carbon-carbon *pi* bond.

34. A is correct.

Both alkanes and alkenes have *sigma* bonds.

The *pi* (i.e., double) bond in the alkenes stabilize a negative charge (as an anion) and therefore, are more acidic.

The increased *s* character on the hybridization of a sp^2 orbital of an alkene (pK_a = 45) allows the orbital to accommodate the negative charge with more stability than for the sp^3 of an alkane (pK_a = 50).

Furthermore, the increased *s* character on the hybridization of a *sp* orbital of an alkyne (pK_a = 28) allows the orbital to accommodate the negative charge with more stability than for the sp^2 of an alkene

35. C is correct.

The compound has five carbons, seven hydrogens, and one nitrogen.

Use the following formulae to calculate the degrees of unsaturation:

C_nH_{2n+2}: for an alkane (0 degrees of unsaturation)

C_nH_{2n}: for an alkene or a ring (1 degree of unsaturation)

C_nH_{2n-2}: for an alkyne, 2 double bonds, 2 rings or 1 ring and 1 double bond (2 degrees of unsaturation)

The molecule has 3 degrees of unsaturation.

Because one of the unsaturation elements is a ring, the molecule contains two *pi* bonds.

36. B is correct.

Benzene is a cyclic aromatic hydrocarbon that has 4 degrees of unsaturation.

The *pi* bonds in the molecule are delocalized and impart aromaticity to the molecule.

37. C is correct. Treatment of salicylic acid (i.e., aspirin) with methanol and dry acid are conditions for synthesizing an ester in a mechanism known as *Fischer esterification*:

Fischer esterification

38. B is correct.

When ketones and aldehydes are alkylated by Grignard nucleophiles, the number of C–O bonds decreases by one, and the number of C–C bonds increases by one.

Oxidation proceeds towards the right, while reduction is shown proceeding to the left

39. B is correct.

Exposing a carboxylic acid to sodium hydroxide produces water and the sodium carboxylate conjugate base. This ionic base has a higher affinity for the aqueous layer due to the negative charge, and this charge forms hydrogen bonds to the hydrogen atoms of water molecules.

40. B is correct.

As the acidity of a group increases, its basic properties decrease.

The carbonyl group of the amide withdraws electron density from the nitrogen atom inductively and through conjugation. This causes the N–H bond of the amide to be much less basic (pK_a of an amine ≈ 10 and pK_a of an amide ≈ 35).

41. D is correct.

Hydrogens, bonded directly to F, O or N, participate in hydrogen bonds.

The hydrogen is partial positive (i.e., delta plus or ∂+) due to the bond to these electronegative atoms. The lone pair of electrons on the F, O or N interacts with the ∂+ hydrogen to form a hydrogen bond.

None of the other molecules can form hydrogen bonds because hydrogen is not attached directly to F, O or N.

42. C is correct.

Unless anchored by a high priority group (e.g., carboxylic acid, ketone or alcohol), the numbering of the longest carbon chain starts at the end that results in the lowest numbering (i.e., sum of the digits) for the substituent groups.

Therefore, the molecule has two methyl groups at the second position and one methyl group in the third position: 2,2,3-trimethylbutane.

43. A is correct.

The oxygen atom contains 4 regions of electron density (i.e., two lone pairs and two methyl substituents) and adopts a tetrahedral configuration.

This configuration has an angle between substituent groups to be approximately 109.5 degrees.

44. B is correct.

The chlorine atom occupies the internal (i.e., 2nd) carbon on the first molecule, and the chlorine atom is bonded to a terminal (i.e., 1st) carbon on the second molecule.

Constitutional (i.e., structural or configurational) isomers have the same molecular formula, but different connectivity of the atoms.

A: conformational isomers involve free rotation around a single bond (e.g., Newman projections).

C: diastereomers are chiral molecules (i.e., attached to four different groups) with two or more chiral centers and are non-superimposable non-mirror images (i.e., *R,R* and *S,R*).

D: enantiomers are chiral molecules (i.e., attached to four different groups) and are non-superimposable mirror images (i.e., *R* and *S*).

The exception of the two or more chiral center requirement for diastereomers is geometric isomers that contain double bonds (i.e., *cis* and *trans*).

45. D is correct.

Collagen is a protein that supports hair, nails, and skin.

Collagen is composed of a triple helix, and the most abundant amino acids in collagen include glycine, proline, alanine and glutamic acid.

Much of the excess protein that is consumed in an animal's diet is used to synthesize collagen.

46. D is correct.

Dietary triglycerides are composed of glycerol and three fatty acids.

The hydrolysis of triglycerides yields glycerol and three fatty acid chains.

Hydrolysis of a triglyceride

47. B is correct.

Mutarotation occurs when cyclic hemiacetals form from monosaccharides with different configurations around the anomeric carbon (i.e., carbonyl carbon in the straight chain).

The reaction mechanism for the interconversion of α and β anomers

The bond to the anomeric carbon is easily broken in aqueous solutions, as either α (hydroxyl points downward) or β (hydroxyl points upward) anomer becomes an open chain.

In an aqueous solution, especially if it is slightly acidic, this open chain is easily recyclized, forming a mixture containing both anomers (α or β) in their equilibrium concentrations.

Thus, the initial opening and subsequent closing of the chain results in a mixture of anomers, known as mutarotation.

A: reduction is the decrease in the number of bonds to oxygen (or gain of electrons in inorganic chemistry).

Examples of reduction in organic chemistry include the conversion of an aldehyde to a primary alcohol, a carboxylic acid to either an aldehyde or primary alcohol or a ketone to a secondary alcohol.

C: hemiacetals are formed as a result of the nucleophilic addition of oxygen of a hydroxyl to a carbonyl (aldehyde or ketone).

D: the open chain form has a carbonyl group, and therefore an aldehyde is already formed.

48. C is correct.

Thymine is a pyrimidine nucleotide base that occurs in DNA but does not occur in RNA.

Instead, RNA has uracil.

49. B is correct.

Secondary structure for proteins involves localized bonding.

The most important intermolecular interaction is hydrogen bonding which is responsible for maintaining both the alpha helix and beta pleated (parallel and antiparallel) sheet structures.

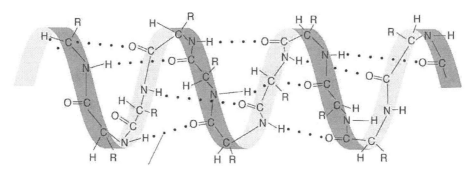

Alpha helix structure with hydrogen bonding shown as dotted lines

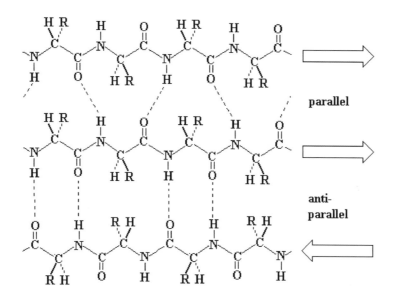

Beta pleated sheets (parallel and antiparallel) with hydrogen bonding shown

50. B is correct.

The *cis* double bond of unsaturated fatty acids causes these molecules to stack less efficiently and less tightly. The melting point for these compounds is lower than for saturated fats.

Therefore, most unsaturated fatty acids are liquids at room temperature.

The presence of double bonds indicates unsaturated fatty acids

The unsaturated fatty acid contains a *cis* double bond at the 6th position.

51. D is correct.

The cyclic hemiacetal forms of sugars exist as either five-membered (furanose) or six-membered (pyranose) rings. A furanose is a carbohydrate that has a chemical structure with a five-membered ring system consisting of four carbon atoms and one oxygen atom.

Formation of pyranose hemiacetal and representations of β-D-glucopyranose

A ketopentose is an open-chain five-carbon sugar that has a ketone carbonyl group.

An aldopentose is an open-chain five-carbon sugar with an aldehyde carbonyl group.

A cyclic hemiacetal is derived from an aldehyde; if the anomeric carbon (i.e., carbon attached to two oxygen) has an H attached – it is an aldose.

If the anomeric carbon lacks an H attached – it is a ketose.

The structure is a furanose form of sugar that has a ketone carbonyl in its open-chain structure.

A: the furanose (five-membered ring) form of an aldopentose is a structure that lacks the H on the anomeric carbon necessary in an aldose.

B: the pyranose (six-membered ring) form of an aldopentose is a structure that lacks the H on the anomeric carbon necessary in an aldose.

D: the pyranose form of a ketopentose is a six-membered ring.

52. C is correct.

In DNA, thymine hydrogen bonds with adenine.

However, in RNA, the thymine is exchanged for uracil.

Uracil (RNA)   Thymine (DNA)

53. C is correct.

The standard conditions for breaking the covalent bonds during peptide hydrolysis are concentrated HCl and several hours of reflux.

The reaction time depends on partial or complete hydrolysis of the peptide.

54. C is correct.

Glycerol is an alcohol that possesses three hydroxyl groups; one hydroxyl group is bonded to each of the carbon atoms of glycerol.

Glycerol is, therefore, a triol molecule, and this molecule is a key component in the structure of triglyceride molecules.

55. B is correct.

The cyclic and acyclic isomers of glucose exist as an equilibrium mixture in aqueous solutions.

Because the cyclization of monosaccharides is reversible, the cyclic isomer also exists as a mixture of diastereomers; α and β isomers.

56. C is correct.

Nucleic acids determine the sequences of amino acids because groupings of nucleotides along a sequence corresponding to a particular amino acid.

The information of certain nucleic acids (i.e., mRNA) is translated on ribosomes with tRNA.

Prions are infectious, disease-causing agents of misfolded proteins.

57. B is correct.

Essential amino acids are those that are obtained from the diet.

Nonessential amino acids can be synthesized by the body and do not need to be consumed.

58. C is correct.

Phospholipids are important lipids that make up the bilayer structure of the membranes of cells, organelles, and other enclosed cellular structures.

Phospholipids are composed of two (same or different) fatty acid molecules, a phosphate group and a glycerol backbone.

The phospholipid contains both a hydrophobic (i.e., fatty acid tail) region and hydrophilic (polar head) region.

The hydrophobic regions point toward each other in the membrane bilayer while the polar heads point towards the inside (i.e., cytosolic) or outside (i.e., extracellular) sides of the bilayer.

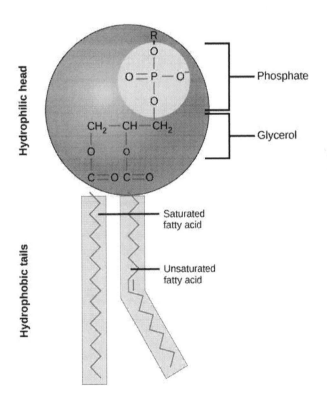

59. C is correct.

Isomers have identical atoms in different arrangements.

The double bond and hydroxyl groups shift positions, which indicates that one carbon was oxidized, and another was reduced.

In glycolysis, the phosphoglucose isomerase assists in the removal of a hydrogen anion (i.e., hydride ion), which attacks a carbonyl group to form a hydroxyl group.

The carbon where the hydride ion is removed – now a cation – is attacked by a water molecule.

A: $CH_3CH_2COCl + H_2O$ reaction is hydration.

B: the number of carbons in the products is one greater than in the reactants; therefore, this is not an example of an isomerization reaction which requires the number of all atoms to remain constant.

D: $CH_3CH_2CH_2CHOHCH_3$ reaction is a transesterification reaction.

60. A is correct.

The sugar component of nucleic acid, the ribose or deoxyribose sugar, is the portion that contains many alcohol groups.

The nitrogenous base contains a basic nitrogen atom (i.e., amino group) that hydrogen bonds with complementary nitrogen bases.

There are two hydrogen bonds between the nitrogenous base's adenine and thymine (A=T) and three hydrogen bonds between cytosine and guanine (C≡G).

Explanations: Diagnostic Test #3

1. D is correct.

Draw the four-carbon chain with the double bond at the second position in the chain.

The second and third position each have a chlorine atom, and these are the highest priority substituents of the alkene. They must be oriented on the same side of the double bond because the molecule is *cis*.

2. C is correct.

The dipole moment is determined by the magnitudes of the individual bond dipoles and the spatial arrangement of the substituents on the molecule.

The dipole moment is greatest when there is a large difference in electronegativity of the bonded atoms.

Therefore, a carbon–carbon bond (i.e., same electronegativity) has no dipole moment, while carbon–halogen bonds have moderately large dipole moments because of the electronegativity difference between carbon and halogen.

(1*R*,2*S*)-1,2-dichloro-1,2-diphenylethane is effectively *cis* due to the restricted rotation.

(1*R*,2*S*)-1,2-dichloro-1,2-diphenylethane has two phenyl rings attached on one side and two chlorine groups attached on the other side.

The (*R/S*)-designation indicates that the two highest priority substituents (i.e., chlorine) attached to the same side (priority according to molecular weight, so chlorine has higher priority). The highly electronegative chlorines pull electron density, creating a net dipole.

A: (1*S*,2*S*)-1,2-dichloro-1,2-diphenylethane contains only single bonds. The (*R/S*)-designation indicates that the two highest priority substituents (i.e., chlorine) attached on opposite sides (with restricted rotation due to the size of the phenyl substitutes). The highly electronegative chlorines pull electron density in different spatial orientations, canceling a net dipole.

B: 1,2-dichlorobutane has carbon–chlorine bonds that are highly polar, but free rotation about the carbon–carbon single bond cancels any net dipole.

D: (*E*)-1,2-dichlorobutene differs from the *Z* configuration (or 1*R*,2*S* in the correct answer) because the two highest priority substituents are on opposite sides of the double bond. As the chlorine pulls electron density, both dipoles cancel each other for a net dipole of zero.

3. A is correct.

The carbon attached to the leaving group is tertiary (bonded to 3 carbons) and chiral because it is bonded to 4 different substituents, and the molecule is optically active. Tertiary alkyl halides undergo S_N1 reactions (forming a trigonal planar carbocation) but do not undergo S_N2 reactions because of steric hindrance.

In the first step of the S_N1 reaction, the bromine dissociates to form a stable tertiary carbocation, which results in the loss of optical activity. A positively charged carbon is sp^2 hybridized (trigonal planar) and always achiral because it has only three substituents.

In the second step, the HCN nucleophile attacks the trigonal planar (flat) carbocation from either side of the plane (i.e., top or bottom) with approximately equal probability. As a result, the reaction yields approximately equal amounts of two chiral products.

The products are enantiomers (i.e., chiral molecules that are non-superimposable mirror images), and each enantiomer rotates the plane of polarized light to the same extent but in opposite directions. Therefore, the product is an optically inactive racemic mixture (i.e., both enantiomers are present in the solution), and there is a loss of optical activity in the solution.

Racemization means loss of optical activity and often involves a carbocation intermediate (S_N1 reaction), whereby the incoming nucleophile attacks from either side of the trigonal planar carbocation.

B: mutarotation occurs in monosaccharides (i.e., sugars) and involves the equilibrium between open-chain forms and cyclic hemiacetal forms (e.g., Haworth projections) in aqueous solutions.

D: inversion of absolute configuration only occurs in S_N2 reactions, whereby a nucleophile attacks the substrate from the side opposite the leaving group (backside) in a one-step reaction. From the concerted S_N2 reaction, the products have the same absolute configuration (often inverted from the backside attack), and the product is considered chiral.

4. A is correct.

UV spectroscopy is useful for identifying compounds that have conjugated double bonds. Neither dimethyl ether nor bromoethane has conjugated double bonds, so UV is not a good analytical technique to distinguish them.

B: mass spectrometry (MS) provides information about the molecular weight, the number, and size of molecular fragments, and a unique fingerprint pattern.

C: infrared (IR) spectroscopy determines if the molecule contains certain functional groups and also gives a unique fingerprint pattern for a molecule.

D: proton nuclear magnetic resonance (NMR) examines the molecular environment of the hydrogens and is related to where the signal is located on the spectrum. NMR is useful in determining the connectivity of the atoms and identifies the relative numbers of each kind of hydrogen (i.e., integration number given by the area under each signal) and the number of hydrogen atoms on adjacent atoms (i.e., splitting pattern as determined by n + 1, where n = number of adjacent Hs).

5. C is correct.

To separate two compounds, consider their chemical and physical properties. From the question stem, at atmospheric pressure, they both decompose before they reach their boiling point.

Vacuum distillation occurs at very low pressure and causes compounds to boil at lower temperatures – this allows these molecules to reach their boiling point before they decompose.

A: sublimation is the direct conversion of a solid into a gas. This often requires lower pressures and/or higher temperature than vacuum distillation, meaning it is more difficult to carry out and would carry more risk of the compounds decomposing.

B: fractional distillation separates compounds that have boiling points very close together (differences less than 25 °C). It is usually performed at atmospheric pressure, so (like for simple distillation) these compounds would decompose instead of distilling (evaporating and moving from the liquid to gaseous phase).

D: in simple distillation, a mixture is heated until each component boils (moves from liquid to gaseous phase) separately and each fraction is collected. Since both of these molecules decompose before they reach their boiling point at atmospheric pressure, they cannot be separated by simple distillation (they decompose before being separated).

Simple distillation is an effective technique to separate molecules with boiling point differences greater than 25 °C.

6. C is correct.

A *trans* isomer requires that the substituents point in opposite directions (up and down). Therefore, one substituent is located axial, while the other substituent is equatorial.

In this substituted cyclohexane, the molecule is more stable when the larger substituents are in the equatorial position.

When comparing a methyl and an isopropyl, the isopropyl is larger and therefore is located equatorially.

7. D is correct.

Carbon-carbon *pi* bonds are elements of unsaturation, and unsaturated compounds can be reduced to give more reduced molecules (e.g., alkanes).

Alkenes have a higher oxidation state than the alkane and are equivalent to a C–O or C–X bond, where X is a more electronegative atom.

8. A is correct.

The Grignard reagent (CH_3CH_2MgBr), as a carbanion, is a strong base.

In the presence of the terminal alkyne shown, an acid-base reaction occurs by deprotonating the alkyne and producing ethane.

9. D is correct. The double bonds in benzene are less reactive than in a non-aromatic alkene because addition (e.g., hydrogenation) disrupts the aromaticity (i.e., delocalization) of the ring making it less stable.

The application of heat and high pressure in the presence of the Rh catalyst permits benzene to overcome the energy of activation necessary to transform the highly stable benzene molecule to a non-aromatic product.

10. A is correct. The electronegativity of the oxygen atom in alcohol helps stabilize the negative charge of the conjugate base (i.e., negative oxygen) of the alcohol.

A more stable conjugate base results in a stronger acid (more readily dissociating its proton).

Secondary alcohols are more acidic than tertiary alcohols.

11. D is correct. The oxidation of aldehydes to carboxylic acid can be done by exposing aldehydes to chromic acid in water and acetone, or to potassium permanganate.

12. A is correct. Secondary alcohols cannot be oxidized further.

B: primary alcohols undergo oxidation by strong oxidizing agents (e.g., potassium permanganate, O_3 or Jones's reagent) to yield carboxylic acids.

C: acidic or basic hydrolysis of a nitrile yields carboxylic acids.

D: Grignard reagents reacting with CO_2 is a method for preparing carboxylic acids. The carbonation of a Grignard reagent (adding CO_2) forms the magnesium salt of a carboxylic acid. In a subsequent step, the magnesium salt is protonated and converted to a carboxylic acid when treated with mineral acid (e.g., H^+ from HCl).

13. A is correct. Consider the susceptibility of different compounds to nucleophilic attack. All of the molecules undergo nucleophilic attack, but the molecule that undergoes attack the easiest is propionyl bromide.

Out of all the carboxylic acid derivatives (acyl halides, anhydrides, esters, carboxylic acids, and amides), acyl halides are the most reactive towards nucleophiles due to the electron withdrawing effects of oxygen and the stability of the halide anion as a leaving group.

B: benzyl bromide is susceptible to nucleophilic attack because of the electronegative substituents, but not to the same extent as propionyl bromide. Acid halides are more electrophilic than alkyl halides, aldehydes or ketones.

C: propanal is susceptible to nucleophilic attack since it has a carbonyl carbon, but no electronegative substituents as does propionyl bromide.

D: butanoic acid has a carbonyl carbon that is slightly susceptible to nucleophilic attack because the double bonded oxygen has an electron-withdrawing effect. However, comparing butanoic acid and its functional derivative propionyl bromide, propionyl bromide has withdrawing effects from the oxygen and the bromide.

14. C is correct.

The molecule has a basic site on the nitrogen atom.

The lone pair of electrons on the nitrogen atom can be protonated to form an ammonium cation.

15. A is correct.

The longest continuous carbon chain in this molecule is six atoms long, making it a substituted hexane chain.

The molecule contains a ketone carbonyl (designated by the suffix *–one*), with the carbon atoms numbered from the end of the chain closest to the carbonyl.

The ethyl substituent is located at carbon 3, while the carbonyl is at carbon 2.

Therefore, the IUPAC name for this molecule 3-ethylhexan-2-one.

16. D is correct.

Benzene with *sigma* and *pi* bonds shown

17. B is correct.

Draw the structure of each of the possibilities and count the total number of isomers.

Two isomers can be formed from the geminal substitution of the chlorine atoms; three isomers result from the (1,2), (1,3) and (1,4) disubstitution.

The last isomer involves a (2,3) dichloro substitution.

The (2,3) disubstitution can exist as a pair of diastereomers.

18. D is correct.

The compound is an ester.

The 3.8 ppm septet corresponds to the single C–H bond near the oxygen atom of the ester.

The singlet at 2.2 ppm suggests that the CH_3 group is near the carbonyl group.

The doublet at 1.0 ppm corresponds to the methyl groups of the isopropyl portion of the molecule.

19. B is correct.

Water has a (p$K_a \approx 18$).

The nitrogen atom of the amine (p$K_a \approx 10$) can be protonated by the acid to become positive.

The positively charged nitrogen is more soluble in water.

The nitrogen atom of the amine (p$K_a \approx 25$-35) can be protonated by the acid, but not the water, to become positive.

20. A is correct.

E_1 and S_N1 reactions are strongly favored by highly branched carbon chains and good leaving groups.

E_2 reactions are largely independent of the structure of carbon chains and are favored by good leaving groups which can easily be eliminated by basic conditions.

S_N2 reactions are strongly favored by substrates with unbranched carbon chains.

($CH_3CH_2CH_2$)$_3CBr$ is a tertiary alkyl halide.

B: $CH_3CH_2CH_2CH_3$ is a hydrocarbon, where alkanes do not undergo either elimination or nucleophilic substitution.

Alkanes are unreactive to most organic chemistry reagents and can either undergo combustion (i.e., burning of propane) or free radical halogenation to introduce a halogen as a leaving group.

C: (CH_3CH_2)$_3COH$ is a highly branched tertiary alcohol carbon chain, so it cannot undergo S_N2. Also, ^-OH is a very poor leaving group, so it does not readily undergo substitution.

With heat, alcohols undergo elimination via dehydration (i.e., removal of water).

D: $CH_3CH_2CH_2CH_2Br$ is a primary alkyl halide that undergoes S_N2 and E_2, but neither S_N1 nor E_1.

21. A is correct.

An *alkoxide* is the conjugate base of an alcohol and therefore consists of an organic moiety (i.e., group) bonded to a deprotonated (i.e., negatively charged) oxygen atom.

Secondary halides undergo bimolecular elimination (E_2) with strong bases, especially hindered ones like potassium *tert*-butoxide, $KOC(CH_3)_3$.

B: E_1 designates unimolecular elimination, generally observed in protic (i.e., H$^+$ donating) solvents (e.g., water or alcohols) and not when subjected to a strong alkoxide base.

C: S_N2 designates bimolecular nucleophilic substitution.

D: S_N1 designates unimolecular nucleophilic substitution.

22. C is correct. The hydration of the terminal alkyne proceeds with Markovnikov regioselectivity to produce a ketone.

A: the enol intermediate tautomerizes to the keto product.

B: $CH_3CH_2CH_2CH=CHOH$ is the enol intermediate of the *anti*-Markovnikov reaction (hydroboration with BH_3).

D: $CH_3CH_2CH_2CH_2CHO$ is the aldehyde product of the *anti*-Markovnikov reaction (hydroboration with BH_3).

23. D is correct.

$CH_3C_6H_5 + H_2$, Rh/C is a reduction reaction with a powerful reducing agent capable of disrupting the stability of the aromatic ring. The regents reduce the benzene ring catalytically via hydrogenation to form cyclohexane. Therefore, this is not an electrophilic aromatic substitution.

In general, an aromatic ring is especially susceptible to electrophilic aromatic substitution (EAS) in the presence of a Lewis acid (e.g., $FeBr_3$, $AlCl_3$ or H_2SO_4).

A: $CH_3C_6H_5 + C_6H$ $CH_2CH_2Cl/AlCl_3$ is an example of Friedel-Crafts alkylation (EAS), whereby toluene (benzene with a methyl substituent) reacts with an alkyl chloride in the presence of the Lewis acid aluminum trichloride ($AlCl_3$). The Lewis acid removes chloride from the alkyl halide, forming a carbocation which is then attacked by the benzene ring.

B: $CH_3C_6H_5 + Br_2/FeBr_3$ is an example of EAS. $FeBr_3$ (like $AlCl_3$) is a Lewis acid. Toluene is activating, and the Br substitutes in the *ortho / para* position.

C: $CH_3C_6H_5 + CH_3CH_2CH_2COCl/AlCl_3$ is an example of Friedel-Crafts acylation (EAS), whereby toluene reacts with an acyl chloride in the presence of the Lewis acid aluminum trichloride ($AlCl_3$). The Lewis acid removes chloride from the acyl halide, forming a carbocation which is then attacked by the benzene ring, and then a proton is removed to restore aromaticity of the original ring structure.

24. A is correct.

Pyridinium chlorochromate (PCC) is a gentle oxidizing agent which converts primary alcohols to aldehydes.

PCC is also used to convert secondary alcohols to ketones.

B: is a carboxylic acid that would require a more powerful oxidizing agent (e.g., Jones reagent; CrO_3, H_2SO_4 and acetone)

C: is an alkene and would proceed via E_1 when the alcohol is subjected to mineral acid (e.g., H_2SO_4)

D: is a terminal alkyl halide produced in two steps. First, the alcohol becomes an alkene (E_1 when the alcohol is subjected to a mineral acid, H_2SO_4). Then, the alkene is halogenated in *anti*-Markovnikov regiochemistry when peroxides (H_2O_2) are included in the reaction.

25. A is correct.

Nucleophiles attack sterically hindered alkyl halides at a much slower rate.

Less sterically hindered substrates undergo reactions with nucleophiles at the fastest rate.

Bromobenzene undergoes the addition reaction at a negligible rate because the ring lacks an electron-withdrawing group that can activate the ring towards nucleophilic aromatic substitution.

Furthermore, the bromide of bromobenzene does not undergo S_N2 displacement reactions because the ring blocks access to the carbon-bromine *sigma** orbital.

26. B is correct.

Acids with smaller alkyl chains have lower boiling points.

Hydrogen bonding also increases the boiling point.

Increased molecular mass and hydrogen bonding are the factors which increase the boiling point.

Formic acid (below) has the molecular formula of CH_2O_2: it contains one carboxylic acid functional group and a hydrogen atom for the *R* group.

Formic acid

A: oxalic acid (below) has the molecular formula of $C_2H_2O_4$.

C: benzoic acid (below) has the molecular formula of $C_7H_6O_2$

D: acetic acid (below) has the molecular formula of $C_2H_4O_2$.

27. C is correct.

Acyl halides and alcohols form esters.

This addition-elimination reaction begins with the nucleophilic attack of the hydroxyl group to the electrophilic carbonyl of the acid halide in an addition reaction.

This is followed by the elimination of chloride to generate the corresponding ester.

Pyridine (below) is a common basic solvent used in organic chemistry:

HCl is generated as a byproduct in this reaction; therefore a base (e.g., pyridine) is needed

28. A is correct.

Hydrogen bonding increases the boiling point of a molecule.

Amines that have N–H bonds typically have higher boiling points compared to tertiary amines.

Tertiary amines can only accept a hydrogen bond, while primary and secondary amines can donate and accept hydrogen bonds.

29. B is correct.

The longest carbon chain is seven carbon atoms and includes an alkene.

The alkene is the highest priority functional group and is assigned the lowest number (i.e., 1 in this example).

Therefore, the molecule has a chlorine substituent in the fourth position.

30. D is correct.

Formal charge = group # – nonbonding electrons – ½ bonding electrons

Nitrogen is in group V on the periodic table.

The ammonium cation has four bonds or eight bonding electrons.

The formal charge for the nitrogen atom is $5 - 0 - 8/2 = +1$.

31. C is correct.

An asymmetric (i.e., chiral) carbon is bonded to four different substituents.

There are three asymmetric carbons in this molecule.

The methylene is symmetrical, the isopropyl group and the geminal dimethyl groups have symmetrical carbons as well.

32. B is correct.

Conjugated polyenes absorb light at longer wavelengths than unconjugated alkenes because the additional *p* orbital overlap present in larger *pi* systems decreases the energy difference between the highest occupied molecular orbital (*HOMO*) and the lowest unoccupied molecular orbital (*LUMO*).

The *LUMO* is an antibonding orbital and has more energy than the *HOMO*, which is a bonding orbital.

The longer the conjugated system, the smaller the energy gap between the two molecular orbitals (MO); this requires radiation of less energy (and longer wavelength) for electron transitions.

When a molecule absorbs UV/visible radiation, electrons are promoted from one orbital to a higher energy orbital.

33. A is correct.

In a complete combustion reaction, a compound reacts with an oxidizing element (e.g., oxygen), and the products are compounds of each element in the fuel combined with the oxidizing element.

General formula:

$$C_nH_{2n+2} + [(3n + 1) / 2]O_2 \rightarrow (n +1)H_2O + nCO_2 + \text{energy}$$

For example, methane yields:

$$CH_4 + 2\ O_2 \rightarrow CO_2 + 2\ H_2O + \text{energy}$$

Nonane:

$$C_9H_{20} + [(3 \times 9 + 1) / 2]O_2 \rightarrow (9 + 1)H_2O + 9\ CO_2 + \text{energy}$$

$$C_9H_{20} + 14\ O_2 \rightarrow 10\ H_2O + 9\ CO_2 + \text{energy}$$

Since nonane has the molecular formula C_9H_{20}, the combustion of 1 mole of neopentane produces 9 moles of CO_2 and 10 moles of H_2O.

34. B is correct.

The bromine adds to the internal position of the epoxide because the partial positive charge is greater at the more substituted position.

The mechanism follows *anti*-addition stereochemistry and would be shown in the final product if both the alcohol and halogen were attached to chiral carbons.

35. B is correct.

Alkynes can undergo bromination to yield compounds with four bromine atoms incorporated in their structures.

The first halogenation is expected to proceed more quickly than the second halogenation.

Bromine atoms are quite large (about the size of a tertbutyl group), and the first bromination increases the steric bulk of the reactant to form the intermediate alkene.

Furthermore, the bromine atoms are more electronegative than carbon, so the *pi* bond of the alkene intermediate is less electron rich and less nucleophilic than the alkyne *pi* bond.

36. D is correct.

A: of the two substituents, the chloro group is *para*-directing, so it should be substituted first.

Additionally, Na / NH_3 results in the single *trans* hydrogenation of alkenes but does not substitute a nitro group in an EAS reaction.

B: of the two substituents, the chloro group is *para*-directing, so it should be substituted first.

C: while HCl / H_2O adds H and Cl across the double bonds of alkenes, these conditions do not substitute Cl in EAS reactions.

37. C is correct.

Tertiary alcohol undergoes E_1 reactions at a faster rate (i.e., due to the stability of the carbocation intermediate) than secondary alcohols, which can dehydrate at a faster rate than primary alcohols.

38. D is correct.

Benedict's test (or Tollens' reagent) is used to detect reducing sugars. An oxidized copper reagent is reduced by a sugar's aldehyde, and the aldehyde is oxidized to a carboxylic acid in the process.

Reducing sugars (and alpha hydroxyl ketones) give a positive Benedict's test: a red-brown precipitate forms. Fehling's solution also gives a positive test for reducing sugars by changing from blue to clear and forming a red-brown precipitate.

The copper complex is reduced to form a red copper product that is less soluble in aqueous solutions.

The detection of this precipitate means the molecule was oxidized.

39. D is correct. This reaction is the Fischer esterification reaction.

Water is given off as the byproduct in this transformation.

To drive the equilibrium of the reaction forward, water should be removed from the reaction or a large excess of one of the two components should be used.

40. C is correct.

This reduction requires two equivalents of lithium aluminum hydride (i.e., powerful reducing agent).

The reactive intermediate involved after the first addition of hydride is a hemiacetal.

This hemiacetal may reversibly open to form the aldehyde, and this aldehyde can be subsequently reduced to form the second primary alcohol.

Reduction:

carboxylic acid / ester → aldehyde → primary alcohol

ketone → secondary alcohol

Reduction of a carboxylic acid, ester requires $LiAlH_4$.

Reduction of an aldehyde or ketone can proceed with either $LiAlH_4$ or the milder reducing agent $NaBH_4$.

41. B is correct.

The most basic site in the molecule is the *N*-methyl tertiary amine because the lone pair of this nitrogen atom is not in conjugation with an electron-withdrawing group or part of an aromatic ring.

42. C is correct.

The longest carbon chain is six carbon atoms.

The two substituents are the chlorine atom and the methyl group.

The highest priority group is chlorine and therefore assumes the lowest number.

43. B is correct.

Pyrrolidine (shown below) is not an aromatic compound, so the lone pair of electrons on nitrogen is available for bonding (i.e., function as a base).

The molecule is a secondary alkyl amine, and the nitrogen atom has sp^3 hybridization.

44. C is correct.

Because one of the stereocenters has a different *R/S* configuration, the molecules are diastereomers.

45. D is correct.

All the described causes of protein denaturation involve inducing changes in the intermolecular forces between the side chains of the residues or amino and carboxylic acid groups.

This denaturation is accomplished through breaking weak bonds or by changing the polarity or charge character of key stabilizing groups.

46. B is correct.

Amphipathic refers to molecules that possess both hydrophobic and hydrophilic elements (e.g., detergents, phospholipids of biological membranes).

Lipid molecules are common examples of amphipathic compounds because they possess hydrophobic tails and polar heads. The polar head group is often composed of electronegative heteroatoms, such as oxygen and nitrogen atoms.

47. D is correct.

Multiple bonds and rings introduce degrees of unsaturation.

Using a subscript of n for the number of carbons, the degrees of unsaturation can be determined from the following formulae:

Alkane: C_nH_{2n+2} = 0 degree of unsaturation

Alkene: C_nH_{2n} = 1 degree of unsaturation

Alkyne: C_nH_{2n-2} = 2 degrees of unsaturation

Rings = 1 degree of unsaturation

Double bonds = 1 degree of unsaturation

Acarbose has one double bond and four rings and therefore has a total of five degrees of unsaturation.

48. B is correct. There are three general components of nucleotides: a phosphate group, a cyclic five-carbon sugar, and a nitrogenous base.

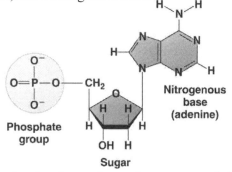

Fat molecules are biomolecules that make up the structure of phospholipid membranes, storage fat molecules, and other lipid molecules.

49. D is correct.

None of the amino acids in the peptide chain contain R groups that have charges in them.

Therefore, the only charges that should exist in the molecule should be the ammonium cation ($^+NH_4$) and the carboxylate anion (COO^-).

50. D is correct.

Saturated fats tend to be solid at room temperature because they lack alkene groups.

The presence of alkene groups in fat molecules lowers the melting point for these compounds.

For example, butter is a dairy product made from the fat of cow's milk. It is solid at room temperature and is mostly composed of saturated fat molecules.

51. D is correct.

Monosaccharides are the basic unit of carbohydrates.

Subjecting these compounds to acids or bases will not hydrolyze them any further; however, they can undergo oxidative decomposition by treating them with periodic acid to form formaldehyde and formic acid.

52. A is correct.

There are three major components of a nucleotide, the subunit that makes up nucleic acids.

All nucleic acids have a nitrogen base used for hydrogen bonding, a hexose sugar (ribose or deoxyribose) and a phosphate group that contains a phosphate linkage with the sugar.

Ester linkages are found in fats, glycosidic linkages are found in sugars, and peptide linkages are found in proteins.

53. C is correct.

The general structure of an amino acid (where R is the side chain):

Amino acid – by convention, the amino terminus is drawn on the left

The three amino acids with basic side chains are lysine (K), arginine (R) and histidine (H).

The side chain of threonine (below) contains a secondary alcohol.

Threonine

Alcohols can be protonated upon exposure to strong acids but are not basic at neutral pH.

54. C is correct.

Although waxes are lipid molecules that contain esters as part of their structure, waxes only contain a single ester functional group.

A monoalcohol is used to form waxes, whereas glycerol is used to form triglycerides and phospholipids.

55. B is correct.

The suffix *ose* is used to denote sugars.

The highest priority functional group in the molecule is a ketone.

Therefore, the sugar is a ketose sugar.

The sugar ($C_nH_{2n}O_n$) has a carbon chain of 5, so it is a pentose.

If the molecule had an aldehyde instead of a ketone, the molecule would be an aldose sugar.

56. B is correct.

One of the two complementary codes important for the construction of peptide chains is the codon made up of three RNA nucleotides that are complementary to the anticodon of tRNA molecules.

57. A is correct.

A zwitterion is a neutral molecule with both a positive and negative charge.

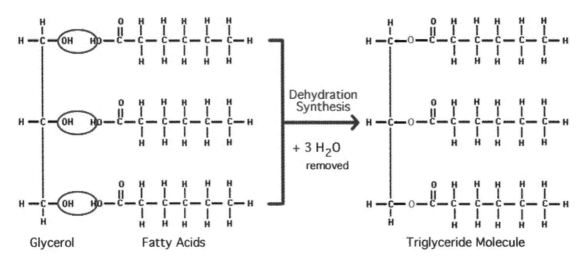

The isoelectric point of an amino acid is the average of the pK_a of the ammonium group and the carboxylic acid.

The isoelectric point is the pH where the carboxylate ion and ammonium cation are dominant in solution.

58. D is correct.

Fatty acids are used to make fat molecules known as triglycerides.

Formation, via dehydration (removal of H_2O), of triglyceride from glycerol and 3 fatty acids

Fatty acids are made from one equivalent of a triol known as glycerol and three equivalents of acid-containing groups known as fatty acids.

59. D is correct.

Carbohydrates can be more specifically described as organic compounds that contain carbon, hydrogen, and oxygen.

The general molecular formula may vary depending on the type of carbohydrates, but many examples have the formula of $C_nH_{2n}O_n$.

60. C is correct.

Because RNA contains uracil, this nitrogenous base forms hydrogen bonds with adenine.

It is important to note that RNA molecules are single-stranded, and DNA molecules are double-stranded.

In DNA:

Adenosine (A) forms two hydrogen bonds with thymine (T).

Cytosine (C) forms three hydrogen bonds with guanine (G).

Please, leave your Customer Review on Amazon

Notes

Explanations: Diagnostic Test #4

1. B is correct.

The longest chain of carbon atom is the cyclohexane ring, hence the root of the molecule's name.

There are two methyl substituents located at the first and second positions in the ring.

The groups are on the same side of the ring, so they have a *cis* orientation.

2. A is correct.

In carbon–carbon double bonds, there is an overlap of sp^2 orbitals and a p orbital on the adjacent carbon atoms.

The sp^2 orbitals overlap head-to-head as a *sigma* (σ) bond, whereas the p orbitals overlap sideways as a *pi* (π) bond.

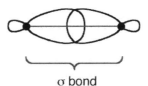

σ bond

Sigma bond formation showing electron density along the internuclear axis

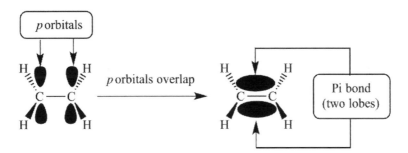

Two *pi* orbitals showing the *pi* bond formation during sideways overlap – note the absence of electron density (i.e., node) along the internuclear axis.

Bond lengths and strengths (σ or π) depends on the size and shape of the atomic orbitals and the density of these orbitals to overlap effectively.

The σ bonds are stronger than π bonds because head-to-head orbital overlap involves more shared electron density than sideways overlap.

The σ bonds formed from two $2s$ orbitals are shorter than those formed from two $2p$ orbitals or two $3s$ orbitals.

Carbon, oxygen, and nitrogen are in the second period ($n = 2$), while sulfur (S), phosphorus (P) and silicon (Si) are in the third period.

Therefore, S, P and Si use $3p$ orbitals to form π bonds, while C, N, and O use $2p$ orbitals.

The $3p$ orbitals are much larger than $2p$ orbitals, and therefore there is a reduced probability for an overlap of the $2p$ orbital of C and the $3p$ orbital of S, P and Si.

B: S, P, and Si can hybridize, but these elements can combine *s* and *p* orbitals and (unlike C, O and N) have *d* orbitals.

C: S, P and Si (in their ground state electron configurations) have partially occupied *p* orbitals which form bonds.

D: carbon combines with elements below the second row of the periodic table. For example, carbon commonly forms bonds with higher principal quantum number ($n > 2$) halogens (e.g., F, Cl, Br and I).

3. C is correct.

For Fischer projections, horizontal lines represent bonds projecting outward (i.e., wedges), whereas vertical lines represent bonds going back (i.e., dashed lines).

A Fischer projection does not include a carbon specified at the cross of the vertical and horizontal lines (i.e., a C is implied, but no C is written on the structure).

For assigning *R/S* in Fischer projections, read the ranked ($1 \rightarrow 3$) priorities as either clockwise (*R*) or counterclockwise (*S*).

If the lowest priority is vertical (i.e., points into the page), then assign *R/S*. If the lowest priority is horizontal (i.e., points out of the page), then reverse ($R \rightarrow S, S \rightarrow R$).

Compound I: the order of priority is hydroxyl, carboxyl, methyl, and hydrogen. The order of increasing priority is counterclockwise, and the configuration appears S.

However, the lowest priority (group 4 is H) is horizontal (pointing outward), so the absolute configuration is *R*.

Compound II: the order of priority is nitrogen, carboxyl, methyl, and hydrogen. The order of increasing priority is counterclockwise.

The lowest priority (group 4 is H) is vertical and therefore points away. The absolute configuration is *S*.

Compound III is achiral because the carbon is not attached to four different groups, and therefore the molecule is neither *R* nor *S*.

Compound IV: the order of priority is hydroxyl, carbonyl (aldehyde), methyl (methanol), and hydrogen. The order of increasing priority is counterclockwise.

The lowest priority (group 4 is H) is horizontal and therefore points towards the viewer. The absolute configuration is *R*.

Compounds I and IV have the same absolute configuration.

4. A is correct.

IR active molecules must have polarized covalent bonds to absorb IR. When a Cl–Cl bond with atoms of the same electronegativity stretches or bends, no dipole is created and therefore the molecule is IR inactive.

B: CO (C≡O) contains covalent bonds whereby carbon is attached to the electronegative oxygen, which creates a dipole generating an IR signal.

C: $CH_3CH_2CH_2OH$ contains covalent bonds that are also attached to an electronegative oxygen, which creates a dipole generating an IR signal.

D: CH_3Br contains covalent bonds that are also attached to electronegative bromines, which create a dipole generating an IR signal.

5. A is correct.

Simple distillation can separate liquids which boil below 150 °C and at least 25 °C apart.

Gas chromatography is used to analyze volatile (i.e., boiling at low temperatures) liquids.

Recrystallization is commonly used to purify solids, not liquids.

Vacuum distillation is useful when the boiling points are high and close in magnitude. Since there is a difference of 80 °C between the boiling points of the two liquids (i.e., boil at 140 °C and 60 °C), it is not necessary to use vacuum distillation.

Electrophoresis establishes an electrical field and separates molecules based upon charge. It is used to analyze charged species, such as nucleic acids (DNA and RNA) and denatured amino acids (after treatment with SDS, which disrupts hydrophobic interactions).

6. C is correct.

Strong nucleophiles have a negative formal charge (i.e., lone pairs excess), while weak nucleophiles are neutral species with a lone pair of electrons.

7. A is correct.

Product A is an example of Markovnikov addition, whereby the hydrogen adds to the least substituted carbon because the most stable carbocation is formed. The bromine then adds to the (most stable) carbocation.

In this example, the hydrogen adds to the secondary carbon, and the bromine adds to the tertiary carbon.

Product B involves free radical intermediates because of the presence of hydrogen peroxide (H_2O_2). Hydrogen peroxide causes the reaction to proceed via a radical intermediate (not carbocation), and the regiochemistry (where the substituents add) is *anti*-Markovnikov. The bromine adds to the least substituted carbon, and the H adds to the most substituted carbon radical.

Product C yields 2-methyl-2-butanol, according to Markovnikov addition.

8. D is correct.

The hydration of the terminal alkyne with BH_3 proceeds with *anti*-Markovnikov regioselectivity.

Enol is on the left and the keto on the right

The enol intermediate tautomerizes to the keto product, whereby the keto product (more stable) is over 99% of the observed product.

9. C is correct.

The reactivity of aromatic molecules toward electrophilic aromatic substitution (EAS) depends on the presence of substituents on benzene.

Electron-donating substituents increase the electron density of the benzene ring and therefore activate benzene towards EAS.

Electron-withdrawing substituents deactivate the ring, making it less susceptible to EAS.

The benzene ring is deactivated by the electron withdrawing effects of the Cl and NH_3^+ substituents, and the ring is deactivated (compared to benzene) to EAS.

A: p-H_3CCH_2O–C_6H_4–O–CH_2CH_3 contains two electron-donating ethoxy substituents and is highly reactive to EAS.

B: p-O_2N–C_6H_4–NH–CH_3 contains strong electron-withdrawing effects from the nitro (NO_2).

The N of the NO_2 group has a formal charge of +, while the single bonded O has a formal charge of –.

The NO_2 group offsets the strong electron-donating amino group (lone pair of electrons on N), so the molecule is only slightly reactive to EAS.

D: p-CH_3CH_2–C_6H_4–CH_2CH_3 contains two electron-donating (i.e., activating) ethyl substituents and is more reactive towards EAS.

10. D is correct.

Alcohols of the same chain length as alkanes, alkenes, and alkynes have higher boiling points due to hydrogen bonding of the –OH group.

Alkanes, alkenes, and alkynes are not able to form hydrogen bonds.

11. B is correct.

Carbonyl groups contain lone pairs on the oxygen atom for hydrogen-accepting capabilities.

However, these groups lack a polarized *sigma* bond to hydrogen atoms (assuming the ketone is in the keto tautomer).

Since these molecules cannot donate hydrogen bonds, they cannot form hydrogen bonds with each other.

12. C is correct.

All of the molecules contain the carboxylic acid functional group, which can hydrogen bond and also ionize to increase its solubility in water.

Besides benzene, the choices differ only in the length of the carbon chain attached to the carboxylic acid.

Saturated carbon chains are hydrophobic, and therefore the shortest-chain carboxylic acid is most water soluble.

13. A is correct.

The amide linkage is present between individual amino acids, and these bonds are commonly known as peptide bonds.

The amide bond is formed when the lone pair of electrons on the nitrogen of the amino group makes a nucleophilic attack on the carbonyl of the other amino acid.

This process is classified as a condensation (via dehydration) and results in the loss of water as the peptide bond forms.

14. C is correct.

The conjugate base of an acid is essentially the deprotonated form.

The most acidic protons of the molecule are the N–H protons, with a pK_a in the mid-30s.

15. A is correct.

The longest carbon chain is 8 carbon atoms.

The only substituent is the isopropyl group.

16. D is correct.

It is helpful to draw all the C–H bonds for this compound.

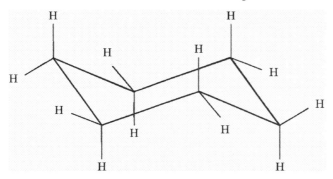

Each carbon atom of the cyclohexane bonds to two hydrogen atoms, because there is one degree of unsaturation (the ring).

Six *sigma* bonds exist in the ring, so the total number of σ bonds is 18.

17. A is correct.

The root name of the compound is cyclopentane because the ring possesses 5 carbons.

The chlorine substituents are adjacent (i.e., position 1,2) on the ring and must be oriented on opposite sides of the ring.

18. A is correct.

Electromagnetic spectrum:

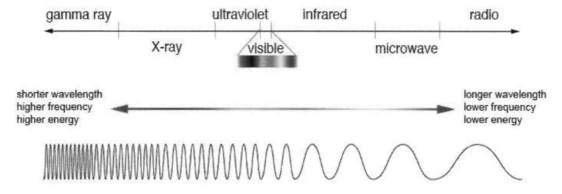

On the electromagnetic spectrum, radio waves have the lowest energy, infrared radiation has more energy than radio waves, and ultraviolet light has more energy than infrared radiation.

19. C is correct.

The free-base form of caffeine is deprotonated and neutral.

Therefore, it has greater solubility in the nonpolar diethyl ether solvent.

Caffeine (neutral)

The protonated form of caffeine is positively charged and more soluble in the aqueous layer.

Resonance forms of protonated caffeine

20. A is correct.

E_1 refers to unimolecular elimination that proceeds via a carbocation intermediate in a two-step reaction.

Substitution of the substrate ($3° > 2° > 1° >>$ methyl) increases the rate of E_1 (and S_N1) reactions because highly branched carbon chains (with more substituted carbons) form more stable carbocations.

S_N2 refers to the bimolecular nucleophilic substitution that proceeds via a one-step (concerted mechanisms) displacement of a leaving group by a nucleophile.

S_N2 is favored by unbranched carbon chains because the nucleophilic displacement of a leaving group by a nucleophile is favored due to less steric hindrance.

Secondary carbons could undergo both E_1 and S_N2.

The cyanide group is a very poor leaving group because it is an unstable anion and therefore is unlikely to dissociate via E_1 or be displaced via S_N2.

Br^- forms a stable anion and can dissociate via E_1 or be displaced by S_N2.

B: $(CH_3CH_2CH_2)_3CBr$ is a tertiary alkyl halide and is not favored.

C: $(CH_3CH_2CH_2)_3CCH_2Cl$ is a primary alkyl halide which lacks β-hydrogens and therefore cannot form a double bond by elimination (E_1 or E_2).

D: $(CH_3CH_2CH_2)_2CHCN$ has the leaving group (cyanide) bonded to a secondary carbon.

21. A is correct.

Vinyl refers to an atom attached to carbon on the double bond.

Allylic refers to an atom attached to a carbon adjacent (β) to the double bond.

The chlorine substituent is directly attached to the alkene carbon atoms in vinyl chloride.

22. B is correct.

1-butyne is a terminal alkyne.

Terminal alkynes have additional chemical properties, such as their ability to form anions when exposed to strong bases (e.g., the acetylide anion that forms with $NaNH_2$).

23. C is correct.

The carbon atoms of benzene are sp^2 hybridized.

Non-planar molecules cannot be aromatic because the *pi* system must be planar (i.e., flat).

A Kekule structure is a Lewis structure in which bonded electron pairs in covalent bonds are drawn as lines.

The Kekule structures illustrate the two most significant resonance contributors of benzene.

Benzene with alternating double and single bonds – hybrid structure as bottom structure

The alternating single and double drawn for benzene exist as a hybrid resonance structure from the delocalization.

24. B is correct.

Carbonyl groups are indicative of ketones, aldehydes, or carboxylic acid derivatives (acyl halides, anhydrides, esters, and amides).

Ethers are noted as R–O–R and do not contain carbonyl groups.

25. A is correct.

The larger the alkyl portion of an organic molecule, the less likely it is able to dissolve in water.

When ketones and aldehydes are dissolved in water, they are in equilibrium with their hydrated forms.

The hydrated form enhances the solubility of the compound in water.

26. B is correct.

The most polar molecule is the molecule that possesses the smallest alkyl portion.

Acidic functional groups also enhance the intermolecular forces that exist among molecules, with hydrogen bonding being the largest contributing factor.

The more polarized a hydrogen-heteroatom bond is, the more acidic it is and the stronger the intermolecular forces the molecule experiences.

Therefore, the carboxylic acid is the most polar molecule.

27. C is correct.

The benzene ring (aromatic group) is bonded to the carbonyl of an amide functional group.

28. B is correct.

Amines are one of several functional groups that contain nitrogen atoms.

The other answer choices only contain carbon, hydrogen or oxygen atoms.

29. C is correct.

When numbering the longest carbon chain of a molecule, start on the end that results in the lowest possible numbering for the substituent groups.

Therefore, the correct molecule should have two methyl groups at the second position and one methyl group in the third position.

30. B is correct.

There are four regions of electron density around the nitrogen atom (including the lone pair). Therefore, the nitrogen atom is sp^3 hybridized.

The bonding angles of molecules that possess nonbonding lone pairs of electrons is slightly smaller than what is predicted by the hybridization state. The nonbonding electrons exert a greater repulsive force than the bonding electrons between the central atom and the substituent groups. However, the presence of bulky ethyl substituents increases the bond angle from approximately 107° to approximately 109.5°.

Ammonia has a bond angle of approximately 107° due to the electrostatic repulsion of the nitrogen's lone pair on the hydrogen atoms. In amines, as substituents become larger (e.g., $(CH_3CH_2)_3N$), the bond angle between bulky groups increases and the molecular shape approaches a tetrahedral with a bond angle of approximately 109.5°.

31. B is correct.

Chiral molecules include carbons that are bonded to four different substituents.

This molecule contains no stereogenic centers (i.e., chiral centers), and therefore the molecule cannot be chiral.

32. D is correct.

The type of electromagnetic radiation (EMR) needed to excite an electron in the molecule from the highest energy occupied molecular orbital (*HOMO*) to the lowest energy unoccupied molecular orbital (*LUMO*) corresponds to UV-visible light.

Exciting an electron from the *sigma* bond is more difficult because the *sigma* bond has very low energy and requires higher energy radiation to be promoted to a vacant orbital.

Furthermore, the *sigma** orbital has very high energy, and promoting electrons to this vacant orbital requires stronger radiation as well.

33. D is correct.

Boiling requires the molecules in the liquid phase to overcome the attractive intermolecular forces (e.g., hydrogen bonding, dipole-dipole & London dispersion forces) and move into the gas phase.

The stronger these interactions are, the more energy (i.e., heat) is needed for the molecules to separate from their neighbors and migrate into the gaseous state. Molecules have lower boiling points when branching increases because branching disrupts the spatial packing of molecules in the solid and liquid phase, and therefore branching reduces intermolecular attractions.

A: *cis*-2-pentene has a slightly higher boiling point because unsaturation establishes a dipole moment that raises their relative boiling point compared to alkanes.

B: 2-pentyne has a slightly higher boiling point because unsaturation establishes a dipole moment that raises their relative boiling point compared with alkanes.

C: pentane is a hydrocarbon and only experiences weak London dispersion forces.

34. B is correct.

An *anti*-Markovnikov addition of water across the alkene double bond is needed.

Peroxides (H_2O_2) are a characteristic reagent for *anti*-Markovnikov regiospecificity.

35. D is correct.

The bond order for an alkyne is larger than for an alkene.

The larger the bond order, the shorter the bond.

Therefore, the *pi* bond in an alkyne is shorter.

Furthermore, there is less *p* orbital overlap present in an alkyne than in an alkene.

Because the internuclear overlap is lower, the *pi* bond is weaker.

36. A is correct.

Addition reactions are typically not observed for aromatic compounds because the aromaticity is restored during their substitution reactions.

When aromatic functional groups react, they may temporarily lose their aromaticity (i.e., high-energy resonance hybrids are the intermediates) and its restoration greatly increases the stability of the molecule.

Electrophilic aromatic substitution (EAS) reactions are favored over nucleophilic aromatic addition (NAS) reactions for aromatic compounds.

37. A is correct.

With respect to alkenes, allylic refers to an atom attached to a carbon adjacent (β) to the double bond.

For carbonyl compounds (aldehydes, ketones, acyl halides, anhydrides, carboxylic acids, esters, and amides) the position adjacent to the C of the C=O is the α position.

The hydroxyl group of allylic alcohols is one carbon-carbon *sigma* bond away from the double bond.

Vinyl refers to an atom attached to a carbon on the double bond.

38. B is correct.

Grignard + nitrile → imine salt + H_3O → ketone

$$R\,MgX \;+\; R'\!-\!C\!\equiv\!N \longrightarrow \underset{\substack{\text{imine}\\\text{salt}}}{\overset{\displaystyle \overset{\text{NMgX}}{\overset{\|}{\underset{R\;\;\;R'}{C}}}}{}} \xrightarrow[\text{work-up}]{H_3O^+} \underset{\text{ketone}}{\overset{\displaystyle \overset{O}{\overset{\|}{\underset{R\;\;\;R'}{C}}}}{}}$$

Unlike esters, the nitrile is not subject to over-alkylation, because the negatively charged imine intermediate generated from the alkylation is less electrophilic than the starting nitrile.

39. A is correct.

Nucleophilic acyl substitution reactions are the most common type of reactions that carboxylic acid derivatives undergo.

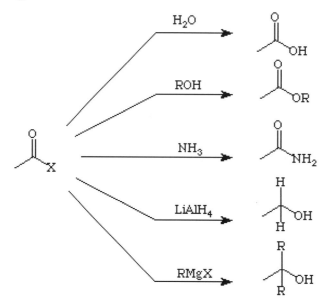

Example reactions involving acyl halides

40. C is correct.

Amides are carboxylic acid derivatives made up of amines, which are carboxylic acid components.

The hydrolysis of carboxylic acid derivatives always results in the formation of the corresponding carboxylic acid and heteroatom-containing component (e.g., an amine or alcohol).

41. D is correct.

Ammonia groups enhance the water solubility of compounds because of the hydrogen bonding and molecular dipoles that amines possess.

The greater the number of N–H bonds (i.e., primary > secondary > tertiary > quaternary) an amine possesses, the more hydrogen bonds the amine can form and the more soluble it is.

Furthermore, acid can be added to aqueous solutions of amines to enhance the solubility of the molecule.

42. B is correct.

The longest carbon chain in the compound is composed of four carbon atoms.

The highest priority group in the molecule is the amine.

The amine is attached to carbon number 2 (i.e., *sec*- position).

The 5 common names recognized by IUPAC are isopropyl, isobutyl, *sec*-butyl, *tert*-butyl, and neopentyl.

2-butanamine is the IUPAC name for the molecule

43. A is correct.

Three degenerate *p* orbitals exist for an atom with an electron configuration in the second (n = 2) shell or higher.

The first (n = 1) shell only has an *s* orbital.

The *d* orbitals become available from the third shell (n = 3).

44. A is correct.

The observed rotation is half the value of the specific rotation for the pure enantiomeric substance.

While the effect of the combined opposite enantiomers is canceled, the mixture should have a 50% excess of the pure substance.

Therefore, the mixture must have 75% of the pure enantiomeric substance, where 25% of the rotation cancels the effect of the 25% opposite rotation of its enantiomer.

45. A is correct.

This covalent bond is a disulfide linkage that contributes to the protein's tertiary (3°) and quaternary (4°) structure (for multiple polypeptide chains).

Disulfide linkage of S–S covalent bond between two cysteine residues

46. A is correct.

Glycerol can condense with fatty acids to expel water.

The new functional group produced is an ester joined by a glycosidic bond.

Condensation reaction (via dehydration) of glycerol and three fatty acids showing a glycosidic (ester) linkage

47. A is correct.

Glycosidic bonds join carbohydrates and are formed between the hemiacetal group of a saccharide and the hydroxyl group of some organic compound, such as an alcohol.

α is the designation when the hydroxyl attached to the anomeric carbon points down.

β is the designation when the hydroxyl attached to the anomeric carbon points up.

C: acetal refers to a carbon that is attached to two ethers (RO–C–OR').

D: hemiacetal refers to a carbon that is attached to an ether and a hydroxyl (RO–C–OH).

Formation of a glycosidic bond: glucose and ethanol combine to form ethyl glucoside and water

The reaction often favors the formation of the α-glycosidic bond (as shown pointing down), due to the anomeric effect.

The size of the arrow indicates the relative direction of the equilibrium

The anomeric effect describes the tendency of an element with lone pairs of electrons adjacent to a heteroatom (e.g., oxygen within a ring) of a cyclohexane ring to prefer the *axial* orientation instead of the less-hindered *equatorial* orientation expected from steric considerations.

The axial orientation permits molecular orbital overlap that increases the overall stability of the molecule.

48. B is correct.

The intermolecular forces among the nitrogen base pairs are hydrogen bonds.

Adenine forms 2 hydrogen bonds with thymine (A=T).

Cytosine forms 3 hydrogen bonds with guanine (C≡G).

49. A is correct.

Peptide bonds are amide bonds that link individual amino acid molecules together.

Two amino acids with the peptide bond indicated by the arrow

The peptide bond involves 4 atoms: C=O, N and H.

The hydrogen must be antiperiplanar (180°) relative to the carbonyl oxygen to permit the lone pair on the nitrogen to participate in a resonance structure and confer rigidity on the peptide bond.

Resonance structure of peptide bond involving the lone pair of electrons on nitrogen

The number of bonds between each amino acid (i.e., or any monomers) equals n – 1 (where n is the number of monomers).

Therefore, 10 – 1 = 9 peptide bonds.

50. D is correct.

Amphipathic refers to molecules that possess both hydrophobic and hydrophilic elements.

Biological molecules, such as fatty acids and some amino acids, have hydrophobic and hydrophilic regions.

A: amphoteric substances can act as either an acid or a base, depending on the medium. Examples include metal oxides or hydroxides, which are amphoteric depending on the oxidation state of the element.

B: enantiomeric compounds are chiral molecules whose molecular structures have a non-superimposable mirror image relationship to each other.

C: amphiprotic molecules can either donate or accept a proton (H^+), depending on the conditions (e.g., amino acids).

51. C is correct.

Glycogen is a polymer of glucose that functions as the energy store of carbohydrates in animal cells (plant cells use starch). Glycogen is common in the liver, muscle, and red blood cells.

Glycogen is a large biomolecule consisting of repeating glucose subunits

Copyright © 2020 Sterling Test Prep. Any duplication (copies, uploads, PDFs) is illegal.

52. C is correct.

The peptide chain is assembled depending on the amino acid residue order, dictated by the mRNA sequence.

rRNA is the nucleic acid that comprises the ribosome used during translation (conversion of the codon into a corresponding amino acid in the growing polypeptide chains of the nascent protein).

Each codon of RNA has a corresponding anticodon located on the tRNA.

tRNA molecules have the 3-nucleotide sequence of the anticodon and the appropriate amino acid at its 3' end that corresponds to the anticodon.

The genetic code is the language for the conversion of DNA (i.e., nucleotides) to proteins (i.e., amino acids).

DNA → mRNA → protein

DNA to mRNA is transcription.

mRNA to protein is translation.

There are 20 naturally occurring amino acids. There is one start codon (methionine) and three stop codons (containing releasing factors which dissociate the ribosome).

53. D is correct.

The primary structure of proteins refers to the linear sequence of amino acids.

Hydrogen bonding is important for the secondary (alpha helix and beta-pleated sheet) and for tertiary (i.e., overall 3-dimensional shape) structure of proteins.

The hydrophobic interactions involved in tertiary and quaternary (i.e., two or more polypeptide chains) structure arise from the hydrophobic side chains of the amino acid residues.

54. B is correct.

Lipids (i.e., fats) is a term used to describe long chain ester-linked molecules such as triglycerides. The term "lipid" is sometimes used interchangeably with the word "fat."

However, lipids also include cyclic biomolecules, such as steroids (e.g., cholesterol and its derivatives such as estrogen and testosterone).

Triacylglycerol is a lipid that can undergo saponification, which is the breakdown of fatty esters with bases, such as sodium hydroxide or potassium hydroxide.

D: terpenes are small alkene-containing hydrocarbon building blocks that can be combined and cyclized to form steroids. Terpenes are simple lipids.

55. C is correct.

If a compound has only one chiral center, it must be chiral.

A *meso* compound has an internal symmetry requiring the presence of at least 2 chiral centers. This internal symmetry yields an achiral molecule, even though it contains chiral centers.

56. D is correct.

Because RNA utilizes uracil (U) nitrogenous base instead of thymine (T) nitrogenous base, thymine should not appear in the codon.

57. B is correct.

The isoelectric point of an amino acid deals with the average pK_a of the acidic functional groups present in the molecule, and this includes the ammonium and carboxylic acid functional groups as well.

The isoelectric point is a characteristic of the entire protein molecule (not just the side chain) where the net charge is zero.

58. D is correct.

Fatty acids are long molecules containing a hydrophobic chain and a hydrophilic region terminating in a carboxylic acid.

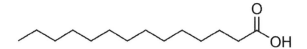

Myristic acid: an unsaturated 14 carbon fatty acid

Soaps are formed from the hydrolysis of fatty acids under basic conditions, in a process known as saponification.

The positively charged counterion (e.g., Na^+, K^+) of the hydroxide base added to the reaction becomes the counter ion of the soap.

A: emollient is a topical agent designed to increase the hydration of the epidermis.

B: ether is a functional group in organic chemistry: R–O–R'.

59. D is correct.

Disaccharides contain a glycosidic linkage that is an ether group.

The ether can be protonated with Brønsted acids and hydrolyzed in the presence of water.

All polysaccharides can be hydrolyzed to produce monosaccharides (i.e., individual monomers of the polymer).

60. A is correct.

Thymine is a pyrimidine nitrogenous base pair that forms two hydrogen bonds with adenine (purine) in the base-paired structure of DNA.

In RNA molecules, the nitrogenous base thymine is replaced by uracil.

Purines (A, G) are single ring structures,
while pyrimidines (C, T, U) are double-ring structures.

Explanations: Diagnostic Test #5

1. B is correct.

Pentanal:

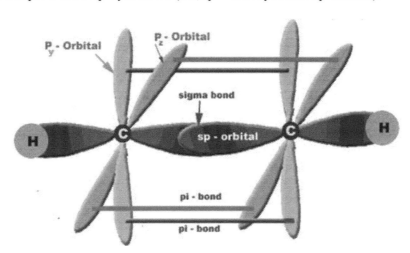

The longest carbon chain in the molecule is five carbon atoms; the molecule contains an aldehyde, so the suffix is ~*al*.

The suffix ~*one* signifies a ketone and ~*oic acid* is for carboxylic acid.

2. B is correct.

Acetylene is the common name for ethyne (C_2H_2).

Alkynes are linear and contain a bond angle of 180°.

$$H-C{\equiv}C-H$$

Acetylene has a triple bond and therefore contains sp hybridized carbons

A carbon of a triple bond is *sp* hybridized (i.e., *sp* + 2 unhybridized *p* orbitals).

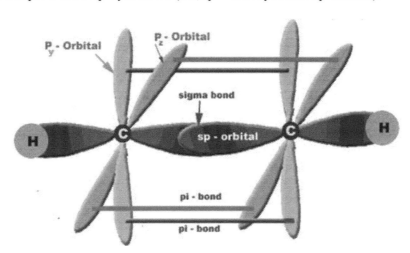

Molecular orbital structure for ethyne showing one sigma bond and two pi bonds

The atoms in a triple bond use *sp* hybridized orbitals from the 2*s* orbital merging (i.e., hybridizing) with a 2*p* orbital.

A: 1,3,5–heptatriene contains sp^2 hybridized orbitals (i.e., double bonds) and sp^3 orbitals for single bonds.

Bond angles of 120° are trigonal planar and originate from sp^2 orbitals. The molecule also contains single bonds which are sp^3; therefore, a portion of the molecule is tetrahedral.

C: 2-butyne is an alkyne, but only two carbons are *sp* hybridized, while the remaining carbon is *sp³* hybridized, which results from the combination of the 2*s* and the 2*p* orbitals. Four *sp³* carbons form and the bond angle is 109.5° with tetrahedral geometry.

D: dichloromethane has a carbon that is *sp³* hybridized because it is attached to two hydrogens and two chlorine atoms. For the greatest separation between the substituents, the geometry is tetrahedral, and the bond angle is 109.5°.

3. D is correct.

Structural isomers have the same molecular formula, but a different connection of the atoms. With molecular formula $C_4H_8Cl_2$, the carbon skeleton is butane.

Eight structural isomers exist: three isomers have chiral carbons.

From top left and moving to the right: molecules 2, 3 and 6 are chiral (i.e., a carbon attached to four different substituents). Molecule 2 has one chiral carbon; molecule 3 has one chiral carbon.

Structural isomer 6 contains two chiral carbons. One of the stereoisomers of 2,3-dichlorobutane has an internal plane of symmetry, making it the *meso* compound of R/S (or S/R, which is the same molecule) and therefore is achiral and optically inactive. The other stereoisomer is R/R (or S/S, which is the same molecule) and therefore is chiral and exhibits optical activity.

Therefore, there are three optically active isomers of $C_4H_8Cl_2$.

4. C is correct. IR spectroscopy provides information about functional groups.

A: mass spectrometry (MS) provides information about molecular weight.

B: nuclear magnetic resonance (NMR) spectroscopy provides information about protons.

D: UV spectroscopy provides information about conjugated (i.e., *sp²* hybridization) double bonds.

5. D is correct.

Higher temperature increases the solubility of most substances because an increase in the kinetic energy allows the solvent molecules to break apart the solute molecules that are held together by intermolecular attractions (e.g., hydrogen bonds, dipole-dipole, and hydrophobic interactions).

For example, a compound is always more soluble at 40 °C than at 10 °C. The laboratory technique of recrystallization relies upon the principle that a molecule is more soluble at a higher temperature. Therefore, solubility increases with increasing temperature.

The statement "like dissolves like" refers to compounds that are either polar (or ionic) and dissolve in solvents that are also polar (or ionic) or non-polar (hydrophobic) and dissolve in non-polar solvents.

Therefore, molecules and solvents with similar polarities (ionic or hydrophobic) have increased solubility.

The molecular mass of a compound is independent of its ability to dissolve in a given solvent.

6. D is correct.

S_N2 reactions are favored with primary substrates, strong nucleophiles, good leaving groups, and polar aprotic solvents. 1-bromobutane is a primary alkyl halide, ⁻CN is an extremely strong nucleophile, and bromine is a good leaving group.

S_N2 occurs exclusively over elimination E_2 because ⁻CN is a strong, linear nucleophile; ⁻CN is not sterically hindered as a base. Only when strong, bulky bases (e.g., *tert*-butoxide) are used, elimination (e.g., E_2) is favored over substitution (e.g., S_N2).

S_N1 and E_1 reaction mechanisms are not favored with primary alkyl halides because a primary carbocation is unstable.

7. A is correct.

Hydrogen bromide will not substitute onto an alkane because alkanes are highly unreactive molecules. Alkanes either undergo substitution only under extreme conditions (e.g., *hv* as UV light) or yield combustion products CO_2 and H_2O.

N-bromosuccinimide (NBS) adds bromine to the allylic position (i.e., one away from a double bond). The product is: butene + NBS → 3-bromobutene

Reaction 2: at high temperatures, alkanes undergo combustion to form CO_2 and H_2O.

Reaction 3: free radical substitution is initiated for highly reactive free radicals (e.g., Br_2 or Cl_2), with Br_2 being more selective, whereby the Br radical adds to the more substituted carbon of the alkene.

Reaction 4: Br_2 in CCl_4 adds bromines to an alkene as a bromonium intermediate, with the second bromide adding to the more substituted carbon of the alkene.

8. C is correct.

Use the following formulae to calculate the degrees of unsaturation:

C_nH_{2n+2}: for an alkane (0 degrees of unsaturation)

C_nH_{2n}: for an alkene or a ring (1 degree of unsaturation)

C_nH_{2n-2}: for an alkyne, 2 double bonds, 2 rings or 1 ring and 1 double bond (2 degrees of unsaturation)

Molecular formula $C_{10}H_{16}$ (C_nH_{2n-6}) has 3 degrees of unsaturation. It is consistent with an acyclic molecule that contains two alkyne functional groups or three alkenes or two alkenes and one ring, etc.

A molecule with two triple bonds has 4 degrees of unsaturation (C_nH_{2n-8}) or $C_{10}H_{14}$.

9. D is correct.

Halogens are electron-withdrawing and deactivate a benzene ring toward electrophilic aromatic substitution, so bromobenzene undergoes nitration slower than benzene.

10. D is correct.

Primary alcohols can be oxidized to the carboxylic acid functional group with an oxidizing agent (e.g., CrO_3 in HCl).

Oxidation:

primary alcohol → aldehyde → carboxylic acid

secondary alcohol → ketone

tertiary alcohol → no reaction

11. D is correct.

The substituents on the carbonyl carbon can be alkyl, alkenyl or aryl groups.

The R groups do not need to be the same group (i.e., R and R').

Asymmetric ketones form chiral secondary alcohols if reduced or if alkylated by a carbon nucleophile that is unlike the structure of the ketone alkyl groups.

Asymmetric ketones are known as "prochiral" electrophiles.

A: carboxylic acid functional group.

B: ester functional group.

C: aldehyde functional group.

12. C is correct.

The high pH (basic conditions) of the aqueous solution causes the carboxylate to deprotonate and assume its conjugate base form.

This carboxylate form (i.e., an anion of the carboxylic acid) has a higher affinity for the aqueous layer than for the organic layer.

13. C is correct.

The first step in this reaction involves the substitution of the OH group in benzoic acid by the Cl group from thionyl chloride ($SOCl_2$).

The resulting compound is benzoyl chloride – a highly reactive acyl halide which undergoes nucleophilic substitution. Treating this molecule with NH_3 (ammonia) results in the substitution of the Cl group by NH_2 group to form an amide (benzamide).

A and B: benzoyl chloride is highly susceptible to nucleophilic substitution, so chlorine is not part of the final product if another nucleophile (NH_3) is present.

D: *p*-aminobenzaldehyde is a benzene ring with an NH_2 substituent *para*- to the aldehyde group which would have replaced the carboxylic acid. The carboxylic acid would not be reduced to the aldehyde. The condition for electrophilic aromatic substitution (EAS) requires an electrophile (e.g., Cl_2) and a Lewis acid (e.g., $FeCl_3$).

14. A is correct. Amines are typically bases due to the lone pair of electrons on the nitrogen.

The name suggests that three methyl groups are bonded to the central nitrogen atom.

15. C is correct.

The three substituent groups attached to the nitrogen atom include the two methyl groups and the *tert*-butyl group.

16. A is correct.

Two resonance Kekule structures of benzene

Six *sigma* bonds connect the carbon atoms in benzene.

Furthermore, the delocalized *pi* electron density in the ring is described by three *pi* bonds in resonance.

17. C is correct.

Chiral carbon atoms have four different groups bonded to a carbon atom.

The molecule is named with the alcohol as the highest priority group and designated carbon 1.

The carbon atoms with two or more hydrogen atoms (i.e., carbons 1 and 5) are achiral because at least two of the groups are the same.

18. A is correct.

The fragmentation pattern of the spectra provides structural information and determination of the molar weight of an unknown compound. Cleavage occurs at alkyl substituted carbons reflecting the order generally observed in carbocations.

3,3-dimethyl-2-butanone

The base peak for this molecule is the acetyl intermediate. This intermediate results from the ionization of the carbonyl oxygen atom to form an oxygen-centered radical cation.

The carbon-carbon bond between the *tert*-butyl group and the carbonyl can homolytically cleave to give the acylium cation.

For example:

acetone sample	radical cation	acylium ion	methyl radical
MW = 58	(molecular ion)	$m/z = 43$	(not detected)
	$m/z = 58$		

19. D is correct.

Compounds with carboxylic acid ($pK_a \approx 5$) functional groups are soluble in aqueous sodium bicarbonate ($pK_a \approx 10.4$).

The proton of the phenol ($pK_a \approx 9.8\text{-}10$) is not acidic enough to be deprotonated by sodium bicarbonate and impart solubility by creating the alkoxide anion.

20. B is correct.

S_N1 proceeds when the substrate forms a carbocation.

Iodide is the best leaving group (i.e., most stable anion) and therefore forms the cation the fastest.

21. C is correct.

Use the following formulae to calculate the degrees of unsaturation:

C_nH_{2n+2}: for an alkane (0 degrees of unsaturation)

C_nH_{2n}: for an alkene or a ring (1 degree of unsaturation)

C_nH_{2n-2}: for an alkyne, 2 double bonds, 2 rings or 1 ring and 1 double bond (2 degrees

of unsaturation)

There are two degrees of unsaturation for the compound C_6H_{10}.

22. D is correct.

A catalytic system, which may also produce alkenes from alkynes, is Lindlar catalyst (i.e., H_2, Pd, $CaCo_3$, quinolone, and hexane).

An alkyne yields a *cis* alkene when subjected to the Lindlar catalyst.

Hydrogenation reactions catalyzed by platinum or palladium result in the formation of alkane products.

23. C is correct.

In electrophilic aromatic substitution, the aromatic ring acts as a nucleophile, attacking an electrophile that has been treated with a Lewis acid (e.g., $FeBr_3$, $AlCL_3$).

Deprotonation of the aromatic ring at the site of the attack reforms the double bond (an elimination reaction) and restores aromaticity.

The overall reaction substitutes an electrophile (e.g., Br, CH_3, RCO, HSO_3) for a hydrogen on the aromatic ring.

24. D is correct.

Boiling points of compounds are determined by two general factors: molecular weight and intermolecular interactions.

The higher the molecular weight, the harder it is to "push" it into the gas phase, and hence the higher the boiling point.

Similarly, the stronger the intermolecular interactions, the more energy is required to disrupt them and separate the molecules in the gas phase, hence the higher the boiling point.

Alcohols participate in hydrogen bonding due to the hydroxyl group.

The alkane, alkene, ether, and alkyl halide only participate in dipole-dipole interactions and London forces.

25. C is correct.

A reducing sugar can act as a reducing agent because it has a free aldehyde group or a free ketone group. All monosaccharides are reducing sugars, while some disaccharides, oligosaccharides, and polysaccharides are also reducing sugars.

A reducing sugar becomes oxidized (e.g., aldehyde → carboxylic acid) from reducing another compound.

Benedict's test (or Tollens' reagent) is used to detect reducing sugars. An oxidized copper reagent is reduced by a sugar's aldehyde, and the aldehyde is oxidized to a carboxylic acid in the process.

Reducing sugars (and alpha hydroxyl ketones) give a positive Benedict's test: a red-brown precipitate forms. Fehling's solution also gives a positive test for reducing sugars by changing from blue to clear and forming a red-brown precipitate.

The Tollens' test for aldehydes involves the reduction of silver cations [Ag^+] to reduced silver; the metal precipitates out of solution and coats the inner surface of the reaction flask. Tollens' reagent forms silver ions (mirror) as a positive test for reducing sugars. The aldehyde is oxidized to the carboxylic acid when this occurs.

26. D is correct.

The carboxylic acid contains the most acidic functional group among the molecules listed.

Any proton has the potential to protonate a base, given that the base is sufficiently strong to remove the proton from an acid. This requires comparing the pK_a of the acid and base, whereby the base must have a higher pK_a.

Amines can deprotonate carboxylic acids; amide bases can deprotonate alcohols.

Use of strong organometallic bases (e.g., Grignard reagent) may be necessary for the deprotonation of neutral amines and hydrocarbons.

27. D is correct.

The compound contains an aromatic ring called benzyl.

The amide functional group is denoted by:

Where R is an alkyl chain (or H).

An ether functional group is denoted by R–O–R'

Additionally, the molecule contains an aromatic ring, phenol group (i.e., hydroxyl attached directly to a benzene ring) and an alkene (i.e., double bond as a *trans*-alkene).

28. C is correct.

Amine salts are compounds containing a positively charged, tetravalent nitrogen atom and an anionic counterion.

1°, 2° and 3° amines are neutral species.

dimethylammonium bromide

A: sulfanilamide (below)

B: thioacetamide (below)

D: histamine (below)

29. A is correct.

The longest carbon chain for this molecule is the cyclohexene.

The highest priority group of the molecule is the carboxylic acid, and the carbon atom it is bonded to should be labeled as carbon one.

Therefore, the *oxo* (i.e., prefix for the ketone) group is positioned at carbon two.

30. C is correct.

Draw each of the bonds in the structure, where the electrons are distributed to satisfy the octets of the carbon and heteroatoms:

$$CH_3C\equiv N$$

The nitrile has a triple bond composed of a *sigma* bond and two *pi* bonds.

31. A is correct.

Achiral compounds cannot rotate the plane of polarized light.

The solutions of achiral compounds are always optically inactive.

B: there is no relationship between absolute configuration (*R/S*) and the specific rotation (+/−) of light in the polarimeter.

C: *meso* compounds are achiral, but not all achiral molecules are *meso*.

D: *meso* compounds are achiral and contain two or more chiral centers and have an internal plane of symmetry.

32. C is correct.

Topicity is the stereochemical relationship between substituents. These groups, depending on the relationship, can be *heterotopic, homotopic, enantiotopic,* or *diastereotopic.*

The protons are chemically equivalent or homotopic because the groups are equivalent.

If labeling the protons of a methylene group as H_a and H_b does not lead to the formation of "enantiomers," the molecule is homotopic.

33. C is correct.

Acetate anion

Dimethyl sulfoxide (DMSO) is an organosulfur compound with the formula $(CH_3)_2SO$.

The colorless liquid is an important polar aprotic solvent that dissolves both polar and nonpolar compounds and is miscible with water and a wide range of organic solvents.

34. C is correct.

Conjugated (alternating double and single) bonds are more thermodynamically stable than the unconjugated double bonds.

B: adjacent double bonds of allenes are not conjugated but cumulated because the *pi* bonds are oriented 90 degrees apart.

Allenes tend to be less stable, especially when confined to cyclic structures.

The other structures are isolated double bonds with (one or more) intervening sp^3 hybridized carbons between the sp^2 carbons of the double bonds.

35. C is correct. The acetylide anion has a $pK_a \approx 28$.

Due to the large differences in electronegativity between oxygen and carbon atoms, ions that possess negatively charged oxygen atoms are relatively more stable than carbon anions.

The sodium methoxide is the most stable conjugate base, and therefore the least basic.

The CH_3Li is the Gilman reagent, and CH_3MgBr is the Grignard. Both are strong bases with a pK_a greater than 40.

36. D is correct.

The halogens are deactivating due to their high electronegativity. However, like all *ortho / para*-directors, the halogens have a lone pair of electrons on the atom attached to the ring.

Alkyl chains do not have lone pairs of electrons on the C attached to the ring but are *ortho / para* directors due to hyperconjugation.

37. C is correct.

2-hexanol is a secondary alcohol and can be oxidized to a ketone with an oxidizing agent (e.g., CrO_3 in HCl).

The carbon atom of the alcohol is only bonded to one other hydrogen atom; therefore, the highest oxidation state it can acquire is the ketone oxidation state (i.e., +2).

Oxidation: primary alcohol → aldehyde → carboxylic acid

secondary alcohol → ketone

tertiary alcohol → no reaction

38. D is correct.

The classes of compounds that contain carbonyl group are ketones, aldehyde, carboxylic acids and carboxylic acid derivatives (acyl halide, anhydride, ester and amide).

Other groups may also contain carbonyl groups, such as carbonate, carbamate, urea, etc., and these groups have the same oxidation state like carbon dioxide with four C–X bonds.

39. A is correct.

Citric acid is a chemical involved in the citric acid (TCA or Krebs) cycle.

Citric acid

The TCA cycle is a metabolic process responsible for ATP production and commonly occurs in most aerobic organisms.

40. A is correct.

Fischer esterification involves a carboxylic acid and alcohol, with an acid catalyst.

Ethyl propanoate

Esters have the general formula: R–COO–R'

The suffix for an ester is *–oate*. The prefix is the substituent attached to the oxygen adjacent to the carbonyl carbon, and the root is the substituent attached to the carbonyl oxygen.

Fischer esterification

Excess alcohol is used to drive the chemical equilibrium forward.

41. A is correct.

Amines tend to be basic and also nucleophilic if they are not sterically bulky.

The attachment of acyl groups to amines causes the nitrogen lone pair to delocalize into the carbonyl π^* orbital, thus greatly reducing the nitrogen's nucleophilic and basic properties.

The amide ($RCONR_2$) group tends to react with electrophiles on the carbonyl oxygen atom because a more stable cationic intermediate is generated.

42. B is correct.

The longest carbon chain is composed of seven carbon atoms.

The remaining carbon groups are substituent methyl groups located at the second, fourth and fifth positions along the carbon chain.

43. C is correct.

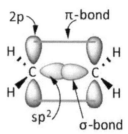

ethene

Hybridization and sigma and pi bonds indicated

Hybridization	Bond angle	Geometry
sp^3	109.5°	tetrahedral
$sp^2 + p$ (unhybridized)	120°	trigonal planar (flat)
$sp + p + p$ (two unhybridized)	180°	linear

44. A is correct.

The stereochemistry about the alkene is '*E*' (highest priority groups are on opposite sides of the alkene).

The priority groups are ranked according to the Cahn-Ingold-Prelog rules for prioritization based for the atomic number of atoms attached to the alkene.

The chain possessing the heaviest atoms proximal to the alkene generally have higher priority. In this example, the bromomethyl group has a higher priority.

The alcohol and methoxy groups contain oxygen atoms, but the methoxy oxygen atom is closer to the double bond.

45. B is correct.

Amino acids contain an amino (~NH$_2$) and a carboxylic acid (~COOH) functional groups.

The α carbon is between the amino and carboxyl groups and is attached to the R (sidechain) group.

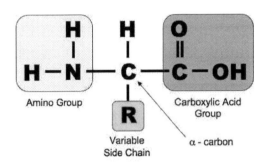

46. B is correct.

There are two overall categories of lipids: long chain lipids (e.g., triglycerides) and smaller, polycyclic lipids, such as steroids (e.g., cholesterol and its derivatives, such as estrogen and testosterone).

Lipid molecules are fat soluble, and these molecules are largely soluble in organic/hydrophobic environments.

47. C is correct.

Cyclic carbohydrates typically have ether and alcohol functional groups.

(a) Fischer projection   (b) Three-dimensional representantion   (c) Cyclic monosaccharide

The hemiacetal and aldehyde forms of these compounds can equilibrate.

48. D is correct.

Ribose differs from deoxyribose sugars in that ribose lacks one alcohol (i.e., hydroxyl) group.

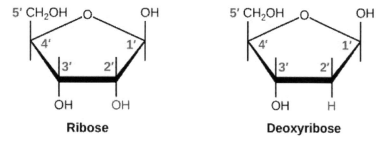

Both ribose sugar (RNA) and deoxyribose sugar (DNA) are used to synthesize nucleic acid polymers.

49. B is correct.

The π electron clouds of aromatic rings are not very basic because the aromatic molecule is stable.

Lone pairs on carbonyl oxygen (sp^2 hybridized) are more basic than π electrons but not as basic as the lone pair on nitrogen (sp^3 hybridized).

The nitrogen on an amine is more basic than the nitrogen on the amide because the electrons on the amide participate in resonance.

50. D is correct.

In hydrogenation reactions, *Z* and *E* alkenes are reduced to alkanes, and this process is catalyzed by transitions metals, such as nickel or palladium.

In this reaction, hydrogen (H_2) is added across the double bond of the alkene.

51. D is correct.

The numbering of carbohydrates begins at the terminal carbon closest to the most oxidized carbon (i.e., anomeric carbon).

It is an α-linkage because the linking oxygen is pointing down (axial) in the Haworth (i.e., ring) representation.

52. B is correct.

Replication: DNA → DNA during the S phase of the cell cycle.

A: translation is the process of synthesizing proteins from mRNA.

C: transcription is the process of synthesizing mRNA from DNA.

D: complementation is observed in genetics when two organisms with different homozygous recessive mutations that produce the same mutant phenotype (e.g., thorax differences in

Drosophila flies), when mated or crossed, produce offspring with the wild-type phenotype.

Complementation only occurs if the mutations are in different genes.

Each organism's genome supplies the wild-type allele to *complement* the mutated allele of the other.

Since the mutations are recessive, the offspring display the wild-type phenotype.

Complementation (i.e., *cis/trans*) test can be used to test whether the mutations are in different genes.

53. C is correct.

The amino acid valine (below):

Valine has an R group (i.e., side chain) of isopropyl attached to the α carbon of the amino acid backbone.

The first step in the reaction sequence below is the *Hell-Volhard-Zelinsky reaction.*

The mechanism for the Hell-Volhard-Zelinsky reaction

The phosphorus tribromide (PBr₃) is electrophilic and can be attacked by the carboxylic acid to generate the acid bromide.

The enol tautomer of this acid bromide can be brominated at the alpha position to give the α-bromo acid bromide.

The acid bromide can be subjected to water to hydrolyze the group to the carboxylic acid.

Finally, in the presence of excess ammonia, the alpha bromide can be displaced to produce the valine amino acid product.

54. A is correct. Many unsaturated fats are omega fats because they contain alkene groups.

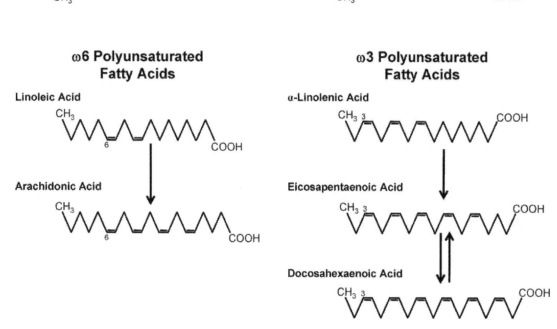

Sample fatty acids showing the positions of double bonds

Omega-3 fats have double bonds that appear three carbon atoms from the methyl end.

Omega-6 fatty acids contain double bonds that are six carbon atoms away from the methyl end.

The double bonds tend to have Z (*cis*) geometry.

55. B is correct.

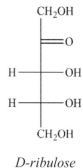

D-ribulose

The prefix *keto~* indicates that the molecule contains a ketone (RCOOR').

The root *pent~* indicates that the molecule contains five carbon atoms.

The suffix *~ose* indicates that the molecule is a sugar.

56. C is correct.

When NADH is oxidized, it loses an equivalent of hydrogen.

Because NADH is a neutral compound, a loss of hydride (H^-) means that the substrate develops a positive charge.

57. A is correct.

The primary structure of proteins consists of the linear sequence of amino acids (i.e., residues) in the polypeptide chain.

The secondary structure of proteins involves the regularly occurring motifs (*alpha* helix and *beta* pleated sheets) that are derived from intramolecular localized (within 10 amino acids) hydrogen and disulfide bonding.

The tertiary structure involves interactions of amino acid R groups and interactions across different motifs (*alpha* helix, *beta* pleated sheets, and loop structures).

The quaternary structure of proteins involves two or more polypeptide chains.

The quaternary structure is maintained between the different polypeptide chains (e.g., 4 chains of 2 α and 2 β in hemoglobin) by hydrophobic interactions and by disulfide bridges between cysteines.

Two cysteine residues form a cystine covalent bond

58. C is correct.

Long alkyl chains present on the alkoxy portion and the carboxyl backbone of the ester are characteristic features of molecules that are waxes.

59. A is correct.

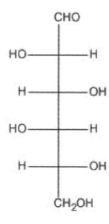

D-glucose

The prefix *aldo~* indicates that the molecule contains an aldehyde.

The root *hex~* indicates that the molecule contains six carbon atoms.

The suffix *~ose* indicates that the molecule is a sugar.

60. D is correct.

The central dogma of molecular biology:

DNA → RNA → protein

DNA → RNA is known as transcription.

RNA → protein is known as translation.

DNA is the nucleic acid biomolecule that can give rise to other nucleic acids and proteins.

DNA strands are synthesized from DNA parental strands during replication.

Please, leave your Customer Review on Amazon

Notes

Explanations: Diagnostic Test #6

1. D is correct.

Cyclopropane is the only compound listed that contains three carbons.

Cyclopropane with the stereochemistry of hydrogens indicated

All other answer choices have four carbons.

2. B is correct.

Carbocations are stabilized by resonance and by hyperconjugation.

Relative stabilities of carbocations

The phenyl ring offers additional stability due to resonance structures with the delocalization of the *pi* electrons.

The primary non-conjugated carbocation will be the least stable.

3. A is correct.

There are two possible stereoisomers for the vicinal disubstituted alkene (i.e., *cis* and *trans*).

cis- and trans-dichloroethylene

There is only one possible isomer of the geminal (i.e., on the same atom) disubstituted alkene.

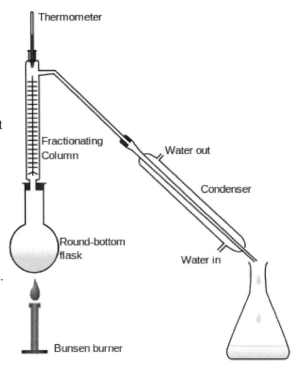

1,1-dichloroethene

4. A is correct.

NMR spectroscopy provides information about the local environment of the proton.

Equivalent hydrogens (i.e., hydrogens in identical locations in relation to other atoms) produce a single NMR signal.

Nonequivalent hydrogens give separate NMR signals on the spectrum.

Since the molecule produces one signal for NMR, all hydrogens are equivalent. In $(CH_3)_3CCCl_2C(CH_3)_3$, the methyl groups are equivalent, and this molecule produces only one signal in NMR.

B: $(CH_3)_2CHCH_2CH_2CH(CH_3)CH_2CH_3$ produces eight signals. Additionally, the splitting produces a complex NMR pattern indicating the number of adjacent Hs.

C: $(CH_3)_2CHCH_2(CH_2)_4CH_3$ produces eight signals. Additionally, the splitting produces a complex NMR pattern indicating the number of adjacent Hs.

D: $CH_3(CH_2)_7CH_3$ produces five signals. For symmetrical molecules, one signal is for the terminal $CH_3(1,9)$, one for the $CH_2(2,8)$, one for the $CH_2(3,7)$, one for the $CH_2(4,6)$ and one for the CH_2 at 5.

5. C is correct.

For a given class of compounds (e.g., hydrocarbons), the lower the molecular weight, the lower the boiling point.

For a mixture containing compounds of different boiling points, the smallest and most volatile components have the lowest boiling points.

Molecules with the lowest boiling points (most volatile) vaporize first and travel first up the fractionating column.

In the fractionating column, natural gas has the lowest boiling point; therefore, it is isolated first.

The next most volatile hydrocarbon is gasoline. Therefore, it has a boiling point that is lower than that of kerosene.

6. B is correct.

To form propyl chloride, any one of six hydrogens (3 on each methyl group) can be substituted.

To form isopropyl chloride, the hydrogen extracted must be one of the two on the middle carbon. Based on statistical probability, propyl chloride forms in a 3:1 ratio compared to isopropyl chloride.

However, when a terminal hydrogen is extracted (to form propyl chloride), a primary radical intermediate is formed. When an internal hydrogen is extracted (to form isopropyl chloride), a secondary radical intermediate is formed.

Carbon radicals are electron-deficient because they do not have a full octet.

Alkyl groups are electron-donating (via hyperconjugation), so a secondary radical is more stable than a primary radical, and therefore the formation of a secondary radical is more likely.

The reaction proceeding through the secondary radical intermediate is faster. Therefore, the reaction leading to the formation of isopropyl chloride proceeds more readily. This is contrary to strictly statistical considerations, and more isopropyl chloride is formed than the predicted 25%.

Note: it is impossible to predict exactly what percentages form because other factors (e.g., temperature) are important for the empirical yield determination for each product.

7. D is correct.

A bromonium ion is a cyclic (three-membered ring) structure of a bromine atom attached to two unsaturated carbons (i.e., an alkene).

The bromonium ion is formed when the nucleophilic double bond adds to a bromine atom of Br_2, releasing Br^-.

The resulting bromine anion (or solvent if it is a nucleophile – contains lone pairs of electrons: H_2O, NH_3 or CH_3OH) bonds to the more substituted carbon of the bromonium structure to give the dibrominated product. Cl_2 follows the same reaction mechanism.

An *anti*-product is always formed because the Br^- (or nucleophilic solvent with lone pairs) must approach the three-membered ring of the bromonium ion from the side opposite the bromonium ion.

$CH_3CH_2CH=CH_2 + HBr \rightarrow CH_3CH_2CHBrCH_3$: HBr adds to alkenes via a Markovnikov mechanism. First, the double bond attacks the proton, and hydrogen adds to the carbon of the double bond with fewer alkyl substituents (i.e., less substituted carbon).

As a result, a carbocation intermediate forms on the more substituted carbon.

Second, Br^- adds to the carbocation (more substituted carbon) to form the alkyl halide. The mechanism involves a carbocation and not a bromonium ion.

Unlike a bromonium ion, which always yields the *anti*-stereochemistry, the trigonal planar carbocation undergoes nucleophilic attack from either face (e.g., the top and bottom) and produces enantiomers (a racemic mixture) if the product contains a chiral center on the carbon that was the carbocation.

8. C is correct.

Using a subscript of n for the number of carbons, the degrees of unsaturation can be determined from the following formulae:

Alkane: C_nH_{2n+2} = 0 degrees of unsaturation

Alkene: C_nH_{2n} = 1 degree of unsaturation

Alkyne: C_nH_{2n-2} = 2 degrees of unsaturation

The formula C_nH_{2n-2} is the general formula for acyclic alkynes.

The general molecular formula for cyclic alkynes is C_nH_{2n-4}.

Cyclic alkynes (i.e., bond angle of 180°) are typically larger sized rings with at least 8 carbon atoms in the ring.

9. C is correct. Halides are electron-withdrawing (i.e., deactivating) and are *ortho/para*-directing.

Halogens are the exception to the general rule, which states that all electron-withdrawing species are deactivating and *meta*-directing.

The reason that the halogens (despite being electron-withdrawing due to their high electronegativity) are *ortho/para*-directing is the lone pair of electrons that localize, via resonance, the electron density at the *o/p* positions.

Resonance hybrids show the anion at both *ortho* positions. Note that the resonance structures also include an anion at the *para* position.

Therefore, like all atoms that have lone pairs of electrons attached to the ring, halogens are *ortho-para* directors.

The resonance structure involves forming a double bond between the halide bearing a formal positive charge and the phenyl ring. Therefore it is not a significant resonance structure and is unable to overcome the deactivating (due to electronegativity) effect caused by induction (along the *sigma* bond).

10. D is correct. For a given class of compounds, the lower the molecular weight, the lower the boiling point.

Alcohols follow the same trend for the boiling point as alkanes.

Ethanol is a two-carbon chain (i.e., lowest molecular weight) with hydrogen bonding (e.g., alcohols and carboxylic acids). It has the lowest molecular weight of all choices and therefore has the lowest boiling point.

11. D is correct.

Ketones and aldehydes have similar chemical properties because both contain a carbonyl group that is not in conjugation with a heteroatom. They undergo similar reduction and alkylation reactions, although the products of these reactions may be slightly different.

Conversely, aldehydes can undergo an additional oxidation reaction to form carboxylic acids, unlike ketones, which cannot be oxidized further.

12. A is correct.

Acid strength is increased by the inductive effect of electron-withdrawing groups on the neighboring carbon atoms.

Factors that affect the acidity of a molecule:

      1) the more electronegative the substituents, the greater the inductive effect;

      2) the closer the electronegative group is to the carbonyl carbon, the greater the effect;

      3) the greater the number of electronegative substituents, the greater the inductive effect.

Fluoroacetic acid has a $pK_a \approx 2.6$ and is more acidic than others because of the inductive influence of the electronegative fluorine atom.

B: acetic acid (i.e., table vinegar) has a $pK_a \approx 5$ and is the least acidic since it has no electronegative substituents.

C: bromoacetic acid has a $pK_a \approx 3.6$.

D: methoxyacetic acid has a $pK_a \approx 3.6$

13. B is correct.

The reactant benzoyl chloride is an acyl halide that forms a ketone when reacted with an equimolar quantity of a Grignard reagent. Excess Grignard reagent converts the ketone to a tertiary alcohol.

      Acyl halide + Grignard reagent → ketone + Grignard reagent → tertiary alcohol

Sample addition reactions of carbonyl compounds and excess Grignard:

      Formaldehyde + excess Grignard → primary alcohol

      Aldehyde + excess Grignard → secondary alcohol

      Ketone + excess Grignard → tertiary alcohol

14. C is correct.

Amine salts are soluble in water because the nitrogen has a positive charge and can form ion–dipole interactions with water.

A: nitrogen donates its lone pair of electrons when forming a salt; a positive charge forms on the nitrogen, not a negative charge.

B: the amine salt has a higher molecular weight than the amine, but it is not the reason why the amine salt is more soluble.

D: some amines are soluble in water. Amines follow a similar solubility pattern to carboxylic acids: up to 6 carbons, they are relatively soluble.

15. B is correct.

The longest carbon chain in the molecule is six carbon atoms long.

The two methyl substituents at the second and fourth positions in the chain.

16. D is correct. The hybridized orbital is a combination of one *s* and three *p* orbitals.

Therefore, the energy of the hybridized orbital is between the energy of the combined orbitals.

The *s* orbital has lower energy than the *p* orbital.

17. B is correct.

To determine the enantiomer of the compound, draw the mirror image of the compound.

This requires inverting the two stereocenters, as inverting only one results in a diastereomer.

18. A is correct.

Note: the displayed masses on the mass spectrum corresponds to the molecular fragments that have a charge of +1.

It is possible to generate dications from the ionization in the mass spectrometer, and therefore an additional calculation may be required to determine the true mass of the fragment.

19. D is correct.

Fractional (as compared to simple) distillation is used to separate molecules with similar boiling points (BP). Simple distillation is effective for separating molecules with differences in BP of at least 25 °C.

In fractional distillation, a mixture of liquids is heated slowly to separate the more volatile products from less volatile ones (based on differences in boiling points).

The extra surface area in the fractional distillation column forces some of the less volatile components to condense and reenter the liquid phase, thus enhancing the separation of molecules with differences in boiling points.

20. D is correct.

S_N1 reactions proceed via a carbocation in the first step of the mechanism.

In the second step, the nucleophile forms a new bond by attacking the carbocation.

S_N1 undergoes first-order kinetics, whereby:

rate = k [substrate]

where k is a rate constant determined experimentally.

21. C is correct.

cis-3-methyl-2-hexene undergoes Markovnikov addition because the first step is protonation to give the more stable (more substituted) carbonium ion. It gives *syn*- and *anti*-addition products because in the second step the bromide ion attacks both the top and bottom faces of the carbonium ion.

The addition of a hydrogen halide to an asymmetrical alkene leads to either a halogenated alkene in which the halide is on the more substituted carbon, or to a product in which the halide is on the less substituted carbon.

The former addition follows Markovnikov's rule.

The latter is an example of an *anti*-Markovnikov addition.

If a mixture of the two products is formed, with a predominance of one product, the reaction is said to be regioselective.

22. C is correct.

The higher is the pK_a of a compound, the less acidic is the molecule, and the stronger is the conjugate base.

The pK_a of water is $\approx$ 15-16.

The pK_a of the terminal alkynes is $\approx$ 25.

The pK_a of the N-H bonds of neutral amines is $\approx$ 36-38.

Therefore, water and the terminal alkyne (but-1-yne or butyne) are more acidic.

23. A is correct.

When 1,3-cyclopentadiene reacts with sodium metal, it is converted from nonaromatic to aromatic.

According to Hückel's rule, a planar cyclic compound is aromatic if it is conjugated (adjacent sp^2 hybridized carbon atoms) and has 4n + 2 *pi* electrons (where n is any whole number).

24. D is correct.

HBr is a strong acid that protonates the oxygen atom of the alcohol. Then, either the bromide displaces the water to give 1-bromo-2-methylpropane, or a hydride shift occurs to form the tertiary carbocation, which can be trapped by the bromide, resulting in 2-bromo-2-methylpropane.

25. B is correct.

Tollens' reagent or Benedict's test are used to detect reducing sugars (i.e., aldehydes).

The aldehyde is oxidized to a carboxylic acid during the reaction.

All monosaccharides are reducing sugars, while some disaccharides, oligosaccharides, and polysaccharides are also reducing sugars.

The Tollens' test for aldehydes involves the reduction of silver cations [Ag^+] to reduced silver; the metal precipitates out of solution and coats the inner surface of the reaction flask (i.e., mirror) as a positive test for reducing sugars.

The Tollens' test does not give a positive test with ketones because the ketone is already fully oxidized and lacks a C–H bond to be further oxidized and be converted to C–O bonds (e.g., aldehydes to COOH).

26. A is correct.

When dissolved in the basic solution, the carboxylic acid is deprotonated to form the carboxylate salt.

The salt is charged and this ion can engage in ion–dipole interactions with the solvent and is therefore soluble.

The aldehyde may also react with the base to form charged species (either the geminal diol or the enolate), but these charged species are formed reversibly. Therefore, the acid is able to dissolve, while the aldehyde is not.

27. A is correct. There are 4 alcohol functional groups present.

A cyclic ester is also present. A cyclic ester is known as a lactone.

$$
\begin{array}{c}
H \\
| \\
R - C - O - R \\
| \\
OH
\end{array}
$$

Hemiacetal: alcohol and ether on the same carbon

$$
\begin{array}{c}
OR'' \\
| \\
R - C - H \\
| \\
OR'
\end{array}
$$

Acetal: two ethers on the same carbon

28. C is correct.

The most notable intermolecular force for water is hydrogen bonding.

$CH_3–CH_2–NH_2$ interact with water through hydrogen bonding. Hydrogens, bonded directly to F, O or N, participate in hydrogen bonds. The hydrogen is partial positive (i.e., delta plus or $\partial+$) due to the bond to these electronegative atoms.

The lone pair of electrons on the F, O or N interacts with the $\partial+$ hydrogen to form a hydrogen bond.

$CH_3–CH_2–NH_2$ is ethylamine. Amines (i.e., nitrogen) can form hydrogen bonds, but thiols (i.e., sulfur) cannot.

29. D is correct.

The longest carbon chain that includes the double bond (i.e., alkene functional group) is a five-carbon molecule. The chain is numbered with the alkene given the lowest number.

An ethyl (i.e., 2 carbon) substituent is at the second position in the carbon chain.

30. C is correct.

The two allylic cations are resonance forms of each other.

Resonance involves the movement of conjugated *pi* systems, not of the atoms.

A and B are constitutional isomers (i.e., same molecular formula, but different connectivity).

31. B is correct.

All *meso* compounds are molecules with chiral centers and require an inversion center or a plane of symmetry.

These elements of symmetry make molecules with asymmetric carbon atoms achiral overall.

32. B is correct.

The two nuclear spin states for protons are *alpha* and *beta*.

The *alpha* spin state has less energy than the *beta* spin state because the *alpha* spin state has the same direction as the applied external field.

33. C is correct.

Conformations in which the single bonds are staggered are more stable than those in which they are eclipsed, due to steric repulsion and torsional strain (i.e., bonding electron between adjacent atoms – such as observed in eclipsed Newman projections).

Torsional strain is present in Newman projections when the substituents are eclipsed. It originates from the repulsion of the bonding electrons (i.e., not the steric interactions of the substituents).

Conformations that put the largest substituents in an *anti* (180° offset) arrangement are more stable than those in a gauche (60° offset) arrangement.

1,2-dibromoethane is shown anti in the Newman projection

34. A is correct.

Addition reactions require two or more reagents to combine to form a single product.

For the oxidation of an alkene (e.g., epoxidation or dihydroxylation), only the oxygen atoms of a reagent are transferred to the alkene.

A reagent byproduct is normally given off in the reaction, such as the carboxylic acid from *m*CPBA oxidation (i.e., peroxy acid) or the reduced metal from potassium permanganate ($KMnO_4$) or osmium tetraoxide (OsO_4) oxidation.

Ozonolysis (O_3 or Cr_2O_7) is a type of oxidation of alkenes that results in splitting the alkene into two separate carbonyl containing products (i.e., cleavage reaction) and is not an addition reaction.

35. B is correct.

When an alkyne is reduced by sodium in liquid ammonia, a single electron is transferred to the alkyne to produce an anion. The intermediate is a vinyl anion because it is on the atom that is in the double bond.

The anion protonates to give the vinyl radical.

The only cations produced during the course of the reaction are the Na^+.

36. B is correct.

Carbonyl compounds are *meta*-directing in EAS reactions.

Since both the nitro and carbonyl groups are deactivating, disubstitution is slow, and single *meta* substitution is the predominant product.

37. D is correct.

The reaction between propanol and PBr_3 (phosphorous tribromide) proceeds via an S_N2 reaction mechanism.

An addition-elimination sequence occurs to the P–Br bond, then substitution by Br^- of the alcohol gives the inverted (*R/S*) product (i.e., bromopropane).

38. A is correct.

The hydrocyanation (i.e., adding ⁻C≡N) of ketones and aldehydes is essentially an alkylation reaction.

This alkylation reaction is sensitive to the steric environment of the carbonyl electrophile.

Formaldehyde (shown below) contains two hydrogen substituents and is the most reactive.

Aldehydes (below) are the second most reactive.

Unhindered ketones (below) are the next most reactive.

Hindered ketones (below) are the least reactive.

These alkyl groups block access to the *pi** orbital of the carbonyl, and the more sterically-hindered substrates react more slowly because the nucleophile (e.g., ⁻C≡N) is impeded in its approach to the delta plus of the carbonyl carbon.

Carbonyl carbon with delta plus carbon (electrophile) indicated

39. C is correct.

Carboxylic acids exchange protons with bases.

When a neutral compound ionizes through the loss of a proton (H^+), the remaining charge of the larger fragment is negatively charged. The proton is positively charged, so the resulting ion is H^+.

The hydroxyl group of a carboxylic acid (or of an alcohol) can be replaced (i.e., substitution reaction) with special reagents (e.g., $SOCl_4$ or PBr_3) to form acyl halides (or alkyl halides for alcohol functional groups).

40. A is correct.

In the addition reaction between water and benzoyl chloride, water donates electrons (acting as a nucleophile) to the electrophilic carbonyl of benzoyl chloride.

The chlorine atom, which is not present in the product, acts as a leaving group during the subsequent elimination step whereby the carbonyl carbon reforms.

41. D is correct.

Salts form as solids with tightly compact repeating unit structures, thus requiring more heat to boil compared with other substances, typically liquids.

42. B is correct.

The longest carbon chain has 5 carbons and is cyclopentane – the root name of the molecule.

It also possesses two substituent groups: the chloride and the methyl group.

Stereochemistry is indicated in the structure; the *cis-* notation is necessary for the compound's name.

43. B is correct.

acetamide

The resonance structures for carboxylic acids and their derivatives cause the carbonyl to adopt a bond length that is between a C–O single and C=O double bond.

Resonance structures of acetamide

The orbitals involved in resonance are the filled, donating *p* orbital of the nitrogen atom and the adjacent electron-accepting carbonyl *pi** orbital.

44. D is correct.

Any molecule that has a non-identical mirror image is chiral and has an enantiomer.

Draw the structure of the cyclic compound:

cis-1,2-dimethylcyclopentane

Comparison of the molecule reveals an internal plane of symmetry.

A *meso* compound and its enantiomer (i.e., a non-superimposable mirror image of a chiral molecule) are the same molecule. Therefore, a *meso* compound does not have an enantiomer.

45. B is correct.

Peptide bonds link the primary sequence of amino acids in a protein.

These bonds form between individual amino acids that then form a peptide chain.

Peptide bonds are not altered when a polypeptide bends or folds to form a secondary structure.

Also, when the polypeptide folds into a three-dimensional shape (the tertiary structure of a protein), new peptide bonds do not form.

A: interactions between charged groups (electrostatic interactions) can arise, especially in the tertiary structure of a protein.

C: hydrogen bonds are involved in both the secondary and tertiary structure of a protein. In the secondary structure, the polypeptide chain folds to allow the carbonyl oxygen and amine hydrogen to lie nearby.

As a result, hydrogen bonding occurs to form sheets, helices, or turns. Likewise, hydrogen bonding may serve to stabilize the tertiary structure of a protein.

D: hydrophobic interactions also play an important role in the tertiary structure of a protein.

For example, in an aqueous environment, the hydrophobic side chains of the amino acids may interact to arrange themselves towards the inside of the protein.

46. C is correct.

Triacylglycerols are molecules composed of a glycerol substructure and three fatty acids that are condensed to form a triester.

47. A is correct.

In an α-1,1 linkage, both anomeric carbons are in an acetal linkage.

Therefore, mutarotation (i.e., interconversion between the open chain and ring form) is not possible, and no free aldehyde is available to react with Benedict's reagent.

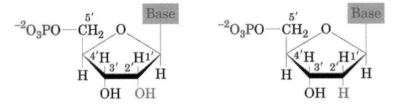

Mutarotation of glucose (α-glucose on the left; β-glucose on the right)

All monosaccharides are reducing sugars, while some disaccharides (e.g., lactose and maltose), oligosaccharides and polysaccharides are also reducing sugars.

B: β-1,4-glucose-glucose is a disaccharide, whereby one glucose unit has its C-1 bound as an acetal and therefore cannot mutarotate, existing only as a ring. Therefore, the aldehyde is unavailable for reaction with Benedict's reagent. However, the other glucose unit is bonded at its C-4 hydroxyl.

C: glucose has a hemiacetal linkage which allows mutarotation. Therefore, the aldehyde group is free to react in the test for reducing sugars.

D: fructose has a hemiacetal linkage which allows mutarotation. Therefore, the aldehyde group is free to react in the test for reducing sugars.

48. C is correct.

After transcription (DNA → mRNA), the synthesized mRNA is transported out of the nucleus and to the ribosome, so that proteins can be synthesized during translation (mRNA → protein).

RNA contains ribose, a sugar similar to deoxyribose of DNA molecules, except that it has a hydroxyl group (~OH) at the 2' position on the sugar.

Ribonucleotide (left) and deoxyribonucleotide (right): note the 2' position of the sugars

Nucleic acids (DNA and RNA) bind to each other via hydrogen bonds between bases (A=T/U and C≡G).

The sugar and phosphate group form the backbone and do not affect (to any appreciable degree) the hydrogen bonding between bases.

The presence of a hydroxyl group (~OH) in RNA causes the backbone to experience steric and electrostatic repulsion. Therefore, the grooves formed in helixes or hairpin loops between chains are larger.

The larger groove permits nucleases (i.e., enzymes that digest DNA or RNA) to more easily bind to the RNA chain and digest the covalent bonds between the alternating sugar-phosphate monomers.

49. C is correct.

Amino acids are the basic building blocks for proteins.

Three amino acids (trimer) with 2 peptide bonds indicated by arrows (above)

The peptide bond is rigid due to the resonance hybrids involving the lone pair of electrons on nitrogen forming a double bond to the carbonyl carbon (and oxygen develops a negative formal charge).

50. D is correct.

Triacylglycerol is a lipid that can undergo saponification, which is the breakdown of fatty esters with bases, such as sodium hydroxide or potassium hydroxide.

Saponification reactions are base promoted because sodium hydroxide is consumed in the reaction and not regenerated.

The amount of base needed to saponify 1 gram of fat is known as the saponification number.

51. A is correct.

For a chiral molecule with n chiral centers, the number of stereoisomers is calculated by 2^n, where n is the number of chiral centers. For example, a molecule with 3 chiral centers has 8 (2 × 2 × 2) stereoisomers. The relationship (relative to the original molecule) is 1 enantiomer and 6 diastereomers.

If there were any *meso* (i.e., internal plane of symmetry) carbohydrates, the number of *meso* forms would be subtracted from the total number of stereoisomers.

52. B is correct.

The nitrogen bases of nucleotides are responsible for the hydrogen bonding that keeps one nucleic acid strand attracted to the other. The number of hydrogen bonds that exist between the pairs varies between two and three bonds.

Adenine and thymine nitrogenous base pairs bond with two hydrogen bonds (A=T).

Cytosine and guanine nitrogenous base pairs bond with three hydrogen bonds (C≡G).

53. D is correct.

The isoelectric point is a pH when the amino and carboxyl end of the protein (and/or the side chains) results in a net neutral charge on overall the protein. Only charged species (i.e., anion and cations) migrate under the influence of an electric field in gel electrophoresis.

Ions are molecules that possess a certain charge, either positive (cation) or negative (anion).

The zwitterion ion (containing both a positive and negative region within the same molecule) form is the dominant form at the isoelectric point, and it possesses two charges. However, the charges are opposite and cancel one another, forming an overall electrically neutral compound.

Neutral proteins do not migrate within the electric field during gel electrophoresis.

54. A is correct.

In esterification reactions, the ester is made from the condensation of carboxylic acids and alcohols.

Fats are formed from the condensation (via dehydration) of fatty acids and glycerol.

For the reaction to take place, an acid catalyst (or enzyme) normally needs to be used. An acid catalyst is needed because carboxylic acids are not electrophilic, and the group needs to be activated by protonation.

Protonation of the carboxylic acid carbonyl oxygen atom causes the carbon-oxygen dipole to increase, allowing an alcohol to add to the group.

Protonation of one of the geminal hydroxyl groups and loss of the group as water leads to the formation of the ester.

55. C is correct. Lactose (shown below) is a disaccharide composed of glucose and galactose.

The glycosidic linkage in lactose is a β(1→4) linkage.

56. A is correct.

Three nucleotides are combined to make a codon or anticodon required for translation.

A larger segment of coding DNA (transcribed into mRNA) is called a gene, and sections of different genes make up the nucleic acid strands.

Two single strands of DNA are used to make one DNA double helix.

57. C is correct.

Protonation or deprotonation of an amino acid residue change its ionization state: it may either become positively or negatively charged or neutral. The process may lead to changes in the interactions among amino acid side chains, as some ionic bonds may be compromised from the lack of opposite charge pairing.

Certain hydrogen bonding interactions may also be modulated if Lewis bases are protonated with Brønsted acids, impairing their ability to accept hydrogen bonds from nearby amino acid residues.

58. A is correct.

Oils are isolated from plant sources and may consist of several different fatty acids. These oils may contain saturated fat, but other fats present in the mixture are unsaturated fat molecules.

The saturated fats that may be present in oil are palmitic and stearic acid and the unsaturated fats found in these oils include oleic, palmitoleic and linoleic acids, as well as others.

59. B is correct.

Ribose is an important monosaccharide that contains an aldehyde and five carbon atoms. This sugar can be found in the structure of mRNA.

The 2'-deoxygenated form of ribose (i.e., deoxyribose), is found in the structure of DNA.

60. B is correct.

In any given molecule of DNA, each of the thymine nitrogen bases forms two hydrogen bonds with adenine.

Because each thymine pairs with an adenine residue, there is an equal number of both nitrogen bases in the molecule.

Notes

Explanations: Diagnostic Test #7

1. A is correct.

The molecule has four carbon atoms and two alkenes, hence the root name butadiene.

The double bonds of alkenes are in the first and third positions of the carbon chain.

2. C is correct.

Multiple bonds and rings introduce degrees of unsaturation.

Using a subscript of n for the number of carbons, the degrees of unsaturation can be determined from the following formulae:

Alkane: C_nH_{2n+2} = 0 degrees of unsaturation

Alkene: C_nH_{2n} = 1 degree of unsaturation

Alkyne: C_nH_{2n-2} = 2 degrees of unsaturation

Rings = 1 degree of unsaturation

Double bonds = 1 degree of unsaturation

There is one degree of unsaturation for this compound (the ring).

Therefore, with no other degrees of unsaturation present, there are no alkenes or double bonds present in the molecule.

3. D is correct.

The number of each different kind of atom must be consistent among a pair or group of isomers, meaning that the oxidation state of the carbon atoms of the compound is consistent as well.

A change in the oxidation state of the compound suggests that the hydrogen count is different.

For instance, the isomer of the given alcohol is another alcohol, and not an aldehyde or a ketone.

4. B is correct.

In the IR spectrum, the various peaks between 900 and 1500 cm^{-1} correspond to the unique fingerprint region. The prominent peak at 1710 cm^{-1} indicates the carbon-oxygen double bond of a carbonyl group (aldehyde, ketone, acyl halide, anhydride, carboxylic acid, ester or amide).

Note: the presence of a similar (prominent and broad peak) between 3300 and 3500 cm^{-1} is characteristic of alcohol.

The alcohol of a carboxylic acid would show an IR absorption peak around 2800 and 3200 cm^{-1}.

5. D is correct.

Higher temperature increases the solubility of most substances because the increase in the kinetic energy of higher temperatures allows the solvent molecules to break apart the solute molecules which are held together by intermolecular attractions (i.e., hydrogen bonds, dipole-dipole, and hydrophobic interactions).

For example, a compound is always more soluble at 40 °C than at 10 °C. The technique of recrystallization relies upon the principle that a molecule is more soluble at a higher temperature. Therefore, solubility increases with increasing temperature.

The statement "like dissolves like" refers to compounds that are either polar (or ionic) and dissolve in solvents that are also polar (or ionic) or non-polar (hydrophobic) and dissolve in non-polar solvents. Therefore, molecules and solvents with similar polarities (ionic or hydrophobic) have increased solubility.

The density of the solvent is independent of its ability to dissolve a given solute.

6. D is correct.

Structural isomers have the same molecular formula (C_7H_{16}) but different atomic connections. Molecular mass would be a consideration if the molecules were not isomers (same molecular formula).

Branching in alkanes lowers the boiling point because branched molecules cannot interact as effectively as unbranched molecules and have less surface area. 2,2,4-trimethylpentane has the lowest boiling point because it is the most highly branched.

Hydrogen bonding is a strong, attractive force between molecules (intermolecular force) but requires hydrogen to be attached to an electronegative atom (fluorine, oxygen or nitrogen). The next most attractive intermolecular force is dipole-dipole interaction.

7. D is correct.

Geometric isomers have the same molecular formula, but different connectivity between the atoms due to the orientation of substituents around a carbon-carbon double bond (or ring).

In *cis* isomers, the same substituents are on one side of the double bond or ring, while in *trans* isomers, the same substituents are on opposite sides of the double bond or ring.

Isomers (same molecular formula, but different molecules) which have no double bonds cannot be geometric isomers.

Isomers include:

Constitutional isomers – different connectivity of the backbone or containing different functional groups;

Enantiomers – mirror images of chiral molecules;

Diastereomers – non-mirror chiral molecules with 2 or more chiral centers or geometric isomers that contain double bonds (i.e., designated as *cis/trans* or *E/Z*).

8. B is correct.

Although hydroxide and high temperatures are employed in this reaction, the potassium hydroxide base is not strong enough to catalyze the isomerization of the triple bond, which is why the internal, not terminal, alkyne is recovered from the reaction.

9. A is correct.

The two arenes activated by nitrogen heteroatoms are more nucleophilic.

The amide does not donate as strongly as the amine, so ring 1 is less nucleophilic than ring 3.

Ring 2 is only activated by the alkyl group and is the least reactive of the three.

10. B is correct.

Ethers follow the same trend as alkanes, so dihexyl ether has the highest boiling point because it has the greatest molecular weight and has the largest surface area.

11. D is correct.

Benedict's test (or Tollens' reagent) is used to detect reducing sugars.

The aldehyde is oxidized to a carboxylic acid in the process.

All monosaccharides are reducing sugars, while some disaccharides, oligosaccharides, and polysaccharides are also reducing sugars.

Reducing sugars (and alpha hydroxyl ketones) give a positive Benedict's test: a brown precipitate forms (as does for Fehling's solution).

Tollens' reagent forms silver ions (mirror) as a positive test for reducing sugars.

The Tollens' test for aldehydes involves the reduction of silver cations [Ag^+] to reduced silver; the metal precipitates out of solution and coats the inner surface of the reaction flask.

The ethyl formate has a terminal (HC=O) group, but this group does not oxidize in the Tollens' test conditions because the group is an ester and not an aldehyde. The C–H of the formate ester cannot be oxidized to an O–H bond.

The mechanism for the oxidation of carbonyl C–H bonds typically proceeds through either the hydrate or nucleophilic attack on the carbonyl carbon atom, both of which are not easily done because of the presence of the ester alkoxyl group.

The ester is much less electrophilic than the aldehyde, so it is less reactive.

12. B is correct.

Molecules that possess the hydroxyl group are alcohols and carboxylic acids.

13. D is correct.

Nitriles ($-C \equiv N$) have the prefix cyano and are similar to alkynes in that both functional groups contain triple bonds, but the nitrile possesses an *sp* hybridized nitrogen atom, giving rise to its alternate chemical reactivity ($pK_a = 25$).

Nitriles are more electron deficient than alkynes and are more susceptible to nucleophilic attack by molecules such as organolithium compounds and Grignard reagents.

Alkynes undergo addition reactions with strong electrophiles, such as bromine.

14. A is correct.

Carbonyl groups are indicative of aldehydes, ketones, carboxylic acid or the four carboxylic acid derivatives (i.e., acyl halide, anhydride, ester, and amide).

Amines do not contain carbonyl groups.

15. A is correct.

The carboxylic acid (~*oic* acid) is considered the 1 position.

The hydroxyl group is in the *ortho* or the 2 position.

16. C is correct.

Hydrogen atoms only bond with other atoms using their 1*s* orbital.

The nitrogen atoms hybridize their atomic orbitals to produce *sp³* orbital hybrids for bonding.

sp³ orbitals are used because the nitrogen atom forms bonds of equal length with 4 other atoms.

17. B is correct.

There are two possible stereoisomers for the vicinal disubstituted alkene (1,1-chlorofluoroethene), and there is only one possible isomer of the 1,2 disubstituted alkene (*cis* and *trans*).

18. B is correct.

Spectroscopy (e.g., NMR) generally is used in the identification of compounds.

Distillation, crystallization, and extraction are commonly used techniques to isolate and purify compounds.

19. C is correct.

Fractional distillation would be the only reasonable method because each product would have a different boiling point.

All the products would have a similar polarity, so it would be difficult to separate by either chromatography or extraction.

20. D is correct.

S_N2 reactions are concerted reactions that have a single step and do not involve the formation of charged intermediates.

Carbocation intermediates are a feature of S_N1 and E_1 mechanisms.

21. A is correct.

The methyl group adjacent to the carbocation migrates via a methide shift to give a tertiary carbocation, which then loses a proton to form the most substituted alkene (i.e., both carbons of the alkene are tertiary).

22. D is correct.

The oxymercuration-demercuration [$Hg(OAc)_2$] of alkynes occurs with Markovnikov addition to generate a ketone enol.

This enol tautomerizes to form a ketone.

23. A is correct.

The reaction is a Friedel-Crafts acylation using acetic anhydride, $(CH_3CO)_2O$, as an acylating agent. The product is a methyl ketone.

All halogens are deactivators, but direct *ortho / para* because the halogen (like all *ortho- / para-* directors) has lone pairs of electrons (on the atom attached to the ring).

The lone pair helps stabilize the positive charge on the ring present in the resonance hybrid intermediates.

In general, deactivators (except for the halogens) are *meta*-directors.

24. C is correct.

The most notable intermolecular force for water is hydrogen bonding. Alcohols donate and receive hydrogen bonds.

Thiols (S–H bonds) have much smaller dipoles compared to O–H bonds, so they do not participate in hydrogen bonding.

25. A is correct.

The first step in the reaction is the coordination of the carbonyl oxygen atom with the positively charged counter ion of the reducing reagent and introduction of the hydride to the group.

The second step involves the protonation of the alkoxide (negative oxygen atom) intermediate with a weak acid.

26. A is correct.

In addition to the presence of polar functional groups, the molecular weight of a compound is an important influence on its boiling point.

Because carboxylic acids are compared, the one with the highest molecular weight has the highest boiling point.

27. A is correct.

Esters are similar in structure to carboxylic acids, but instead of having a hydroxyl group bonded to the carbonyl carbon atom, an alcohol derived group is present.

These groups are less electrophilic than ketones and aldehydes, and they have the same oxidation state as carboxylic acids.

Important esters in the body include triacylglycerides or triglycerides.

28. B is correct.

A quaternary ammonium salt has no lone pairs of electrons on the nitrogen atom and therefore cannot function as a nucleophile.

1°, 2° or 3° amines can attack alkyl halides by donating their lone pairs of valence electrons.

Ammonium salts have no available valence electrons and can act as acids (proton donors), but not a nucleophile.

29. B is correct.

The word *acetone* has two important components. The *ace~* part is similar to *acetyl* and indicates that the structure includes a methyl group that is bonded to a carbonyl group.

The suffix *~one* indicates that the carbonyl group is a ketone.

30. C is correct.

The bond dipole in H–F is the largest because of the large difference in electronegativity between hydrogen and fluorine. The electrostatic attraction pulls the atoms closer together, so the bond is the shortest and the strongest.

The bond dipole in H–I is the smallest because the electronegativity between the atoms is the lowest; therefore, H–I bond is the longest and weakest.

31. D is correct.

Use the rotation rule (clockwise = *R*, counterclockwise = *S*) to determine the configuration after assigning priorities.

When the lowest priority group is on the horizontal bond, the assigned configuration is reversed.

32. C is correct.

For carboxylic acid derivatives, the presence of the heteroatom either increases or decreases the stretching frequency of the carbonyl group.

If the lone pair conjugation with the carbonyl is the more dominant effect (e.g., amides), then the carbonyl stretching frequency is lower than 1710 cm^{-1}.

If the inductive effect of the heteroatom outweighs the conjugation effect into the carbonyl group (e.g., esters and acid chlorides), then the stretching frequency is higher than 1710 cm^{-1}.

33. B is correct.

The twist-boat is located at a local energy minimum (or trough) for the conformers of cyclohexane.

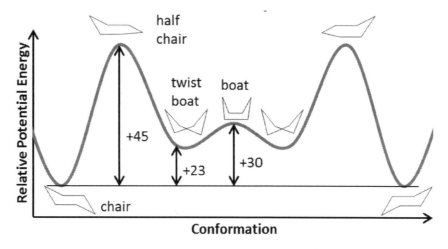

Relative energy diagram for conformers (i.e., chair flips) of cyclohexane

34. B is correct.

The reaction conditions are for halohydration (i.e., halohydrin formation) of an alkene.

The bromonium ion forms first; this is attacked (ring opens) by water as a nucleophile on the more substituted side.

35. B is correct.

Hydrogenation (i.e., reduction) involves the addition of hydrogens (H_2) to an unsaturated molecule.

Catalytic hydrogenation (H_2 / Pd or Pt) of an alkyne is susceptible to a further reduction to yield an alkane.

Alkynes can be reduced to stereospecific products with special reagents.

An alkyne yields a *cis* alkene which requires the Lindlar catalyst (i.e., H_2, Pd, $CaCo_3$, quinolone, and hexane) and a *trans* alkene with Ni (or Li) metal over NH_3 (*l*).

A: oxidation is an increase in the number of bonds to oxygen.

Increasing the number of bonds to oxygen often results from decreasing the number of bonds to hydrogens.

C: adding H_2 (i.e., hydrogenation) is an addition, not a substitution, reaction.

D: a hydration reaction adds water to an unsaturated (i.e., alkene or alkyne) molecule.

36. D is correct.

In electrophilic aromatic substitution, the aromatic ring acts as a nucleophile attacking an electrophile.

Due to its aromaticity, however, the aromatic ring is relatively unreactive and is a poor nucleophile.

Extremely reactive electrophiles (and the addition of a Lewis base) are used to overcome this limitation.

37. B is correct.

The tosyl group is added with the retention of stereochemistry because the C–O bond is not broken.

Tosylation of secondary alcohol makes it a better leaving group.

The chloride anion is a good nucleophile, able to displace the tosylate leaving group to form the secondary alkyl chloride.

D: shows a product that has retained stereospecificity (no inversion).

This retention of stereochemistry occurs when an S_N2 reaction (i.e., inversion) is followed by a second S_N2 reaction.

38. D is correct.

A Michael acceptor is an α, β unsaturated carbonyl – the double bond is between the first and second carbons from the carbonyl carbon.

The best Michael acceptor is the electrophile that best stabilizes the resulting negative charge at the alpha position when a nucleophilic attack (i.e., by Michael donor) occurs at the beta position.

The mechanism for the Michael reaction (below):

The Michael donor participates in a nucleophilic attack on the Michael acceptor

39. D is correct.

Carboxylic acids are more acidic than phenols.

The pK_a of carboxylic acids is ≈5 and the pK_a of phenols is ≈ 10.

The aryl (on the C=O) proton of benzaldehyde has a pK_a near the lower 40s, while the ketones (e.g., acetone) have pK_a values of ≈ 20.

40. C is correct.

Saponification (shown below) is the name for the base-promoted hydrolysis of esters.

This type of hydrolysis is typically applied to the formation of soap compounds.

For example, triacylglycerol is a lipid that can undergo saponification, which is the breakdown of fatty esters with bases, such as sodium hydroxide or potassium hydroxide.

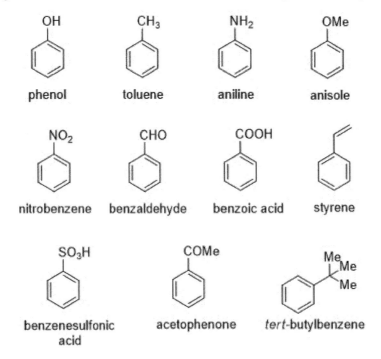

Base hydrolysis (saponification) of an ester to form a carboxylate salt and an alcohol

41. D is correct.

Ammonia is a basic compound with a low boiling point and exists as a gas at room temperature.

It is basic, colorless, has a pungent smell and can be toxic if ingested.

42. A is correct.

The names below each benzene derivative are the common names for the benzene-derived compounds (e.g., toluene is the common name for a benzene ring with a methyl substituent).

Common names for benzene derivatives

For the IUPAC name, the longest carbon chain in the compound is the six-membered benzene ring.

There are two substituent groups present in the molecule: the ethyl group and the methyl group.

Therefore, the IUPAC name is 1-ethyl-3-methylbenzene.

43. D is correct.

Tertiary carbocations are more stable than secondary carbocations, which are more stable than primary carbocations.

Carbocation stability: 3° > 2° > 1° > methyl

The more substituted the cation, the more it benefits from hyperconjugation stabilizing factors.

44. C is correct.

Enantiomers are chiral molecules (i.e., attached to four different groups) and are non-superimposable mirror images (i.e., *R* and *S*).

The two molecules are mirror images of each other, so they are enantiomers.

45. C is correct.

The primary structure of a protein is the amino acid sequence, which is formed by covalent peptide linkages.

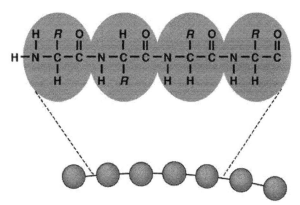

The amino acids (circles) are joined by covalent peptide bonds (lines)

A: only proteins containing more than one peptide subunit have a quaternary structure.

B: proteins are denatured by heating, and they lose their conformation above 35-40 °C, not retain it.

D: many proteins contain more than one peptide chain (i.e., have quaternary structure).

46. B is correct.

Not all lipids are entirely hydrophobic.

The ionic and polar heads of soaps and phospholipids, respectively, enable the molecules to interact with aqueous or polar environments.

Nevertheless, the bulk of these molecules are hydrophobic, because they largely consist of hydrocarbon chains or rings.

47. A is correct.

An aldotetrose is a four-carbon carbohydrate with an aldehyde.

D-(–)-tartaric acid converts to aldotetrose

48. A is correct.

Nucleotide consisting of sugar, phosphate and nitrogenous base

The hexose sugar, nitrogen base, and phosphoric acid group make up nucleotides, and these nucleotides are used to make larger molecules known as nucleic acids.

49. C is correct.

The reaction mechanism by which 2,4-dinitrofluorobenzene reacts with an amine is known as nucleophilic aromatic substitution (NAS).

The nitro groups are electron withdrawing, and therefore the benzene ring is electrophilic.

50. A is correct.

For unsaturated fats, the molecules are more likely to exist as oils (i.e., liquids) at room temperature.

Saturated fats tend to be solid at room temperature because the reduced forms of these molecules have better stacking properties, which allow them to form solid states.

51. C is correct.

The key to determining a monosaccharide's category involves counting the number of carbon atoms in the structure.

There are four carbon atoms in the five-membered ring, and there is a methylene-containing ($\sim CH_2 \sim$) substituent bonded to the ring.

Because there are five carbon atoms present, the molecule is a pentose.

52. D is correct.

Identical copies of DNA are necessary for the division of cells; these cells are also known as daughter cells.

When the daughter strand is synthesized, complementary nitrogenous base containing nucleotides (A↔T and C↔G) are incorporated into the growing strand.

Replication (i.e., synthesis of DNA) occurs during the S phase (i.e., within interphase) of the cell cycle.

53. B is correct.

Amino acids are the building blocks of proteins.

Humans need 20 amino acids, some are made by the body (i.e., nonessential), and others must be obtained from the diet (i.e., essential).

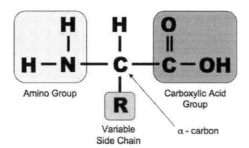

Amino acids contain an amine group, a carboxylic acid, an α-carbon, and an R group

See the diagram below for examples of the 20 common amino acids divided into the nonpolar, polar and electrically charged side chains.

Nonpolar side chains

Glycine (G)
Gly

Alanine (A)
Ala

Valine (V)
Val

Leucine (L)
Leu

Isoleucine (I)
Ile

Methionine (M)
Met

Phenylalanine (F)
Phe

Tryptophan (W)
Trp

Proline (P)
Pro

Polar side chains

Serine (S)
Ser

Threonine (T)
Thr

Cysteine (C)
Cys

Tyrosine (Y)
Tyr

Asparagine (N)
Asn

Glutamine (Q)
Gln

Electrically charged side chains

Acidic

Aspartate (D)
Asp

Glutamate (E)
Glu

Basic

Lysine (K)
Lys

Arginine (R)
Arg

Histidine (H)
His

The 20 naturally occurring amino acids

The above table is shown not for memorization but identification of characteristics (e.g., polar, nonpolar) for the side chains.

54. B is correct.

The alkene molecules typically found in fatty acids tend to be *Z* alkenes.

Saturated Fatty Acid

Unsaturated Fatty Acid

Saturated versus unsaturated fatty acids

The double bond of the alkene (i.e., unsaturated) prevents the fatty acid molecules from stacking closely together.

The double bond of the alkene results in lowering the melting point for the fat molecule.

This may also influence the state of matter of the oil, as unsaturated fats tend to be liquid at room temperature and saturated fats tend to be solids.

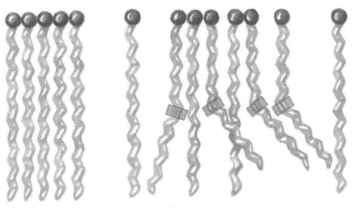

Saturated fatty acids   Mixture of saturated and unsaturated fatty acids

55. D is correct.

If the chiral carbon farthest from the carbonyl points to the right, then it is a D-sugar.

If the chiral carbon farthest from the carbonyl points to the left, then it is an L-sugar.

The terminal alcohol is not an asymmetric carbon atom, because it is typically bonded to two hydrogen atoms.

D-Glucose   L-Glucose

D-glucose and L-glucose are enantiomers (i.e., non-superimposable mirror images)

56. B is correct.

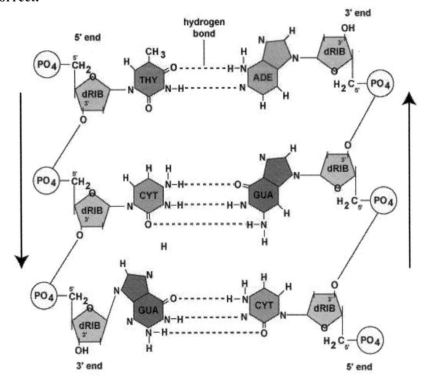

Two antiparallel strands of DNA are shown with the vertical arrows to indicate the 3'-hydroxyl of the sugar (i.e., from the point of chain elongation). The nucleotide is the building block of DNA and is comprised of sugar (i.e., deoxyribose), phosphate and base (adenosine, cytosine, guanine, and thymine).

For nucleotide pairs that contain adenine and thymine, there are two hydrogen bonds (A=T) holding the base pairs together. Cytosine and guanine nitrogen base pairs use three hydrogen bonds (C≡G) to support the nucleic acid structure.

57. A is correct.

Human hair can be curly without the application of reducing agents due to the cross-linking positions of the disulfide bonds.

The notation [O] represents oxidation (i.e., from reducing agent such as *beta*-mercaptoethanol), while [H] represents reduction (i.e., from an oxidation agent such as O_3).

The reducing agents cleave the disulfide bond linkages between peptide strands, enabling the hair to be restructured.

58. D is correct.

For omega acids, the number indicates the position of the first double bond from the non-carboxylic acid end (i.e., near the alkyl chain end) of the molecule (hence the "omega" part of the name).

Examples of omega-3 and omega-6 fatty acids

59. B is correct.

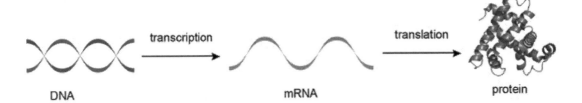

Deoxyribose is the sugar of DNA, while ribose is the sugar of RNA.

The difference is the absence of a 2'-hydroxyl (DNA) or the presence of the 2'-hydroxyl (RNA).

Both DNA and RNA have a 3'-hydroxyl necessary for chain elongation.

Deoxyribose is a monosaccharide that contains one fewer hydroxyl group than ribose.

Deoxyribose is the sugar in DNA, and ribose is the sugar contained in RNA.

60. B is correct.

```
                 transcription                    translation
DNA      ─────────────────────→    mRNA    ─────────────────────→    protein
```

The central dogma of molecule biology: DNA → RNA → protein

tRNA and ribosomes are used to make peptide chains from mRNA.

Nucleotide triplets known as codons are combined with a complementary tRNA (i.e., containing the anticodon that is complementary in base pairing with the codon of the mRNA).

Each tRNA brings an appropriate (i.e., anticodon ↔ amino acid) to the growing polypeptide during translation.

The amino acid residues are combined in the order of the codon sequence.

Please, leave your Customer Review on Amazon

Explanations: Diagnostic Test #8

1. A is correct.

Drawing the line formula of the carbon chain and proper interpretation of the subscripts.

There are two methyl groups and five methylene (~CH_2~) in the molecule for a total of seven carbons.

Use the following formula to calculate the degrees of unsaturation:

C_nH_{2n+2}: for an alkane (0 degrees of unsaturation)

2. D is correct.

Except for structure D, the other structures are intermediates for electrophilic aromatic substitution.

These resonance intermediates typically have one cation and no negative charges in the ring.

Resonance hybrids of aniline during electrophilic aromatic substitution

---

3. D is correct.

There are only two possible ways to draw butane, either as the straight chain or the tertiary alkyl constitutional isomer. Note that the term "constitutional isomers" is recognized by IUPAC, while the term "structural isomers" was commonly used historically.

Two constitutional isomers of n-butane (left) and isobutene (right)

4. C is correct.

1-chlorobutane (below) has a chiral center and produces four (4) NMR peaks.

$$H-\overset{\overset{\displaystyle H}{|}}{\underset{\underset{\displaystyle H}{|}}{C}}-\overset{\overset{\displaystyle H}{|}}{\underset{\underset{\displaystyle H}{|}}{C}}-\overset{\overset{\displaystyle H}{|}}{\underset{\underset{\displaystyle H}{|}}{C}}-\overset{\overset{\displaystyle H}{|}}{\underset{\underset{\displaystyle H}{|}}{C}}-Cl$$

A: 3,3-dichloropentane (below) is a symmetrical molecule that produces two (2) NMR proton peaks.

B: 4,4-dichloroheptane (below) is a symmetrical molecule that produces three (3) NMR proton peaks.

D: 1,4-dichlorobutane (below) produces two (2) NMR proton peaks.

5. C is correct.

The extraction with sodium bicarbonate ionizes the carboxylic acid by deprotonating it to its carboxylate form.

This negatively charged anion has a greater affinity for the aqueous layer.

$$H_3C \overset{CH_3}{\diagup}\overset{O}{\diagdown} OH \quad -H^+ \text{ (loss of proton)} \rightarrow \quad H_3C \overset{CH_3}{\diagup}\overset{O}{\diagdown} O-$$

6. D is correct.

Unimolecular elimination occurs via E_1 and involves the formation of a carbocation in the slow (rate determining) step.

A: a single step (concerted) process describes bimolecular (E_2), not E_1 elimination.

B: homolytic (compared to the more common heterolytic) cleavage of a covalent bond yields free radicals.

C: free radicals occur with peroxides (H_2O_2) or dihalides / UV, and radicals are an intermediate in unimolecular (E_1) elimination.

7. A is correct.

A conjugated system contains two or more double or triple bonds separated by a single bond (i.e., sp^2 hybridization at each carbon in the conjugated system).

1,2-butadiene is not conjugated because the double bonds are adjacent to each other (not separated by a single bond). Adjacent double bonds are cumulated and are unstable.

B: cyclobutadiene is conjugated because the molecule has two double bonds separated by single bonds.

C: benzene is conjugated because a single bond separates each double bond.

D: 1,3-cyclohexadiene is conjugated because a single bond separates the double bonds between carbons 1-2 and carbons 3-4.

8. B is correct.

The substrate contains a carbon-carbon triple bond at the end of the chain. Therefore, to synthesize 2-hexanone from 1-hexyne, oxygen is introduced to the internal carbon atom of the alkene. This reaction requires aqueous acidic conditions so that the addition proceeds as a Markovnikov addition.

The protonation of the alkyne results in the formation of a secondary vinyl cation. This cation is trapped by water to produce an enol that tautomerizes to form the ketone product.

9. D is correct.

The methyl group is as an electron-donating substituent and therefore is an *ortho / para* director.

Due to steric hindrance at the *ortho* position, the formation of the *para* product is the major product.

10. C is correct.

Carboxylic acids are also functional groups that contain an –OH group bonded to carbonyls (C=O).

Oximes C=N–OH are functional groups that can contain an –OH group; they are used for reductive amination.

11. A is correct.

The treatment of a terminal alkyne with a dialkyl borane results in the formation of a vinyl borane.

The vinyl borane is oxidized to the enol through exposure to hydrogen peroxide (H_2O_2) and the hydroxide (^-OH) base.

This group tautomerizes to form an aldehyde.

12. C is correct.

The reaction used to combine alcohols and carboxylic acids is the Fischer esterification reaction.

Acid catalysis is needed to activate the carboxylic acid carbonyl group for the nucleophilic attack.

13. C is correct.

An amide is an amine that is directly bonded to a carbonyl group.

The carbonyl group accepts the lone pair of electrons on the nitrogen atom through resonance action.

Amides ($pK_a \approx 20–25$) are less electrophilic than esters.

Primary and secondary amides have acidic N–H protons ($pK_a \approx 35$).

14. A is correct.

Boiling points of compounds are determined by two general factors: molecular weight and intermolecular interactions.

The higher the molecular weight, the harder it is to "push" it into the gas phase, and hence the higher the boiling point.

Similarly, the stronger the intermolecular interactions, the more energy is required to disrupt them and separate the molecules in the gas phase, hence the higher the boiling point.

Dimethylamine has one N–H bond (donor) and one lone pair on the nitrogen (acceptor):

The other answer choices can also accept and donate hydrogen bonds, which increases their boiling points.

15. B is correct.

The longest carbon chain is composed of five carbon atoms.

There are two alkenes, so the root name is "pentadiene."

There is a methyl group in the second position along the carbon chain.

16. C is correct.

The bonds between atoms (i.e., intramolecular) are stronger than the bonds between molecules (i.e., intermolecular).

Examples of intermolecular bonds are hydrogen, dipole-dipole, dipole-induced dipole and van der Waals.

Sigma bonds are single bonds and involve overlap along the internuclear axis between the atoms.

S*igma* bonds are stronger than the *pi* bond of a double bond.

A: hydrogen bonding is a common intramolecular *bond* in which a *hydrogen* atom of one molecule is attracted to an electronegative atom (nitrogen, oxygen or fluorine).

B: dipole-dipole bonds are attractive forces between the positive end of one polar molecule and the negative end of another polar molecule.

D: ionic bonds result from the complete transfer of valence electron(s) between atoms; it generates two oppositely charged ions. The metal loses electrons to become a positively charged cation, whereas the nonmetal accepts those electrons to become a negatively charged anion.

Ionic bonds can be disrupted in water and are much weaker in aqueous solutions than in a dry environment.

17. C is correct.

Geometric (configurational) isomers have the same molecular formula, but different connectivity between the atoms due to the orientation of substituents around a carbon-carbon double bond (or ring).

In *Z* (*cis* when substituents are the same) isomers, the same substituents are on one side of the double bond or ring, while in *E* (*trans* when substituents are the same) isomers, the same substituents are on opposite sides of the double bond or ring.

18. B is correct.

Carboxylic acid protons are some of the most deshielded protons.

These functional groups can partially ionize, causing the hydrogen to develop a high degree of positive (cationic) character.

19. C is correct.

Molecules with greater molecular mass and that experience stronger intermolecular forces (e.g., hydrogen bonding) tend to have higher boiling points.

These compounds are less volatile and found near the bottom of the fractioning tower.

20. C is correct.

Since an S_N1 reaction proceeds through a planar, sp^2 hybridized carbocation intermediate (which can be attacked from either side), it forms a racemic mixture (i.e., both *R* / *S* stereoisomers are present).

21. A is correct.

In $(CH_3)_2C=C(CH_3)CH_2CH_3$, both carbons of the alkene are equally substituted (i.e., tertiary), so the two putative carbocations are approximately equally stable.

The addition of a hydrogen halide across a double bond also has the potential to create two chiral centers, one at each of the former sp^2 carbons.

The carbocation forms preferentially at the more substituted carbon.

22. A is correct.

Radical hydrogenation of a C≡C triple bond in the presence of sodium metal and liquid ammonia adds two hydrogen atoms (i.e., reduction) across the double bond with *anti*-stereoselectivity, producing an *E* alkene.

The mechanism for reducing an alkyne to a trans (E) alkene

Lindlar reagent (i.e., H_2, Pd, $CaCo_3$, quinolone, and hexane) reduces the alkyne to the *cis* (Z) alkene.

The reaction for reducing an alkyne to a cis (Z) alkene

The Lindlar reagent, unlike the reagents of Na and NH_3, can be used to reduce a terminal alkyne to an alkene. Na and NH_3 is a "poison catalyst" and are unreactive with a terminal alkyne.

23. C is correct.

The unknown cyclic hydrocarbon does not react with bromine in dichloromethane, carbon tetrachloride, or water. This means that it cannot contain any non-conjugated double or triple bonds; otherwise, the bromine would have added across the double bonds.

Since the unknown compound reacts when $FeBr_3$ is added, it must be benzene. The $FeBr_3$ acts as a Lewis acid and catalyzes aromatic electrophilic addition reactions.

Bromine is not a strong enough electrophile to disrupt the conjugated double bonding in the benzene ring, but the addition of the iron (III) bromide catalyst converts the bromine into a strong enough electrophile that it adds to the benzene ring.

24. B is correct.

The reaction between (S)-2-heptanol and $SOCl_2$ (thionyl chloride) proceeds via an S_N2 reaction mechanism.

An addition-elimination sequence occurs at the S=O double bond, then substitution by Cl^- of the alcohol gives the inverted (R)-2-chloroheptane product.

25. B is correct.

The iodoform reaction involves trihalogenating the methyl group to turn it into a good leaving group.

After tribromination of the methyl group has occurred, the group is expelled from the molecule by the addition of hydroxide to the ketone.

Molecule 4 undergoes tribromination before being replaced by the ⁻OH

Acidic conditions only provide the monobrominated compound from the starting ketone; therefore, basic conditions need to be used during the reaction.

26. B is correct.

Carboxylic acids have some of the highest boiling points due to their ability to hydrogen bond and form dimeric structures.

Alcohols also contain the polar O–H bond and form hydrogen bonds, thus contributing to their high boiling point.

27. D is correct. The hydrolysis of esters using basic conditions (e.g., sodium hydroxide) is not a catalytic reaction. It is a base-promoted reaction because the hydroxide is consumed in the reaction and is not regenerated.

On the contrary, acid-catalyzed hydrolysis reactions of esters regenerate the acid catalyst.

28. C is correct.

Tertiary amines possess no N–H bonds, while secondary amines have one N–H bond, and primary amines contain two N–H bonds.

29. C is correct.

The longest carbon chain is composed of five carbon atoms.

The highest priority group is an aldehyde.

The substituent groups are the hydroxymethyl group, the ethyl group, the alkene, and the alkyne.

30. D is correct.

Trimethylamine is similar to ammonia, which has a central nitrogen atom attached to three hydrogens; trimethylamine has three methyl substituents. The central nitrogen in both examples retains a lone pair of electrons. As lone pairs, the electrons occupy more space than electrons bonded to a substituent. Therefore, the negatively charged electrons repel the bonds holding the substituents attached to the central nitrogen atom.

The hydrogens on ammonia have small van der Walls radii and are forced closer together – bond angle is 107°. For trimethylamine, the methyl groups are larger and cannot be forced as close together by the lone pair of electrons on the central nitrogen atom. Therefore, the bond angle is approximately 108°.

31. A is correct.

Isomers are molecules with the same molecular formula but different connections (e.g., functional groups) between the atoms. Therefore, the number of carbon atoms, hydrogen atoms, and any heteroatoms present must be the same.

32. C is correct.

The stretching frequency is much higher than a typical carbonyl group.

The chlorine atom is a poor electron donor to the carbonyl through lone pair conjugation, and it tends to withdraw more electron density through induction.

The lone pair of electrons on the oxygen atom can donate to carbon-chlorine *sigma* orbital, thus shortening the bond.

The shorter (or stronger) a bond, the higher is its stretching frequency in the IR spectrum.

If the lone pair conjugation with the carbonyl is the more dominant effect (e.g., amides), then the carbonyl stretching frequency is lower than 1710 cm^{-1}.

If the inductive effect of the heteroatom outweighs the conjugation effect into the carbonyl group, the carbonyl stretching frequency is higher than 1710 cm^{-1}.

33. B is correct.

S_N1 reactions favor substituted alkyl halides because of the stability of the carbocation intermediates, whereas S_N2 reactions favor unsubstituted reactants due to minimal steric hindrance for the approaching nucleophile.

A: S$_N$1 reaction rates are greatly affected by electronic factors (degree of substitution and inductive influence of electronegative atoms), while S$_N$2 reaction rates are greatly affected by steric (hindrance) factors.

C: S$_N$1 reactions proceed via a carbocation intermediate, but S$_N$2 reactions (by definition as bimolecular) proceed via a single-step reaction involving a concerted mechanism with a transition state instead of a carbocation.

D: S$_N$2 reactions are bimolecular reactions that proceed via a single-step reaction with a transition state (i.e., bond making and breaking events) rather than via an intermediate.

34. C is correct. Oxymercuration-reduction of an alkene yields Markovnikov orientation and *anti*-addition, as shown in the cycloalkene below.

By comparison, hydroboration-oxidation of an alkene is consistent with *anti*-Markovnikov and *syn*-addition.

Step one uses BH$_3$ to add BH$_2$ and H as *syn* addition across the double bond of the alkene.

Step two uses peroxides and nucleophilic oxygen for *syn* addition of a hydroxyl. Note other nucleophiles (e.g., methanol) can add with *syn*-addition as an ether substituent across the double bond.

35. C is correct. When terminal alkynes are treated with Lewis acids, such as mercury salts in aqueous conditions, the ketone forms as the major product instead of the aldehyde.

The mercury cation is electron deficient and forms a complex with the alkyne. This coordination increases the electrophilicity of the carbon atoms of the alkyne, and water adds to the internal carbon atom because the partial positive charge is larger at this position. This addition results in the formation of an enol (i.e., hydroxyl attached to a carbon in a double bond) that tautomerizes to the ketone.

A reduction step with sodium borohydride (NaBH$_4$) is not necessary, because the carbon-mercury bond could break (to give Hg^{2+} and the enolate) when the ketone forms.

36. D is correct.

The activating, deactivating and directing (*ortho-* / *para-* and *meta*-directing) properties of aromatic substituents in electrophilic aromatic substitutions (EAS) and nucleophilic aromatic substitutions (NAS) are based on resonance stabilization or destabilization.

Through resonance, electron-withdrawing groups introduce a partial positive charge on positions *ortho* and *para*.

Resonance forms of nitrobenzene during EAS

The *pi* bonds undergo delocalization for two hybrid structures:

In EAS, the aromatic ring acts as a nucleophile, and the partially positive sites are less nucleophilic, making the electron-withdrawing group *meta*-directing. In NAS, the aromatic ring acts as an electrophile, and the partially positive sites are more electrophilic, making the electron-withdrawing group an *ortho-* / *para*-director.

37. A is correct.

The reaction of 1-pentanol + acetic acid

The alkoxy group has five carbon atoms, and an acyl portion is an acetyl group.

Acetyl group

Acetate is the root for this molecule.

38. A is correct.

Hemiacetals (shown below) are intermediates that can be produced in acetal formation reactions of aldehydes with two equivalents of alcohols.

hemiacetal   acetal

Hemiacetals are not stable groups and typically cannot be isolated. The hemiacetal O–H bond collapses to expel alcohol and regenerates the carbonyl of the aldehyde. This normally occurs because the carbonyl formation increases the entropy of the system (starting from one molecule and converting it to two molecules), and the carbonyl is almost as thermodynamically stable as the hemiacetal form.

39. D is correct.

The negative charge of the carboxylate anion is stabilized by the electronegativity of the oxygen atom and by resonance stabilization. The negative charge delocalizes over the two oxygen atoms of the carboxylate functional group.

Resonance structures of the carboxylate anion

40. B is correct.

Group 1 is a ketone; 2 is an amide and 3 is an ester.

Ketones are more electrophilic functional groups than esters.

Esters are more electrophilic than amides.

41. D is correct.

The nitrogen atom of amines is basic because it possesses a lone pair of electrons that add to the acidic protons of acids, resulting in its protonation.

Ammonium cation

The conjugate acid of amines is the ammonium cation, and the nitrogen atom is covalently bonded to four other atoms. Because the nitrogen atom is bonded to four other atoms, it develops a positive formal charge.

Although the nitrogen atom has a formal charge, this positive charge character is distributed over the less electronegative substituent groups.

42. B is correct.

The longest carbon chain has 6 carbon atoms.

There are two methyl substituents in the molecule, and there is an isopropoxide substituent at the C_4 position.

The stereochemistry of the alkene is *E*.

43. A is correct.

Only the hydrogen atom can bond to other atoms with its unhybridized $1s$ orbital.

The *sigma* bonding of all other elements is described by the hybridization of their atomic orbitals before bonding with other atoms.

Therefore, when a carbon atom forms a *sigma* bond, it does so through the overlap of one of its hybridized orbitals.

However, *pi* bonding involves the indirect overlap of unhybridized *p* orbitals.

44. C is correct.

Cis means that the groups are on the same side of the alkene (or face of a cyclic structure).

Trans means that the groups are on opposite sides.

Cis and *trans* isomerism can occur with disubstituted cycloalkanes.

cis-2-butene   *trans*-2-butene

Cis and *trans* isomerism can occur with alkenes (or with respect to a ring).

45. C is correct.

A pH of 8 indicates a basic solution whereby the carboxylic acid is deprotonated, and the amino group remains protonated (until the pH reaches the pK_a of the amine at ≈ 9.8).

Zwitterion: carboxyl is deprotonated (negative), and the amino is protonated (positive)

46. B is correct.

This fatty acid is omega three because a *Z* alkene double bond appears three carbon atoms away from the methyl end of the molecule.

Linolenic is an omega-3 fatty acid while both oleic and linoleic acid are omega-6 fatty acids

Because these molecules contain one or more double bonds, they are unsaturated fats.

47. A is correct.

Monosaccharides cannot be broken down into simpler sugar subunits.

However, monosaccharides can undergo oxidative degradation to produce carbon dioxide and carbon monoxide when treated with nitric acid.

48. D is correct.

DNA	DNA	mRNA	tRNA
A	T	A	U
C	G	C	G
G	C	G	C
T	A	U	A

Complementary base pairing for nucleotides

DNA → DNA (replication); DNA → RNA (transcription); RNA → protein (translation)

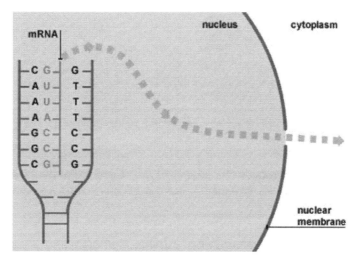

Guanine and Cytosine

Adenosine (left) and Uracil (replaces thymine in RNA)

A single strand of DNA is the template for RNA synthesis during transcription.
The mRNA (after processing) is translocated to the cytoplasm for translation to proteins.

49. D is correct.

Amino acids with hydrophobic side chains are not typically found near the external regions of proteins, but rather in the interior regions.

Hydrophobic side chains containing amino acids are located along the protein interfaces with lipid layers, such as the external amino acids of proteins embedded in lipid membranes.

50. D is correct.

Estradiol (shown below) is a steroid hormone derived from cholesterol.

Cholesterol (shown below) is a lipid made up of four fused rings. Three of the fused rings are six-membered rings, and the fourth ring is a five-membered ring.

Cholesterol is a steroid, which makes up one of two types of lipid molecules.

A triglyceride (i.e., glycerol backbone with three fatty acid chains) is the other type of lipid.

51. C is correct.

This is how monosaccharide sugars exist as two different diastereomers.

These diastereomers are classified as α (alpha) and β (beta) diastereomers.

Two diastereomers are possible because the alcohol that cyclizes (i.e., mutarotation) to form the ring may add to either face of the aldehyde.

Epimers are isomers that differ at a single chiral center (shown below):

Epimers of D-glucose (left) and D-galactose (right) with inversion at the 4th chiral carbon

52. B is correct.

Cellular respiration involves the breakdown of sugar molecules to produce energy. When this occurs, water and carbon dioxide are given off as byproducts.

A campfire (i.e., wood is mainly the sugar of cellulose) gives off the same byproducts of carbon dioxide and water because it is a combustion reaction.

$$\text{wood} + O_2 \rightarrow CO_2 + H_2O$$

53. B is correct.

The isoelectric point is the pH at which the net charge of the amino acid is 0.

Aspartic acid is an amino acid that contains an additional carboxylic acid in the side chain.

For this amino acid to maintain an overall neutral polarity, the carboxylic acid must maintain its protonated form, which requires the solution to be acidic.

Therefore, the isoelectric point of aspartic acid is the lowest for the given list of amino acids.

54. C is correct.

When micelles form in aqueous environments, the hydrophobic tails cluster together.

The polar head regions of these molecules are exposed on the surface of the micelle and exposed to the aqueous environment.

55. B is correct.

Reducing sugars possess a free aldehyde or a free ketone group. All monosaccharides are reducing sugars, along with some disaccharides, oligosaccharides, and polysaccharides.

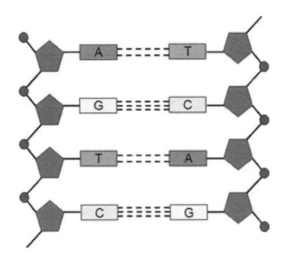

Maltose exists in equilibrium between the closed ring (left) and open form.
Open form (with the aldehyde on the far right) is the reducing sugar.

If a cyclic sugar possesses an acetal instead of a hemiacetal at the anomeric carbon, the sugar will not be a reducing sugar.

56. A is correct.

Double-stranded DNA with two hydrogen bonds between A=T and three hydrogen bonds between C≡G. The backbone is comprised of deoxyribose sugar and phosphates (shown as circles between the sugars).

57. D is correct.

In glutamate metabolism, the amino group of glutamic acid is removed through an oxidative deamination reaction with glutamate dehydrogenase.

Ammonia is released during this process and forms urea to be excreted as urine from the body.

58. D is correct.

Triacylglycerides (also known as triglycerides) are made from one equivalent of glycerol and three equivalents of fatty acids.

The molecule contains a three-carbon chain that is flanked by oxygens. The three fatty acids (–COR chains) are attached via an ester linkage.

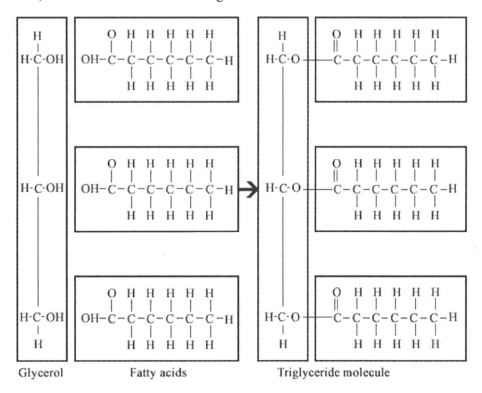

Glycerol Fatty acids Triglyceride molecule

A triester is produced when condensation (via dehydration) occurs between the glycerol and three fatty acids.

59. D is correct.

People who cannot produce the lactase enzyme are known to be lactose intolerant. This protein is responsible for the catalytic breakdown of lactose.

Lactose is a β(1→4) disaccharide comprised of galactose (left) and glucose.

Both lactose and cellulose are two forms of sugar that possess the difficult to digest β(1→4) glycosidic linkage.

60. D is correct.

Codons (schematic shown below) are three nucleotide sequences located on the mRNA, while anticodons are three nucleotides sequences on the tRNA. The codon-anticodon sequences hybridize by forming hydrogen bonds to the complementary base pair.

Relationship between codon (on mRNA), anticodon (on tRNA) and the resulting amino acid:

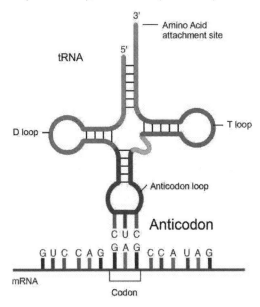

Codon (mRNA):	5'–AUG–CAA–CCC–GAC–UCC–AGC–3'
Anticodon (tRNA):	3'–UAC–GUU–GGG–CUG–AGG–UAG–5'
Amino acids:	Met–Gln–Pro–Asp–Phe–Ser

	U	C	A	G
U	UUU = phe UUC = phe UUA = leu UUG = leu	UCU = ser UCC = ser UCA = ser UCG = ser	UAU = tyr UAC = tyr UAA = stop UAG = stop	UGU = cys UGC = cys UGA = stop UGG = trp
C	CUU = leu CUC = leu CUA = leu CUG = leu	CCU = pro CCC = pro CCA = pro CCG = pro	CAU = his CAC = his CAA = gln CAG = gln	CGU = arg CGC = arg CGA = arg CGG = arg
A	AUU = ile AUC = ile AUA = ile AUG = met	ACU = thr ACC = thr ACA = thr ACG = thr	AAU = asn AAC = asn AAA = lys AAG = lys	AGU = ser AGC = ser AGA = arg AGG = arg
G	GUU = val GUC = val GUA = val GUG = val	GCU = ala GCC = ala GCA = ala GCG = ala	GAU = asp GAC = asp GAA = glu GAG = glu	GGU = gly GGC = gly GGA = gly GGG = gly

The genetic code is the nucleotide sequence of the codon (mRNA) that complementary base pairs with the nucleotide sequence of the anticodon (tRNA). From the genetic code, the identity of the amino acid encoded by a gene (synthesized during translation into mRNA) can be deduced.

Explanations: Diagnostic Test #9

1. D is correct.

A: the molecule is *ortho*-fluorobenzoic acid.

B: the substituents should be given the lowest possible numbering system and alphabetized to give 2-chloro-1,3-dinitrobenzene.

C: the substituents should be alphabetized to give 1-bromo-2-iodobenzene.

2. D is correct.

Reasonable resonance forms do not allow nuclei to change positions and satisfy the octet rule.

Based on the valence number, hydrogen can only have one bond, and carbon can only have four bonds.

Negative charges should be placed on more electronegative atoms.

3. A is correct.

These molecules are isomers because they have the same number and kinds of atoms, but the bonding is different for each.

B: epimers are two isomers that differ in configuration at only one stereogenic center. All other stereocenters in epimer molecules, if any, are the same.

C: anomers are diastereoisomers for cyclic forms of sugars differing in the configuration at the anomeric carbon (C–1 atom of an aldose or the C–2 atom of a 2-ketose). The cyclic forms of carbohydrates can exist in either α– or β–, based on the position of the substituent at the anomeric center. α–anomers have the hydroxyl pointing down, while β–anomers have the hydroxyl pointing up.

D: allotropes are two or more different physical forms in which an element can exist. Graphite, charcoal, and diamond are all allotropes of carbon.

4. C is correct.

3,3-dibromoheptane (below) produces 6 NMR signals.

A: 1,1,2-tribromobutane (below) produces 4 NMR signals.

B: bromobutane (below) produces 4 NMR signals.

H₃C〰〰Br

D: dibutyl ether (below) produces 4 NMR signals.

H₃C〰〰O〰〰CH₃

5. B is correct.

Fractional distillation separates compounds that have boiling points very close together (differences less than 25 °C).

The extra surface area in the instrument enhances the separation of the compounds.

6. B is correct.

The concentrations of both the substrate and nucleophile control the rate of the reaction because the rate-determining step is bimolecular.

S_N2 undergoes second-order kinetics whereby:

$$\text{rate} = k \, [\text{substrate}] \times [\text{nucleophile}]$$

7. C is correct.

Conjugation is the alternation of double and single bonds, which results in delocalization of electrons via resonance through the sp^2 hybridized carbons, resulting in increased stability for the molecule.

1,3-hexadiene has two conjugated double bonds.

A: 1,2-hexadiene has two cumulated, rather than conjugated, π bonds. Cumulated molecules have a sp carbon in the center of the two double bonds – this is unstable and increases the overall energy of the molecule.

B: 1,3,5-heptatriene has three π bonds.

D: 1,5-hexadiene has two isolated π bonds.

8. C is correct.

1-butyne is a gas at room temperature, and 1-propyne has an even lower boiling point, so it is also a gas.

9. D is correct.

Phenol (i.e., hydroxybenzene) has an OH group on the benzene ring. The hydroxyl oxygen has two nonbonded pairs of electrons, either of which can be donated (via resonance) to the aromatic ring after addition of an electrophile.

Electron-donating groups stabilize the cations formed upon addition of a substituent to the *ortho* and *para* positions and therefore are *ortho/para*-directing activators.

The OH group is not particularly bulky, and there is a limited steric hindrance that reduces substitution at the *ortho* position.

10. A is correct. The molecule has an alkene on the right side, an alcohol near the lower right portion, and a fused ether functional group.

11. C is correct.

Benedict's test is used to detect reducing sugars. An oxidized copper reagent is reduced by a sugar's aldehyde, and the aldehyde is oxidized to a carboxylic acid in the process. All monosaccharides are reducing sugars, while some disaccharides (e.g., lactose and maltose), oligosaccharides and polysaccharides are also reducing sugars.

Reducing sugars (and alpha hydroxyl ketones) give a positive Benedict's test: a red-brown precipitate forms. Fehling's solution also gives a positive test for reducing sugars by changing from blue to clear and forming a red-brown precipitate.

Tollens' reagent forms silver ions (mirror) as a positive test for reducing sugars. The Tollens' test for aldehydes involves the reduction of silver cations [Ag^+] to reduced silver; the metal precipitates out of solution and coats the inner surface of the reaction flask.

Benedict's test, like the Tollens' test, involves the oxidation of an aldehyde to form a carboxylic acid. Sugars able to do this are those that have the aldehyde or hemiacetal functional groups, and these molecules are known as reducing sugars.

12. B is correct.

The carboxylic acid functional group accounts for at least two sites of hydrogen bonding.

Because all the answers include carboxylic acids, the hydrocarbon regions of the molecules must be considered.

The molecule with the largest hydrocarbon region has more intermolecular forces (most of which are London forces) and has the largest boiling point.

Stearic acid is a saturated fatty acid and has the highest boiling point.

13. A is correct.

Both acid chlorides and anhydrides combine with alcohols to form esters and with amines to form amides.

Acid chlorides are more reactive than anhydrides, and the chloride is a better leaving group than the carboxylate anion.

These factors contribute to the enhanced reactivity of the acid chloride.

14. C is correct.

Oxygen and nitrogen atoms can act as proton acceptors if they are not conjugated with electron withdrawing groups.

The amine is the most basic and nucleophilic functional group.

15. A is correct.

The longest chain is the cyclohexane; the chlorines are on the same side (*cis*) and are three carbons (1,3) apart.

16. B is correct.

The nitrogen atom does not contain a formal charge (the formal charge calculation for this atom is 0).

However, the charge is slightly negative because the nitrogen atom withdraws electron density from substituent groups via induction, and the lone pair represents a region of electron density.

17. D is correct.

The bromine and hydrogen atom alternate the carbon atoms they are bonded to, so they are constitutional isomers.

These molecules cannot be chiral because they have a mirror plane of symmetry.

18. C is correct.

Molecules containing the carbonyl functional groups, such as ketones, typically have C=O resonance frequencies at 1710 cm^{-1}.

However, if the carbonyl group is in conjugation with another group (in this case, the alkene), then the stretching frequency is lower.

Resonance contributes to the carbon-oxygen single bond character of the carbonyl, and single bonds are weaker than double bonds.

19. A is correct.

Although amines are organic molecules, they have enhanced water solubility in the presence of acid.

The protonation causes the nitrogen to develop a positive formal charge, which enhances its dipole interactions with water.

20. D is correct.

The heat of combustion ($\Delta H_c°$) is the energy released (as heat) when a compound undergoes complete combustion with oxygen.

The chemical reaction is typically a hydrocarbon reacting with oxygen to form carbon dioxide, water, and heat. General formula:

$$C_nH_{2n+2} + ((3n + 1)/2)O_2 \rightarrow (n + 1)H_2O + nCO_2 + \text{energy}$$

The heat of combustion of a compound depends on three main factors: molecular weight, angle strain, and degree of branching.

In most cases, the compound with a higher molecular weight (i.e., more C–C and C–H bonds) has the larger heat of combustion.

For straight-chain alkanes, each addition of methylene groups ($\sim CH_2\sim$) adds approximately – 157 kcal/mole to the heat of combustion.

For cycloalkanes, the heat of combustion also increases with increasing angle strain.

Reference: $1 \text{ kJ·mol}^{-1} = 0.239 \text{ kcal·mol}^{-1}$

$\Delta H_c°$ for alkanes increase by about 657 kJ/mol (157 kcal/mol) per $\sim CH_2\sim$ group.

For example, heptane has 4 more $\sim CH_2\sim$ groups than propane:

$$4 \times -157 \text{ kcal per mole} = -628 \text{ kcal/mol}$$

Yields:

$$-530 \text{ (propane)} + -628 = -1{,}094 \text{ kcal/mol (heptane)}$$

21. A is correct.

Water, methanol, and acetic acid are poor solvents because they can react as nucleophiles and add to the alkenes.

22. C is correct.

Two *pi* bonds use one mole of H_2 each, so 2 moles of hydrogen are consumed in the conversion.

23. C is correct.

C: contains 4 π electrons and therefore does not satisfy Hückel's rule for aromaticity ($4n + 2$ π electrons). Additionally, the silicon atom is sp^3 hybridized and would not participate in aromatic conjugation.

24. B is correct.

Molecules containing rings or multibonds are molecules that have degrees of unsaturation.

A completely saturated compound only consists of single bonds (*sigma* bonds).

25. A is correct.

A common ylide is the phosphonium ylide as a Wittig reagent.

$$Ph_3\overset{+}{P}\text{---}\overset{\overset{\displaystyle\cdot\cdot}{-}}{C}\overset{\displaystyle R^1}{\underset{\displaystyle R^2}{<}}$$

Phosphonium ylide

The double-charged (+ and –) resonance structure is the more dominant resonance contributor because the orbitals of phosphorus are larger than the valence orbitals of carbon, thus making the overlap of the carbon and phosphorus p orbitals less favorable.

The minor resonance contributor for this functional group is the charge-neutral pentavalent phosphorus-containing structure formed from the overlap of the C and phosphorus p orbitals.

26. B is correct.

Acetic acid is a neutral compound, with all the atoms in the molecule having no formal charge.

Carboxylic acids are charged when protonated by other acids, as is the case in Fischer esterification reactions or when deprotonated by bases.

27. B is correct.

$$CH_3\text{---}CH_2\text{---}\overset{\overset{\displaystyle O}{\|}}{C}\text{---}OH \;+\; H\text{---}\underset{\underset{\displaystyle H}{|}}{N}\text{---}CH_3 \;\longrightarrow\; CH_3\text{---}CH_2\text{---}\overset{\overset{\displaystyle O}{\|}}{C}\text{---}\underset{\underset{\displaystyle H}{|}}{N}\text{---}CH_3 \;+\; H_2O$$

carboxylic acid   amine   →   amide   water

The synthesis of amides from carboxylic acids and amines usually requires heating the reaction to high temperatures. This is necessary for the creation of the amide bond and to possibly drive away the water byproduct, so the chemical equilibrium continues to favor the product formation.

28. B is correct.

Amines are compounds that contain basic nitrogen atoms that can act as nucleophiles as long as steric interactions don't prevent them from doing so.

The nitrogen lone pair of electrons of the amides are tied up in conjugation with the carbonyl group and are therefore not basic or nucleophilic.

29. D is correct.

The longest carbon chain has five carbon atoms.

The alcohol is attached to the carbon at the second position, and the methyl group is attached to the carbon in the fourth position.

30. B is correct.

Compounds that tend to be polar possess electronegative heteroatoms and more carbon-heteroatom bonds. If these groups can ionize to form charges, then they become even more polar.

31. A is correct.

The *anti*-conformer (180° offset) has the lowest energy because it minimizes steric strain (i.e., bulky substituents within van der Waals radii) and torsional strain (i.e., repulsion of bonding electrons when eclipsed).

Gauche refers to a dihedral angle of 60°.

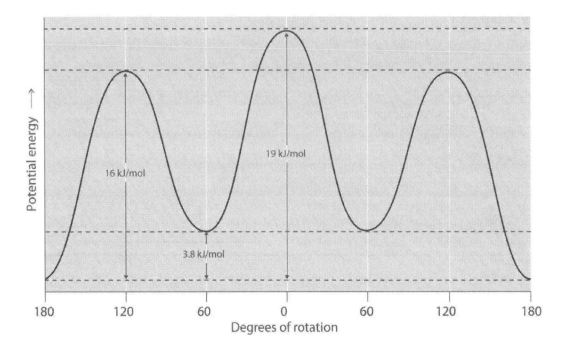

32. A is correct.

The topicity of the protons can be determined by labeling them as H_a and H_b to produce a "chiral center." If this causes the molecule to have two or more chiral centers, then the protons are diastereotopic.

If the labeling causes the molecule to have only one stereocenter, the labeled protons are enantiotopic.

If labeling the protons as H_a and H_b does not lead to the formation of a chiral center (as in the case of methane), then the protons are homotopic.

33. D is correct.

Identify the molecules that contain nitrogen or oxygen heteroatoms because these atoms enable molecules to participate in hydrogen bonding and contribute to dipolar interactions.

The cyclopentane is only composed of hydrogen and carbon, so it is the least water soluble.

34. C is correct.

The hydration proceeds with Markovnikov addition.

The first step in the reaction is protonation to form the tertiary carbocation; this is trapped by water.

35. D is correct.

Bromine atoms are added to both sides of the triple bond to produce a vicinal dibrominated alkene.

The addition product has the bromine atoms on opposite sides of the double bond.

Therefore, this addition proceeds through an *anti*-addition mechanism.

36. A is correct.

Four requirements for aromaticity:

　　1) molecule is cyclic

　　2) molecular is planar (flat)

　　3) each atom is sp^2 hybridized (i.e., conjugated)

　　4) the number of *pi* electrons satisfies Hückel's rule ($4n + 2$ *pi* electrons)

Aromatic rings can be positively or negatively charged if the four criteria are satisfied.

Aromatic compounds have no saturated carbon atoms present in the aromatic ring. The hybridization state of aromatic carbon atoms is sp^2, and the total number of electrons in the aromatic system is consistent with Hückel's rule ($4n + 2 \pi$ electrons).

37. C is correct.

Primary alcohols have an ~OH group attached to a carbon that is connected to another carbon atom.

Secondary alcohols possess an ~OH group that is bonded to a carbon attached to two other carbon atoms.

Tertiary alcohols have ~OH groups that are bonded to carbon atoms attached to three other carbon atoms.

38. D is correct.

Hydrocarbons tend to have lower boiling points than molecules containing heteroatoms because hydrocarbons lack large molecular dipoles.

These dipoles strengthen the intermolecular forces and raise boiling points.

Furthermore, molecules that can hydrogen bond have the highest boiling points because the hydrogen bond is a strong type of dipole interaction.

39. B is correct.

$$R-\underset{\underset{O}{\|}}{C}-OH \;+\; ROH \;\underset{}{\overset{H^+}{\rightleftharpoons}}\; R-\underset{\underset{O}{\|}}{C}-OR \;+\; H_2O$$

Ester formations from alcohols and carboxylic acids are condensations, so an equivalent of water is lost as a reaction byproduct as well.

40. B is correct.

6-APA is the core of penicillin and is the chemical compound (+)-6-aminopenicillanic acid.

Since amides are more stable than carboxylic acids, their hydrolysis is higher in energy.

Penicillin with 2 amide bonds

41. A is correct.

When amines are added to water at neutral pH, the solution becomes basic, and hydroxide ions ($^-$OH) are produced.

Alternatively, carboxylic acids, when added to water at neutral pH, generate hydronium ions (H_3O^+).

42. B is correct.

The longest carbon chain is a four-carbon cyclo derivative (i.e., cyclopentane).

There are four substituents located at the first and third positions in the molecule.

43. C is correct.

For symmetric compounds like acetylene, no molecular dipole moment exists, because the electron density is evenly distributed on either side of the triple bond.

Asymmetric molecules have molecular dipoles.

44. D is correct.

Draw each of the possible isomers and be cognizant of equivalent structures.

ortho-dibromobenzene   *meta*-dibromobenzene   *para*-dibromobenzene

There are only three possible isomers that can be drawn for the given molecular formula.

45. A is correct.

The amine N–H bond is acidic because the nitrogen atom is in conjugation with the carbonyl group.

However, the N–H bond of saccharine is much more acidic because the functional group overall is an amide and a sulfonamide.

The sulfone group (SO_2) also acts as an electron-withdrawing group to stabilize the negative charge that is generated from deprotonation.

The pK_a of saccharin is 1.6.

46. D is correct.

Saturated fats lack the alkene double bond. Unsaturated fats convert to saturated fats through a process known as hydrogenation.

In this process, hydrogen gas is catalytically added to the alkene groups of the fatty acids to convert them to alkane groups.

47. A is correct.

When a six-carbon sugar cyclizes (yielding a pyranose), a hemiacetal bond is formed (–linkage between the –OH at carbon number 5 and the anomeric carbon (C_1)) and the carbonyl of C_1 is converted to an alcohol.

The resulting C_1 hydroxyl may be in the axial or equatorial positions on the ring with the two possible positions called anomers.

α-D-glucopyranose   β-D-glucopyranose

If the –OH at carbon number 1 is in the down position (which is axial in the case of D-glucopyranose, or glucose), the ring is referred to as the α anomer.

When the –OH is in the axial (up) position, it is the β anomer.

A monosaccharide in solution freely converts between the open chain form and the two anomeric forms (mutarotation). It is necessary to specify the anomeric form because the acetal linkage (glycosidic bond) between monosaccharides in di- and polysaccharides prevents mutarotation.

Enzymes accept only one of the two anomers in the formation and hydrolysis of glycosidic linkages. Hence, all the linkages in starch and glycogen (except at branch points) are α(1→4) glycosidic linkages, whereas all the bonds in cellulose are β(1→4).

Even though all these macromolecules are simple glucose polymers, humans can digest only the former two, since humans lack enzymes for the hydrolysis of β glycosidic linkages (therefore, humans can digest starch but not grass or wood).

48. D is correct.

The common base pairing that is observed in DNA is adenine-thymine and guanine-cytosine.

Adenine-thymine forms two hydrogen bonds (A=T).

Guanine-cytosine forms three hydrogen bonds (G≡C).

This pairing is consistent with the structure of DNA, and this complementary pairing is what guides the formation of daughter strands of DNA.

49. C is correct.

2,4-dinitrofluorobenzene is used to identify the *N*-terminus of a peptide.

2,4-dinitrofluorobenzene reacts with the *N*-terminal amino acid and remains attached even after complete acid hydrolysis, which allows for isolation of the *N*-terminal amino acid from the rest of the polypeptide.

In 1945, Frederick Sanger used 2,4-dinitrofluorobenzene for determining the N-terminal amino acid in polypeptide chains.

Dinitrofluorobenzene reacts with the amine group in amino acids to produce dinitrophenyl-amino acids.

50. D is correct.

The hydrogenation of unsaturated fats adds hydrogen across the double bonds of the fat. This causes the fats to be saturated and increases their melting points.

Because of their ability to form solids more easily, consumption hydrogenated fats should be limited for health concerns.

51. D is correct.

Glycogen (below) contains $\alpha(1\rightarrow6)$ linkages:

Cellulose (below) contains $\beta(1\rightarrow4)$ linkages:

Sucrose (below) contains β(1→2) linkages:

Amylose (below) contains α(1→4) linkages:

Maltose (below) contains α(1→4) linkages:

52. D is correct.

Because adenine forms two hydrogen bonds with thymine, and cytosine forms three hydrogen bonds with guanine, the complementary nitrogen base is used by DNA polymerase (in the S phase of interphase) to synthesize the new strand.

53. A is correct.

Hormones are substances secreted by a gland and released into the blood to affect a target tissue/organ.

Insulin (below) is a hormone composed of amino acids (i.e., peptide hormones) and therefore is a protein molecule. Insulin is composed of two peptide chains (A chain and B chain).

The chains are linked together by two disulfide bonds, and an additional disulfide is formed within the A chain.

In most species, the A chain consists of 21 amino acids and the B chain of 30 amino acids.

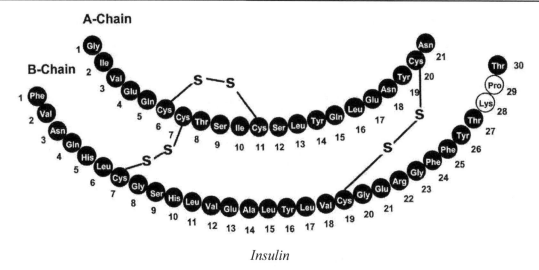

Insulin

Hormones can be lipid molecules, such as steroid derivatives (e.g., testosterone, progesterone, estrogen).

54. B is correct.

Triglycerides (or triacylglycerides) are used for storage and exist in the adipose tissue of animals.

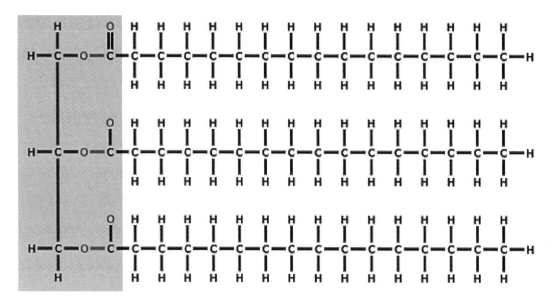

Triglyceride (glycerol and three saturated fatty acid chains)

Phospholipids (below) are the largest component of semi-permeable cell membranes.

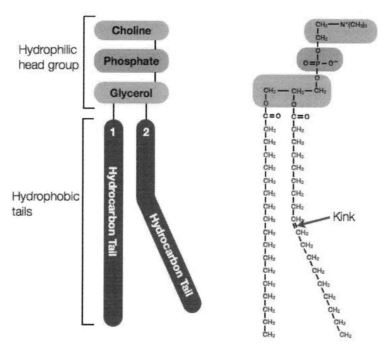

Phospholipids differ mainly in the composition of the polar head region

Steroids are lipids used for cell-signaling (e.g., testosterone, estradiol).

(a) Cholesterol

(b) Testosterone

(c) Estradiol

Cholesterol is the precursor molecule for several steroid hormones
(e.g., progesterone, aldosterone)

55. D is correct.

Humans are unable to digest cellulose because the appropriate enzymes to breakdown the beta acetal linkages are lacking. The enzyme responsible for cleaving this glycosidic linkage is known as cellulase. Cellulase is produced by plants, bacteria, fungi, and protozoans.

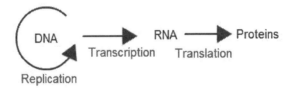

56. C is correct.

DNA molecules hold the genetic information of organisms.

RNA molecules are synthesized from the DNA strand to make proteins for the cell.

Genes are the sections of DNA responsible for the synthesis of proteins in cells.

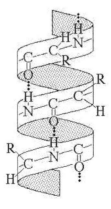

The central dogma of molecular biology (designates information flow)

57. B is correct.

The *alpha* helix structure is one of the two common types of secondary protein structure.

The *alpha* helix is held together by hydrogen bonds between every N–H (amino group) and the oxygen of the C=O (carbonyl) in the next turn of the helix; four amino acids along the chain.

The typical *alpha* helix is about 11 amino acids long.

alpha helix

The other type of secondary structure is the *beta* pleated sheet.

Beta pleated sheets are either parallel or anti-parallel (with reference to the amino terminus)

58. C is correct.

The straight chain fatty acid that possesses the greatest number of alkenes in its structure is fat (lipids) that most likely is a liquid at room temperature.

Stearic acid is fully saturated, while linoleic acid has two double bonds.

The triacylglyceride of these fatty acids is a liquid (or oil) at room temperature.

Saturated fat (stearic acid)

Unsaturated fat (linoleic acid)

59. A is correct.

Mutarotation is possible because the anomeric carbon is a hemiacetal.

When dissolved in water, hemiacetals are known to reversibly open to the acyclic form, allowing the formation of the cyclic diastereomer.

Mutarotation (open chain in the center) with the less stable α-glucose anomer
(left) and more stable β-glucose anomer on the right

The process is accelerated from the addition of acid or base.

60. D is correct.

There are five known nucleotides, four of which appear in DNA.

These nucleotides are cytosine, guanine, adenine, and thymine.

In RNA molecules, the thymine is replaced with another pyrimidine nucleotide known as uracil.

Nucleotides consisting of a phosphate group (note the negative charge on oxygens), deoxyribose sugar (lack a 2'-hydroxyl) and a nitrogenous base (adenine, cytosine, guanine or thymine)

Please, leave your Customer Review on Amazon

Explanations: Diagnostic Test #10

1. A is correct.

The longest carbon chain of the molecule is the 3-carbon propane.

There are three substituents in this molecule: two methyl groups are on the nitrogen atom, and one methyl group is at the second position.

2. B is correct.

Tertiary carbocations are more stable than secondary and primary benzylic carbocations, which are more stable than primary or vinylic carbocations.

Methyl cations are the least stable of the carbocations.

3. B is correct.

Isomers are compounds that have the same molecular formula but a different structure.

A: "hydrocarbons" refers to organic molecules containing only carbon and hydrogen (i.e., no heteroatoms such as oxygen or nitrogen).

C: homologs are a series of compounds with the same general formula, usually varying by a single parameter (e.g., length of the carbon chain).

D: isotopes have different mass numbers due to differences in the number of neutrons.

The number of protons determines the identity of the element.

4. D is correct.

The most deshielded protons in the NMR spectrum have the largest δ shift (i.e., downfield).

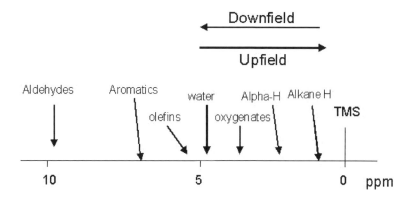

NMR with the approximate δ shifts of some functional groups

5. C is correct.

The distillation chamber in the fractionating tower has a constant volume.

Therefore, the pressure is directly proportional to the temperature.

The less volatile components have higher boiling points and therefore require higher temperatures to vaporize them. These high temperatures mean that the pressure will be greater near the bottom of the tower.

6. B is correct.

The order of stability of carbocations is $3° > 2° > 1°$.

Therefore, more substituted carbocations are more stable.

7. A is correct.

The rate law may not reveal anything about the total number of steps in a reaction mechanism.

Furthermore, the bromination of alkenes proceeds in two steps, not one.

8. B is correct. Alkynes are triple bonded molecules made of hydrogen and carbon atoms.

The electronegativity difference between carbon and hydrogen is low, resulting in the molecule being less polar.

Molecules with little polarization may be more soluble in organic solvents as opposed to water.

9. C is correct.

Compared to benzene, electron-donating groups (such as –OH) activate the ring towards EAS reactions.

Electron-withdrawing groups (such as the acetyl group) deactivate the ring, slowing EAS reactions.

Benzene can undergo the bromination reaction as well; however, its rate of bromination is less than the rate for the phenol bromination.

10. B is correct.

The –OH group is characteristic of both alcohol and carboxylic acids, but the latter also includes a carbonyl group.

11. A is correct.

The compounds ending in *–one* suggests that the highest priority functional group is the molecule is the ketone.

Compounds that end in *–ol* may possess an alcohol as the highest priority group.

12. D is correct.

All the acids contain a carboxylic acid functional group, which largely contributes to the boiling points of all of the molecules.

The molecule with the largest hydrocarbon region has more intermolecular forces (most of which are London forces) and has the largest boiling point.

The alkyl region of stearic acid consists of 17 saturated carbon atoms

Stearic acid is a saturated fatty acid and has the highest boiling point.

Among the answer choices, no other acid possesses an alkyl region this large, and this molecule has the largest boiling point.

13. C is correct.

The reaction above is a hydrolysis reaction, and it is the reverse process for the Fischer esterification reaction.

In the presence of excess water, the acid catalyst activates the ester carbonyl group to promote nucleophilic attack by water.

This produces the corresponding alcohol and carboxylic acid components (in the presence of H^+).

14. B is correct.

The polar amino group of *p*-toluidine makes it slightly soluble in water:

p-toluidine

p-toluidine is soluble in acidic water due to the formation of ammonium salts.

15. B is correct.

The highest priority groups are *trans* to one another.

The longest carbon chain has seven carbon atoms, and the alkene is in the fourth position (fourth carbon from the alcohol, which is the highest priority group).

---

16. B is correct.

Nodes only form between the orbitals of atoms if the orbital phases have the opposite sign.

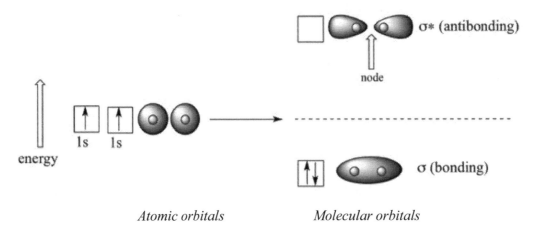

Atomic orbitals   *Molecular orbitals*

17. B is correct.

(Z)-1-bromo-1-chloropropene   *(E)-1-bromo-1-chloropropene*

These molecules can only adopt one conformation because of the rotational barrier of the alkene.

Configurational isomers involve a double bond.

If the molecules have optical activity, they may be enantiomers (non-superimposable mirror images) or diastereomers.

If they lack optical activity, they are geometric isomers.

(see diagram below)

A: constitutional isomers have the same molecular formula but different connectivity.

The molecules are not the same, but the connectivity is the same, so they are not constitutional isomers.

C: identical molecules may be drawn with different orientation on the paper but are the same.

D: conformational isomers refer to molecules that are different due to free rotation around single bonds (e.g., Newman projections or chair flips for cyclohexane).

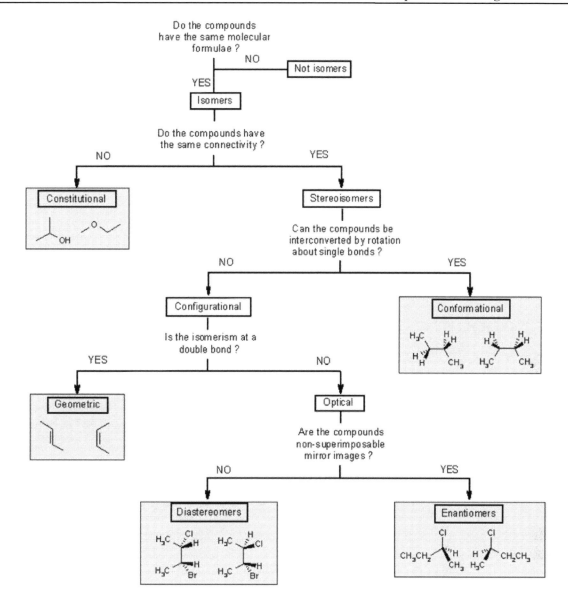

18. A is correct.

The M–18 peak corresponds to the loss of water. The loss of water in a substrate containing an alcohol may suggest that an alkene intermediate is generated during the ionization process.

19. D is correct.

Isomers are compounds that have the same molecular formula but a different structure.

Isomers may or may not have the same physical properties. For compounds that are not isomers of each other, different physical properties should be expected.

Enantiomers are the only types of isomers that have the same physical properties. Enantiomers require a chiral environment (e.g., a chiral substrate such as an enzyme in the body) for their separation.

20. D is correct.

1-bromopropane is a primary halogen and a strong nucleophile, leading to S_N2, which is preferred when there is no steric hindrance.

21. D is correct.

Draw the structures of the starting material and product to determine which reagent is used.

Two halogen atoms are added to the molecule, and an efficient method to achieve this is by exposing the alkene to a diatomic halogen species (e.g., Cl_2 or Br_2).

The chlorine atoms add in an *anti*-orientation from the 3-membered ring of the chloronium ion.

bromoniom ion

Bromonium (like chloronium) ions undergo the same reaction mechanism

22. A is correct.

Whenever a hydrocarbon is burned (adding O_2), the major byproducts of the reaction are water and carbon dioxide. Ash may also form from the reaction, composed of carbon material that cannot undergo further oxidation.

23. D is correct.

The *pi* molecular orbitals of benzene are made from the overlap of six *p* orbitals.

Because the number of molecular orbitals equals the number of atomic orbitals involved in the overlap, there are six molecular orbitals.

24. D is correct.

Sodium dichromate ($Na_2Cr_2O_7$) is a strong oxidizing agent which converts primary alcohols to carboxylic acids.

Sodium dichromate converts secondary alcohols to ketones.

25. D is correct.

These reaction conditions are the Clemmensen reduction reaction conditions.

The Clemmensen reduction mechanism involves the protonation of the ketone oxygen atom.

Clemmensen reduction reaction

26. D is correct.

Carboxylic Acid

Carboxylate Salt
(More soluble in water)

Phenol

Phenolate Salt
(More soluble in water)

The salt is a sodium carboxylate salt of the carboxylic acid. The byproduct in the reaction is water.

Because carboxylic acids are about 10 or more orders of magnitude more acidic than water, the conversion to the carboxylate form by exposing it to sodium hydroxide is irreversible.

Therefore, no equilibrium is associated with this reaction.

27. A is correct.

Sodium hydroxide can act as a base to reversibly deprotonate the N–H of the amide (due to resonance stabilization of the anion).

However, the irreversible reaction pathway involves the formation of carboxylate and amine products.

28. A is correct.

Amines are compounds that are derivatives of ammonia. These compounds contain carbon-nitrogen single bonds and are known to be sufficient bases for strong acids.

Carbonyl-containing compounds are: aldehyde, ketone, acid chloride, anhydride, carboxylic acid, ester, and amide.

29. D is correct.

The longest carbon chain contains five carbons.

The highest priority group in the molecule is the alcohol, so the name of the compound has –*ol* as the suffix and *pent~* as the root name.

The methyl substituent is in the second position.

30. B is correct.

As the number of covalent bonds (i.e., triple > double > single) increases between carbon atoms, the bond order and bond strength increases.

Stronger bonds are shorter, so the two carbon atoms that make up the triple bond have the shortest bond.

31. B is correct.

Chiral carbons refer to asymmetric carbons that are typically bonded to three other atoms.

Carbon 2 cannot be an asymmetric carbon (or chiral carbon), because carbon atoms with trigonal planar configuration possess a plane of symmetry and are achiral.

32. B is correct.

The alpha nitrogen atom makes the neighboring C–H bonds less shielded because the nitrogen atom is electronegative and withdraws electron density through an inductive effect.

Terminal or substituted alkyl C–H bonds (away from electronegative atoms) normally resonate between 1 and 2 ppm.

33. C is correct.

Molecules with double or triple bonds are not able to undergo free rotation because the *pi* bond rigidifies the structure of the compound. To achieve the bond rotation, the *pi* bond(s) must be broken.

Furthermore, for cyclic compounds, the smaller the ring size, the fewer degrees of freedom it has.

Due to strain energy, cyclopropane is unable to rotate freely.

34. A is correct.

The Zaitsev product is one that is the most thermodynamically stable.

Thermodynamically stable alkenes are most substituted ($3° > 2° > 1°$).

2,3-dimethyl-1-butene has a 1° alkene carbon (terminal) and a 3° carbon (at position 2)

2,3-dimethyl-2-butene has two 3° alkene carbons at positions 2 and 3

The hyperconjugation of the neighboring C–H bonds into the pi^* orbital of the alkene lowers the energy of the alkene.

Furthermore, the sp^3 hybridized alkyl groups help to inductively donate electron density to the more electronegative sp^2 hybridized carbon atoms.

35. C is correct.

$$H_3C-\!\!\!\equiv\!\!CH$$

Alkyne: C_nH_{2n-2} = 2 degrees of unsaturation due to the triple bond.

In the name of this molecule, the prefix is *pro–*, which indicates that the molecule is composed of three carbon atoms.

The *–yne* suffix indicates that a carbon-carbon triple bond exists in the molecule.

Therefore, propyne has three carbon atoms and four hydrogen atoms.

36. A is correct.

Four requirements for aromaticity:

    1) molecule is cyclic

    2) molecular is planar (flat)

    3) each atom is sp^2 hybridized (i.e., conjugated)

    4) the number of *pi* electrons satisfies Hückel's rule ($4n + 2$ *pi* electrons)

Aromatic rings can be positively or negatively charged if the 4 criteria are satisfied.

B, C, and D are antiaromatic with $4n$ *pi* electrons.

37. B is correct.

Thionyl chloride ($SOCl_2$) is a reagent that converts primary and secondary alcohols to alkyl chlorides.

Phosphorous tribromide (PBr_3) is a reagent that converts primary and secondary alcohols to alkyl bromides.

38. D is correct.

When Grignard (R–MgBr or R–MgCl) or Gilman (R_2CuLi) reagents are combined with aldehydes, the product is a secondary alcohol.

This alcohol may or may not be chiral, depending on which Grignard reagent is used for alkylation.

The alkylation of ketones yields tertiary alcohols.

The alkylation of epoxides (below) results in an alcohol with an extended carbon chain.

The Grignard reagent (i.e., carbanion in basic conditions) proceeds with the nucleophile (Grignard) attaching the less substituted carbon of the epoxide.

Grignard reaction (RMgX) involving several electrophiles and the resulting products

39. B is correct.

When carboxylic acids and alcohols are combined in the presence of acid catalysts (e.g., H_2SO_4), esters form as the product.

Water is also produced as a byproduct in the reaction, and its removal from the reaction drives the reaction forward because an equilibrium exists.

40. C is correct.

When forming an amide from a carboxylic acid and an amine, higher temperatures are typically needed to drive the reaction forward.

$$\xrightarrow[\text{base}]{SOCl_2}$$

$$R-\overset{\overset{\displaystyle O}{\|}}{C}-Cl$$

$$\xrightarrow[\text{heat}]{RCO_2H}$$

$$R-\overset{\overset{\displaystyle O}{\|}}{C}-O-\overset{\overset{\displaystyle O}{\|}}{C}-R$$

$$R-\overset{\overset{\displaystyle O}{\|}}{C}-OH \qquad \xrightarrow[\text{H}^+\,/\,\text{heat}]{R'OH} \qquad R-\overset{\overset{\displaystyle O}{\|}}{C}-OR'$$

$$\xrightarrow[\text{heat}]{R_2NH}$$

$$R-\overset{\overset{\displaystyle O}{\|}}{C}-NR_2$$

$$\xrightarrow{\text{base}}$$

$$R-\overset{\overset{\displaystyle O}{\|}}{C}-O^-$$

Reactions for a carboxylic acid with specific reagents

The reactivity of the carboxylic acid derivatives is:

acyl chloride > anhydride > carboxylic acid ≈ ester > amide > carboxylate.

An equivalent of water is lost (i.e., dehydration) in the process, so this reaction is a condensation reaction.

41. A is correct.

Although primary and secondary amines can both accept and donate hydrogen bonds, the hydrogen bonding forces are greater for primary amines, because these molecules possess two N–H bonds.

Quaternary ammonium salts cannot form hydrogen bonds because the N has four bonds and no lone pairs of electrons remain on the nitrogen.

42. A is correct.

Propyl substituents (shown below) contain a three-carbon chain.

If the point of attachment (indicated by the squiggle line) is at the second carbon, the groups is an *iso*propyl group.

B: *tert-* butyl

C: *sec*-butyl

D: isobutyl

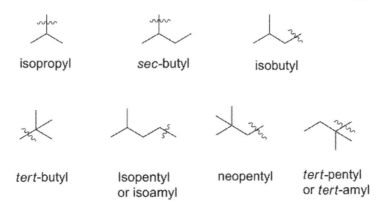

isopropyl   *sec*-butyl   isobutyl

tert-butyl   Isopentyl or isoamyl   neopentyl   *tert*-pentyl or *tert*-amyl

Common names of alkyl substituents (recognized by IUPAC)

43. B is correct.

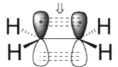

pi bond overlap between the unhybridized orbitals is indicated by the arrow

In organic molecules, the overlap of *pi* bonds is responsible for the formation of carbon-carbon *pi* bonds.

The orbitals of double and triple bonds (alkenes and alkynes, respectively) are unhybridized and are more reactive than the *sigma* bonds of single bonds.

Therefore, the reactions of alkenes typically involve breaking the alkene double bond.

44. D is correct.

The number of possible stereoisomers of a molecule depends on the number of chiral centers, which are defined as a carbon bonded to 4 different substituents.

The number of possible stereoisomers is 2^n, where n is the number of chiral centers.

Number the carbon with the carbonyl carbon as #1.

Carbons 1 and 6 are not chiral centers, because carbon 1 is attached to only three substituents, while carbon 5 has two identical hydrogen substituents.

Carbons 2, 3, 4, and 5 are chiral centers since each is bonded to 4 different groups.

Therefore, the molecule has 4 chiral centers and the number of stereoisomers is $2^4 = 2 \times 2 \times 2 \times 2 = 16$.

45. A is correct.

Amino acids are linked together in peptides by amide bonds.

The peptide forms in a condensation reaction via dehydration (loss of water) when the lone pair on the nitrogen of an amino group of one amino acid makes a nucleophilic attack on the carbonyl carbon of another.

Peptide bond formation from the condensation reaction of 2 amino acids

46. D is correct.

Steroid molecules are one of the two different kinds of fat molecules, which are composed of fused rings.

Triacylglycerides (aka triglycerides) are composed of long hydrocarbon chains with functionalized head groups.

47. A is correct.

Common monosaccharides are composed of five (pentose) or six (hexose) carbon atoms, hydrogen, and oxygen.

This molecule contains a hemiacetal group, which can open reversibly to form an aldehyde.

The presence of the aldehyde makes this carbohydrate a reducing sugar.

48. B is correct.

Four common nucleotides are found in DNA molecules:

   adenine (A), cytosine (C), guanine (G) and thymine (T)

Four common nucleotides are found in RNA molecules:

   adenine (A), cytosine (C), guanine (G) and uracil (U)

49. C is correct.

Valine is the only amino acid listed with a hydrophobic (carbon and hydrogen only) side chain.

Group	Characteristics	Name	Example (-Rx)
non-polar	hydrophobic	Ala, Val, Leu, Ile, Pro, Phe Trp, Met	CH_3 $CH-CH_2-$ CH_3 Leu
polar	hydrophilic (non-charged)	Gly, Ser, Thr, Cys, Tyr, Asn Gln	OH $CH-$ CH_3 Leu
acidic	negatively charged	Asp, Glu	O $C-CH_2-$ O- Asp
basic	positively charged	Lys, Arg, His	NH_3^+ $-CH_2-CH_2-CH_2-CH_2-$ Lys

50. C is correct.

Saponification is the name for the base-promoted hydrolysis of esters. This type of hydrolysis (i.e., saponification) is typically used to form soap compounds.

carboxylate ester   sodium hydroxide   sodium carboxylate   alcohol

Base hydrolysis (saponification) of an ester to form a carboxylate salt and an alcohol

Soap is hard or soft depending on the counter-ion of the carboxylate salt.

If the base used to hydrolyze the fat is sodium hydroxide, a hard soap is produced.

If potassium hydroxide is used for the base hydrolysis reaction, then a soft soap is produced.

Furthermore, other kinds of bases can give rise to these two kinds of soaps.

51. B is correct.

The ratio of these atoms that compose sugars is normally 1:2:1 (carbon : hydrogen : oxygen).

D-ribose: Fisher projections of an example ribose sugar

52. A is correct.
When DNA is replicated in the cell, one of the strands of DNA acts as a template for a new strand synthesized as the replication fork opens. This continuously synthesized strand is known as the leading strand and, when combined with one of the old strands of DNA, makes up one new DNA molecule.

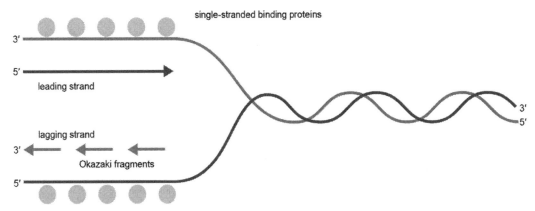

Furthermore, an additional DNA molecule is created in the process, as the other parent strand acts as a template for its complementary strand.

This lagging strand is made up of smaller segments called Okazaki fragments (about 150-200 nucleotides long). Okazaki fragments are combined with the enzyme DNA ligase.

53. C is correct.

Amino acid – glycine

Amino acid with the amino, carboxyl group and α-carbon attached to the side chain (R group)

Glycine has no alkyl substituent at the *alpha* position (R = H); is the smallest amino acid.

54. C is correct.

Cholesterol is a lipid molecule also known as a steroid compound.

Cholesterol

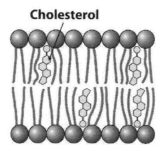

The fused ring structure of steroid molecules is what makes them rigid and have fewer degrees of motion due to the few conformations that are available for cyclic molecules *vs.* acyclic molecules.

Molecules, such as phospholipids, lack fused-ring structures, and they exist as straight-chained molecules.

Therefore, cholesterol in the cell membrane acts as a bidirectional regulator of membrane fluidity: at high temperatures, it stabilizes the membrane and raises its melting point,

At low temperatures, cholesterol intercalates between the phospholipids and prevents them from clustering together and stiffening

55. C is correct.

During the formation of disaccharides, the only configuration that can vary is at the anomeric carbon.

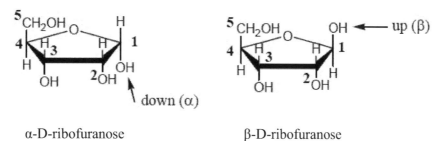

α-D-ribofuranose   β-D-ribofuranose

The other alcohols of the carbohydrate are either primary or secondary alcohols that are not adjacent (i.e., allylic) to an oxygen atom (as in the case of anomeric alcohols).

The neighboring oxygen atom in the ring facilitates the ring opening of the anomeric C_1 alcohol, and this may lead to the formation of the other anomer (α ↔ β).

56. D is correct.

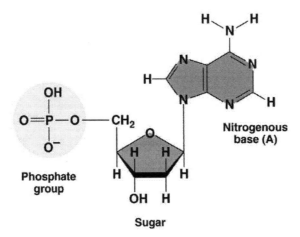

RNA molecules contain ribose as the carbohydrate component of the backbone

DNA contains deoxyribose (lacking a 2'-hydroxy) as part of the backbone

57. D is correct.

The isoelectric point of an amino acid is determined by calculating the average of the pK_a values of the carboxylic acid and the ammonium cation.

When more than one ionizable group is present, the two pK_a that are numerically closer are used for the calculation.

CO$_2$H   pKa$_1$ CO$_2^-$ pKa$_2$ CO$_2^-$

H$_3$N$^+$—H   H$_3$N$^+$—H   H$_2$N—H

R   R   R

acidic media   neutral   basic media

low pH   form   high pH

For instance, for acidic amino acids, the isoelectric point can be calculated by averaging the two lower pK_a values.

For basic amino acids, the two highest pK_a values are averaged to determine the isoelectric point.

Amino acid	α-CO$_2$H pK$_a$^{1}	α-NH$_3$ pK$_a$^{2}	Side chain pK$_a$^{3}	pI
Arginine	2.1	9.0	12.5	10.8
Aspartic Acid	2.1	9.8	3.9	3.0
Cysteine	1.7	10.4	8.3	5.0
Glutamic Acid	2.2	9.7	4.3	3.2
Histidine	1.8	9.2	6.0	7.6
Lysine	2.2	9.0	10.5	9.8
Tyrosine	2.2	9.1	10.1	5.7

pK$_a$ values for the 7 amino acids with ionizable side chains

58. B is correct.

Triglycerides are one of two common types of lipids that are found in the body.

This fat is composed of four components, including one equivalent of glycerol (a triol) and three fatty acid molecules.

These components are combined to form the three ester groups of the triglyceride.

59. B is correct.

Any sugar molecule that lacks the aldehyde or the hemiacetal functional group is a non-reducing sugar. The sugars are not active during chemical tests like the Tollens' test.

When reducing sugars react, they are normally oxidized to carboxylic acid molecules.

All monosaccharides are reducing sugars, while some disaccharides (e.g., lactose and maltose), oligosaccharides and polysaccharides are also reducing sugars.

Reducing sugars (and *alpha* hydroxyl ketones) give a positive Benedict's test: a brown precipitate forms (as does for Fehling's solution).

Tollens' reagent forms silver ions (mirror) as a positive test for reducing sugars.

60. A is correct.

A nucleoside is a nitrogenous base linked to a sugar.

A nucleotide is a nucleoside and 1 or more phosphate groups attached to the ribose or deoxyribose sugar.

The uracil base is directly bonded to the 1' position of 2'-ribofuranose (i.e., RNA sugar) moiety, rather than the 2'-deoxyribofuranose (i.e., DNA sugar) ring.

thymidine (DNA)   uridine (RNA)

Explanations: Diagnostic Test #11

1. B is correct.

The longest carbon chain in the molecule has 4 carbon atoms, and therefore the root is *but–*.

An alkene is positioned at the second carbon with a suffix of *–ene*.

2. B is correct.

The allylic cation is a carbocation that is one *sigma* bond away from a double bond (i.e., alkene).

Resonance hybrids of an allylic carbocation

Methylene groups are points of saturation in the molecule that can prevent the conjugation of nearby alkenes.

is more stable than

is more stable than

3. C is correct.

The naming of the compounds reveals that the compounds are the same:

    4,7-diethyl-3,6-dimethyldecane

4. A is correct.

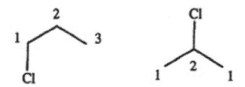

5. C is correct.

Extraction is an organic separation technique that relies on the relative acidity of the molecules.

Aniline is the most basic of the three because it has an amino group, whereby the nitrogen has a lone pair of electrons available for donation to a Lewis acid.

Para-nitroaniline is less basic because the nitro group is electron-withdrawing. The amino group with decreased electron density is less able to donate electrons as needed for a Lewis base.

Nitromethane is not basic because the nitro group is electron-withdrawing.

Acidic extraction makes organic bases soluble in the aqueous phase via protonation of the base to form a soluble ionic salt. Extraction with a sufficiently weak aqueous acid protonates only the most basic compound (aniline), which allows it to migrate into the aqueous phase.

A subsequent extraction with a stronger acid then protonates the less basic (*p*-nitroaniline) of the remaining two molecules, which enters the aqueous phase. The third molecule (nitromethane) remains alone in the organic layer, and distillation completes the separation.

If a strong acid were used initially, both aniline and nitroaniline would be protonated and transfer to the aqueous layer, so the extraction (separation) would not be effective.

Extraction with a base is not effective because both aniline and nitroaniline are bases and are inert to treatment by a base.

6. D is correct.

Only the concentration of the electrophile controls the rate of the reaction because the rate-determining step is the unimolecular formation of the carbocation.

S_N1 reactions proceed via a carbocation in the first step of the mechanism.

In the second step, the nucleophile forms a new bond by attacking the carbocation.

S_N1 undergoes first-order kinetics, whereby:

$$rate = k[\text{substrate}]$$

7. D is correct.

Of the given molecules, HI is the strongest acid, so it protonates the fastest (followed by HBr, then HCl).

Also, I⁻ is the best nucleophile, so it adds to the carbocation most rapidly.

8. A is correct.

One *sigma* bond and two *pi* bonds are used to make the triple bond of alkynes.

Nitriles are another functional group that contains a triple bond.

9. D is correct.

Because the nitrogen lone pair of the aniline is protonated, the group is unable to donate electron density through the *pi* system of the aromatic ring.

Furthermore, the nitrogen atom has a formal charge of +1, and this group can act as a deactivating group because of its inductive effect.

10. A is correct.

No carbon-oxygen *pi* bonds exist in alcohols (hydroxyl) functional groups.

Carbonyl groups (i.e., carbon double bonded to oxygen) are indicative of ketones, aldehydes or carboxylic acid derivatives (acyl halide, anhydride, ester, and amide).

11. B is correct.

For a ketone to be converted to an enolate, a base that is strong enough to remove a proton from the alpha position completely is used.

If hydroxides or alkoxides are used instead of lithium amide bases, an equilibrium exists between both conjugate forms of the ketone.

Methyllithium and diethylamine may add to the ketone instead of deprotonating it; they are too weak to deprotonate the ketone.

12. B is correct.

Carboxylic acids are molecules that contain a terminal carbon atom with three bonds to oxygen.

It consists of a hydroxyl (~OH) group and a carbonyl (~C=O) group.

13. C is correct.

The hydrolysis of an ester is essentially the reverse of Fischer esterification. To drive the reaction forward, excess water and an acid catalyst are used.

The ester hydrolyzes to its two simpler components: the corresponding alcohol and carboxylic acid.

The *R* components of the alcohol product and the alkoxy group of the ester are the same.

14. D is correct.

Arenediazonium salts, which are synthesized from primary aromatic amines, are compounds with an N_2^+ group attached to the aromatic ring. They are useful for synthesizing a wide variety of compounds because they can easily undergo replacement reactions in which molecular nitrogen is released, and a nucleophilic substituent attaches to the aromatic ring in its place.

For example, in the presence of cuprous halides, diazonium salts release molecular nitrogen and form halogen-substituted arenes – the Sandmeyer reaction.

Similarly, in the presence of cuprous cyanide, nitrogen is released and replaced by the cyanide ion, thus forming aromatic nitriles.

In the same way, in cold aqueous solutions, the hydroxyl group replaces the nitrogen to form phenol.

Therefore, compounds I, II, and III can all be obtained by the replacement of nitrogen in arenediazonium salts.

15. C is correct.

The longest carbon chain is composed of five carbon atoms.

The highest priority group is an aldehyde.

The substituent groups are the hydroxymethyl group, the ethyl group, the alkene, and the alkyne.

16. C is correct.

Propene is an example of an alkene, which are molecules that have bonding angles of about 120 degrees. This molecular geometry affords the substituent groups the greatest amount of spatial separation to minimize the intramolecular Van der Waals repulsions among them.

17. C is correct.

The bromine substitution changes from vicinal (on adjacent carbons) to geminal (on the same carbon). Because the connectivity changes, the structures are constitutional isomers.

The first molecules cannot be chiral because it has a mirror plane of symmetry.

18. A is correct.

The n to *pi** transition for ketones is the electron transition that requires the least amount of energy. Antibonding orbitals are vacant and serve as the acceptor orbitals for the electron excitation. The orbitals of nonbonding electrons have more energy than the orbitals for *pi* bonds.

Electron transitions from the *sigma* bond are difficult because the electron energy is low and requires high energy to be promoted.

19. D is correct.

Under basic conditions, the caffeine molecule is deprotonated and neutral. As a result, it dissolves in organic solvents (CH_2Cl_2) rather than in H_2O.

Under basic conditions, heptanoic acid is deprotonated, negatively charged (i.e., an anion) and is soluble in H_2O.

Therefore, in a basic solution, caffeine (i.e., neutral) is miscible in the organic layer, while heptanoic acid (i.e., negatively charged anion) is miscible in the aqueous layer.

Under acidic conditions, caffeine is charged because the NH_2 amine group is protonated, while the heptanoic acid is neutral.

Therefore, the positively charged caffeine is more soluble in H_2O (polar) than in CH_2Cl_2.

Under acidic conditions, heptanoic acid is more soluble in CH_2Cl_2 (nonpolar dichloromethane) when the acid is protonated because heptanoic acid is neutral.

20. B is correct.

Alkanes are only composed of hydrogen and carbon atoms.

Because the electronegativity of these atoms is quite similar, large bond dipoles are not expected.

Hydrogen bonding is a force that acts through highly polarized bonds to form intermolecular bonds to partial positive hydrogen atoms (H attached to F, O or N).

21. D is correct.

In 1,3-butadiene, C_2 and C_3 are both sp^2 hybridized with their unhybridized p orbitals involved in π bonding.

The bond between C_2 and C_3 is a result of the overlap of two sp^2 hybridized orbitals.

There cannot be a partial double-bond character due to σ electrons; double bonds result only from π electrons.

22. A is correct.

Using a subscript of n for the number of carbons, the degrees of unsaturation can be determined from the following formulae:

Alkane: C_nH_{2n+2} = 0 degrees of unsaturation

Alkene: C_nH_{2n} = 1 degree of unsaturation (1 ring or 1 double bond)

Alkyne: C_nH_{2n-2} = 2 degrees of unsaturation (2 double bonds, 1 double bond and 1 ring or 2 rings)

23. A is correct.

Methyl substituents on benzene (toluene) is an *ortho-* / *para*-director and an activator (rate of the electrophilic aromatic substitution is faster than for benzene)

Friedel-Crafts alkylation reactions work best with electron-rich arenes.

Friedel-Crafts alkylation of toluene

24. A is correct.

It is helpful to draw the structure of all known compounds or at least the product of the reaction.

Ethanoate is an ester that has an *n*-propoxy substituent.

Therefore, the alcohol that should be used is 1-propanol.

The remaining component is ethanoic acid.

25. C is correct.

Ketones are molecules that have alkyl or aryl (i.e., ring) substituents on either side of the carbonyl (C=O) functional group.

The IUPAC name for the molecule is butan-2-one or 2-butanone.

26. A is correct.

The carboxylic acid and alcohol starting components for the synthesis of an ester are determined by cleaving the *sigma* bond between the oxygen atom of the alkoxyl (O of the ether) group and the carbonyl (C=O) group.

27. A is correct.

Esters are functional groups that belong to a class of compounds known as carboxylic acid derivatives (along with acyl halides, anhydrides and amides).

Esters have the same oxidation state as carboxylic acids but have different properties compared to carboxylic acid groups, such as enhanced electrophilic properties, decreased polarity, and higher pK_a values.

28. B is correct.

Ethylamine is the product since nitrile reduction adds carbon to the alkyl chain.

Cyanide is nucleophilic and can add to methyl bromide, which results in the expulsion of the bromide leaving group. The product of this reaction is cyanomethane.

The nitrile group can be reduced by lithium aluminum hydride (LiAlH$_4$ or LAH) or hydrogenation to form ethylamine.

29. B is correct.

The cyclohexane is the longest carbon chain, and the alcohol is the highest priority group, making the root name "cyclohexanol."

The chlorine and methyl groups are the substituents.

30. D is correct.

The electronegativity difference decides the distribution of electrons between bonded atoms. This unequal distribution of electrons creates the polarity (∂^+ and ∂^-) of the bond.

31. C is correct.

The molecules shown above are mirror images of each other.

Assign *R* and *S* at each chiral center to verify the answer to any question asking for the relationship between two chiral molecules.

32. B is correct.

The peak area ratios of the spin states correspond to the values derived from Pascal's triangle.

The heights of the peaks may not correspond to the same ratio, but the area does.

n	2^n	multiplet intensities
0	1	1 Singlet (s)
1	2	1 1 Doublet (d)
2	4	1 2 1 Triplet (t)
3	8	1 3 3 1 Quartet (q)
4	16	1 4 6 4 1 Pentet
5	32	1 5 10 10 5 1 Sextet
6	64	1 6 15 20 15 6 1 Septet
7	128	1 7 21 35 35 21 7 1 Octet
8	256	1 8 28 56 70 56 28 8 1 Nonet

Pascal's triangle

33. A is correct.

The sodium methoxide in this reaction acts as a strong base and abstracts a proton on the carbon atom that neighbors the chloride. The mechanism for this process is E_2.

The reaction is not S_N1, because heat is needed to generate the carbocation, and this is not included in the reaction conditions.

34. A is correct.

In the first step of the reaction, the H^+ adds to the double bond creating a carbocation. The nucleophilic water attacks the carbocation, and the acid is regenerated in the last step of the reaction.

2,3-dimethyl-2-butanol

35. D is correct.

Platinum and palladium are used to hydrogenate alkynes to alkenes (or alkanes) or to reduce alkenes to alkanes.

Two moles of hydrogen gas reduces the two pi bonds of the alkyne to an alkane

36. D is correct.

The two arenes (i.e., phenyl moiety) with oxygen substituents are more nucleophilic than the arene with the methyl substituent.

The ester is less nucleophilic than the aryl ether, because of the inductive effect of the oxygen atom on the carbonyl (ester group) that reduces the electron density in the ring.

The lone pair of electrons on the ether resonates into the ring, which increases the electron density for EAS.

37. C is correct.

The 5-carbon molecule of *n*-pentanol has the largest alkyl portion (i.e., the greatest number of London forces) and possesses the hydroxyl group, which allows it to hydrogen bond (increases boiling point).

An overall molecular dipole also exists for this molecule, that contributes to its high boiling point.

38. D is correct.

1,3-dithiane serves as a nucleophilic carbonyl equivalent.

Treatment of 1,3-dithiane with n-BuLi generates a carbanion between both sulfur atoms of the molecule, and this anion can add to electrophiles such as alkyl halides.

Both C–H bonds of the 1,3-dithiane can be substituted with alkyl groups.

The hydrolysis of the dithiane to the carbonyl group requires mercury salts in acidic solution.

39. C is correct.

The initial reaction between the amine and carboxylic acid is neutralization (i.e., proton transfer).

However, at high temperatures, this proton transfer is reversible, and the reaction has enough energy to promote the nucleophilic attack of the carboxylic acid instead, leading to amide formation.

40. D is correct.

Anhydride functional groups (below) have oxygen between two carbonyl carbons.

The anhydride functional group does not exist in the reference molecule.

41. D is correct.

Primary amines have one alkyl group attached to the nitrogen atom; secondary amines have two alkyl groups attached to the nitrogen atom; tertiary amines have three alkyl groups attached to the nitrogen atom.

42. D is correct.

The alcohol of this aromatic compound has the highest priority, and the carbon count starts at this position. The root (and suffix) name of the compound is "phenol."

The ethyl group is numbered as three instead of four because the numbering favors the lower position values.

43. D is correct.

The molecular formula given above is for an acyclic alkyne.

Acyclic alkynes have a linear geometry (i.e., 180 degrees), and the carbon atoms have an *sp* hybridization.

Cyclic alkynes have two fewer hydrogen atoms because those bonds are replaced with carbon-carbon bonds to form a ring.

44. B is correct.

In the polarimeter (i.e., plane-polarized light), enantiomers have the same magnitude of specific rotation, but the opposite sign.

45. A is correct.

The primary structure of a protein is the linear sequence of amino acids.

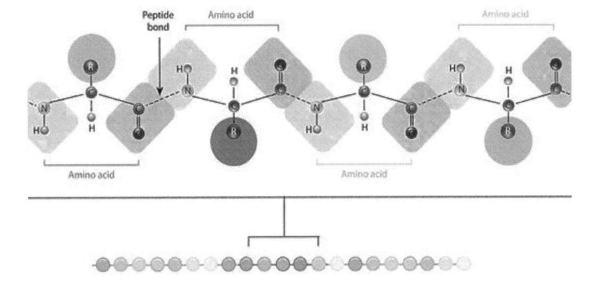

Copyright © 2020 Sterling Test Prep. Any duplication (copies, uploads, PDFs) is illegal.

46. D is correct.

Palmitic acid (below) is a saturated acid, meaning that the molecule does not contain a double bond.

Because palmitic acid lacks a double bond (i.e., saturated), the molecules are better able to stack together to form solids.

Since unsaturated fats are often liquids at room temperature, the fat has a higher melting point.

Linolenic acid (shown below) is polyunsaturated with three double bonds.

Alkenes (i.e., unsaturation) introduce "kinks" in the chain that give the unsaturated fat an overall bent structure. This molecular geometry limits these fats from clustering closely together to form solids.

Therefore, (relative to chain length), polyunsaturated molecules have the lowest melting point.

The position *omega* (ω) of the double bond(s) indicates the number of carbon atoms from the terminal methyl group.

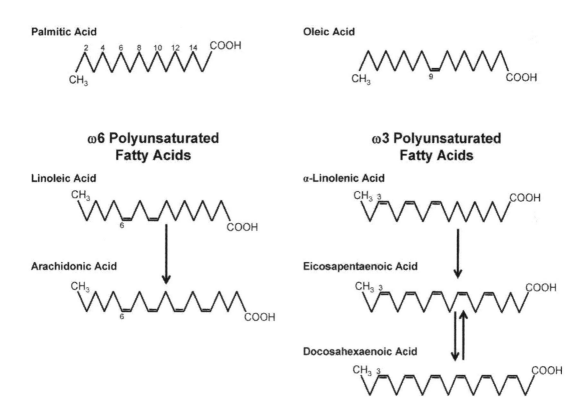

Saturated and unsaturated fatty acids – note the position (omega, ω) of the double bonds

47. D is correct.

Because amylose is a type of polysaccharide that does not have a β(1→4) glycosidic linkage, this polysaccharide can be digested by humans.

Polysaccharides (cellulose) with β(1→4) glycosidic linkages cannot be digested by humans, because they lack the cellulase enzyme to cleave the β(1→4) glycosidic linkages.

48. C is correct.

In double-stranded DNA molecules, adenine nucleotides always pair with thymine and cytosine pairs with guanine nucleotides.

Adenine forms two hydrogen bonds with thymine (A=T).

Cytosine forms three hydrogen bonds with guanine (C≡G).

The strands of DNA are antiparallel with the 5' written on the top left side of the molecule.

5'–ATATGGTC–3'
3'–TATACCAG–5'

49. D is correct.

Hydrophilic amino acids are found near the external regions of proteins and line the walls of protein ion channels because these molecules form more favorable interactions with the aqueous environment than hydrophilic amino acids.

50. D is correct.

As unsaturated fats become hydrogenated to form saturated fats, the melting point increases.

An equivalent of hydrogen is added across the double bonds of unsaturated fats during hydrogenation, increasing the molecular weight of the compound.

Furthermore, saturation helps to enhance the stacking ability of these compounds in the solid state.

The more saturated the compound is, the higher its melting point.

51. A is correct.

Ketohexose, a monosaccharide (shown below), is one of the components of sucrose, which is a disaccharide made from fructose and glucose.

Aldopentose
(5-carbon aldehyde)

Ketohexose
(6-carbon ketone)

Fructose (shown below) is one of the sweetest tasting natural sugars.

Glucose
(an aldohexose)

Fructose
(a ketohexose)

52. D is correct.

The DNA molecule (shown below) has a deoxyribose sugar-phosphate backbone with bases (A, C, G, T) projecting into the center to join the antiparallel strand of DNA (i.e., double helix).

A nucleotide has a deoxyribose sugar, base, and phosphate.

A nucleoside is a deoxyribose sugar and base without the phosphate group.

The deoxyribose sugar-phosphate (DNA) backbone is negatively charged due to the formal charge of the oxygen attached to the phosphate group.

The purine and pyrimidine base structures are shown below:

deoxyadenosine 5'-phosphate

deoxythymidine 5'-phosphate

deoxyguanosine 5'-phosphate

deoxycytosine 5'-phosphate

The purines (adenine and guanine) are double-ringed nitrogenous bases, while the pyrimidines (cytosine and thymine) are single-ringed nitrogenous bases.

53. C is correct.

Nonpolar amino acids are amino acids that have side chains composed of hydrogen and carbon atoms. The incorporation of electronegative heteroatoms, such as oxygen and nitrogen atoms, can make the side groups polar, acidic, or basic.

54. B is correct.

The two ends of a fatty acid compound are the hydrophobic, nonpolar end composed of hydrogen and carbon atoms, and the hydrophilic, polar end of the molecule, which is composed of oxygen atoms and can hydrogen bond with water molecules.

55. C is correct.

Tautomeric forms of a molecule involve changes in the connectivity of a functional group, and this is typically observed for aldehydes, ketones, and imines.

The two cyclic forms of monosaccharides have the same connectivity, but the configuration of the carbons is different. These forms are, therefore, diastereomers.

56. B is correct.

Transcription is a biomolecular event that takes place in the nucleus of the cell.

During transcription, RNA molecules are synthesized using complementary base pairs of DNA single strands.

57. B is correct.

All the molecules in the body are divided into four categories.

These biomolecular categories are: carbohydrates, lipids, nucleic acids, and proteins.

58. B is correct.

Although cholesterol plays a pivotal role in the synthesis of other steroids and the integrity of cell membranes, too much cholesterol in the blood results in the formation of plaque deposits in blood vessels.

59. C is correct.

One exception to the tendency for sugars to have oxygen atoms linked to every carbon atom is in deoxyribose (DNA).

Deoxyribose is similar in structure to a ribose; however, one of the alcohols is replaced with a carbon-hydrogen bond.

60. D is correct.

Amino acids are the monomers that makeup proteins.

Nucleotides are comprised of a nitrogenous base (i.e., adenosine, cytosine, guanine, and thymine or uracil), a phosphate group and a five-carbon sugar (i.e., ribose for RNA or deoxyribose for DNA).

Please, leave your Customer Review on Amazon

Explanations: Diagnostic Test #12

1. D is correct.

The longest carbon chain is composed of seven carbon atoms.

There are chlorine, ethyl and methyl substituent in this compound.

2. D is correct.

The benzylic position is one carbon away from benzene or aromatic ring.

Without the aromatic ring, the cation is considered an allylic carbocation when it is one carbon away from a double bond.

Vinyl means on the double bond.

3. C is correct.

Draw the different isomers of butene.

This compound can be drawn with the double bond terminal (the carbons are numbered according to IUPAC).

The terminal carbon in the double bond is numbered 1.

There are two geometric isomers of butene (i.e., *cis*-butene and *trans*-butene).

cis-2-butene   trans-2-butene

Geometric isomers are a subset of structural isomers. Geometric requires that the substituents from the double bond can be the same (i.e., *cis* and *trans*) or different (i.e., *E* and *Z*).

1-butene or butene (the position 1 is implied by IUPAC)

Isobutylene (not 2-methyl propene) according to IUPAC

Therefore, there are four structural isomers of butene.

4. D is correct.

The local magnetic field generated by the circulating current of the benzene ring causes the protons attached to the ring to be further deshielded (diagram below).

Electron-donating and withdrawing groups attached to the ring may shift the resonances of certain protons up or downfield.

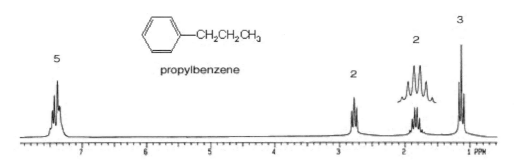

^{1}H NMR spectra with characteristic absorption for the phenyl ring between 6.0-8.0 ppm

5. B is correct.

Statement I: most substances become more soluble at higher temperatures because solubility constants, like other equilibrium constants (Le Châtelier's principle), are a function of temperature.

Statement II: polar or ionic molecules dissolve in solvents that are also polar, whereas non-polar compounds dissolve in non-polar solvents. Therefore, similar polarities increase solubility.

Statement III: molecular weight of the solvent is not related to solubility.

Statement IV: density of the solvent is not related to solubility.

6. C is correct.

A nucleophile donates lone pairs of electrons; therefore, it is a Lewis base.

7. C is correct.

Although these reactions produce the same products and in the same quantities, what is different is the rate of the borane addition for each alkene.

(E)-3-heptene   (Z)-3-hexene

The E has the highest priority substituents on opposite sides, while the Z alkene has both alkyl substituents on the same side.

Therefore, because Z alkenes are less thermodynamically stable than E alkenes, Z alkenes are more reactive.

Furthermore, the approach of the borane to the *Z* alkene is less sterically demanding, because the *Z* alkene is more open to an attack (alkyl groups are on the same side).

8. A is correct.

In the presence of excess hydrogen gas, the triple bond of 3-heptyne is completely reduced to the alkane.

Platinum and palladium catalysts can be used to reduce alkynes to alkenes or alkanes.

9. C is correct.

$FeBr_3$ acts as a catalyst to activate the alkyl bromide for electrophilic aromatic substitution (EAS) in this Friedel-Crafts alkylation.

Since the ethyl substituent on ethylbenzene is slightly electron donating, it functions as an *ortho-*, *para*-director for the substitution reaction.

Due to steric hindrance at the *ortho*-position, *para*-substitution is the major product.

10. B is correct.

Alcohols follow the same trend for boiling points as alkanes with longer chain molecules having higher boiling points.

Hexanol is the longest chain and, therefore, has the highest boiling point.

11. D is correct.

Ketones are functional groups that can no longer be oxidized by Cr^{VI} reagents. These groups do not undergo further reactions because there are no C–H bonds to the carbonyl carbon of the ketone.

Aldehydes, however, may have subsequent oxidations to generate carboxylic acids.

12. C is correct.

Carboxylic acids are acidic functional groups that have a hydroxyl group directly bonded to the carbonyl group.

Carboxylic acids are acidic because the conjugate base is relatively stable due to resonance stabilization of the negative charge on oxygen.

The molecule also contains three hydroxyl groups and an arene.

13. A is correct.

Amides are functional groups that possess an amino group bonded to a carbonyl moiety.

The reference molecule is a tertiary amine because it is bonded to three R groups.

14. B is correct.

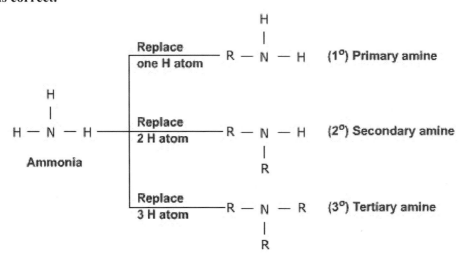

Primary amines are amines that have one alkyl group bonded to the nitrogen atom.

Secondary amines have two alkyl groups bonded to the nitrogen atom.

Tertiary amines contain nitrogen atoms that are bonded to three alkyl groups.

15. C is correct.

The longest carbon chain is composed of six carbon atoms and is the cyclohexene substructure.

The molecule contains a methyl group in the fourth position.

16. B is correct.

The hydrogen atom bonds by overlapping its $1s$ orbital with the orbital of a bonding partner.

The carbon atom is bonded to three atoms and is positively charged, both of which are indications that the carbon atom is sp^2 hybridized.

17. D is correct.

An asymmetric carbon refers to a chiral carbon: carbon bonded to four different substituents.

All the other compounds do not contain asymmetric carbons because at least two of the three atoms or groups bonded to each of their carbon atoms are the same.

18. D is correct.

The shielding effect arises from the electron density associated with the nuclei.

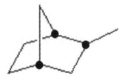

Hydrogen nuclei that have more electron density are more shielded, and their chemical shifts appear more upfield in the spectrum.

19. C is correct.

Thin layer chromatography relies upon the principle that a mobile phase (solvent) flows through a stationary phase (sample on the polar plates) and migrates at different rates depending on the attraction towards these phases.

If components within the sample are polar, then they adhere to the polar plates and are held immobile, producing a spot near the original location.

If components within the sample are nonpolar, then they are weakly attracted to the stationary phase, dissolve in the nonpolar solvent, move up the TLC plate with the solvent, and produce a spot further from the original location.

Each unique molecule has a reference R_f value that is a fraction of the movement of the sample to the total distance of the solvent.

Nonpolar samples move further and have higher R_f values than polar samples, which migrate a shorter distance because they remain bound to the polar plate.

R_f = migration distance of a sample/migration distance of the solvent front

20. D is correct.

There are only three tertiary alkyl positions (i.e., carbon bonded to three other carbons) in this molecule.

21. B is correct.

The addition of deuterium (an isotope of hydrogen) across a C=C double bond is metal-catalyzed and proceeds with *syn*-stereoselectivity, adding both deuterium to the same face of the double bond.

22. C is correct.

Protonation of alkynes with acids generates the more substituted carbocation because this cation is the more stable intermediate. Because the cation exists on a vinyl carbon atom, this cation is known as a vinyl cation.

23. B is correct.

The aromatic stabilization energy of benzene decreases the reactivity of its *pi* system relative to isolated or conjugated/nonaromatic alkenes.

Because of this stabilization, arenes resist metal catalyzed hydrogenation reactions and may require more specialized catalysts to facilitate their reductions.

24. A is correct.

When phenols are deprotonated (i.e., acting as an acid), a phenoxide ion (i.e., phenolate ion) are produced as shown.

The pK_a of phenols is much lower than it is for alcohols.

Methanol has a pK_a of 16, while phenols have pK_a values ≈ 9.9.

25. A is correct.

Aldehydes can convert to the enol form, although the equilibrium constant favors the aldehyde.

Conversion to the enol form destroys the stereocenter because this isomer is achiral.

When the enol form converts back to the ketone, protonation may occur on either face of the group, and this interconverts the configuration (i.e., producing R and S isomers).

The process is catalyzed by the presence of an acid or base.

26. D is correct.

A chemical equilibrium exists for this reaction, and water is given off as a byproduct in the process.

27. D is correct.

The hydrolysis of an ester is essentially the reverse of Fischer esterification.

To drive the reaction forward, excess water and an acid catalyst are used. The ester hydrolyzes to its two simpler components: the corresponding alcohol and carboxylic acid.

The *R* component of the alcohol product and the alkoxy group of the ester are the same.

28. C is correct.

Amines possess nitrogen atoms which have lone pairs that are more basic and nucleophilic than oxygen atoms and halogens such as fluorine.

This is because the nitrogen atom is a less electronegative heteroatom; therefore, the nonbonding valence electrons of nitrogen have more energy and are more reactive.

29. A is correct.

One option is to draw all the atoms to determine the atom count.

Alternatively, using a subscript of n for the number of carbons, the degrees of unsaturation can be determined from the following formulae:

Alkane: C_nH_{2n+2} = 0 degrees of unsaturation

Alkene: C_nH_{2n} = 1 degree of unsaturation

Alkyne: C_nH_{2n-2} = 2 degrees of unsaturation

Rings = 1 degree of unsaturation

The reference molecule has 2 rings and therefore 2 degrees of unsaturation:

C_nH_{2n-2}

$C_8H_{16-2} = C_8H_{14}$

30. A is correct.

Using the formula for calculating the degrees of unsaturation reveals that 2 unsaturation elements (either rings or *pi* bonds) exist.

Structures that contain atoms with satisfied octets are favored.

Molecules with charged carbon atoms tend to be less stable.

31. D is correct.

The total number of possible stereoisomers for a given molecule depends on the number of asymmetric carbon atoms (or chiral centers) present in the molecule.

There is a 2^N number of possibilities, where N is the number of chiral centers present.

The molecule has 4 chiral centers: $2^4 = 2 \times 2 \times 2 \times 2 = 16$ stereoisomers.

For some molecules, symmetry elements in the molecule may be redundant structures, which is why the 2^N calculation gives the maximum possible number of stereoisomers and not necessarily the actual number that exists.

32. D is correct.

2-methylpropanoic acid (or isobutyric acid)

Carbonyl carbons show an IR absorption between approximately 1630 and 1780 cm^{-1}.

The carbonyl of a carboxylic acid is reported to be between 1710 and 1780 cm^{-1}.

Because carboxylic acids contain a hydroxyl group, another signal around 3300 to 3400 cm^{-1} should be expected in the spectrum for this compound.

33. B is correct.

S_N2 is bimolecular;

   rate = k [substrate] × [nucleophile].

Therefore, if the nucleophile ($^-$OH) concentration is doubled, then the reaction rate also doubles.

Since the alkyl halide is primary, a unimolecular (S_N1) reaction occurs.

Water stabilizes the carbocation intermediate and thereby increases the rate of the reaction.

34. D is correct.

The trapping of mercury-alkene cations normally opens on the more substituted side, but the *tert*-butyl group sufficiently blocks access to this side. Therefore, the cation is opened on the more terminal side.

35. C is correct.

Use the following formulae to calculate the degrees of unsaturation:

   C_nH_{2n+2}: for an alkane (0 degrees of unsaturation)

   C_nH_{2n}: for an alkene or a ring (1 degree of unsaturation)

   C_nH_{2n-2}: for an alkyne, 2 double bonds, 2 rings or 1 ring and 1 double bond (2 degrees of unsaturation).

The general chemical formula for alkynes is C_nH_{2n-2} because each *pi* bond of the alkyne represents one degree of unsaturation.

Cyclic alkynes have an additional degree of unsaturation because of the cyclic structure.

Therefore, C_9H_{16} is the molecular formula that describes an acyclic alkyne.

36. B is correct.

Degenerate orbitals are orbitals that have the same energy.

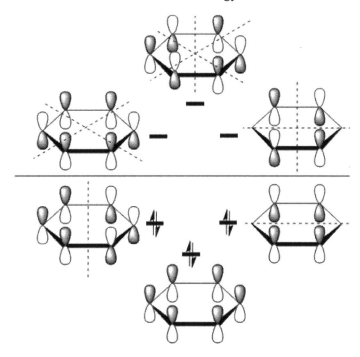

Bonding orbitals are below the horizontal plane, while antibonding orbitals are above

In the molecular orbital (MO) diagram for benzene: MOs π2 and π3 are positioned in the second energy level, and π4 and π5 MOs are positioned on the third energy level.

Therefore, there are two pairs of degenerate MOs.

37. C is correct.

The formation of an inorganic ester by the addition of alcohol and phosphoric acid is an example of dehydration synthesis because an equivalent of water is lost during the process.

38. D is correct.

If a stronger reducing agent, such as lithium aluminum hydride (LiAlH₄), is used, the aldehyde is reduced to the primary alcohol.

Ester is reduced to an aldehyde with the mild reducing agent of DIBAL

39. C is correct.

benzoic acid
insoluble in water

sodium benzoate
soluble in water

40. A is correct.

The reaction best suited to occur under "normal conditions," rather than harsh conditions, is the aminolysis of the ester to form an amide.

Amides are less electrophilic than esters, and basic conditions are needed to convert the amide back to the ester.

41. A is correct.

Quaternary ammonium salts can be formed from the *N*-alkylation of tertiary amines.

When tertiary amines are converted to ammonium salts, the inductive effects of the nitrogen atom are larger, and the magnitude of the carbon–nitrogen dipoles increases.

42. A is correct.

The *para-* notation means that two of the substituent groups are on opposite sides of the aromatic rings in a C_1–C_4 relationship.

When the bromine atoms are adjacent (C_1–C_2), the isomer is *ortho*.

When the bromine atoms are in a C_1–C_3 relationship, the isomer is *meta*.

43. D is correct.

Wohler's experiment is significant because it demonstrated that organic compounds can be created from inorganic compounds.

This result ran counter to the belief that the material that composed life was different from the matter of nonliving things, a theory called vitalism.

44. A is correct.

It is important to remember that if an alkene has geminal disubstitution (i.e., two identical moieties bonded to the same alkene carbon), then *cis-* and *trans*-isomerism is not possible.

45. A is correct.

In this reaction, an amino acid is prepared from a carboxylic acid.

The first step in this reaction is the conversion of the carboxylic acid to the alphabromo acid bromide intermediate.

This intermediate is then hydrolyzed in water to regenerate the carboxylic acid.

The alpha bromide is displaced upon exposure to ammonia and heat to form alanine.

Both enantiomers of the compound are expected for this reaction.

46. D is correct.

$$CH_2 \text{—} OR$$
$$CH \text{—} OR'$$
$$CH_2 \text{—} O \text{—} P(=O)(O^-) \text{—} OR''$$

Glycerophospholipid

The lipid shown is a derivative of the triglyceride molecule.

It is composed of glycerol, two fatty acid groups, and a phosphate group.

The purpose of the phosphate group is to increase the polarity of the molecule so it can be utilized as a part of cell membranes.

Sphingolipids (or glycosylceramides) are a class of lipids containing a backbone of sphingoid bases, a set of aliphatic amino alcohols that includes sphingosine.

They are important for signal transmission and cell recognition.

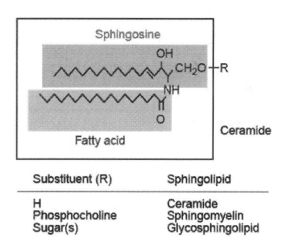

Substituent (R)	Sphingolipid
H	Ceramide
Phosphocholine	Sphingomyelin
Sugar(s)	Glycosphingolipid

Sphingolipid (R group is: H, phosphocholine, sugars, ceramide, sphingomyelin or glycosphingolipid)

Eicosanoids (e.g., prostaglandins and leukotrienes) are signaling molecules made by oxidation of 20-carbon fatty acids.

Eicosanoids are derived from either ω-3 or ω-6 fatty acids.

Prostaglandin E1 (with characteristic 5-membered ring)

Waxes are organic compounds that characteristically consist of long alkyl chains.

Wax

47. C is correct.

The conversion of one cyclic glucose stereoisomer to another involves the formation of an acyclic intermediate form.

When the molecule cyclizes again, the opposite face of the aldehyde is accessed to generate the other cyclic diastereomer.

48. D is correct.

A complementary base pair is used for RNA molecules during transcription and translation.

Errors are sometimes introduced to the sequence, and these errors can lead to mutations in the proteins that are assembled from them.

49. D is correct.

Threonine is an amino acid that contains secondary alcohol as part of the side chain.

The alcohol has a permanent dipole and is capable of hydrogen bonding.

Therefore, the types of intermolecular interactions expected are dipole-dipole interactions (hydrogen bonding is a subset of dipole-dipole interactions).

50. D is correct.

Fatty acids are biological molecules that contain long hydrocarbon groups.

These long hydrophobic chains can have alkene groups, but branching is not typically observed.

51. D is correct.

Glucose is an example of a reducing sugar because it contains an aldehyde that can undergo reduction.

The reduction of its aldehyde produces a sugar known as sorbitol. This is a way for the body to reduce blood glucose levels and is typically observed in diabetic patients with high blood sugar levels.

52. A is correct.

The dipole interactions that join the strands of DNA together are more specifically known as hydrogen bonds.

Hydrogen bonds form from the acid protons between the amides and imide functional groups, and the carbonyl and amide Lewis basic sites of the matched nitrogen base pairs.

53. B is correct.

Glycine is an achiral molecule that lacks a substituent at the alpha position.

The unsubstituted alpha position is methylene, and a methylene group has a symmetrical center (i.e., bonded to two hydrogens).

54. D is correct.

The plasma membrane is made up of lipids known as phospholipids.

Phospholipids mostly possess nonpolar characteristics due to the long hydrocarbon chains, making the membrane permeable to nonpolar materials and semipermeable to polar or charged molecules.

55. C is correct.

Sugar molecules typically contain hydrogen, carbon and oxygen atoms.

Lipids, such as phospholipids, may contain other heteroatom groups (e.g., phosphorus atoms).

Aminosaccharides are sugars that have nitrogen atoms in their structure.

56. C is correct.

Deoxyribose sugars are carbohydrates that are utilized in DNA synthesis, while ribose sugars are used to synthesize RNA molecules.

57. D is correct.

Tyrosine contains a phenol *R* group, phenylalanine has a phenyl group, tryptophan has an indole group, and histidine has an imidazole group.

58. A is correct.

Fatty acids and triglycerides do not contain any stereocenters.

The ester and alkene functional groups that exist in some fats possess a plane of symmetry and therefore do not possess asymmetric carbon atoms.

These molecules are achiral and are not optically active.

59. C is correct.

It may help to use a molecular model to answer this question.

If the hemiacetal is converted to the aldehyde, then the acyclic form of this molecule is represented by the indicated structure.

60. B is correct.

NADH is the biochemical equivalent to a hydride (H^-) reduction reagent for carbonyl groups.

Alternatively, NAD^+ is an oxidizing agent that can accept a hydride equivalent.

Glossary of Terms

A

Acetal – the product formed by the reaction of an aldehyde with an *Alcohol*; the general structure of an acetal is:

$$R-\underset{\underset{H}{|}}{C}\underset{\diagdown OR'}{\overset{\diagup OR'}{}}$$

Achiral – the opposite of *Chiral*; also called *non-chiral;* can be superimposed on its mirror image (e.g., CH_4); does not rotate plane-polarized light.

Acid – an agent able to produce positively charged hydrogen ions (H^+); since the hydrogen ion is a bare proton, it usually exists in a solvated form (such as H_3O^+); a proton donor or an electron pair acceptor; see *Brønsted-Lowry theory of acids and bases,* *Lewis acid* and *Lewis base.*

Acid-base reaction – a neutralization reaction in which the products are salt and water.

Activated complex – molecules at an unstable intermediate stage in a reaction.

Activating group – a group that increases the rate of electrophilic *Aromatic* substitution when bonded to an aromatic ring.

Activation energy – the minimum energy which reacting species must possess in order to be able to form an "activated complex," or "transition state," before proceeding to the products; the difference in potential energy between the ground state and the transition state of molecules; molecules of reactants must have this amount of energy to proceed to the product state; the activation energy (E_a) may be derived from the temperature dependence of the reaction rate using the Arrhenius equation.

Acyl group – a group with the following structure, where R can be either an alkyl or aryl group:

$$R-\overset{\overset{O}{\|}}{C}-$$

Acyl halide – a compound with the general structural formula:

$$R-\overset{\overset{O}{\|}}{C}-X$$

Acylation – a reaction in which an acyl group is added to a molecule.

Acylium ion – the resonance stabilized cation:

$$\overset{+}{R\overset{}{C}} = \overset{..}{\overset{..}{O}} \longleftrightarrow RC \equiv \overset{+}{\overset{..}{O}}$$

Addition – a reaction that produces a new compound by combining all the elements of the original reactants.

Addition elimination mechanism – the two-stage mechanism by which nucleophilic *Aromatic* substitution occurs; in the first stage, the addition of the nucleophile to the carbon bearing the *Leaving group* occurs; an elimination follows in which the leaving group is expelled.

Addition reactions – reactions in which an unsaturated system is saturated or partly saturated by the addition of a molecule across the multiple bond (e.g., the addition of bromine to ethene to form 1,2-dibromoethane).

Adduct – the product of an addition reaction.

Alcohol – a molecule containing a hydroxyl (–OH) group; also a functional group.

Aldehyde – a molecule containing a terminal carbonyl (–CHO) group; also, a functional group.

Alicyclic compound – an *ali*phatic *cyclic* hydrocarbon; a compound contains a ring but not an *Aromatic* ring; see *Aliphatic compound* and *Cyclization*.

Aliphatic compound – a straight- or branched-chain hydrocarbon; an *Alkane*, *Alkene* or *Alkyne*.

Alkaloid – organic substances occurring naturally which are basic, forming salts with acids; the basic group is usually an amino function.

Alkane – a hydrocarbon that contains only single covalent bonds (i.e., containing only C–H and C–C single bonds); the *Alkane* general formula is C_nH_{2n+2}.

Alkene – a molecule containing one or more carbon-carbon double bonds; a functional group.

Alkoxide ion – an anion formed by removing a proton from an *Alcohol*; the RO$^-$ ion.

Alkoxy free radical – a free radical formed by the homolytic cleavage of an *Alcohol* –OH bond; the RO· free radical.

Alkyl group – an *Alkane* molecule from which a hydrogen atom has been removed; abbreviated as "R" in structural formulas.

Alkyl halide – a hydrocarbon that contains a halogen substituent, such as fluorine, chlorine, bromine or iodine.

Alkyl-substituted cycloalkane – a cyclic hydrocarbon to which one or more *Alkyl group*s are bonded; compare with *Cycloalkyl Alkane*.

Alkylation – a reaction in which an *Alkyl group* is added to a molecule.

Alkyne – a molecule containing one or more carbon-carbon triple bonds; a functional group; the general formula is C_nH_{2n-2}.

Allyl group – the $H_2C{=}CHCH_2-$ group; a group containing 3 carbon atoms and a double bond, $C_1{=}C_2{-}C_3$, where C_3 is called the "allylic position" or "*Allylic carbon* atom."

Allylic carbon – an sp^3 carbon adjacent to a double bond.

Allylic carbocation – the $H_2C{=}CHCH_2^+$ ion.

Allylic rearrangement – the migration of a double bond in a 3-carbon system from carbon atoms one and two to carbon atoms two and three (e.g., $C_1{=}C_2{-}C_3{-}X$ to $X{-}C_1{-}C_2{=}C_3$).

Analogue – in organic chemistry, chemicals that are similar to each other but not identical (e.g., the hydrocarbons are all similar to each other, but an *Alkane* is different from the *Alkenes* and *Alkynes* because of the types of bonds they contain; therefore, an *Alkane* and an *Alkene* are analogs).

Angle of rotation (α) – in a polarimeter, the angle right or left in which plane-polarized light is turned after passing through an optically active compound in solution.

Amide – a molecule containing a carbonyl group attached to nitrogen ($-CONR_2$); also, a functional group.

Amine – a molecule containing an isolated nitrogen (NR_3); also, a functional group.

Anion – a negatively charged ion.

Anomers – the specific term used to describe carbohydrate stereoisomers differing only in configuration at the hemiacetal carbon atom.

Anti-**addition** – a reaction in which the two groups of a reagent X–Y add on opposite faces of a carbon-carbon bond.

Anti-**aromatic** – a highly unstable planar ring system with $4n$ *pi* electrons.

Antibonding molecular orbital – a molecular orbital that contains more energy than the atomic orbitals from which it was formed; an electron is less stable in an antibonding orbital than it is in its original atomic orbital.

Anti-**conformation** – a type of staggered conformation in which the two big groups are opposite of each other in a *Newman projection*.

Anti-**Markovnikov addition** – a reaction in which the hydrogen atom of a hydrogen halide bonds to the carbon of a double bond that is bonded to *fewer* hydrogen atoms; the addition takes place via a free-radical intermediate rather than a carbocation; compare with *Markovnikov rule*.

Antiperiplanar (anticoplanar) – the conformation in which hydrogen and a leaving group are in the same plane and on opposite sides of a carbon-carbon single bond; the conformation required for E_2 elimination.

Aprotic solvents – solvents that do not contain O–H or N–H bonds.

Arene – an *Aromatic* hydrocarbon.

Aromatic – an aromatic molecule or ion possesses aromaticity; aromaticity is the special property of planar (or nearly planar) cyclic, conjugated systems having (4n + 2) conjugated *pi* electrons; the delocalization of the (4n + 2) *pi* electrons gives them special stability (aromatic compounds are unusually stable compounds); for benzene, the most common aromatic system (n = 1, therefore 6 *pi* electrons), the aromaticity confers the characteristic reactivity of electrophilic substitution.

Aromatic compound – a compound that possesses a closed-shell electron configuration as well as resonance; obeys *Hückel's rule*.

Aryl – an *Aromatic* group as a substituent.

Aryl group – a group produced by the removal of a proton from an *Aromatic* molecule.

Aryl halide – a compound in which a halogen atom is attached to an *Aromatic* ring.

Association – a term applied to the combination of molecules of a substance with one another to form more complex systems; see *Dissociation* and *Dissociation constant*.

Asymmetry – a term applied an object or molecule that does not possess symmetry.

Asymmetric induction – a term applied to the selective synthesis of one diastereomeric form of a compound resulting from the influence of an existing *Chiral* center adjacent to the developing asymmetric carbon atom; this usually arises because, for steric reasons, the incoming atom or group does not have equal access to both sides of the molecule.

Atom – the smallest amount of an element; a nucleus surrounded by electrons.

Atomic mass (A) – the sum of the weights of the protons and neutrons in an atom; a proton and neutron each have a mass of 1 atomic mass unit.

Atomic number (Z) – the number of protons or electrons in an atom.

Atomic 1*s* orbital – the spherical orbital nearest the nucleus of an atom.

Atomic orbital – a region in space around the nucleus of an atom where the probability of finding an electron is high, which may be described in terms of the four quantum numbers.

Atomic *p* orbital – an hourglass-shaped orbital, oriented on *x, y* and *z*-axes in three-dimensional space.

Atomic *s* orbital – a spherical orbital.

Avogadro's constant – the number of particles (atoms or molecules) in one mole of any pure substance: 6.022×10^{23}.

Axial bond – a bond perpendicular to the equator of the ring (up or down), typically in chair cyclohexane.

B

Baeyer reagent – cold, dilute potassium permanganate; used to oxidize *Alkenes* and *Alkynes*.

Base – a substance that can combine with a proton (i.e., a proton acceptor or an electron pair donor); see *Brønsted-Lowry theory of acids and bases*, *Lewis acid* and *Lewis base*.

Benzene (Benzenoid) ring – an *Aromatic* ring with a benzene-like structure.

Benzyl group – a *Benzene ring* plus a methylene (~CH_2~) unit: $C_6H_5CH_2$.

Benzylic position – the position of a carbon attached to a *Benzene ring*.

Benzyne – an unstable intermediate that consists of a *Benzene ring* with an additional (triple) bond that is created by the side-to-side overlap of sp^2 orbitals on adjacent carbons of the ring.

Bicyclic – a molecule with two rings that share at least two carbons.

Bimolecular reaction – a chemical reaction in which two species (e.g., molecules, ions or radicals) react together to form new chemical species; most reactions are bimolecular or proceed through a series of bimolecular steps.

Bond angle – the angle formed between two adjacent bonds on the same atom.

Bond-dissociation energy – the amount of energy needed to homolytically fracture a bond.

Bond energy – the energy required to break a particular bond by a homolytic process.

Bond length – the equilibrium distance between the nuclei of two atoms or groups that are bonded to each other.

Bond strength – see *Bond-dissociation energy.*

Bonding electron – see *Valence electrons.*

Bonding molecular orbital – the orbital formed by the overlap of adjacent atomic orbitals.

Branched-chain *Alkane* – an *Alkane* with *Alkyl groups* bonded to the central carbon chain.

Brønsted-Lowry theory of acids and bases – A Brønsted-Lowry acid is a compound capable of donating a proton (a hydrogen ion); a Brønsted-Lowry base is capable of accepting a hydrogen ion; in *Neutralization,* an acid donates a proton to a base, creating a conjugate acid and a conjugate base.

Buffer solution – a solution of definite pH made up in such a way that the pH alters only gradually with the addition of an acid or a base.

C

Canonical structures – any of two or more hypothetical structures of *Resonance* theory which can be written for a molecule simply by rearranging the valence electrons of the molecule (e.g., the two Kekule structures of benzene); sometimes called "valence bond isomers."

Carbanion – a carbon atom bearing a negative charge; a carbon anion.

Carbene – a reactive intermediate, characterized by a neutral, electron-deficient carbon center with two substituents - two single bonds and just six electrons in its valence shell (R_2C:).

Carbenoid – a chemical that resembles a carbene in its chemical reactions.

Carbocation – a carbon *Cation*; a carbon atom bearing a positive charge (sometimes referred to as a "carbonium ion").

Carbonyl group – a carbon double bonded to oxygen (C=O); the $-\overset{\overset{\text{O}}{\|}}{\text{C}}-$ group.

Carboxylic acid – a molecule containing a carboxyl (COOH) group; also, a functional group; the $-\underset{\underset{\text{O}}{\|}}{\text{C}}-\text{OH}$ group.

Catalyst – a substance that, when added to a reaction mixture, changes (speeds up) the rate of attainment of equilibrium in the system without itself undergoing a permanent chemical change.

Catalytic cracking – the method for producing gasoline from heavy petroleum distillates; generally, the catalysts are mixtures of silica and alumina or synthetic conjugates, such as the zeolites.

Catalytic reforming – the process of improving the octane number of straight-run gasoline by increasing the proportion of *Aromatic* and *Branched-chain Alkanes*; catalysts employed are either molybdenum-aluminum oxides or platinum-based.

Cation – a positively charged ion.

Cationic polymerization – occurs via a cation intermediate and is less efficient than *Free-radical polymerization*.

Chain reaction – a reaction that, once started, produces enough energy to keep the reaction running; proceed by a series of steps which produce intermediates, energy and products (e.g., the free radical addition of hydrogen bromide to an *Alkene)*.

Chair conformation – typically, the most stable cyclohexane conformation; looks like a chair.

Chemical shift – the location of an NMR peak relative to the standard tetramethylsilane (TMS), given in units of parts per million (ppm).

Chiral – describes a molecule that is not superimposable on its mirror image, as the relationship of a left hand to a right hand; see *Chiral molecule*.

Chiral center – a carbon or other atom with four non-identical substituents.

Chiral molecule – a molecule that is not superimposable on its mirror image; rotate plane-polarized light.

Chirality – a term which may be applied to any asymmetric object or molecule; the property of non-identity of an object with its mirror image.

Chromatography – a series of related techniques for the separation of a mixture of compounds by their distribution between two phases; in gas-liquid chromatography, the distribution is between a gaseous and a liquid phase; in column chromatography, the distribution is between a liquid and a solid phase.

Cis – two identical substituents on the same side of a double bond or ring.

Closed-shell electron configuration – a stable electron configuration in which all the electrons are in the lowest energy orbitals available.

Competing reactions – two reactions that start with the same reactants but form different products.

Compound – a term used generally to indicate a definite combination of elements into a more complex structure (a molecule); also applied to systems with non-stoichiometric proportions of elements.

Concerted – taking place at the same time without the formation of an intermediate.

Condensation reaction – a reaction in which two molecules join with the liberation of a small stable molecule.

Configuration – the order and relative three-dimensional orientation of the atoms in a molecule; given the designation *R* or *S*; "absolute configuration" is when the relative three-dimensional arrangement in the space of atoms in a *Chiral* molecule have been correlated with an absolute standard.

Configurational isomers – a series of compounds which have the same constitution and bonding of atoms, but which differ in their atomic spatial arrangement (e.g., glucose and mannose).

Conformation – the spatial arrangement of a molecule in space at any particular moment in time; most molecules can adopt an infinite number of conformations because of the possible rotation about single covalent bonds; of these possibilities, most compounds tend to spend most time in only one or a few conformational states, called the "preferred conformations."

Conformer – a conformation of a molecule; generally, these will be at energy minima.

Conjugate acid – the acid that results when a Brønsted-Lowry base accepts a hydrogen ion.

Conjugate base – the base that results when a Brønsted-Lowry acid loses a hydrogen ion.

Conjugated double bonds – double bonds separated by one carbon-carbon single bond; also alternating double bonds.

Conjugation – the overlapping in all directions of a series of *p* orbitals; a sequence of alternating double (or triple) and single bonds (e.g., C=C–C=C and C=C–C=O); can also be relayed by the participation of lone pairs of electrons or vacant orbitals.

Conjugation energy – see *Resonance energy.*

Constitution – the number and type of atoms in a molecule.

Constitutional isomers – molecules with the same molecular formula but with atoms attached in different ways.

Coordinate bond – the linkage of two atoms by a pair of electrons, both electrons being provided by one of the atoms (the donor); covalent bonds.

Coupling constant (*J*) – the distance between two neighboring lines in an NMR peak (given in units of Hz); the separation in frequency units between multiple peaks in one chemical shift; this separation results from the spin-spin coupling.

Coupling protons – protons that interact with each other and split the NMR peak into a certain number of lines following the *n* + 1 rule.

Covalent bond – a bond formed by the sharing of electrons between atoms.

Cyano group – the ~C≡N group.

Cyanohydrin – a compound with the general formula:

$$\begin{array}{c} \text{OH} \\ | \\ \text{R}-\text{C}-\text{C}\equiv\text{N} \\ | \\ \text{R'} \end{array}$$

Cyclization – the formation of ring structures.

Cycloaddition – a reaction that forms a ring.

Cycloalkane – a ring hydrocarbon made up of carbon and hydrogen atoms joined by single bonds.

Cycloalkyl *Alkane* – an *Alkane* to which a ring structure is bonded.

Cyclohydrocarbon – an *Alkane*, *Alkene* or *Alkyne* formed in a ring structure rather than a straight or branched chain; the general formula is C_nH_{2n} (*n* must be a whole number of 3 or greater).

D

Deactivating group – a group that causes an *Aromatic* ring to become less reactive toward electrophilic aromatic substitution.

Debye unit (D) – the unit of measure for a dipole moment; one debye equals 1.0×10^{-18} esu · cm (electrostatic units); see *Dipole moment*.

Decarboxylation – a reaction in which carbon dioxide is expelled from a carboxylic acid.

Dehalogenation – the elimination reaction in which two halogen atoms are removed from adjacent carbon atoms to form a double bond.

Dehydration – the elimination reaction in which water is removed from a molecule.

Dehydrohalogenation – the elimination reaction in which a hydrogen atom and a halogen atom (a hydrohalic acid, like HBr, HCl, etc.) are removed from a molecule to form a double bond.

Delocalization – electron systems in which bonding electrons are not localized between two atoms as for a single bond but are spread (delocalized) over the whole group (e.g., *Pi-bond* electrons the delocalized *pi*-electrons associated with *Aromatic* molecules).

Delocalization energy – see *Resonance energy*.

Delta value (*d* value or Δ) – the chemical shift; the location of an NMR peak relative to the standard tetramethylsilane (TMS), given in units of parts per million (ppm).

Deprotonation – the loss of a proton (hydrogen ion) from a molecule.

Deshielding – an effect in NMR spectroscopy that the movement of *sigma* and *pi* electrons within the molecule causes; causes chemical shifts to appear at lower magnetic fields (downfield).

Dextrorotatory – the phenomenon in which plane-polarized light is turned in a clockwise direction.

Diastereomers (diastereoisomers) – stereoisomeric structures which are not enantiomers (mirror images) of one another; often applied to systems that differ only in the configuration at one carbon atom (e.g., *meso-* and *d-* or *l-*tartaric acids).

Diels-Alder reaction – a cycloaddition reaction between a conjugated diene and an *Alkene* that produces a 1,4-addition product.

Diene – a molecule that contains two alternating double bonds; also a reactant in the *Diels-Alder reaction*.

Dienophile – a reactant in the *Diels-Alder reaction* that contains a double bond; often substituted with electron-withdrawing groups.

Dienophile – the *Alkene* that adds to the *Diene* in a Diels-Alder reaction.

Dihalide – a compound that contains two halogen atoms; also called *"dihaloalkane."*

Dihedral angle – the angle between groups attached on adjacent carbon atoms when viewed in a *Newman projection*.

Diol – a compound that contains two hydroxyls (~OH) groups; a *"dihydroxy alkane."*

Dipole moment – a measure of the polarity of a molecule; the mathematical product of the charge in electrostatic units (esu) and the distance that separates the two charges in centimeters (cm) (e.g., substituted *Alkyne*s have dipole moments caused by differences in electronegativity between the triple-bonded and single-bonded carbon atoms).

Disproportionation – a process in which a compound of one oxidation state changes to compounds of two or more oxidation states (e.g., $2\ Cu^+ \rightarrow Cu + Cu^{2+}$).

Dissociation – the process whereby a molecule is split into simpler fragments that may be smaller molecules, atoms, free radicals or ions.

Dissociation constant – the measure of the extent of dissociation, measured by the dissociation constant K. For the process:

$$AB = A + B$$

$$K = ([A] \cdot [B]) / [AB]$$

Dissymmetric – see *Chiral*.

Distillation – separation of a liquid mixture based on differences in boiling points.

Double bond – some atoms can share two pairs of electrons to form a double bond (two covalent bonds); formally, the second (double) bond arises from the overlap of p orbitals from two atoms, already united by a *sigma* bond, to form a *Pi bond*; hydrocarbons that contain one double bond are *Alkenes*, and hydrocarbons with two double bonds are *Dienes*.

Doublet – describes an NMR signal split into two peaks.

Dyestuffs – intensely colored compounds applied to a substrate; colors are due to the absorption of light to give electronic transitions.

E

E₁ elimination reaction – a reaction that eliminates a hydrohalic acid (e.g., HCl, HBr, etc) to form an *Alkene*; a first-order reaction that goes through a *Carbocation* mechanism.

E₂ elimination reaction – a reaction that eliminates a hydrohalic acid (e.g., HCl, HBr, etc) to form an *Alkene*; a second-order reaction that occurs in a single step in which the double bond is formed as the hydrohalic acid is eliminated.

E isomer – *Stereoisomer* in which the two highest priority groups are on opposite sides of a ring or double bond.

Eclipsed – a *Conformation* in which substituents on two attached saturated carbon atoms overlap when viewed as a *Newman projection*.

Eclipsed conformation – *Conformation* about a carbon-carbon single bond in which all the bonds on two adjacent carbons are aligned with each other (0° apart when viewed in a *Newman projection*).

Electron – negatively charged particles of little weight that exist in quantized probability areas around the atomic nucleus.

Electron affinity – the amount of energy liberated when an electron is added to an atom in the gaseous state.

Electronegativity – the measure of an atom's ability to attract electrons toward itself in a covalent bond; the halogen fluorine is the most electronegative element; measured in terms of the highest occupied molecular orbital (*HOMO*) of one molecule and the lowest unoccupied molecular orbital (*LUMO*) energy levels.

Electronegativity scale – an arbitrary scale by which the electronegativity of individual atoms can be compared.

Electronic configuration – the order in which electrons are arranged in an atom or molecule; used in a distinct and different sense from stereochemical *Configuration*; see *Stereochemistry*.

Electronic transition – in an atom or molecule, the electrons only have certain allowed energies (orbitals); if an electron passes from one orbital to another, an electronic transition occurs and there is the emission or absorption of energy corresponding to the difference in energy of the two orbitals.

Electrophile – an "electron seeker;" an atom, molecule or ion able to accept an electron pair to stabilize itself; a *Lewis acid*.

Electrophilic addition – a reaction in which the addition of an *Electrophile* to an unsaturated molecule results in the formation of a saturated molecule.

Electrophilic substitution – an overall reaction in which an *Electrophile* binds to a substrate with the expulsion of another electrophile (e.g., the electrophilic substitution of a proton by another electrophile, such as a nitronium ion, on an *Aromatic* substrate, such as benzene).

Electrostatic attraction – the attraction of a positive ion for a negative ion.

Electrovalent (ionic) bond – bonding by *Electrostatic attraction*.

Element – a substance which cannot be further subdivided by chemical methods.

Element of unsaturation – a *Pi bond*; a multiple bond or ring in a molecule.

Enantiomers – a pair of isomers that are related as mirror images of one another (e.g., isomers differing only in the configuration of the *Chiral* atoms).

Enantiomorphic pair – in optically active molecules with more than one stereogenic center, the two structures that are mirror images of each other.

Endothermic – a reaction in which heat is absorbed.

Energy diagram (or reaction energy diagram) – a graph of the energy of a reaction against the progress of the reaction.

Energy of reaction – the difference between the total energy content of the reactants and the total energy content of the products; the greater the energy of reaction, the more stable the products.

Enol – an unstable compound (e.g., *Vinyl alcohol*) in which a hydroxide group is attached to a carbon bearing a carbon-carbon double bond; these compounds *Tautomerize* to form *Ketones*, which are more stable.

Enolate ion – the resonance stabilized ion formed when an *Aldehyde* or *Ketone* loses an α hydrogen:

Enthalpy (*H*) – a thermodynamic state function, generally measured in kilojoules per mole; in chemical reactions, the enthalpy change (ΔH) is related to changes in the free energy (ΔG) and *Entropy* (ΔS) by the equation: $\Delta G = \Delta H - T\Delta S$.

Entropy (*S*) – a thermodynamic quantity that is a measure of the degree of disorder within any system. The greater the degree of order, the higher the entropy; for an increase in entropy, S is positive; has the units of joules per degree K per mole.

Enzyme – a naturally occurring substance able to catalyze a chemical reaction.

Epimerization – a process in which the configuration about one *Chiral* center of a compound, containing more than one *Chiral* atom, is inverted to give the opposite configuration; the term "epimers" is often used to describe two related compounds that differ only in the configuration about one chiral atom.

Epoxide – a three-membered ring that contains oxygen.

Epoxidation – the addition of an oxygen bridge across a double bond to give an oxirane; achieved by use of a peracid or, in a few cases, by use of a *Catalyst* and oxygen.

Equatorial – the bonds in chair cyclohexane that are oriented along the equator of the ring.

Equilibrium constant – according to the law of mass action, for any reversible chemical reaction, aA + bB = cC + dD, the equilibrium constant (*K*) is defined as:

$$K = ([C]^c[D]^d) / ([A]^a[B]^b)$$

Ester – the $\overset{O}{\underset{}{-\overset{\|}{C}-OR}}$ functional group; a molecule containing a carbonyl group adjacent to oxygen (RCOOR').

Ether – a molecule containing oxygen singly-bonded to two carbon atoms; also, a functional group; the general formula is R–O–R'; epoxyethane, an epoxide, is a cyclic ether; often refers to diethyl ether.

Excited state – the state of an atom, molecule or group when it has absorbed energy and become excited to a higher energy state as compared to the normal ground state; may be electronic, vibrational, rotational, etc.

F

Fischer projection – a convention for drawing carbon chains so that the relative three-dimensional stereochemistry of the carbon atoms is relatively easy to portray as a 2-dimensional drawing.

Fingerprint region – region of an IR spectrum below 1500 cm^{-1}; often complex and difficult to interpret.

Free energy (*delta G*) – a thermodynamic state function; the free energy change (G) in any reaction is related to the *Enthalpy* and *Entropy*: $\Delta G = \Delta H - T\Delta S$.

Free radicals – molecules or ions with unpaired electrons; generally, extremely reactive; "stable" free radicals include molecular oxygen, NO and NO_2; organic free radicals range from those of transient existence only to very long-lived species; alkyl free radicals tend to be very reactive and short-lived.

Free-radical chain reaction – a reaction that proceeds by a free-radical intermediate in a chain mechanism (a series of self-propagating, interconnected steps); compare with *Free-radical reaction.*

Free-radical polymerization – a polymerization initiated by a *Free radical.*

Free-radical reaction – a reaction in which a covalent bond is formed by the union of two radicals; compare with *Free-radical chain reaction.*

Frontier orbital symmetry – the theory that the site and rates of reaction depend on the geometries, the sign of the wave function and relative energies of the highest occupied molecular orbital (*HOMO*) of one molecule and the lowest unoccupied molecular orbital (*LUMO*) of the other.

Functional group – a set of bonded atoms that displays a specific molecular structure and chemical reactivity when bonded to a carbon atom in the place of a hydrogen atom.

G

Gauche – a conformational isomer in which the groups are neither eclipsed nor trans to one another; often taken as the conformation where the dihedral angle between the groups is 60°.

Gauche conformation – a type of staggered conformation in which two bulky groups are next to each other.

Geometrical isomerism – a term describing isomerism owing to the presence of restricted rotation about a bond (e.g., (*Z*) and (*E*) isomers of unsymmetrically substituted *Alkene*s).

Grignard reagent – an organometallic reagent in which magnesium metal inserts between an *Alkyl group* and a halogen (e.g., CH_3MgBr).

Ground state – the lowest energy state of an atom, molecule or ion.

H

Half-life, $t^{1/2}$ – the time taken for the concentration of a substance in a reaction to reduce to half its original value; used in first-order reactions and as a measure of the rate of radioactive decay.

Halide – a member of the VIIA column of the periodic table (e.g., F, Cl, Br, I) or a molecule that contains one of these atoms; also a functional group.

Haloalkane – an *Alkane* that contains one or more halogen atoms; also called an *Alkyl halide*.

Halogen – an electronegative, nonmetallic element in Group VII of the periodic table, including fluorine, chlorine, bromine, and iodine; often represented in structural formulas by an "X."

Halogenation – a reaction in which halogen atoms are bonded to an *Alkene* at the double bond.

Halonium ion – a halogen atom that bears a positive charge; highly unstable.

Hard and soft acids and bases – a classification of acids and bases depending on their polarizability; hard bases include fluoride ions; soft bases include triphenylphosphine; hard acids include Na^+, whilst an example of a soft, polarizable acid is Pt^{2+}; hard-hard and soft-soft interactions are favored; hardness and softness can be described in terms of the *HOMO* and *LUMO* interactions.

Heat of reaction – the amount of heat absorbed or evolved when specified amounts of compounds react under constant pressure; expressed as kilojoules per mole; for exothermic reactions, the convention is that the *Enthalpy* (*H*) change (heat of reaction) is negative.

Hemiacetal – a functional group of the structure:

$$-\overset{\displaystyle |}{\underset{\displaystyle H}{C}}\!\!\overset{\displaystyle OR}{\underset{\displaystyle OH}{\big<}}$$

Hemiketal – a functional group of the structure:

$$-\overset{\displaystyle |}{\underset{\displaystyle R}{C}}\!\!\overset{\displaystyle OR}{\underset{\displaystyle OH}{\big<}}$$

Hertz – a measure of a wave's frequency; equals the number of waves that pass a specific point per second.

Heteroatom – in organic chemistry, an atom other than carbon.

Heterocyclic compound – a class of cyclic compounds in which one of the ring atoms is not carbon (e.g., epoxyethane).

Heterogeneous reaction – a reaction that occurs between substances that are mainly present in different phases (e.g., between a gas and a liquid).

Heterogenic bond formation – a type of bond formed by the overlap of orbitals on adjacent atoms. One orbital of the pair donates both electrons to the bond.

Heterolytic cleavage – the fracture of a bond in such a manner that one of the atoms receives both electrons; in reactions, this asymmetrical bond rupture generates carbocation and carbanion mechanism.

Heterolytic reaction – a reaction in which a covalent bond is broken with unequal sharing of the electrons from the bond.

HOMO – the highest occupied molecular orbital of a molecule, ion or atom.

Homologous series – a set of compounds with common compositions (e.g., the *Alkane*s, the *Alkene*s and the *Alkyne*s).

Homolog – one of a series of compounds in which each member differs from the next by a constant unit.

Homolytic cleavage – the fracture of a bond in such a manner that both atoms receive one of the bond's electrons; this symmetrical bond rupture forms free radicals; in reactions, it generates *Free-radical* mechanisms.

Homolytic reaction – a reaction in which a covalent bond is broken with equal sharing of the electrons from the bond.

Hückel's rule – a rule stating that a compound with 4n + 2 π electrons will have a closed-shell electron configuration and will be *Aromatic*.

Hybrid orbitals – orbitals formed from mixing together atomic orbitals, like the sp^x orbitals, which result from mixing *s* and p orbitals.

Hydration – the addition of the elements of water to a molecule.

Hydride shift – the movement of a hydride ion (a hydrogen atom with a negative charge) to form a more inductively-stabilized carbocation.

Hybridization – the process whereby atomic orbitals of different types but similar energies are combined to form a set of equivalent hybrid orbitals; these hybrid orbitals do not exist in the atoms, but only in the formation of molecular orbitals by combining atomic orbitals from different atoms.

Hydroboration – the *Cis*-addition of B–H bonds across double (or triple) C–C bonds.

Hydroboration-oxidation – the addition of borane (BH_3) or an alkyl borane to an *Alkene* and its subsequent oxidation to produce the *Anti-Markovnikov* indirect addition of water.

Hydrocarbon – a molecule that exclusively contains carbon and hydrogen atoms; the central bond may be a single, double or triple covalent bond, and it forms the backbone of the molecule.

Hydrogenation – the addition of hydrogen to a multiple bond.

Hydrogenolysis – the cleaving of a chemical bond by hydrogen, generally carried out in the presence of a hydrogenation *Catalyst*.

Hydrohalogenation – a reaction in which a hydrogen atom and a halogen atom are added to a double bond to form a saturated compound.

Hydrolysis – the addition of the elements of water to a substance, often with the partition of the substance into two parts (e.g., the hydrolysis of an *Ester* to an acid and an *Alcohol*).

Hydrolyze – to cleave a bond via the elements of water.

Hyperconjugation – weak interaction (electron donation) between *sigma* bonds with p orbitals; explains why alkyl substituents stabilize carbocations.

I

Inductive effect – an electronic effect transmitted through bonds in an organic compound due to the electronegativity of substituents and the permanent polarization thereof; the substituent either induces charges towards or away from itself with the formation of a dipole.

Infrared spectroscopy (IR) – the study of the absorption of infrared light by substances; since this corresponds to vibrational (and some rotational) changes, infrared spectroscopy provides valuable information about the structure of a substance; detailed correlation tables exist relating infrared bands (absorbances) to functional groups.

Inhibitor – a general term for any compound that inhibits (slows down) a reaction; can be used to slow or stop free radical chain reactions.

Initiation step – the first step in the mechanism of a reaction.

Initiator – a material capable of being easily fragmented into free radicals, which in turn initiate a *Free-radical reaction*.

Insertion – placing between two atoms.

Intermediate – a species that forms in one step of a multistep mechanism; unstable and cannot be isolated.

Ion – an atom or group of atoms that has lost or gained one or more electrons to become a charged species.

Ionic bond – a bond formed by the transfer of electrons between atoms, resulting in the formation of ions of opposite charge; the electrostatic attraction between these ions.

Ionization energy – the energy needed to remove an electron from an atom.

IR spectroscopy – an instrumental technique that measures IR (infrared) light absorption by molecules; can be used to determine functional groups in an unknown molecule.

Isolated double bond – a double bond that is more than one single bond away from another double bond in a *Diene*.

Isomers – compounds having the same atomic composition (*Constitution*) but differing in their chemical structure; includes structural isomers (chain or positional), tautomeric isomers and stereoisomers (including geometrical isomers, optical isomers, and conformational isomers).

IUPAC nomenclature – a systematic method for naming molecules based on a series of rules developed by the International Union of Pure and Applied Chemistry; not the only system in use, but the most common.

J

***J* value** – the coupling constant between two peaks in an NMR signal; given in units of Hz.

K

Kekulé structure – the structure for benzene in which there are three alternating double and single bonds in a six-membered ring of carbon atoms.

Ketal – the product formed by the reaction of a *Ketone* with an *Alcohol*; the general structure is:

Keto-enol tautomerization – the process by which an *Enol* equilibrates with its corresponding *Aldehyde* or *Ketone*.

Ketone – a compound in which an oxygen atom is bonded via a double bond to a carbon atom, which is itself bonded to two more carbon atoms.

Kinetic product – the product that forms the fastest; has the lowest *Activation energy*.

Kinetics – the study of the rate of reactions.

Kinetically controlled product – the product formed as the result of the fastest reaction in a set of competing reaction pathways.

L

Levorotatory – the phenomenon that turns plane polarized light in a counterclockwise direction.

LCAO – a method for the calculation of molecular orbitals from a "Linear Combination of Atomic Orbitals."

Leaving group – the negatively charged group that departs from a molecule, which is undergoing a *Nucleophilic substitution* reaction.

Lewis acid – an agent capable of accepting a pair of electrons to form a *Coordinate bond*.

Lewis base – an agent capable of donating a pair of electrons to form a *Coordinate bond*.

Lone pair – a pair of electrons in a molecule that is not shared by two of the constituent atoms.

Linear – the shape of a molecule with *sp* hybrid orbitals; an *Alkyne*.

LUMO – the lowest unoccupied molecular orbital in a molecule or ion.

M

Markovnikov rule – the positive part of a reagent (e.g., a hydrogen atom) adds to the carbon of the double bond that already has more hydrogen atoms attached to it; the negative part adds to the other carbon of the double bond; such an arrangement leads to the formation of the more stable *Carbocation* over other less-stable intermediates; useful in the prediction of the major product from such reactions; *Free radical reactions* proceed in the opposite sense, giving rise to *Anti-Markovnikov addition*.

Mass number – the total number of protons and neutrons in an atom.

Mass spectrometry – a form of spectrometry in which, generally, high energy electrons are bombarded onto a sample, generating charged fragments of the parent substance; these ions are then focused by electrostatic and magnetic fields to give a spectrum of the charged fragments.

Mechanism – the series of steps that reactants go through during their conversion into products.

Meso **compounds** – molecules that have *Chiral* centers but are *Achiral* as a result of one or more planes of symmetry in the molecule.

Mesomerism – see *Resonance*.

Meta – describes the positions of two substituents on a *Benzene ring* that are separated by one carbon.

Meta-directing substituent – any substituent on an *Aromatic* ring that directs incoming *Electrophile*s to the *meta* position.

Methylene group – a ~CH_2~ group.

Microwave spectroscopy – the interaction of electromagnetic waves with wavelengths in the range 10^{-2} to 1 meter; this energy range corresponds to rotational frequencies; useful in studying the structure of materials (generally gases) and in their characterization.

Molecular ion – the fragment in a mass spectrum that corresponds to the *Cation* radical (M+) of the molecule; gives the molecular mass of the molecule.

Molecular orbitals (MO) – the electron orbitals belonging to a group of atoms forming a molecule.

Molecular orbital theory – a model for depicting the location of electrons that allows electrons to delocalize across the entire molecule; a more accurate but less user-friendly theory than the *Valence bond theory*.

Molecule – a covalently-bonded collection of atoms that has no electrostatic charge; the smallest particle of matter that can exist in a free state; in the case of ionic substances, such as sodium chloride, the molecule is considered as a pair of ions (e.g., NaCl).

Multiple bond – a double or triple bond; involve the atomic *p* orbitals in side-to-side overlap, preventing rotation.

Multistep synthesis – a synthesis of a compound that takes several steps to achieve.

N

n+1 rule – rule for predicting the coupling for a proton in ^{1}H NMR spectroscopy; an NMR signal will split into n+1 peaks, where n is the number of equivalent adjacent protons.

Natural product – a compound produced by a living organism.

Neutralization – the reaction of an acid and a base; the products of an acid and base reaction are a salt and water.

Neutron – an uncharged particle in the atomic nucleus that has the same weight as a proton; additional neutrons do not change an element but convert it to one of its isotopic forms.

Newman projection – a projection obtained by viewing along a carbon-carbon single bond.

Nitrile – a compound containing a cyano group (a carbon triply-bonded to nitrogen ($\sim$C$\equiv$N); also, a functional group.

NMR – nuclear magnetic resonance spectroscopy; a technique that measures radiofrequency light absorption by molecules; a powerful structure-determining method; see *Nuclear magnetic resonance spectroscopy*.

Node – a region of zero electron density in an orbital; a point of zero amplitude in a wave.

Nonbenzenoid aromatic ring – an *Aromatic* ring system that does not contain a *Benzene ring*.

Nonbonding electrons – *Valence electrons* that are not used for covalent bond formation.

Nonterminal Alkyne – an *Alkyne* in which the triple bond is located somewhere other than the 1 position.

Nuclear magnetic resonance (NMR) spectroscopy – a form of spectroscopy that depends on the absorption and emission of energy arising from changes in the spin states of the nucleus of an atom; for aggregates of atoms, as in molecules, minor variations in these energy changes are caused by the local chemical environment; the energy changes used are in the radiofrequency range of the electromagnetic spectrum and depend upon the magnitude of an applied magnetic field.

Nucleofuge – see *Leaving group*.

Nucleophile – a "nucleus lover;" a molecule with the ability to donate a lone pair of electrons (a *Lewis base*).

Nucleophilic substitution – an overall reaction in which a *Nucleophile* reacts with a compound displacing another nucleophile; such reactions commonly occur in aliphatic chemistry; if the reaction is unimolecular, they are known as S_N1 *reactions*; for reactions which are bimolecular, they are known as S_N2 *reactions*.

Nucleophilicity – a measure of the reactivity of a *Nucleophile* in a *Nucleophilic substitution* reaction.

Nucleus – the central core of an atom; the location of the protons and neutrons.

O

Optical activity – the property of certain substances to rotate plane polarized light; associated with asymmetry; compounds that possess a *Chiral* carbon atom of all the same "handedness" will rotate plane polarized light; isomers that rotate light in equal but opposite directions are sometimes called "optical isomers," although the better term to use is "enantiomers."

Orbit – an area around an atomic nucleus where there is a high probability of finding an electron; also called a "shell;" divided into *Orbitals*, or "subshells."

Orbital – an area in an *Orbit* where there is a high probability of finding an electron; a "subshell;" all the orbitals in an orbit have the same principal and angular quantum numbers.

Organic compound – carbon-containing compound.

Ortho – describes the positions of two substituents on a *Benzene ring* that are on adjacent carbons.

Ortho-para **director** – an *Aromatic* substituent that directs incoming *Electrophile*s to the *ortho* or *para* positions.

Outer-shell electron – see *Valence electrons*.

Overlap region – the region in space where atomic or molecular orbitals overlap, creating an area of high electron density.

Oxidation – a chemical process in which the proportion of electronegative substituents in a compound is increased (the loss of electrons by an atom in a covalent bond), the charge is made more positive, or the oxidation number is increased; in organic reactions, this occurs when a compound accepts additional oxygen atoms.

Oxonium ion – a positively-charged oxygen atom.

Ozonide – a compound formed by the addition of ozone to a double bond.

Ozonolysis – the cleavage of double and triple bonds by ozone, O_3.

P

Paired spin – the spinning in opposite directions of the two electrons in a bonding orbital.

Para – describes the positions of two substituents on a *Benzene ring* that are separated by two carbons.

Parent name – the root name of a molecule according to the *IUPAC nomenclature* rules (e.g., hexane is the parent name in *trans*-1,2-dibromocyclohexane).

Peroxide – a compound that contains an oxygen-oxygen single covalent bond.

Peroxyacid – an acid of the general form:

$$\underset{R-\overset{\displaystyle O}{\overset{\|}{C}}-O-OH}{}$$

Phenyl ring – a *Benzene ring* as a substituent, abbreviated Ph.

Photochemical reaction – a chemical reaction brought about by the action of light.

Pi (π) bond – a bond formed by the side-to-side overlap of atomic *p* orbitals (with electron density above and below the two atoms, but not directly between the two atoms); weaker than a *Sigma* bond because of poor orbital overlap caused by nuclear repulsion; create unsaturated molecules; found in double and triple bonds.

Pi (π) complex – an intermediate formed when a *Cation* is attracted to the high electron density of a *Pi bond*.

Pi (π) molecular orbital – a molecular orbital created by the side-to-side overlap of atomic *p* orbitals.

p*K*a – the scale for defining a molecule's acidity (p*K*a = –log *K*a).

Plane-polarized light – light that oscillates in a single plane.

Plane of symmetry – a plane cutting through a molecule in which both halves are mirror images of each other.

Polar covalent bond – a bond in which the shared electrons are not equally available in the overlap region, leading to the formation of partially positive and partially negative ends on the molecule.

Polarimeter – an instrument used to measure the amount of rotation of plane-polarized light by a compound, generally prepared in a solution.

Polarity – the asymmetrical distribution of electrons in a molecule, leading to positive and negative ends on the molecule.

Precursor – the substance from which another compound is formed.

Preparation – a reaction in which the desired chemical is produced (e.g., the dehydration of an *Alcohol* is a preparation for an *Alkene)*.

Primary carbocation – a *Carbocation* to which one *Alkyl group* is bonded.

Primary (1°) carbon – a carbon atom that is attached to one other carbon atom.

Product – the substance that forms when reactants combine in a reaction.

Propagation step – the step in a free radical reaction in which both a product and energy are produced; the energy keeps the reaction going.

Protecting group – a group that is formed on a molecule by the reaction of a reagent with a substituent on the molecule; the resulting group is less sensitive to further reaction than the original group, but it must be able to be easily reconverted to the original group.

Protic solvent – a solvent that contains O–H or N–H bonds.

Proton – an H^+ ion; also a positively-charged nuclear particle.

Protonation – the addition of a proton (a hydrogen ion) to a molecule.

Pure covalent bond – a bond in which the shared electrons are equally available to both bonded atoms.

Pyrolysis – the application of high temperatures to a compound.

R

R group – abbreviation given to an unimportant part of a molecule; indicates rest of molecule; see *Alkyl group*.

Racemate –a 50:50 mixture of two enantiomers; another name for *Racemic mixture*.

Racemic mixture – an equimolar mixture of the two enantiomeric isomers of a compound; because of the equal numbers of *levo-* and *dextro*-rotatory molecules present in a *Racemate*, there is no net rotation of plane-polarized light (i.e., they are optically inactive).

Radical – a term applied to an atom or molecule having one or more free valences; see *Free radicals*.

Rate-determining step – the step in a reaction's mechanism that requires the highest activation energy and is, therefore, the slowest.

Rate of reaction – the speed with which a reaction proceeds.

Reactant – a starting material.

Reaction energy – the difference between the energy of the reactants and that of the products.

Reagent – the chemicals that ordinarily produce reaction products.

Rearrangement reaction – a reaction that causes the skeletal structure of the reactant to change in converting to the product.

Reduction – chemical processes in which the proportion of more electronegative substituents is decreased, the charge is made more negative, or the oxidation number is lowered.

Resolution – the separation of a *Racemate* into its two enantiomers by means of some *Chiral* agency.

Resonance – 1) the representation of a compound by two or more canonical structures in which the *Valence electrons* are rearranged to give structures of similar probability; the actual structure is considered to be a hybrid of the resonance forms; 2) the process by which a substituent either removes electrons from or gives electrons to a *Pi bond* in a molecule; a delocalization of electrical charge in a molecule.

Resonance energy – the difference in energy between the calculated energy content of a *Resonance structure* and the actual energy content of the hybrid structure.

Resonance hybrid – the actual structure of a molecule that shows resonance; possesses the characteristics of all possible drawn structures (and consequently cannot be drawn); lower in energy than any structure that can be drawn for the molecule and is more stable than any of them.

Resonance structures – various intermediate structures of one molecule that differ from each other only in the positions of their electrons; used to better depict the location of *pi* and nonbonding electrons on a molecule; a molecule looks like a hybrid of all resonance structures; none of the drawn resonance structures are correct, and the best representation is a hybrid of all the drawn structures.

Reversible process – a process in which the forward reaction can reach an equilibrium with the reverse reaction.

Ring structure – a molecule in which the end atoms have bonded, forming a ring rather than a straight chain.

Rotamers – isomers formed by restricted rotation.

Rotation – the ability of carbon atoms attached by single bonds to freely turn, which gives the molecule an infinite number of *Conformations*.

R/S convention – a formal non-ambiguous nomenclature system for the assignment of the absolute configuration of structure to *Chiral* atoms using the Cahn, Ingold and Prelog (CIP) priority rules.

S

s-*cis* conformation – a *Conformation* in which the two double bonds of a conjugated *Diene* are on the same side (*cis*) of the carbon-carbon single bond that connects them; the required conformation for the *Diels-Alder reaction*.

s-*trans* conformation – the *Conformation* in which the two double bonds of a conjugated *Diene* are on opposite (*trans*) sides of the carbon-carbon single bond that connects them.

Saturated – the term given to organic molecules that contain no multiple bonds.

Saturated compound – a compound containing all single bonds.

Saturation – the condition of a molecule containing the most atoms possible; a molecule made up of single bonds.

Sawhorse projection – the sideways projection of a carbon-carbon single bond and the attached substituents; gives a clearer representation of stereochemistry than the *Fischer projection*; see *Newman projection*.

Secondary carbocation – a carbocation to which two *Alkyl group*s are bonded.

Secondary (2°) carbon – a carbon atom that is directly attached to two other carbon atoms.

Separation technique – a process by which products are isolated from each other and from impurities.

Shielding – an effect, in NMR spectroscopy, caused by the movement of *sigma* and *pi* electrons within the molecule; causes chemical shifts to appear at higher magnetic fields (upfield).

***Sigma* (σ) antibonding molecular orbital** – a *sigma* molecular orbital in which one or more of the electrons are less stable than when localized in the isolated atomic orbitals from which the molecular orbital was formed.

***Sigma* (σ) bond** – a bond formed by the linear combination of orbitals in such a way that the maximum electron density is along a line joining the two nuclei of the atoms.

***Sigma* (σ) bonding molecular orbital** – a *sigma* molecular orbital in which the electrons are more stable than when they are localized in the isolated atomic orbitals from which the molecular orbital was formed.

Singlet – describes an NMR signal consisting of only one peak.

Skeletal structure – the carbon backbone of a molecule.

S_N1 – a *Substitution reaction* mechanism in which the slow step is a self-ionization of a molecule to form a *Carbocation*; the rate-controlling step is unimolecular.

S_N1 **reaction** – a first-order substitution reaction that goes through a *Carbocation* intermediate.

S_N2 – a *Substitution reaction* mechanism in which the rate-controlling step is a simultaneous attack by a *Nucleophile* and a departure of a *Leaving group* from a molecule; the rate-controlling step is bimolecular.

S_N2 **reaction** – a second-order *Substitution reaction* that takes place in one step and has no intermediates during the reaction pathway.

sp **hybrid orbital** – a molecular orbital created by the combination of wave functions of an *s* and a *p* orbital.

sp² **hybrid orbital** – a molecular orbital created by the combination of wave functions of an *s* and two *p* orbitals.

sp³ **hybrid orbital** – a molecular orbital created by the combination of wave functions of an *s* and three *p* orbitals.

Spectrometer – an instrument that measures the spectrum of a sample (e.g., a *Mass spectrometer*).

Spectrophotometer – an instrument that measures the degree of absorption (or emission) of electromagnetic radiation by a substance. The measuring system generally includes a photomultiplier; UV, IR, visible and microwave regions of the electromagnetic spectrum may be measured in this way.

Spin-spin splitting – the splitting of NMR signals caused by the coupling of nuclear spins on neighboring nonequivalent hydrogens.

Stability constant – when a complex is formed between a metal ion and a ligand in solution, the equilibrium may be expressed by a constant that is related to the free energy change for the process: $M + A = MA : \Delta G = -RT\ln K$.

Staggered conformation – conformation about a carbon-carbon single bond in which bonds off one carbon are at a maximum distance apart from bonds coming off an adjacent carbon (60° apart when viewed in a *Newman projection*).

Stereochemistry – the study of the spatial arrangements of atoms in molecules and complexes.

Stereoisomers – molecules that have the same atom connectivity but different orientations of those atoms in three-dimensional space. Another name for *Configurational isomer*.

Stereospecific reactions – reactions in which bonds are broken and made at a particular carbon atom and that lead to a single stereoisomer; if the configuration is altered in the process, the reaction is said to involve inversion of configuration; if the configuration remains the same, the transformation occurs with retention of configuration.

Steric hindrance – the phenomenon of a physical blockage of a site within a molecule by the presence of local atoms or groups of atoms; therefore, a reaction at a particular site will be impeded.

Straight-chain *Alkane* – a saturated hydrocarbon that has no carbon-containing side chains.

Structural isomer – also known as a *Constitutional isomer;* have the same molecular formula but different bonding arrangements among their atoms (e.g., C_4H_{10} can be butane or 2-methylpropane, and C_4H_8 can be 1-butene or 2-butene).

Subatomic particles – a component of an atom; either a proton, neutron or electron.

Substituent – a piece that sticks off the main carbon chain or ring.

Substituent group – any atom or group that replaces a hydrogen atom on a hydrocarbon.

Substitution – the replacement of an atom or group bonded to a carbon atom with a second atom or group.

Substitution reactions – reactions in which one atom or group of atoms is replaced by another atom or group of atoms; see *Electrophilic substitutions* and *Nucleophilic substitutions*.

***Syn* addition** – a reaction in which two groups of a reagent X–Y add on the same face of a carbon-carbon double bond.

T

Tautomerism – a form of structural isomerism where the two structures are interconvertible by means of the migration of a proton.

Tautomers – molecules that differ in the placement of a hydrogen and double bonds and are easily interconvertible; keto and *Enol* forms are tautomers; see *Keto-enol tautomerization*.

Terminal *Alkyne* – an *Alkyne* whose triple bond is located between the first and second carbon atoms of the chain.

Terminal carbon – the carbon atom on the end a carbon chain.

Termination step – the step in a reaction mechanism that ends the reaction, often a reaction between two free radicals.

Tertiary carbocation – a *Carbocation* to which three *Alkyl group*s are bonded.

Tertiary (3°) carbon – a carbon atom that is directly attached to three other carbon atoms.

Tetrahaloalkane – an *Alkane* that contains four halogen atoms on the carbon chain; the halogen atoms can be located on vicinal or non-vicinal carbon atoms.

Thermodynamic product – the reaction product with the lowest energy.

Thermodynamically controlled reaction – a reaction in which conditions permit two or more products to form; the products are in an equilibrium condition, allowing the more stable product to predominate.

Thermodynamics – the study of the energies of molecules.

Thiol – a molecule containing an ~SH group; also, a functional group.

Tosyl group – a *p*-toluenesulfonate group:

Tosylation – a reaction that introduces the toluene-4-sulphonyl group into a molecule, generally by the reaction of an *Alcohol* with tosyl chloride to give the tosylate *Ester*.

Transition state – the point of highest energy on an energy against reaction coordinate curve; the least stable point (peak) on a reaction path; a reaction path may involve more than one transition states.

Trigonal planar – the shape of a molecule with a sp^2 hybrid orbital; in this arrangement, the *Sigma bonds* are in a single plane separated by 60° angles.

Triple bond – a multiple bond composed of one *Sigma bond* and two *Pi bond*s; rotation is not possible around a triple bond; hydrocarbons that contain triple bonds are called *Alkyne*s.

Triplet – describes an NMR signal split into three peaks.

U

Ultraviolet light (UV) – radiation of a higher energy range than that of visible light but lower than that of ionizing radiations, such as X-rays; many substances absorb ultraviolet light, leading to electronic excitation; useful both as a means for characterizing materials and for stimulating chemical reactions (*Photochemical reactions*).

Ultraviolet spectroscopy – spectroscopy that measures how much energy a molecule absorbs in the ultraviolet region of the spectrum.

Unsaturated – the term is given to an organic compound containing multiple bonds.

Unsaturated compound – a compound that contains one or more multiple bonds (e.g., *Alkene*s and *Alkyne*s).

Unsaturation – refers to a molecule containing less than the maximum number of single bonds possible because of the presence of multiple bonds.

V

Valence bond theory – the mechanical wave basis of *Resonance* theory.

Valence electrons – the outermost electrons of an atom (e.g., the valence electrons of the carbon atom occupy the $2s$, $2p_x$ and $2p_y$ orbitals).

Valence isomerization – the isomerization of molecules that involve structural changes resulting only from a relocation of single and double bonds; if a dynamic equilibrium is established between the two isomers it is also referred to as "valence *Tautomerism*" (e.g., the valence tautomerism of cyclo-octa-1,3,5-triene).

Valence shell – the outermost electron orbit.

Vinyl Alcohol – $CH_2=CH–OH$

Vinyl group – the ethenyl group: $\sim CH=CH_2$.

W

Walden inversion – a Walden inversion occurs at a tetrahedral carbon atom during an S_N2 *reaction* when the entry of the reagent and the departure of the leaving group are synchronous; the result is an inversion of configuration at the center under attack.

Wurtz reaction – the coupling of two *Alkyl halide* molecules to form an *Alkane*.

X

X group – "X" is often used as the abbreviation for a halogen substituent in the structural formula of an organic molecule.

Y

Ylide – a neutral molecule in which two oppositely charged atoms are directly bonded to each other.

Z

Z isomer – an isomer in which the two highest-priority substituents are on the same side of a double bond or ring.

Zaitsev's rule – the major product in the formation of *Alkenes* by elimination reactions will be the more highly substituted alkene or the alkene with more substituents on the carbon atoms of the double bond.

To access online MCAT tests at a special pricing visit:
http://www.OnlineMCATprep.com/bookowner.htm

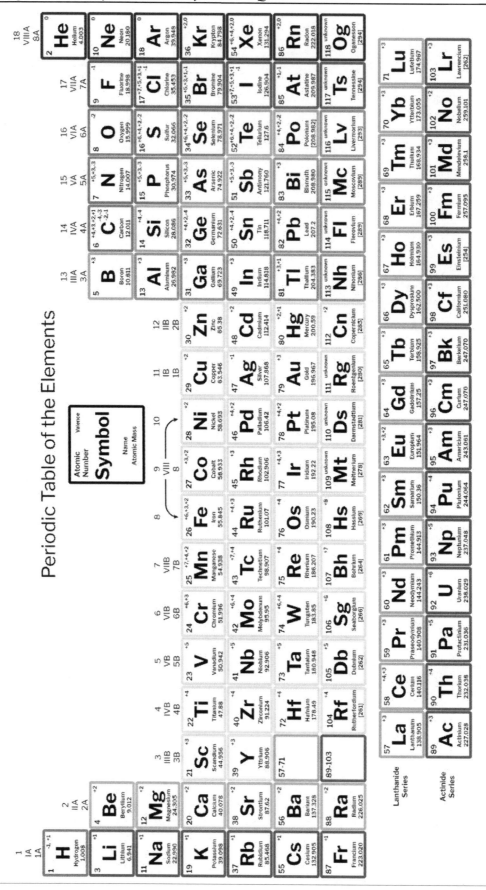

Periodic Table of the Elements

We want to hear from you

Your feedback is important to us because we strive to provide the highest quality prep materials. Email us if you have any questions, comments or suggestions, so we can incorporate your feedback into future editions.

Customer Satisfaction Guarantee

If you have any concerns about this book, including printing issues, contact us and we will resolve any issues to your satisfaction.

info@onlinemcatprep.com

We reply to all emails – please check your spam folder

Thank you for choosing our products to achieve your educational goals!

Please, leave your Customer Review on Amazon

Made in the USA
Middletown, DE
17 January 2020